£19.99

...COMPANIES 1995–2014

BRITISH THEATRE COMPANIES 1995–2014

Mind the Gap, Kneehigh Theatre, Suspect Culture, Stan's Cafe, Blast Theory, Punchdrunk

Liz Tomlin

Series Editors: John Bull and Graham Saunders

Bloomsbury Methuen Drama
An imprint of Bloomsbury Publishing Plc

B L O O M S B U R Y
LONDON • NEW DELHI • NEW YORK • SYDNEY

Bloomsbury Methuen Drama

An imprint of Bloomsbury Publishing Plc

Imprint previously known as Methuen Drama

50 Bedford Square	1385 Broadway
London	New York
WC1B 3DP	NY 10018
UK	USA

www.bloomsbury.com

BLOOMSBURY, METHUEN DRAMA and the Diana logo are trademarks of Bloomsbury Publishing Plc

First published 2015

British Library Cataloguing-in-Publication Data

A catalogue record for this book is available from the British Library.

ISBN: HB: 978-1-4081-7728-0
PB: 978-1-4081-7727-3
ePDF: 978-1-4081-7730-3
ePub: 978-1-4081-7729-7

Library of Congress Cataloging-in-Publication Data

A catalog record for this book is available from the Library of Congress.

Typeset by Fakenham Prepress Solutions, Fakenham, Norfolk NR21 8NN
Printed and bound in Great Britain.

CONTENTS

ACKNOWLEDGEMENTS

I would like to thank the University of Birmingham for the research leave that enabled me to get started on this volume, and to gratefully acknowledge the support from colleagues in the Department of Drama over the course of the project. I'd also like to thank the university for funding a research studentship to help with the initial research for this volume, and to thank Isabelle Taylor for her extremely helpful contributions and committed approach to the work.

Thanks are also due to staff at the Arts Councils of England and Wales, Creative Scotland and the British Council for their support in enabling me to access archive material, and to Neil Webb from the British Council for granting me an interview.

Many thanks are also due to Mark Dudgeon of Bloomsbury Methuen Drama, and to the series editors, Professor John Bull and Dr Graham Saunders, for inviting me on board, and for their help and guidance over the course of this project.

Thanks must go as always to Joseph for his unfailing patience and support.

Liz Tomlin
Sheffield 2014

SERIES EDITORS' PREFACE

In the first major study of John McGrath's theatre company 7:84 Scotland, published in 1996, Maria DiCenzo notes a curious omission in scholarship: 'While it is not unusual to find book-length studies of the work of playwrights (often an analysis of plays with a bit of socio-political context thrown in), alternative theatre *companies* in the same period have received comparatively little detailed coverage' (DiCenzo, 1996, 6). Despite the remarkable proliferation of companies that emerged from the late 1960s until the end of the 1980s, a phenomenon that undoubtedly reshaped the ecology of British theatre, the area has only ever partially been addressed in edited collections such as Catherine Itzin's *Stages in the Revolution* (1980) and Sandy Craig's *Dreams and Deconstructions: Alternative Theatre in Britain* (1980), or in monographs, principally Andrew Davies's *Other Theatres: The Development of Alternative and Experimental Theatre in Britain* (1987) and Baz Kershaw's *The Politics of Performance: Radical Theatre as Cultural Intervention* (1992). However, in all these cases, the companies themselves are rarely considered collectively, comprising instead one strand of an alternative theatre culture that included arts labs/centres, individual practitioners and dramatists.

In recent years, this situation has changed through the endeavours of Susan Croft's exhaustive online project Unfinished Histories, which concentrates on the work of companies operating between 1968 and 1988. The project seeks to archive and document materials relating to these companies including posters and photographs of productions as well as interviews with former company members. However, being a website, Unfinished Histories, despite providing both valuable focus and scope, cannot provide a clear chronological and contextual account of the overall development of these groups, how they related to each other, or how funding policies and shifts in cultural agendas changed their evolution in the course of over 40 years.

This three-volume series aims to address this lacuna. Individually, each volume charts the progress – and sometimes demise – of small- to medium-scale touring companies, who from the late 1960s took to the road in a fleet of transit vans and established a network of performance venues for themselves throughout the British Isles. These included theatres, community centres, youth clubs, arts centres as well as urban and rural outdoor spaces.

These companies have been variously described as 'alternative' or 'fringe', yet over the years both their work and more significantly much of their influence, has been assimilated into mainstream British theatre culture. For some groups, including Complicite, Cheek by Jowl and Punchdrunk, their move from the margins to international status has been easy to identify. However, more often than not, the process has been more subtle, and so consequently unrecognized and unacknowledged. A good example of this has been the gradual absorption of black and Asian work into the repertoires of many major subsidized London and regional theatres since the late 1990s. This did not happen by accident: rather it came about through a long succession of gruelling one-night stands by pioneering companies including Tara Arts, Temba and the Black Theatre Co-operative during the 1970s and 1980s.

Each volume covers a distinct historical era. The first discusses the period 1965–79; volume two 1980–94, while volume three covers 1995–2014. The format for all three includes an opening chapter written by each editor that provides a contextual political and cultural background to the period in which the companies operated. The second chapter gives a broad outline and discussion of the many types of companies operating within the given period. Here, the editors have endeavoured not only to include familiar names, but other lesser-known documented groups. The final section of each volume includes a series of case studies from chosen contributors on the work of a particular theatre company active in the period covered.

Archival sources, both from holdings dedicated to a specific company and from the Arts Council of Great Britain, largely inform the choice of companies and approach taken in volumes one and two. This has come out of a larger five-year AHRC funded project, Giving Voice to the Nation: The Arts Council of Great Britain and the Development of Theatre and Performance in Britain 1945–1995, that the editors Bull and Saunders have been engaged on since 2009. It soon became clear that, for the period covered between 1965 and 1994, the Arts Council archive would provide a unique and, up until recently, unexplored resource for the study of theatre companies active in those areas: materials include minutes of company meetings, funding proposals for projects, records of tour dates, statistics on box-office takings and audience attendance, newspaper and magazine reviews, publicity materials, as well as Arts Council, memos, letters and records of meetings. These frequently reveal much about the Arts Council's often cryptic assessment methods and more tellingly their attitudes towards particular companies, or the types of work they produced. The archive also offers insights into wider questions relating to changing priorities in policy towards alternative/ fringe theatre in Britain from the late 1960s to the mid-1990s. Contributors, where possible (and where relevant), have made use of this resource, as well as individual company archives in assessing their work.

As editors, we are mindful of what we have left out. We also fully recognize that some of our decisions will be highly contentious. For instance, with hindsight, the first two volumes could perhaps have been retitled *English Theatre Companies*, as relatively little space is accorded to Scottish, Welsh or Northern Irish companies. This has been influenced by a number of factors: for one thing, we wanted each of the volumes to look at the *kinds* of work produced, rather than the geographical location they came out of. While it also might be assumed that the Arts Council archive would have provided a detailed national survey of British companies, in reality the archive resembles more of a Domesday Book on English theatre. The reasons for this are both historical and administrative, in that the Welsh, Scottish and Northern Ireland offices of the Arts Council, while answerable to London, were in effect autonomous bodies with their own allocated budgets and set of policies. This meant (with the often-made exception for the annual Edinburgh Festival) that a company such as 7:84 Scotland would be funded on the proviso that they tour exclusively within Scotland, unless prior arrangements had been made between other regional offices, or the company had secured necessary funds to tour within England. The third volume begins as the Arts Council of Great Britain devolved into three distinct Arts Councils for England, Scotland and Wales, and so looks at how arts policy develops in each of these three nation states and the impact of this on the independent theatre ecology that emerges across the UK (with the exception of Northern Ireland) in this period.

The editors have also endeavoured to provide as comprehensive an insight as possible into the types of work produced in any given period; yet this will always mean that certain companies will be privileged over others. Sometimes this is reflected in the priorities operating in a given period: for instance, in volume two, the second chapter places more emphasis on black, Asian and women's companies simply because these were areas that experienced the largest growth and afforded greater priority in terms of funding allocation than companies specializing in Live Art or Theatre in Education, whereas volume three takes particular account of the participation and access agenda that supported a growth in theatre for children and young people, as well as more widespread experimentation with audience involvement.

The editors are also aware of the problems of adopting a chrono-logical approach. While the majority of companies only enjoyed a comparatively short life span, others such as C.A.S.T., The Women's Theatre Group and Temba continued to work over the course of several decades. While each editor's second chapter concentrates on the work of groups who were formed within the period covered by their respective volumes (with some leeway given between companies who formed on the cusp), the contributors' chapters on particular companies assess the work on the basis of what they consider to be their most significant or celebrated of the period.

PREFACE TO VOLUME THREE

This volume examines the field of British theatre companies after the Arts Council of Great Britain devolved in 1994, and so continues the narrative beyond the Giving Voice to the Nation project, which produced the archive drawn on in Volumes One and Two. In this narrative, the transfiguration of the alternative theatre movement into the independent theatre sector makes conclusive rules about inclusion and exclusion impossible. In the 1980s, according to Sara Freeman, alternative theatre replaced political theatre as the preferred label among artists as it 'points to an "otherness" from commercial theatre or from the establishment theatre of the subsidized nationals but it leaves the details of that otherness open to a broad range of possibilities' (Freeman, 2006, 374). The notion of alternative, however, becomes ever more slippery in this period, as the influence of experimentation in small-scale and emergent companies conclusively permeates those very establishment theatres. In the absence of a better term, I have followed Baz Kershaw (2004, 371) in defining the companies discussed in this volume as independent, suggesting, for the most part, that they are not building-based or, at least, that the company identity pre-dates any building that has been acquired. The building-less Scottish and Welsh National Theatres are exceptions to this rule due to their evident establishment status.

There are also difficulties with what is defined as a *'theatre* company' in this period, given the proliferation of performance that positions itself outside of, or in opposition to, the theatre tradition; the rising influence of gaming and participation models and the increasingly porous distinctions between the fields of live art and theatre. In a real sense, these ambiguities and developments best characterize the trajectory of the theatre company over the last two decades, so I have attempted to be as inclusive as possible, using theatre in its very broadest sense, while keeping the emphasis on companies, rather than solo artists, for the purpose of this series.

Although Chapter 2 of this volume makes structural use of sub-headings, the vast majority of companies in this period work across many different categorizations and may crop up in unexpected places, so readers are advised to take the chapter as a whole. The narrative that I have chosen to tell is only one of a number of possible ways of reading this period of unprecedented growth and diversity, but I hope it offers a number of productive, and sometimes provocative, starting points for further research into the field.

Chapter 1

HISTORICAL AND CULTURAL BACKGROUND

Liz Tomlin

PART ONE:
POLITICS, SOCIETY AND CULTURE

Introduction

By 1995, the seemingly unstoppable march of globalization was well underway, and it becomes impossible, in this final volume, to neatly extricate British politics of the period from events of global significance such as the expansion of the European Union, the terrorist attack on New York's World Trade Center, and the financial banking crisis that struck the economies of the developed world in 2008. Since the Maastricht Treaty in 1993, the people of the 12 member states had been European citizens, with common passports and the right to move, live and vote in any country in the European Union (EU). The Treaty also defined the stages that would be required to achieve economic and monetary union, which finally arrived for the majority of member states with the advent of the Euro in 1999. In 2004, the EU expanded to incorporate member states from much of Eastern Europe, with Romania and Bulgaria joining in 2007 and Croatia in 2013.

The dissolution of many of the national boundaries that had previously existed on the continent did have an impact on British artists and cultural organizations over this period, who found partnerships and movement across and within the continental European countries significantly easier than had previously been the case. The expansion of European festivals, and the development of British Council support for overseas touring, both discussed in Chapter 2, offered British companies opportunities to embed themselves in an increasingly unified European network of theatre and performance, develop international partnerships, and benefit from the often significantly greater financial rewards that accompanied commissions of their work from countries where art enjoyed greater subsidy than was the case at home.

If the identity of a distinctly *British* theatre ecology was to shift under European expansion and increased integration, it was also to be further complicated by the devolution of Wales and Scotland and the prospect of Scottish independence. On 11 September 1997 the referendum for an independent Scottish Parliament was held and proved a decisive victory (63.5 per cent of voters voting yes) which granted Scotland devolution and tax-varying powers. A week later, the Welsh vote for devolution was also won, albeit by a tiny margin of 50.3 per cent against 49.7 per cent, for a Welsh Assembly that would be without the tax-varying powers of the Scottish Parliament.

In the 2007 elections, the Scottish National Party (SNP), under Alex Salmond, formed the government in Scotland for the first time, bringing Labour dominance in Scotland to an end. The SNP's vision of a fully independent Scotland was arguably strengthened by the Conservative/ Liberal coalition victory in Westminster in 2010; the coalition's politically regressive austerity measures further alienated Scottish voters always well to the left of the majority of the English. This shift in Westminster was perhaps one catalyst for the SNP's more decisive 2011 victory, this time with an overall majority, which pushed the UK government to recognize Scotland's right to hold an independence referendum (Curtice et al., 2013, 141). The referendum took place on 18 September 2014 with a startlingly high turn out of 84.59%. Although the vote for independence was lost by 55.3% to 44.7%, the strength of support for the 'Yes' vote forced Westminster to promise further devolutionary powers for Scotland.

Political devolution had been pre-empted by the devolution of the Arts Councils of Great Britain in 1994, and would further consolidate the distinct cultural trajectories that were already emerging in line with the different national agendas, linguistic contexts and political colours of England, Scotland and Wales, as will be discussed throughout this chapter. In all three nation states, however, the fields of politics, society and culture were to become increasingly difficult to distinguish from one another. One of the most significant characteristics of the New Labour era that dominates this period was the appropriation of society and culture into the politics of government across all departments and in each of the three nation states in question. This chapter examines, above all else, how culture was fashioned into an essential political instrument for the advancement of social objectives, economic prosperity and national prestige, both under the Blair government of Great Britain, and the devolved administrations of Scotland and Wales.

New Labour

After 18 years of Conservative government in Britain, the 1997 victory of Labour under Tony Blair was greeted with some relief by the artistic community. Not only did New Labour, towards the end of its first term, virtually double the grant-in-aid available for arts funding, but there was a sense that this government understood culture to be central to the country's status and prosperity in a way that had not previously been the case. Before looking in detail at the ways in which arts and culture were to be largely transformed under Blair's 'Cool Britannia' branding exercise and New Labour's influence on Arts Council policy, it is useful to outline the more general political direction of Britain under New Labour, which was not entirely as anticipated in the celebratory spirit of 1997, the year that we were promised by Labour's election anthem that things could only get better.

Blair's rebranding of the Labour Party was marked decisively at the 1994 annual conference by the removal of a central commitment within Clause IV of the Party's constitution to 'common ownership of the means of production'. This was the turning point between 'Old' and 'New' Labour; between 'old' socialist principles of nationalization and state ownership and Labour's 'new' neoliberalist embrace of the free market and privatization as endorsed by Margaret Thatcher. If politics up to 1989, in the context of alternative cultural movements, had generally been seen in terms of left-wing/right-wing dichotomies, New Labour was to expedite the increasing suspicion of such binaries that had been growing since the failure of socialism in Eastern Europe. Will Leggett argues that Tony Blair's New Labour agenda 'led this tendency, with [its] frequent ... claims that social change has consigned left and right to history' (Leggett, 2005, 15). This, of course, was the decisive move in Blair's proposal of a 'third way politics'; less historical truth than an ideological strategy that resulted in successfully manoeuvring Labour to the centre of the political spectrum, and outlawing everything that stood to the left of it. New Labour's appropriation of the neoliberalist agenda set by Thatcher was presented by Blair's ubiquitous spin doctors as a centre-left third way, in order to rebrand what had been previously seen as a right-wing ideology as a new kind of politics which 'transcended' the traditional notions of ideological class conflict and, in Blair's own words, 'left the redundant twentieth-century battles between capitalism and communism behind' (Cockerell, 2001, 574).

Despite New Labour's embrace of the doctrine of neoliberalism, to which I will return, there is also ample evidence throughout Blair's term of office of a genuine commitment to the redistributive social democracy that had historically characterized the Labour movement. In the wake of nearly two decades of Conservative rule, initiatives such as Sure Start, the minimum wage, the New Deal, the Educational Maintenance Allowance, tax credits, Education Action Zones and significant public investment in health and education all contributed to this government's success in stalling the income gap between the best and worst paid, reducing levels of child and pensioner poverty, and maintaining high levels of employment (see Astle and Murray, 2006). However, despite ten years of huge public investment, and the wide reach of the government's social inclusion agenda across all areas of policy, at the end of Blair's term of office there remained, from a social democratic perspective, notable failures.

Although the economy was strong, there were indicators of the financial crash that was to follow, including high levels of consumer debt, and a housing market bubble that was always fated to be unsustainable. While levels of income inequality had been stalled, if not reversed, wealth inequality, partly due to the rising value of property, was 'higher even than in the 1980s' (Astle and Murray, 2006, 24), with the richest 5 per cent of the population owning 70 per cent of the country's wealth by 2001 (Astle and Murray, 2006, 26–7). Social mobility had declined and looked set to decline further, and residual pockets of poverty and social deprivation showed stubborn resistance to Blair's reforms, particularly in black and minority ethnic communities where persistent educational underachievement threatened to sustain the higher than average levels of poverty and unemployment for future generations (Astle and Murray, 2006, 26). New Labour's social inclusion agenda, both in its successes and failures, was hugely significant in shaping arts policy, particularly in the areas of widening participation for black and ethnic minorities, those from less privileged socio-economic backgrounds and children and young people. A brief examination of the ideological basis of New Labour's policies, at their most fundamental level, can clarify both why the arts became so vital as a means of improving social inclusion, and the reasons behind the rather limited success of New Labour's endeavours.

'Education education education' was Blair's personal mantra, and his passion to improve the life-chances of the less privileged in society, from the earliest point possible, lay at the heart of his government's drive for social inclusion, and its emphasis and significant expenditure on early years schemes such as Sure Start. However, as Astle and Murray observed in 2006: '[d]espite the government's efforts, class and wealth remain key determinants of British children's educational prospects' (Astle and Murray, 2006, 30). Eric Shaw argues likewise that 'while the outcome [of Labour's redistributive policies] has been a substantial movement of resources to the least well endowed, it falls well short of any significant advance towards equality of opportunity' (Shaw, 2007, 202). Shaw identified a key reason for this as the persistent and growing inequality of wealth distribution, which rendered Blair's rhetorical emphasis on 'equal opportunity' at the start of a child's life unable to counter the hierarchy of economic privilege into which that child is born.

The problem, it appears, was that Blair's efforts to follow a progressively redistributive agenda was counterpointed at every turn by his contradictory embrace of the neoliberalist notion of meritocracy. Tony Wright argues, 'among socialists who have taken values seriously, there has been wide agreement that equality should be regarded as a key socialist value, perhaps even *the* socialist value' (Wright, 1986, 33 in Eatwell, 1989, 61). Blair, however, was no socialist, and his rhetoric and policy were directed not towards equality of outcome (a levelling of the gap between the poorest and the wealthiest) but towards equality of opportunity, in the belief that if everyone was given equal opportunity, then the meritocratic principle could be left to itself to 'level up' those who took best advantage of such opportunity. However, as Shaw explains 'relational equality was impossible in a society characterized by cumulative, persisting and entrenched inequalities in the distribution of income and wealth' (Shaw, 2007, 35).

While Wales, and Scotland in particular, used their new legislative powers under devolution to operate within a more traditional Labour model of social democracy, instigating progressive national policies on health, social care and education, England, under the unfettered control of New Labour, was forced to embrace Blair's preference for the market-driven, neo-liberalist model of capitalism, as advocated by the Anglo-American politics of Reagan and Thatcher (Norris, 1999, 27–8). It is not, as Colin Leys notes, that the state becomes impotent in the face of market-driven politics, but more worryingly that 'it is constrained to use its power to advance the process of commodification' (Leys, 2001, 2). Leys describes how the total capitulation of the New Labour government to the market-driven politics of neoliberalism opened the floodgates for firms to 'constantly explore ways to break out of the boundaries set by state regulation, including the boundaries that close non-market spheres to commodification and profit-making' (Leys, 2001, 4).

The most significant cultural consequence of this intrusion of the marketplace into previously non-market spheres, as Colin Leys warns, is the danger that it threatens 'the destruction of non-market spheres of life on which social solidarity and active democracy have always depended' (Leys, 2001, 4). Education and cultural activities, alongside health and welfare benefits, have historically been considered to be public goods which, under 'ethical socialist thinking' (Shaw, 2007, 36), should be 'contrasted with commodities in that they were defined by their intrinsic value: they were particularly "human" in that they were essential to human well-being and fulfilment' (Keat, 2000, 26–7 in Shaw, 2007, 39). As such, they represented vital non-market spheres, in Eric Shaw's words, 'from which market exchange and the commercial ethos should be barred *as a matter of principle*' (Shaw, 2007, 36, original emphasis). David Marquand concurs that '[t]he attempt to force these relationships into a market mould undermines the service ethic, degrades the institutions that embody it and robs the notion of common citizenship of part of its meaning' (Marquand, 1999, 254). These are the fundamental and deeply ideological consequences of the commercialization of Britain's public services that began under a Labour government, from the creeping privatization that invaded the NHS and state education to the commodification of English universities, a process that began with the introduction of student fees in 2006.

The creep of the market into traditionally non-market spheres has also impacted on the independent theatre ecology across the UK. A sector which had been staunchly oppositional and collectivist under Thatcher was incorporated by New Labour into a creative or cultural 'industry' in which companies were now expected to be run like small businesses, with entrepreneurial leadership, mission statements, 'diverse income streams', and sustainable strategies for growth. As Michael McKinnie argues, such a shift enabled the notion of 'culture' and the 'arts' to be captured within a market sector, to subdue its potential to oppose market structures, or function beyond them (McKinnie, 2004). No longer were theatre companies expected to challenge the politics of the state, as had been the case under Thatcher. Rather, under Blair's leadership of the Labour Party, the arts had become, as Robert Hewison notes, 'entirely instrumental, a matter of "value for money", and the opposition between culture and industrial society ha[d] disappeared' (Hewison, 1994, 30). Precisely how the arts were to be transformed into instruments of government policy, I shall now detail, by first examining their key role in the national branding exercises that were to define

'Cool Britannia' as a union, and Wales and Scotland as newly devolved nations, in the early 2000s.

Cool Britannia and the Creative Industries

The creative industries were central to Tony Blair's 'Cool Britannia' project, but as Andrew Ross proposes, the rebranding of artists and so-called 'creatives' in the UK was part of a much wider global shift that grew out of the surge in internet-based operations that constituted the 'dot-com boom' of the late 1990s (Ross, 2009, 16). This new 'composite "creative economy"', as Ross argues, was 'perfectly adapted to the freelancing profile favored by advocates of liberalization', because of the 'self-directed work mentality of artists', and so 'occupied a key evolutionary niche on the business landscape' (Ross, 2009, 16). Ross credits Tony Blair with creating the most definitive packaging of the 'CI [Creative Industries] policy paradigm', which was then rolled out as a viable development strategy across the globe, 'to persuade bureaucrats that human capital and IP [Intellectual Property] are the keys to winning a permanent seat in the knowledge-based economy' (Ross, 2009, 20). The arts, of course, could not stand alone in this brave new branding exercise as they were renowned for their resistance to market place imperatives – that is to say that they have always, whether via private patronage or public funding – needed subsidy to survive. The incorporation of the arts into the creative industries enabled a whole range of other more profit-making enterprises, including software, computer services and advertising, to support the balance sheet of the new business model, which became a 'revenue powerhouse' that generated £60–112 billion per year (Ross, 2009, 24).

The arts were required in this portfolio of creative activity to add the kind of international prestige that names like Damien Hirst, Irvine Welsh and Oasis could offer. Britpop and Britart, in particular, were vital to the marketing side of 'Cool Britannia', which became, as Ross argues, 'a massive PR campaign to persuade the world that the country Napoleon once mocked as a nation of shopkeepers was now a nation of artists and designers, with the future in their enterprising bones' (Ross, 2009, 24). Blair had seized the Cool Britannia initiative as key to his party's electoral victory in 1997, as Ken Urban, among other commentators observes (Urban, 2008, 39–41). The marketing emphasis on the young, the cutting edge and the risky was cleverly designed to separate Blair's government-in-waiting both from the previous Tory administration and the socialist identity of 'Old' Labour, and it bled into all aspects of artistic and cultural life.

Stephen Daldry, then-director of the Royal Court, towed the Cool Britannia line, seeking to create a 'cult of youth' characterized by work such as Sarah Kane's *Blasted* (1995), which caused such critical uproar when it opened at the Court in 1995 (Urban, 2008, 42). However, Graham Saunders suggests that theatre always held an 'outsider status on the fringes' of the Cool Britannia project (Saunders, 2008, 9), with writer Mark Ravenhill specifically satirizing the superficiality of Blair's branding in *Shopping and Fucking* (1996) and *Some Explicit Polaroids* (1999) (Saunders, 2008, 11). Ravenhill, along with Sarah Kane, was at the core of what came to be known as the 'in yer face theatre' generation (Sierz, 2000), whose violent and often sexually explicit new writing developed concurrently with the Cool Britannia project in the mid- to late-1990s. Their writing, however, was always regarded, according to Saunders, 'with some degree of circumspection' by New Labour, arguably because, unlike in Britpop and Britart, they saw themselves implicitly or explicitly satirized in much of the work that was produced (Saunders, 2008, 12). Ken Urban also concurs that Kane, Ravenhill and their contemporaries resisted being co-opted by Blair's rebranding but formed instead 'a youth-based counter-politics to the cynicism and opportunism of Cool Britannia' (Urban, 2008, 39).

The most significant legacy of Cool Britannia was the success of London's bid to host the 2012 Olympics, a prize won by New Labour at the height of the boom years, and delivered by the Lib–Con coalition at the peak of austerity. The Olympic opening ceremony, directed by Danny Boyle (who had made his name directing Irvine Welsh's *Trainspotting* in 1996), was a masterclass in brand-Britain promotion. Interspersed with the stalwarts of traditional Britishness – the industrial revolution, Shakespeare, a politically astute homage to the NHS, and a brilliant fusion of James Bond and the Queen – Boyle's opening ceremony presented twenty-first-century Britain first and foremost as a land of cultural expertise (particularly in digital developments) and ethnic diversity.

Ben Pitcher notes how central the notion of race was to the success of the 'Cool Britannia' project in his examination of the 1997 Demos pamphlet written for New Labour by Mark Leonard, the self-declared inventor of the term (Pitcher, 2009, 46–8). Leonard's *Britain*, as Pitcher discusses, proposes the slogan 'United Colours of Britain' (Leonard, 1997, 56), after the famous Benetton advertisement campaign. In this way he 'weaves the nation's brand identity on a multicultural loom: both "edgy" and "contemporary", the "United Colours of Britain" perfectly articulates a pluralist approach to national identity as refracted through the imagery of the advertising world' (Pitcher, 2009, 47). This new national identity, Pitcher argues, was required to distinguish itself from an out-of-date nationalism that was known for its implicit racism and essentialism, in order that Blair could reclaim the 'One Nation Britain' that had formerly belonged to right-wing politics. To this end,

> the subject of race has recently been approached in a new register that claims an ethos of cultural, religious and racial pluralism as its own. That which had stood outside of or in opposition to the state has become articulated as one of its core principles.(Pitcher, 2009, 34)

New Labour's co-option of cultural diversity was central to Blair's image of a Cool Britannia, a project that was particularly vital to construct in the light of devolution. In an article analysing the displacement of a traditional English identity in UK tourism literature at the turn of the millennium, José Igor Prieto Arranz concludes that:

> It is a new Britannia aiming to cover all of the British nations; a new Britannia trying to come to terms with Britain's postcolonial reality, fully recognising the richness and variety to be found in an essentially cosmopolitan society; a new Britannia that seems to have left behind the traditional rural presumption and that has taken the great industrial city as a powerful emblem for everything that Englishness was not. (Arranz, 2006, 196)

This was a rejection of 'Englishness', historically associated with a 'bad' brand of nationalism and insular pockets of mono-cultural rural heritage, in favour of an urban, multicultural and pluralist Britain that encompassed all of its parts. As such, Cool Britannia was the pro-Union counterpoint to the emerging and influential branding and nation-building exercises undertaken by Wales and Scotland on the road to ever-greater independence, as detailed later in this chapter. No degree of emphasis on cultural diversity within this New Britain, however, could neutralize the political and media hostility to those whose citizenship lay outside of it. For not everyone, it seems, was welcome in New Labour's Cool Britannia.

Immigration and Asylum

Andrew Geddes describes the increasing politicization of migration since the 1990s as a result of the 'third-wave' of postwar migration, 'with a particularly noticeable increase in asylum seeking migration and migration defined by state policies as illegal' (Geddes, 2003, 17). As the numbers of refugees seeking asylum in the UK began to rise, so did the intensity of the press hostility, fed by often spurious statistics from anti-immigration groups such as Migration Watch, to create a climate where the notion of asylum seeker became synonymous with non-white, third-world, bogus interlopers who would put pressure on housing, schools, and other public services, drain the welfare system and threaten the 'British' way of life (Finney and Simpson, 2009). Stratham and Morrison's review of media coverage in the mid-1990s concludes that immigration and asylum politics made up '37% of news coverage in the *Guardian*, 46% in *The Times*, and 55% in the *Daily Mail*' (in Finney and Simpson, 2009, 51). Whether the media was following or creating public opinion is a question beyond the scope of this chapter, but responses to a 2009 MORI poll evidence that '[m]ore than a third of the public now regularly cite race and immigration as among the most important issues facing the country, significantly higher than in most European countries and a sharp increase from a decade ago' (Spencer, 2011, 1).

Public hostility to immigrants was further exacerbated by New Labour's spectacularly conservative estimate of the number of Polish migrants who would come to the UK for work after Poland's accession to the EU in 2004. The predicted figure was 26,000 over the first two years; the total figure over that time was estimated (not including spouses and children) at between 427,000 and 600,000 (when self-employed were included) and resident communities in particularly affected areas were woefully unprepared for the volume of migration they experienced (Marr, 2007, 593). The public hostility to asylum seekers and economic migrants, stoked by the right-wing press, and particularly evident in economically disadvantaged communities who saw themselves in direct competition with the newcomers for housing and other resources, led to a rise in popularity for Britain's right-wing parties and a swing to the right by the mainstream parties in an attempt to appease public opinion. Electoral support for the United Kingdom Independence Party's (UKIP) stance on immigration and their desire to leave the EU, evidenced by the party's gains in the 2013 local elections and the 2014 European elections, has already played into the hands of the Tories on the right of the Conservative Party and might yet move the national debate for all parties towards increasingly isolationist policy making in the future.

Between 1993 and 2002 there were four attempts to adapt the 1971 immigration legislation in response to asylum seeking, each one seeking to impose tighter controls on entry, and more punitive containment of those refugees who had succeeded in obtaining illegal entry to Britain. The media hostility and the legal sanctions imposed by governments in response have had the effect of galvanizing support for refugees and asylum seekers within the artistic community, and precipitated the growth of refugee theatre on a global scale, particularly in the UK and Australia (Jeffers, 2012, 43). Refugee Week, first held in London in 2002, was repeated annually across numerous cities in the UK as Alison Jeffers reports, growing from 225 events in 2002 to 450 events attended by an estimated 250,000 people by 2006 (Jeffers, 2012, 113). Annual refugee arts festivals were also established in London, Birmingham and Manchester (Jeffers, 2012, 113) and there was evidence of a significant growth in companies working in this area. Banner Theatre – *Wild Geese* (2005) and *They Get Free Mobiles ... Don't They?* (2007); Red Room Theatre – *The Bogus Woman* (2001) and *Unstated* (2009); Ice and Fire – *I Have Before Me a Remarkable Document Given to Me by a Young Lady from Rwanda* (2003) and *Crocodile Seeking Refuge* (2005); and Cardboard Citizens – *Pericles* (2003) are examples of just four companies that have developed ongoing projects with refugees and engaged explicitly with the politics of refuge and asylum over the 2000s.

War on Terror

Almost 3,000 people were killed as a result of the terrorist attacks on the World Trade Center on 11 September 2001. The direct economic cost ran into billions of dollars, and the global political consequences, which were to continue into the next decade and most probably well beyond, immediately began to take shape. The military reprisals were the most visible manifestations of these consequences. On 7 October 2001, less than a month after the attacks and the subsequent identification of Osama bin Laden and al-Qaeda as the perpetrators, British and American air attacks against the Taliban in Afghanistan, where bin Laden and his organization were believed to be hiding, began. To prove more controversial still was the invasion of Iraq on 19 March 2003, undertaken by British and American troops regardless of the absence of a UN mandate, raising serious questions surrounding the legality of the invasion and inspiring the biggest ever anti-war demonstration in the UK. Protestors voiced suspicions that this was as much about instigating the regime change that Bush's father had neglected to accomplish in the first Gulf War, and the protection of oil revenues in the Middle East, as it was about Saddam Hussein's harbouring of weapons of mass destruction that constituted a real and genuine threat to either country's national security. Such suspicions were not eased by Bush's insistence on linking Iraq with al-Qaeda without the slightest grounds for so doing, in attempts to justify the invasion as part of his ill-advised declaration of a 'war on terror', mounted in response to the terrorist attacks on America.

In the UK, the impact of Tony Blair's decision to stand 'shoulder to shoulder' with Bush was far reaching. First and foremost, it engendered a deep distrust of Blair and New Labour that almost certainly played a key role in Blair's own subsequent fall in popularity, and arguably had some lasting impact on the fortunes of the party itself. Suspicions surrounding the government's claim that the UK was imminently at threat from weapons of mass destruction (WMD) held by Saddam Hussein were exacerbated by a report by Andrew Gilligan on the BBC *Today* programme which alleged that intelligence documents presented as evidence of this threat had been largely fabricated, or at the very least 'sexed-up' for the purpose of justifying the invasion to the public. Moreover, ten years after the defeat of Saddam Hussein's regime, no weapons of mass destruction have yet been located and few would now hold to the argument that they ever existed in the first place. The alleged suicide of Dr David Kelly, purportedly as a result of his being outed as the senior government scientist who was the source of Gilligan's report, led to the Hutton Inquiry. This ultimately castigated the BBC while leaving the government exonerated, but did nothing to counter public opinion, which remained largely cynical of the WMD claim and the legitimacy of the government's course of action.

The Tricycle Theatre in London was at the heart of a resurgence of verbatim and documentary theatre that arose in response to the events following 9/11; its productions included Richard Norton-Taylor's *Justifying War* (2003), a dramatization of the Hutton Inquiry, and his *Called to Account: The Indictment of Anthony Charles Lynton Blair for the Crime of Aggression Against Iraq – a Hearing* (2007). Another was Victoria Brittain and Gillian Slovo's *Guantanamo – Honor Bound to Defend Freedom* (2004), which was constructed from interviews with British citizens who had been imprisoned without trial in America's infamous Guantanamo Bay. David Hare's *Stuff Happens* (2004), produced by the National Theatre, Robin Soans' *Talking to Terrorists* (2005), commissioned by Out of Joint, Steve Gilroy's *Motherland* (2009) and the National Theatre of Scotland's *Black Watch* (2006) also used verbatim techniques to dramatize issues arising from the British invasion of Iraq and subsequent events.

An ongoing consequence of Blair's complicity in Bush's 'war on terror' was the growing hostility of the Muslim diaspora to the West's arguably unjustified and illegal military intervention in the Middle East. Tensions between Islam and the West did not begin with 9/11; rather the attacks were, in part, one result of long-standing tensions, most notably the West's support of Israel in the long-running conflict over Israel's occupation of Palestinian territory. Nevertheless, it has been claimed by many commentators that the retaliatory action of Bush and Blair supported the growth of al-Qaeda and related terrorist cells better than any recruitment campaign bin Laden could have devised, particularly in light of ensuing scandals such as the Abu Ghraib images, where American soldiers posed for photographs with Iraqi prisoners forced to adopt humiliating and degrading positions. In February 2003, one month before the Iraq invasion, the Joint Intelligence Committee warned the government that 'al Qaeda and associated groups continued to represent by far the greatest terrorist threat to Western interests, and that threat would be heightened by military action against Iraq' (Jones, 2003 in Hewitt, 2008, 77), and it has been calculated that there was 'a sevenfold increase in worldwide terrorism in the four years following March 2003' (Hewitt, 2008, 5). In 2004, a Joint Foreign Office–Home Office report, 'Young Muslims and Extremism', cited the double standards of Western foreign policy, the bias for Israel in the ongoing dispute over Palestinian territories and the recent 'war on terror' as core grievances that underpinned a growing hostility to Western governments, even when these governments were their own (Hewitt, 2008, 78). Consequently, it is difficult to dismiss a causal link between the invasion of Iraq and the terrorist attacks that subsequently occurred in Madrid (2004), London (2005) and Glasgow (2007). One of the London bombers, indeed, made the link explicit in his posthumous video posting on the Arabic news channel, Al Jazeera.

The London bombings on 7 July 2005, later explored in Simon Stephens's play *Pornography* (2008), were unprecedented and unanticipated. The government's anti-terror legislation had been targeted predominantly at foreign nationals, and on 6 July, the head of MI5 had assured a group of Labour MPs that no imminent terror attacks were on the horizon. London was celebrating the news that it had been chosen to host the 2012 Olympic games when, at 8.50 a.m., three bombs exploded at different points on the London Underground; the fourth detonated on a crowded bus passing through Tavistock Square at 9.47 a.m. In total, there were 52 deaths and over 700 people injured, many seriously. All four bombers were British citizens from British Muslim communities, who had launched an indiscriminate suicide attack on their own people.

After the attacks of 11 September, and reinforced by the subsequent London bombings, the figure of the terrorist, in the popular imagination, became increasingly synonymous with the Muslim identity, a conflation that was enhanced by the media, the security forces and, arguably, the government, to the significant detriment of community and race relations in the UK. The growing suspicion of multiculturalism, with specific regard to Islam, was, of course, already well established by this point in time, as most infamously proposed in Samuel Huntington's 'clash of civilizations' thesis, which claimed that the values of Islam and the values of the Western world were fundamentally incompatible (Huntington, 1993). The sense, within the UK, that the narrative of multiculturalism was being re-written as 'solving the problem' of Islam became more acute following the riots in Bradford, Burnley and Oldham in 2001, when the focus turned onto the alleged 'self-segregation' of Muslim communities, rather than any attempt being made to address the well-documented discrimination and disadvantage such communities were facing. As Charles Husband and Yunis Alam make clear in their study 'Social Cohesion and Counter Terrorism', the riots were in large part understood by those in power as the result of a 'collective failure' on the part of the Muslim communities 'to embrace their "Britishness"' (Husband and Alam, 2011, 3).

After 9/11 came new legislation in the form of the Anti-Terrorism, Crime and Security Act 2001, in which the government proposed draconian new powers for detaining international terrorist suspects without charge, much like the Americans were able to do inside the infamous Guantanamo Bay. The Terrorism Act 2006 swiftly supplanted its 2005 predecessor as the government responded to the threat of home-grown terrorism evoked by the London bombings, and proposed, among other measures, that the police could now hold terrorist suspects for up to 90 days without trial. This proposal was eventually overturned in the worst government defeat since 1978 in favour of a 28-day compromise that was still double the previous maximum, and quadruple the seven-day maximum in place prior to the Terrorism Act

2000 (Hewitt, 2008, 55). Days into Gordon Brown's taking up of the Labour leadership in June 2007, Kafeel Ahmed, who later set himself alight, and Bilal Abdulla, a diabetes specialist at the Royal Alexandra hospital in Paisley, drove a car bomb into the passenger terminal of Glasgow International Airport in an attempted terrorist attack, following their previous failed car bomb attempts in London early that month. Brown then continued the swathe of Labour's anti-terrorist legislation by swiftly proposing new legislation that would, among other things, create a border police force, and renew the government's attempts to further double the duration of the detention without charge period from 28 to 56 days. The impact of Labour's counter-terrorism agenda on Muslim communities throughout the UK in this period was to be far reaching and, arguably, counter-productive, a topic I return to later in this chapter.

The Age of Austerity

If 11 September 2001 marked the first millennial moment when events in America sparked off a catastrophic chain of global events, then 15 September 2008 could be characterized as the second. When Lehman Brothers went into liquidation, the global banking crisis, already foreshadowed by the nationalization of Northern Rock (UK) and the rescue of Bear Stearns (US) earlier that year, was now inevitable. Loans lent to those unable to pay them back had been sold from bank to bank around the world, traded in 'the belief ... that these collater-alised securities offered high returns at minimal risk. The belief was that not all mortgage borrowers would default at the same time. That belief was wrong' (Elliott and Treanor, 2013). As Lord Turner, who took over as chairman of the Financial Services Authority in the UK concluded, 'we had created a system by 2006 with such a build-up of debt that it was inherently unstable, and that was going to produce a massive crisis' (Elliott and Treanor, 2013). On the 7 October 2008, the Chancellor, Alistair Darling, took a phone call from Sir Tom McKillop, chairman of the Royal Bank of Scotland, telling him that within two to three hours the bank was going to run out of cash, and would have to cease trading by the end of the day (Elliott and Treanor, 2013). RBS and Lloyds proved to be too big to fail, and were bailed out by the government, and are still, at the time of writing, being paid for by the British taxpayer. The banking collapse was followed by the credit crunch – banks refusing, or unable, to lend, and businesses starved of cash. As businesses began to fail, unemployment began to rise and the economy began to plummet, and there were real fears that the Great Depression following the Wall Street Crash of 1929 might be repeated. While this was ultimately averted, in significant parts of Europe the impact of the banking crisis was not so far removed from that caused by the slump in the 1930s.

For it was not only businesses that were no longer able to borrow the finance they required. National governments had long enjoyed low interest rates and had borrowed heavily over the boom years, building up significant levels of national debt. In this new age of austerity and uncertainty, it became clear that these debt levels were so high in certain countries and the economies now so weak, that there was a risk that they could never be repaid. This was the sovereign debt crisis that hit the Eurozone in 2009, with first Greece, and subsequently Spain, Portugal, Ireland and Cyprus requiring bailouts from the European Union to save them from national bankruptcy and the ultimate collapse of the Euro. Conditions in the UK never reached the degree of economic and humanitarian crisis experienced in these countries, but the Tory-led coalition, elected in 2010, took their opportunity to impose severe, and many believed substantively ideological, fiscal cuts on government spending, ostensibly designed to reduce the country's deficit and maintain its credit rating and financial credibility. Swathing cuts to public services included the decimation of local authorities and local government funding, the withdrawal of government subsidy for university fees, and sweeping cuts to welfare and disability benefits as well as to Arts Council budgets. While education, along with the NHS, was ring-fenced from direct cuts, initiatives that had been introduced by Labour, such as the Educational Maintenance Allowance to enable those from poorer backgrounds to be supported in post-16 education, were axed. Educational support services and social care, provided in the main by local authorities, suffered severely. Given the spending restraints they were now under, many local authorities withdrew significant amounts of funding previously spent on the arts that were now required to plug the gap to enable them to continue to offer essential services in social care and basic urban maintenance. Newcastle and Nottingham were two city councils that were driven to publicly threaten the withdrawal of 100 per cent of their arts spending to balance budgets elsewhere. The knock-on impact of such cuts across the UK was the closure of libraries and other cultural and leisure centres, the retrenchment of urban regeneration projects and local participatory arts projects, and a reduction in the levels of match funding required for Arts Council support for regional theatres and companies.

The banking crisis, and the austerity politics that prioritized deficit reduction over the maintenance of essential public services, inspired a whole new wave of global radical activist protest, unseen at this level of visibility for at least a generation. On Saturday 17 September 2011, 5,000 Americans set up a semi-permanent protest camp in a park on Liberty Street, as close as they could get to their symbolic target of Wall Street, which had been barricaded by police. By October, the occupation was being replicated in 47 US states, and similar protests in Canada, the UK, Germany and Sweden were in the planning (McVeigh, 2011). On 15 October, it was claimed that more than 950 protests were being held in over 80 countries, including Rome, Sydney and Madrid, and the Occupy London movement gathered outside St Paul's Cathedral, ready to march to occupy the London Stock Exchange (Batty, 2011). In the event, they found their way barred, and so set up camp outside St Paul's, calling for systemic change to the financial system, on behalf of 'the ninety nine per cent' who were currently being failed by it. On 18 January the City of London finally won its court case to evict the protestors and by the end of February 2012 the camp was gone, but not before it had caused the resignation of both the Canon and the Dean of St Paul's, who felt their positions had become untenable in light of the church's own public statements on the immorality of the global banking system, which seemed irreconcilable with the state's constant threat of forcible removal of the protestors on behalf of St Paul's.

The occupy movement was possibly the first globally co-ordinated protest movement to benefit from the developments in social media technology, and similar direct-action campaigns against tax-evading multinational corporations such as Starbucks and Amazon have been likewise co-ordinated by civil disobedience organizations such as UK Uncut since the economic crisis in 2008. A new wave of environmental activism was also mounted against the multinational oil corporations awarded fracking contracts in parts of the UK where reserves had been identified, including Lancashire, Scotland, South Wales, Sussex and Kent. The protestors argued that not only would fracking increase our reliance on fossil fuels that were responsible for rising carbon emissions, but it was a method of extraction that threatened significant local environmental disturbance including devastation of landscapes, air pollution and water contamination.

This resurgence of political activism is also evident in theatre, although not always undertaken by theatre companies, as would have been the case in the alternative theatre movements of the 1960s and 1970s. This current generation of artists tends to commit to political action as individuals within more loosely based collectives, perhaps as a direct result of the ways in which company identities and bodies of work have been co-opted into the capitalist marketplace of the creative industries, as earlier described. The most high-profile example of such collectivist practice is Theatre Uncut, which was formed in 2010 as a direct response to the 'brutal cuts in public spending'. Theatre Uncut requests protest plays from well-known playwrights (the 2013 event included work from Tanika Gupta, Neil LaBute, Tim Price and Mark Thomas) to be made available for public performances within a limited period of time. This creates a Theatre Uncut mass action event each year with the plays performed simultaneously around the world, predominantly in the UK, continental Europe and North America, but with some reaching as far as Africa, South America and Australia.

Discrimination and Equal Rights

Improving the quality of life for people with disabilities was high on New Labour's social agenda. John Major's government had already introduced the Disability Discrimination Act in 1995, an act which was amended in 2005 following Labour's earlier establishment of the Disability Rights Commission, extension of the definition of disability and introduction of 'a public duty to promote disabled people's equality' and 'involve disabled people in decision making' (Close, 2011, 13). In 2010, the UK government ratified the United Nations Convention on the Rights of Persons with Disabilities, and passed the Equality Act, which covered characteristics including 'age, disability, gender reassignment, pregnancy and maternity, race, religion or belief, sex and sexual orientation' (Government Equalities Office, 2010, 3). New Labour's commitment to raising levels of participation for people with disabilities led to a raft of arts funding being prioritized for theatre companies working with disabled artists and audiences, as I outline in more detail later in this chapter. In 2003, the European Year of Disabled People, the Labour government allocated £2 million to promote partnerships and activities designed to raise awareness of disability issues, many of which were arts based. A period that was characterized by the growing visibility of disabled artists, and growing public awareness of disability rights, culminated in the 2012 Paralympics. This potential high-point of progress, however, was already undermined by mass protests and rallies against the increasingly brutal welfare cuts and 'fit-for-work' regime (soon to be joined by the 'bedroom tax') imposed by the coalition government; these were austerity policies that were disproportionately devastating to the lives of those with disabilities and long-term physical and mental illness.

However, unquestionable progress in equality legislation during this period was made in the recognition of greater rights for the gay community and significantly increased levels of public tolerance for homosexual partnerships, lifestyles and parenthood. The first gay pride events took place in Manchester in 1990, and Brighton and London in 1992, and in 1994 the Criminal Justice and Public Order Act reduced the age of consent for male homosexual sex from 21 to 18, reducing it finally to 16 in 2001. Reversing the homophobic trend of the Thatcher years, the controversial Clause 28 of the Local Government Act 1988 was repealed by Labour in England and Wales in 2003, with the equivalent already having been taken off Scottish statute books in 2000. In 2004 the Civil Partnership Act was passed, giving same-sex couples equivalent legal rights to married couples, and in 2013, a Marriage (Same-Sex Couples) Bill was introduced to both the UK and Scottish Parliaments, making lesbian and gay rights in Britain 'among the best in Europe' (Park and Rhead, 2013, 14–15). Consequently, the politically activist gay theatre companies of the 1970s and 1980s are not much in evidence in this period, and the gay presence within the independent theatre environment tends towards the exploration or celebration of queer culture, rather than the political argument for its legitimation, with venues such as the Drill Hall, companies such as Duckie, and festivals such as Glasgow's Glasgay and Manchester's Queer Up North platforming artists from across the LGBT (Lesbian, Gay, Bisexual, Transgender) community and beyond, with an emphasis on queer and transgressive performance, including a rise in the popularity of neo-burlesque.

Race Relations and Cultural Tensions in the UK

Following the Metropolitan Police's gross mismanagement of the investigation of the murder of black teenager Stephen Lawrence in 1993, the Macpherson Report was commissioned by the Blair government and published in 1999. Macpherson's inquiry concluded that institutional racism had been at the heart of the investigation, and could be defined as

the collective failure of an organisation to provide an appropriate and professional service to people because of their colour,
culture, or ethnic origin. It can be seen or detected in processes,
attitudes and behaviours which amount to discrimination through
unwitting prejudice, ignorance, thoughtlessness and racist stereo-
typing which disadvantage minority ethnic people. (Macpherson,
1999, para. 6.34)

Subsequently, the Race Relations (Amendment) Act 2000 required a
pro-active approach on the part of all public organizations and services
to ensure that they were fully complicit with a commitment to the
eradication of racism, however implicit, 'invisible' or unintentional that
racism might be. This legislation, and the spirit behind it, had a significant effect on arts organizations, as I shall later detail, in that it obliged
them to put race and diversity at the forefront of their artistic policies.

Racist discourse within wider society, as Chris Allen argues, tended
to shift over the period of this study, from an emphasis on race and
colour, as had been the case in the 1960s, 1970s and 1980s, to an
emphasis on race and religion which became much more publicly
explicit and visible, and was often justified with recourse to grounds
of reasoned cultural difference as opposed to irrational prejudice
(Allen, 2005). Even within traditionally liberal contexts such as the
Independent and *Guardian* newspapers, criticism of Islam, often from
feminist, libertarian or secular positions, was socially tolerated, or even
supported (Allen, 2005, 61). For some, such as Allen, this was racism
hiding under liberal colours; for others, it was vital defence of the right
to free speech and the right to oppose cultural traditions that were at
odds with your own belief systems, without fear of being called a racist
for so doing.

In the wider theatre context, similar tensions were exposed. In 2004,
Birmingham Rep pulled their production of *Bhetzi* (Dishonour), written
by the young female Sikh playwright Gurpreet Kaur Bhatti, following
an evacuation of the theatre in the face of violent protests by the Sikh
community incensed by the play's depiction of rape and violence
in a gurdwara, a Sikh place of worship. Artists almost unanimously
condemned the closure of the play as cowardice and capitulation to
censorship of the mob, with 700 signatures endorsing a letter of protest,
including those of Southbank director Jude Kelly, and Richard Eyre.
The Christian rallies and protests that greeted the BBC's screening of
Jerry Springer: The Opera (2005), and dogged the subsequent theatre
tour, were also often couched in terms that suggested that the militancy

of Islamic and Sikh groups had galvanized a traditionally less-vocal religious community into action. To cite Stephen Green, national director of Christian Voice, 'If this show portrayed Mohammed or Vishnu as homosexual, ridiculous and ineffectual, it would never have seen the light of day' (BBC, 2005).

Despite the theatre community's condemnation of Birmingham Rep, there was nevertheless a notable absence of plays that directly challenged religious fundamentalism in the name of free speech. One notable exception was the theatre company DV8, which produced two courageous and highly critical pieces of work, *To Be Straight With You* (2007) and *Can We Talk About This?* (2011). The first addressed the often-fatal extent of homophobia within fundamentalist African/Asian Christian and Muslim communities; the second addressed the murder and persecution of individuals who had been seen to commit offence by their representations of Islam in artistic material. In both cases, the company explicitly charged its audience with cowardice in permitting prejudice and censorship rather than risking being castigated as racist.

Community Cohesion

In 2011, the worst riots in 30 years erupted in London, Birmingham, Liverpool, Nottingham, Manchester and Salford, with public order temporarily suspended as police struggled to deal with thousands of youths on the rampage, and the Army was placed on alert to intervene. The riots were initially seen as a response to the shooting of Mark Duggan, a young black man who was killed by a Metropolitan Police officer who mistakenly thought he was armed, and austerity politics were also widely considered to have played their part, but a study undertaken by the *Guardian* and the London School of Economics evidenced that a more widespread anger against the police, and in particular their day-to-day treatment of black and Asian communities, was a much more significant factor (Prasad, 2011).

This would be borne out by Steve Hewitt's report that within a nine-month period in 2006, '22,700 stops [and searches] led to 27 terrorism-related arrests and the Metropolitan Police Authority described the counter-terrorist programme as doing "untold damage" to community relations' (Hewitt, 2008, 113). The shooting of Jean Charles de Menezes the day after a failed attempt by would-be terrorists to mimic the London bombings on 21 July 2005 had done nothing to instil confidence. De Menezes was a Brazilian plumber, with no terrorist connections, who was mistaken for a suicide bomber and shot dead by armed police in a London tube station. In attempts to alleviate this 'untold damage' to community relations, the ongoing project of community cohesion, galvanized by the 2001 riots and ensuing inner city disturbances such as the Lozells riots in Birmingham in 2005, was now reined into service as a key strand of the counter-terrorism strategy published in 2006.

The need to engage Muslim communities in what were strategically and ideologically defined as 'shared values', and to 'assimilate' them into social arenas that were multi, rather than mono, cultural, became one of the key targets of the community cohesion agenda, and one which was to have a notable impact on arts policy, as will be described later in the chapter. There were significant concerns around certain aspects of this agenda that are worth highlighting here in their wider social context. First, assimilation was always conceived as a one-way street. Community cohesion was less about all communities finding common ground and establishing shared values by mutual compromise and tolerance, and much more about specific communities (Muslims) adopting cultural practices and values that were authorized by the government as desirable and British. As Husband and Alam succinctly paraphrase, '[f]or members of the British Muslim population the message of Community Cohesion appeared to be: *We want you to be more actively engaged as citizens, but we want you to be more like us*' (Husband and Alam, 2011, 3). Secondly, the shift from New Labour's earlier emphasis on 'social cohesion' to 'community cohesion' resulted, as proposed in the Cantle Report, in a move away from addressing socio-economic factors and social class, to a focus on 'identifiable communities defined by faith or ethnicity' (Cantle, 2008, 50). As such, the issues of economic disadvantage underlying many inner-city Muslim communities were sidelined as potential causes of tension. De-segregation, as Kalra and Kapoor observe in their report, was now less about promoting material equality and more about removing cultural difference, a significant departure from the aims of the multicultural project in Britain up to this time (in Husband and Alam, 2011, 55). The ideological basis of the community cohesion project ensured that when government funding was made available to promote wider access to cultural activities for black, Asian and minority ethnic communities, it was done with the clear understanding that only the 'right kind' of cultural development should be supported. As Communities Secretary Ruth Kelly announced in 2006, only those Muslim groups who were seen to be 'taking a pro-active leadership role in tackling extremism and defending our shared values' could expect to receive funding for their activities (Hewitt, 2008, xxi). As Spalek and Lambert have argued:

> It appears that government projects aimed at fostering dialogue and community participation tend to be underpinned by broader questions and debates around what sort of Muslim identities should be encouraged in the UK ... and what kinds of Muslim identities should be actively discouraged and/or suppressed. (Spalek and Lambert, 2008, 261)

Surveillance, Digital Developments and New Technologies

The counter-terrorist agenda heralded a raft of measures that were to infringe the civil liberties of those beyond, as well as within, Muslim communities. The action group Liberty highlights as particularly concerning, the frequent use of 'section 44 of the Terrorism Act 2000 allowing stop and search without suspicion which has been disproportionately used against peaceful protestors and ethnic minority groups', the 'banning of non-violent political organisations' and 'the dangerously broad definition of terrorism' (Liberty, 2013). Identity cards were proposed in 2005 on the back of the London bombings but, despite Blair's best efforts, were never introduced, and the scheme was eventually scrapped by the coalition government, probably due to pressure from the Liberal Democrats, in 2010. Surveillance of other kinds, however, rose steadily throughout New Labour's term of office.

According to Professor Clive Norris, in the mid-2000s the British were under surveillance by approximately 4.2 million closed circuit television (CCTV) cameras – 'one for every four citizens' – with Londoners picked up on average 300 times per day (in Marr, 2007, 580–1). GPS systems in mobile phones and cars could also now easily enable the geographical tracking of their users. In June 2013, the *Guardian* published interviews it had held with Edward Snowden, an employee of defence contractor Booz Allen Hamilton at America's National Security Agency, which drew from internal NSA documents suggesting that the agency had 'direct access' to data held on millions of private citizens by Google, Facebook, Apple and other US internet providers (Gidda, 2013). Snowden was immediately charged with espionage by the US government, who demanded his extradition, but he was granted temporary asylum in Russia. Snowden's initial leaks were followed by revelations in the autumn of 2013 that the NSA routinely spied on its European allies, collecting tens of millions of European phone records, including those of Germany's Chancellor, Angela Merkel. The NSA countered that the European data had been collated by NATO, and that security agencies in Europe were fully complicit with the practice, despite the denials of their leaders.

The developments in new technology, however, could work both ways. The website WikiLeaks, established by Julian Assange and launched in 2006, has established a reputation for publishing high-level secret documents, from government and security organizations, that the public were never intended to see. Most famously, the site released hundreds of thousands of secret US military logs detailing its operations in Iraq and posted a video showing a US Apache helicopter killing Iraqi civilians and journalists during an attack in Baghdad in July 2007. WikiLeaks has also revealed 'a report on toxic waste dumping on the Ivory Coast, Church of Scientology manuals, Guantanamo Bay detention camp procedures and material involving large banks such as Kaupthing and Julius Baer, among other documents' (Hiscock, 2013). Like Snowden, Julian Assange is wanted by the US for espionage, and has been living within the Ecuadorian Embassy in London since June 2012.

It was 1991 when Tim Berners-Lee, celebrated in the London Olympics opening ceremony, launched the World Wide Web browser that was going to change global structures of communication from that point on. By 1995 internet shopping on eBay and Amazon had already begun for a limited market, in 1998 Google was founded, and by 2000, 40 per cent of Britons had accessed the internet at some time. By 2003, nearly half of British homes were connected, and by 2006, 75 per cent of British children had internet access at home (Marr, 2007, 573). The first-ever smartphone was launched in 1994 and in 2001 Apple's iPod was born. Both of these items of technology were to have real impact on performance practice over the first decade of the twenty-first century, as companies began to experiment with audio soundtracks, with iPods provided for the audience, and with interactive models of performance where smartphones were increasingly assumed to be something that every spectator would be carrying.

In 2005, the Facebook social networking site was launched. It grew to boast more than a billion users each year and was valued at more than $104 billion when sold on the stock market only seven years later (*Guardian*, 2012). YouTube was also created in 2005, and in 2006, the micro-blogging service Twitter went live. The advent of social networking media and open-access documentation sites such as YouTube was to change the face of marketing for cultural activity, especially once websites became easy for anyone to create, and digital stills and films could be shot from mobile phones and uploaded directly to the internet. Where theatre companies had previously required professional designers, photographers and technical resources to focus on press releases, flyers and posters, it was now all about spreading the word virally online, getting information and links to promotional footage to vast networks of people at the push of a button, and cultivating an online presence, with friends and followers numbering in the thousands through constant posting and sharing of news and information. Online blogging, made more accessible to large numbers of readers by the advent of Twitter and Facebook, has also significantly changed patterns of reception for performance work, with many blogs such as those by Matt Trueman and Jake Orr now established and respected as sites of theatre criticism that are given at least equal weight to the more traditional critical reviews in the broadsheet media.

The advent of social media also further enhanced the growing appetite for self-promotion and voyeurism that had underpinned reality TV shows like *Big Brother* (2000–) which had first appeared on Channel 4 in 2000, formats described by Richard Kilborn as amalgamating 'game-show, talk-show and peep-show elements while retaining vestiges of the observational documentary' (Kilborn, 2003, 12). The cynicism engendered by the ubiquity of reality TV and talent shows such as *The X Factor* permeates the cultural zeitgeist of the 2000s, also notable in films pre-empting the period, such as *The Truman Show* (1998) and *The Blair Witch Project* (1999). It is also reflected in the deconstructions of 'the real' that underpin the sceptical postmodern aesthetic of many companies in this period, including Forced Entertainment, Stan's Cafe and Desperate Optimists, to name only a few.

The digital economy had been promoted by New Labour through the creative industries, both for its capacity to generate significant levels of income, and for its automatic claim to 'innovation' that is a by-product of all technological development. Seen as vital to the future of theatre from one of its earliest policy appearances in the Boyden Report (2000), by 2008 it featured in the Arts Council's manifesto 'Great Art for Everyone' as one of four development priorities for the next three-year period. The year 2009 saw the launch of NTLive, which enabled filmed versions of National Theatre productions to be screened live in cinemas around the country, and in 2012 the online resource

'The Space' was developed by a partnership of the Arts Council and the BBC, providing free and on-demand access (via computers, tablets, smartphones and connected TV) 'to the work of some of the UK's greatest artists and arts organisations – including full performances and premieres, original commissions and rare archive material' (ACE, 2013, 18).

PART TWO:
ARTS COUNCILS, FUNDING AND POLICY

Grant-in-Aid Funding 1994–7

In 1993, the Arts Council of Great Britain (ACGB) had pre-empted political devolution and set out its plan to dissolve itself into its national constituents. From 1994, the Scottish and Welsh Arts Councils, which had up until then been sub-committees of the ACGB, became independent bodies with their own Royal Charters, to be funded by the Scottish and Welsh Offices. In Wales, this also resulted in the merger of the new Welsh Arts Council with Wales' three existing regional arts associations to form one single Arts Council of Wales/*Cyngor Celfyddydau Cymru*. Art in England would now be funded, under a new Royal Charter, by a newly established Arts Council for England.

For all three countries, the final years of the long-standing Tory government were characterized, in financial terms, by the effects of the recession. The first cut to the ACGB in 1992/3 was initially 2 per cent, and by 1997, the Arts Council of England (ACE) was reporting a cut in real terms, over the previous four years, of 9 per cent (Allen, 1997, 8). Not only was the government cutting its grant contribution to ACE for the first time since the Arts Council's formation in 1946, but local authority partnership funding, sponsorship and earned revenue were also falling due to the economic effects of recession. In a policy document published in 1996, it was estimated that there had been a 32 per cent real-terms reduction in sponsorship and donations income between 1986/7 and 1994/5. The same document reported that 'the persistent real-terms increase in average ticket yields at building-based repertory theatres – up 37% between 1986/87 and 1993/94 – went into reverse in 1994/95', showing a real-terms reduction of 6 per cent (ACE, 1996, 3).

Despite having to endure the same dismal financial climate, with the reorganization of local authorities and steep decreases in local government funding for the arts causing particular headaches in the Welsh and Scottish contexts, independence from the ACGB meant that, unlike their English counterparts, the Arts Council of Wales (ACW) received a small increase in funding at this time, and the Scottish Arts Council (SAC) grant was at least held at a standstill. Over the same period of 1986/7 to 1997/8, spending on drama as an art form in both Scotland and Wales actually enjoyed an 18 per cent rise, compared with a 38 per cent fall in England (ACE, 2000a, 33–5). There were few new franchises offered to English theatre companies over this period, due to the dire funding situation, but companies to buck the trend included motiroti, The Right Size, Open Hand Theatre Company, David Glass Ensemble and Graeae Theatre. In Scotland, a number of emerging companies were allocated special funds to bid for fixed term funding in 1997, out of which Suspect Culture and Boilerhouse were successful, at the expense of the long-standing Wildcat from which revenue funding was removed. There was very little movement in Welsh theatre over this period, with Theatre West Glamorgan joining other Theatre in Education (TIE) companies for regular funding in 1995/6, and no other significant gains or losses.

The National Lottery

In the economic climate of the mid-1990s, the potential of the National Lottery, introduced by John Major in 1993, was heralded as no less than the saviour of the arts. Funding from the Lottery was to come on stream in 1995; the money to be raised from the public's purchase of Lottery tickets to be split among five good causes: art, charity, heritage, millennium projects and sport, with the art component to be administered by the Arts Councils. The financial impact of the Lottery, more than doubling arts funding in its first full year of operation, can be seen by a quick comparison. By 1995/6, the arts Lottery fund of £255.4 million was already exceeding the Arts Council of England's government grant of £191.1 million. By 1997/8, the Lottery funds had increased to £297.6 million, while the government grant had fallen to £185.1 million. In 1995/96 SAC's government grant stood at £24.5 million alongside Lottery income of £27.3 million. By 1997/8, the Lottery funds totalled £32.5 million in comparison with government grant-in-aid of £27.1 million. ACW received £14.2 million in government grants in 1995/96 alongside Lottery income of £15.3 million. By 1997/8, the figures were £14.5 million (government) and £17.8 million (Lottery) (ACE, 2000a,

43). It was no surprise that in the 1996 annual report the Chair of ACE reported nothing less than a 'cultural revolution' (Gowrie, 1996, 6).

For the independent theatre companies, the impact of Lottery funding was somewhat delayed by the terms the Arts Councils themselves had requested. With good reason, given the economic climate and public spending cuts of the time, the Arts Councils, and the arts community in general, had foreseen a danger that Lottery funds would be seized on as a replacement, not an addition, to statutory funding of the arts. To prevent this, and protect the principle of core statutory funding, Lottery proceeds could not be used to fund what was described as 'core' activity, but must work on the principle of what became known as 'additionality'. This meant that the Lottery could not pay for the running costs and ongoing primary activities of companies, but only projects and resources that could be defined as 'additional' to those core costs and activities. Consequently, in the first instance, Lottery funds for the arts were restricted to capital – mainly building – projects, and were not able to be used for revenue, thus effectively preventing the funds from having any significant impact on the level of arts activity itself, which continued to struggle for survival under the public spending cuts and general economic downturn.

However, by 1996 the paradoxical vision of gleaming new buildings with declining numbers of artists to fill them, or companies to run them, was becoming apparent. The Arts Councils entered into conversations with the Secretary of State for the Department of National Heritage, Virginia Bottomley, to discuss how a percentage of Lottery funds might be shifted from capital spend to artistic development and content, albeit practice that could still be defined as 'additional' to the core activities of the company. The subsequent Lottery-funded schemes including Arts for Everyone (A4E), A4E Express, Awards for All and the Regional Arts Lottery Programme (RALP) had much to offer the independent theatre sector. Their objectives (new audiences, increased participation in the arts, skills development, youth projects and new work) were perfectly suited to the development, not only of artistic practice rather than buildings, but of new and experimental artistic practice and new approaches to audience, access and participation which situated independent theatre companies as perfectly placed recipients for the new money.

Of greatest impact on the future of the independent theatre ecology was the introduction of the A4E Express scheme which was targeted at small organizations who could bid for up to £5,000. In its first two rounds, the A4E Express delivered 21 million pounds to over 5,000 small projects (FitzHerbert and Paterson, 1998, 46). As a result, there was to be an explosion of new theatre companies across Britain who were benefiting from funds which were both significantly greater, and significantly easier to win, than anything that had previously been available for start-up companies from the Regional Arts Boards or National Arts Councils. As FitzHerbert and Paterson confirm, 'projects that met the criteria and the necessary technicalities were accepted pretty much on the spot' (FitzHerbert and Paterson, 1998, 46).

The impact of the Lottery went further than funding an explosion of new work; it also, to some degree, began to shape what that new work might be. Certainly for the main programme, the criteria outlined by the A4E application form encouraged projects to be designed with a distinctly greater emphasis on widening audience, access and partici-pation than had previously been the case with Arts Council funding. This can be seen in the nature of the work of the companies that were among the first beneficiaries of generous Lottery awards. Mind the Gap (£302,050) and Strathcona Theatre (£396,797) were both companies supporting people and artists with disabilities; Cardboard Citizens (£253,754) focused on working with and for homeless people; Tara Arts (£605,534) was a leading Asian theatre company; and Pop Up Theatre (£220,218) and Pegasus Theatre (£222, 239) both produced theatre for young people. Mind the Gap and Strathcona, although funded by the Arts Council under its touring scheme, did not receive core funding, and Cardboard Citizens was not funded by the Arts Council at all, so this lottery money, and its particular objectives, can be seen to have made a genuine contribution to the existing theatre ecology of the time, both in the kind of work that met its particular objectives, and in the degree of funds it could make available to support this kind of practice.

Arts Council Policies for Theatre 1995–8

The *Policy for Drama of the English Arts Funding System*, addressing the crisis in funding for drama in England in 1996, offered real seeds of hope for the independent theatre sector in subsequent years (ACE, 1996). Many of its recommendations were picked up and nurtured by the Boyden Report (2000) which was written a few years later in a much more auspicious period for significant financial investment. It emphasized throughout, the importance of new work and new writing for the growth of the theatre ecology in England; it also suggested that a shift in emphasis from allocations of funding according to historical precedent to one which was more responsive to emerging artistic initiatives might be desirable. Perhaps most crucially for independent touring companies in the following decades, it stressed the importance of the development of long-term partnerships between companies and venues, as the venue's traditional role as producing house was under strain and could benefit from a more mixed economy that included receiving and co-commissioning independent touring productions. Many of the additional initiatives which were going to influence the direction of arts strategy and impact on the independent theatre sector into the new millennium were also proposed here – an emphasis on access, audience development, international exchange, diversity and inclusion, and theatre for young people.

The year 1993 had seen the publication of two key strategy documents for Scottish Arts, the Charter for Arts in Scotland and SAC's four-year Corporate Plan. In common with the developments in England noted above, and in common with emerging arts policy in Wales, there was an emphasis on access and education, artist-led innovation, audience development, international exchange and the development of partnerships between building-based organizations and independent companies, co-productions and a greater sharing of existing resources. Where the English strategy's emphasis on access and greater cultural inclusion predominantly focused on the multicultural diversity of its population, in Scotland and Wales strategies highlighted the importance of promoting each nation's indigenous languages. In Scotland, policy was directed towards increasing the momentum for the sustainability of indigenous arts, and for greater support to be given to companies working in Scots or Gaelic. One of the first outcomes of this initiative, in 1995, was the establishment of an umbrella organization to improve the funding, promotion and development of Fèisean, festivals for young people to develop skills in the Gaelic arts of song, dance, drama and traditional music. The development of indigenous arts remained a priority in the subsequent corporate plan covering 1997–2001, leading, among other initiatives, to a commitment to support the newly independent Gaelic touring theatre company, TOSG, by offering it revenue funding from 1999. In Wales, the early initiatives outlined to promote Welsh-language theatre took a little longer to come to fruition, and were not without controversy, as I will later detail.

The other big question for Scotland at this time was the resurgence of discussions around the potential remit and repertoire for a Scottish National Theatre. Before such discussions could progress, however, the ongoing issues with the four existing national companies

(Scottish Ballet, Scottish Opera, Royal Scottish National Orchestra and the Scottish Chamber Orchestra) had to be resolved. In 1998, after two years of arduous conflict and mutual hostility, the Scottish Arts Minister, Sam Galbraith, finally released the additional funding that had been withheld from the companies pending their acceptance of significant changes in their financing, strategic management and infrastructure. This resulted in an agreement whereby, among other things, the companies were obliged to work much more collaboratively and share resources more centrally between them. To some degree, this emphasis on partnership and collaboration might be seen to lay the ground for the conception of the National Theatre that followed, although, significantly, the model of the National Theatre was put forward by the artistic community in the first instance, rather than the Scottish government. Perhaps, more portentously, the distrust expressed by the government in the internal management of these organizations can also be seen, with hindsight, as a key factor in their decision further down the line to take the national organizations, including the new National Theatre, out of the Arts Council's remit, to answer directly to government ministers.

In 1998, the Federation of Scottish Theatres, representing all the professional theatres in Scotland, took the findings of their report into the options for a National Theatre to the Scottish Executive. The plan was, as is now widely acknowledged, a radical departure from existing models, proposing not a building-based producing house but, as Robert Leach describes, 'a kind of parallel Arts Council ... but with "new" money to promote particular productions, and to be controlled by artists rather than bureaucrats' (Leach, 2007, 173). The working group's proposals were accepted by the Executive and in 2003 the Minister for Finance and Public Services was to allocate £7.5 million over two years to develop a National Theatre along the lines that had been recommended. The auspicious start to this national project, as Leach confirms, was that it ensured that pretty much the entirety of the Scottish artistic community 'was deeply committed from the outset to support a venture which complied with virtually all their ideas' (Leach, 2007, 174). Moreover, the collaborative nature of the model (with no building of its own, partnership was virtually a requirement for each of the company's productions) ensured that a comparatively significant percentage of the £4 million annual grant could go directly into artistic costs, rather than overheads. In addition, Scotland's existing theatres and independent companies stood, as it seemed at that time, to benefit significantly – in terms of profile, opportunity and economic dividends

– from the national project that was designed to 'commission existing theatres and theatre companies, or bring together directors, writers, designers, and performers in new combinations to create productions that will play in theatres and other venues up and down the country' (Leach, 2007, 174).

English Arts Policy under New Labour

In the summer of 1998, ACE received its first rise in government grant-in-aid since funds had begun to drop in real terms in 1992–3, with an additional £125 million pledged over the following three years. The immediate rise to grant-in-aid enabled the Arts Council to go some way to redressing the crippling five-year standstill in core funding which had been imposed on regularly funded clients since 1993. In 2000, a further significant spending review took place which resulted in a government commitment to subsequent increases to the arts grant-in-aid budget that would see Treasury spending on the arts rise by 'an additional £100m a year by 2003/4' (ACE, 2000b, 5). Theatre was to be highlighted as one of the three strategic priority areas to benefit from the substantial rise in grant-in-aid funding and was allocated an additional £25 million per year, thus taking the total annual spend on theatre from £40 million in 2000/1 to £70 million in 2003/4. A second priority of the government's additional funding was to address core funding across all arts organizations, so many theatre companies benefited twice over, with their core funding set to increase by an average of 17 per cent in 2002/3. Some companies, such as motiroti and Yellow Earth Theatre were awarded triple their existing grant allocation, and Pilot Theatre for young people went from an allocation of £49,300 in 2001/2 to an allocation of £240,000 in 2002/3. In addition, the rise in funding meant that the number of regularly funded independent theatre companies rose astronomically from around 30 in 2000/1 to well over 100 by 2002/3.

This expansion of the sector was seen as an opportunity for 'theatre to reinvent itself' in accordance with the *National Policy for Theatre*, published in 2000 and drawing on the Boyden Report and the Arts Council's subsequent response, *The Next Stage*. While Peter Boyden's report focused on the crisis facing regional repertory theatres, or producing houses, it addressed these within an assessment of the theatre ecology as a whole (Boyden, 2000). In the Boyden Report, we can see the consolidation of the strategic imperatives that were going to become a regular feature of arts funding policy in the new millennium, in particular, digital experimentation, cultural diversity, grass roots participation and internationalism. One further recommendation stands out as being central to the way in which independent companies were set to develop. Boyden recommended that producing houses, which were to be the main beneficiaries of the additional theatre funding, take on a much more central role in the development of independent companies than had previously been the case, thus leading to significantly increased support for independent companies in the making and touring of new work, as I will discuss further in Chapter 2.

The additional funding allocated to the sector by the government did not come without its own implicit or explicit ring-fenced directives. Under New Labour, the Department of National Heritage was rebranded as the Department of Culture, Media and Sport (DCMS). The four key themes for the department – access, excellence, education, economic value – were precisely replicated in the Arts Council objectives of 1998, and ultimately foregrounded the arts under New Labour as serving two primary purposes: first, their contribution to the economic growth area of the creative industries (Smith, 1998, 50), and secondly, their contribution to the 'cross-governmental attack on poverty and social exclusion' (Smith, 1998, 139). In line with New Labour's balancing act between the neoliberal market and the social-democratic imperative to address disadvantage, discussed earlier in this chapter, it saw artistic practice as likewise serving both agendas. In addition to their economic role within the 'Cool Britannia' project, the arts were committed, as I will now detail, to support government objectives in urban regeneration, reducing unemployment, juvenile crime and social delinquency, improving access for young people to culture and education, supporting diversity initiatives and greater community cohesion, and improving equal rights for minorities and those with disabilities. While such aims undoubtedly have merit, they do, as Michael McKinnie observes, reduce artistic practice to an instrumentalist role that 'is wholly affirmative. [New Labour's] policy does not acknowledge that art might be critical, subversive, or socially dissonant, conceptions of art which Labour Party policy once thought possible, and, to a limited degree, tried to encourage' (McKinnie, 2004, 188).

In the annual report of 2000, the Arts Council declared that it 'no longer simply gives out money. We now set national policy [...]' (ACE, 2000b, 7). No degree of emphasis in Arts Council literature on the 'arms-length from government' principle of arts funding could disguise the government's strategic objectives, which were as evident in their increased funding of the arts as they were in health, education and all other publicly funded services during their administration. From 2004, the Arts Council annual reviews were required to report against the official requirements of its Public Service Agreement that focused, in particular, on its commitment to increase levels of participation and widen social inclusion in the arts. This move towards a more target-driven cultural policy was underpinned by a shift in perspective which, from then on, began to frame the public funding of the arts 'as an "investment" with an anticipated return, as would have been the case with any other industry, rather than a "subsidy" offered to some supplicant, grant-dependent entity' (Ross, 2009, 25). In contrast to the message of the outgoing chairman, Lord Gowrie, who invoked Shakespeare and Wagner in his conclusion that 'the high arts have always been subsidised' (Gowrie, 1998, 8), the subsequent appointment, Gerry Robinson, the first chairman under New Labour, is clear that from this point on 'we don't want to create dependencies: a leg-up from the Arts Council will not mean a free ride for life' (Robinson, 1998, 2). Reconfigured as 'investment', public funding could now legitimately have several strings attached, and arts organizations under New Labour were rather to be seen as small businesses that could support the economy, the education of young people and the social fabric of a multicultural society.

Tony Blair's mantra on the importance of education and opportunities for young people was reflected in the Arts Council's emphasis on provision for this age group – indeed, it remained a strategic priority beyond New Labour's term in office, appearing as one of the four strategic priorities for the period 2008–11. In the wake of the spending review in 2000, and the significant rise in grant-in-aid money allocated to the theatre, the Arts Council committed to a 15 per cent increase in the funding of young people's companies throughout the country. In schools, Creative Partnerships was the flagship programme for New Labour and the Arts Council, and ran from its conception in 2002 until 2009 when it was finally disbanded as the squeeze on public spending began. The scheme placed artists into schools to work with teachers and pupils on often long-term projects and provided a significant funding stream for independent theatre companies and freelance artists over this time period. By the end of its run, it had worked 'intensively with more than 2,700 schools, with a further 10,000 involved. More than 915,000 young people had taken part in over 14,000 sessions' (ACE, 2009, 40). Creative Partnerships was quintessentially New Labour in its vision. Artists, in this instance, were not to teach their artistic practice for its own sake, but to offer schools their creative skills and strategies as a means to enhance educational provision across the curriculum, raising educational standards by re-engaging children in learning and skills acquisition.

The New Labour government's drive for community cohesion, as detailed earlier in this chapter, stepped up the Arts Council's ongoing attempts to establish a much wider ethnic diversity among the artists that it funded and the audiences for that work. The Black Regional Initiative in Theatre (BRIT) was designed to improve opportunities for the national touring of work by black, Asian and minority ethnic (BAME) artists, and gave rise, in 2002, to the Eclipse Theatre project that focused specifically on middle-scale African Caribbean touring theatre, as discussed further in Chapter 2. Decibel, a showcase platform for the work of BAME artists, was first established in 2003, and proved influential in introducing promoters, producers, programmers, artistic directors and venue managers to BAME work across the country.

Although disability theatre had been active on the fringes since the 1980s with companies such as Graeae and Theatre Workshop leading the vanguard, the 1990s and 2000s were to see a significant expansion and increase in the profile of such work in line with increased funding, changes in political legislation and progressive ideological shifts in public and media perception, as noted earlier in the chapter. Companies introduced to regular funding in 2001 included Mind the Gap, New Breed, Heart n Soul, and Full Body and the Voice (renamed Darkhorse in 2012), with Deafinately Theatre brought into the portfolio in 2005. Graeae saw its regular funding rise from £115,000 in 1999 to £225,566 in 2001. An even wider pool of artists benefited from a series of showcases over the 2000s designed specifically to promote the work of disabled and deaf artists. DaDaFest is an annual showcase of disabled and deaf art, supported by the Arts Council and delivered by the North West Disability Arts Forum since 2001. The Unlimited Festival at the Southbank Centre was established in 2009 as part of the run-up to the London Paralympics, and was presented as part of the Cultural Olympiad in 2012 featuring not only specialist disability companies such as Graeae and Mind the Gap, but also productions featuring deaf and disabled artists by the National Theatres of Wales and Scotland.

The Arts Council's strategic initiatives in relation to much of the above activity were informed by its Public Service Agreement with the Labour government and its need to meet the targets which were set for it as a condition of its receipt of public funds. In 2006, the Arts Council

Public Service Agreement targets were to 'increase the proportion of people from priority groups' who took part in, and who attended, arts events. The three priority groups were defined as the disabled; black, Asian and minority ethnic (BAME) communities; and the 'socially excluded' (those from socio-economic groups C2, D and E). What was clear from the Arts Council's annual reporting on these targets was that something was not working: despite the initiatives highlighted above, in the first year (2007) no targets were reached, and black, Asian and minority ethnic rates of participation and attendance actually went into reverse. By 2009, the final assessment of progress against the targets told much the same story, except for one single year when black, Asian and minority ethnic attendance at arts events had shown a slight increase, which the Arts Council credited to its Decibel initiative as mentioned above (ACE, 2009, 57). I will return to a number of possible reasons for the failure of these targets throughout this and the following chapter.

Scottish Arts Policy after Devolution

Both the 1999 election and the subsequent 2003 election produced a Scottish Labour-led coalition government with the Scottish Liberal Democrats. As Gavin Reid notes, in comparison with its Westminster counterpart, Holyrood Labour operated less in the 'post Thatcherite realm of markets' and more in a 'social democratic and ... nationalist environment' (Reid, 2007, 70). This was not all good news for the arts in terms of spending priorities. In defence of the reason Scottish theatres had not received a comparable funding boost to Westminster's additional £75 million, a Scottish Labour Culture Minister retorted that 'England did not benefit from free personal care for the elderly, the abolition of university tuition fees, or generous teachers' pay deal' (Wade 2002 in Reid, 2007, 71). The Executive's National Cultural Strategy, published in 2000, was seen by many, Reid reports, as a 'missed opportunity' that focused on 'discussing culture's role in social policy rather than its evaluation' (Reid, 2007, 72) or simply as 'dour public-service utilitarianism with art tagged onto social policy' (Reid, 2007, 71).

Even more inauspiciously, from the very start of the new Scottish Parliament, the Scottish Arts Council's policies were yoked firmly to the government's Cultural Strategy, with Allan Wilson, MSP and deputy Minister for Sport and Culture, commenting that he was 'pleased to see how well the Scottish Arts Council's Plan for 2001/2 ...

responds to the priorities set out in the [National Cultural] strategy'
(SAC, 2001, 3). The key messages in the Cultural Strategy were to
improve quality, diversity and inclusiveness, and it was clear that the
Arts Council was required to help the government deliver objectives
in this area in return for a significant increase in grant-in-aid funding
which would amount to more than £150 million for the arts in Scotland
over the subsequent five years.

The Scottish Arts Council was set targets between 2003 and 2006 to
increase participation in general, in the numbers of under-represented
groups taking part in cultural activity (in particular children and
young people), and in the number of cultural programmes in areas
of economic and social disadvantage. There was increased financial
support for theatre companies working with children and young
people, and those working with disabled artists were also particularly
well supported over this time. Young people's companies such as Wee
Stories, Catherine Wheels and Visible Fictions were brought into the
core funding portfolio over this period, and Theatre Workshop and
Lung Ha's also gained core funding for their work with disabled artists,
including the former's Degenerate Festival that was launched in 2003.
Unlike its English counterpart, the targets set on access and inclusion
appeared to have been met and exceeded by 2006, perhaps due to a
greater rigour on the part of Scottish funders to tie the strategic objectives directly to the activities of the companies that were allocated core
funding, or perhaps due to the much more pivotal role of local authorities in Scotland's cultural provision, thus enabling more focused,
local-level initiatives.

An additional governmental objective that can be seen to exponentially increase over the 2000s is the importance of arts and culture to
Scotland's national identity and profile as presented to the rest of the
world, with a particular focus on Europe and America. Here there are
clear parallels with Tony Blair's exploitation of the arts in his 'Cool
Britannia' project, and perhaps early signs of the 2007 victory of the
Scottish Nationalist Party, and Scotland's subsequent commitment to a
2014 vote for independence, in which the case for Scotland's capacity
to thrive as a fully independent country in an international climate
would be key to the campaign for a yes vote. In addition to the participation and inclusion objectives, therefore, the final target set was for
the Arts Council to 'develop the means of identifying the number of
Scottish world class artists, companies and institutions for 2006' (SAC,
2004a). The Arts Council also highlighted, among its four objectives,
the necessity of 'promoting Scotland internationally' (SAC, 2004a). It

is noticeable, in the annual reports over this period, how much space is increasingly taken up by a roll call of Scottish cultural success, not only via the Creative Scotland Awards made to individual artists, but also in international recognition for film stars (Sean Connery, Maggie Smith), novelists (Ian Rankin) and popular musicians (Franz Ferdinand, KT Tunstall), who arguably might be less validly claimed as 'recent' subsidized success stories (SAC, 2006). The importance of marketing a 'confident, cultured Scotland' appears many times throughout the Arts Council documents (SAC, 2003, 1), and in the 2004 report the potential of culture to offer a new and important brand to Scotland is explicitly spelt out: 'the arts are a universal language, ideal for promoting the positive image of a contemporary Scotland as an attractive place to visit, and to live and work in' (SAC, 2004b, 3). Gregory Burke's *Gagarin Way* (2001) and *Black Watch* (2006) are two notable Scottish exports over this period. The latter, in particular, has been described by Joanne Zerdy as a 'Scottish operative' whereby 'the production becomes the face of the NTS [National Theatre of Scotland] as the NTS acts as an international delegate for Scotland's performing arts' (Zerdy, 2013, 183). She continues, '[i]t may also stimulate interest in American audiences about Scottish culture and politics, which could lead to financial investment in tourism initiatives such as Homecoming Scotland' (Zerdy, 2013, 190). If *Black Watch* had performed a successful 'outward facing' national identity, then the inaugural production of the National Theatre of Scotland in 2006, *Home,* had been notable in the dialogue it established with all corners of Scotland about itself, made up of work 'by ten different directors, each charged with making a work round the word "home", and each working with local people in a different part of the country' (Leach, 2007, 176).

The early signs that forewarned of the eventual amputation of the arm that was intended to maintain the independence of arts funding and policy from government control came to fruition with the publication of the Scottish Executive's plan for the future of arts funding, *Scotland's Culture,* in 2006. Some of its most inauspicious conclusions had already been foreseen in the recommendations made by the Cultural Commission in 2005, which saw a raft of last-ditch attempts by over 90 leading Scottish organizations, including Scottish National Opera and the Edinburgh International Festival, to urge the Commission to retain the arm's length principle, and preserve the Arts Council or a body like it, which acts, in the words of the Scottish Arts Council's chief executive, 'as a check, or balance, against unhealthy concentrations of power which can skew the ultimate aims or purpose of any endeavour' (Calvi, 2005). In the event, arts organizations might have preferred more, not less, of the Commission's recommendations to be taken up, including the necessity for additional annual funding of £100 million and the maintenance of the arm's length principle which the report did, to some degree, advocate. The Executive's preference, as detailed in *Scotland's Culture*, was to award only an additional £20 million annually, and to fund national arts companies directly from that point on, with, as Reid notes, 'increased funding tied to minimum standards of performance, touring, outreach and governance' (Reid, 2007, 73). All other companies would come under the strategic remit of a new organization, Creative Scotland, which would replace both the Scottish Arts Council and Scottish Screen.

If this was potentially politically catastrophic for the arts in Scotland, the economic impact would be felt even more directly, as it was announced that the 100 plus arts companies currently being core funded would no longer be able to rely on a continuation of automatic funding, but would have to apply for either long-term 'foundation funding', or 'flexible funding' that could last for up to three years. In the event, foundation funding was predominantly reserved for venues and ongoing development initiatives, with previously core-funded theatre companies, other than the NTS which was now going to be taken under the government's remit, being required to apply for flexible funding in the future. Long-standing core-funded companies Borderline and 7:84 were told that they would have their funds withdrawn from March 2007 as part of, in the words of SAC chairman Richard Holloway, 'a root-and-branch investigation of the whole landscape of arts funding in Scotland with a view to getting this logjam moving, as we'll be building in space for the surprises of new talent and new approaches' (BBC, 2006). In the event, the majority of theatre companies on core-funded contracts were re-established on comparable budgets (if not comparable expectations of stability) within the new flexibly funded system, and new beneficiaries of the 'space for surprises' included Grid Iron, Giant Productions, Plan B and Vanishing Point.

Welsh Arts Policy after Devolution

In 1998, Arts Council Wales launched a fundamental review of its support for professional theatre in the context of three years of standstill funding and an unbalanced portfolio of revenue funded companies, with only four out of 20 clients receiving over £150,000 per annum. The review, particularly focused on Theatre in Education (TIE) and new writing, was drawn up after a significant public consultation, but despite the Arts Council's insistence that there was popular support for its view that it was funding too many companies too thinly, its final recommendations were to prove hugely contentious on both fronts.

It was inarguable that the eight TIE companies in Wales – Arad Goch, Clwyd TIE, Cwmni'r Frân Wen, Gwent Theatre, Hijinx, Theatr Iolo, Theatr Powys and Spectacle Theatre – were now experiencing severe financial difficulties due to their historic links with the eight former local education authorities which had recently been dismantled and restructured, resulting in local authority funding for TIE dropping by half. In June 1999, ACW put out tenders for only five fixed-term funding contracts for what was now termed Theatre for Young People, to replace the eight TIE funding agreements that then existed. However, the proposed axing of funding for the long-established Gwent Theatre and Theatr Powys in particular, not least in the light of potential legal challenges to the franchise process itself, sparked a sustained and impassioned assault on the directorship and management of ACW from arts professionals, politicians and the public, with MP Llew Smith calling for the Arts Council to be 'scrapped and replaced with an organisation that is democratic, accountable and fair, with an understanding of the aspirations of communities right throughout Wales' (Theatre-Wales, 1999). With Arts Council staff threatening a vote of no confidence in their own management, and imminent legal challenges to the funding decisions, ACW was forced into a U-turn and reluctantly announced the suspension of the Theatre for Young People element of the Drama Strategy and the reinstatement of three-year funding agreements to all eight existing TIE companies with effect from April 2000.

A similar strategy, running parallel to the developments in young people's theatre, was at the heart of ACW's new theatre writing initiative, which invited three existing revenue-funded companies, Dalier Sylw, Made in Wales and the Sherman Theatre Company, to bid for the running of a single, bi-lingual new-writing centre, producing plays in Welsh and English. In the event, only Made in Wales was to have its funding axed, with Dalier Sylw (renamed Sgript Cymru and ultimately, in 2006/7, to be merged with the Sherman) gaining increased funding, but still £90,000 short of the combined budget that had supported the two companies previously. There was an outcry at the decision from playwrights and supporters of new writing, who saw the new bi-lingual strategy as a cynical money-saving move that actually cut the budget for new writing in both languages under the auspices of a review that purported to be developing the capacity of new writing throughout Wales.

While the concern over the loss of funding for new writing is well documented in the media, less noted was the loss, in the same year, of revenue funding for Brith Gof, arguably the most innovative and politically edgy company in recent Welsh history, with a significant academic and international following. It seemed that as the control over new writing was becoming more and more centralized, as I will further detail, genuinely alternative theatre in Wales – in both a political and aesthetic sense – was to be pushed to the very margins of existence. In 2000, in the wake of the calamitous drama review, a report on the management of ACW was commissioned by the Welsh Assembly and compiled by Richard Wallace, who concluded that 'the council has lost the confidence of those it serves in the arts community and in itself' (BBC, 2000). The report was followed by the resignation of the Chief Executive, Joanna Weston, and the start of a large-scale restructuring process of ACW itself, which was, as in Scotland, to ultimately lead to control over arts funding and strategy being diverted further away from the Arts Council and ever closer to the directives of government ministers.

In 2002, the re-structured Arts Council was rewarded by the Welsh Assembly with a 23 per cent increase in funding – an announcement in the annual report ominously followed by the news of the government's cultural strategy (*Creative Future: Cymru Greadigol*) that would provide 'the framework for the Arts Council of Wales' strategy and includes many challenging targets for ACW' (ACW, 2002, 6). Clearly, in the minds of the National Assembly, the additional money was allocated with some considerable strings attached. One significant project to be launched was the plan for a Welsh-language theatre powerhouse with a national brief. In an unprecedented move, rather than identifying an existing company to take this agenda forward, or putting the opportunity out to tender, the Arts Council itself established a steering committee 'charged with formulating the vision statement of the new company, registering the new company and recruiting the Chair and Board' (ACW, 2002, 21). In effect, the ACW, now tied to some degree at least to government objectives, were creating their own company – Theatr Genedlaethol Cymru – to which they then awarded £430,150 for its first year of trading; a considerable sum in comparison to Sgript Cymru's allocation of only £284,000. The rationale, it might well be argued, was to increase the funding of Welsh-language theatre to somewhere near its English language theatre counterpart – Clwyd Theatr Cymru – which had now been afforded the status of a National Performing Company and was in receipt of revenue funding of £1,383,819, but this could equally have been achieved by raising the funding of existing Welsh-language theatre organizations, such as Sgript Cymru had been before it was required by ACW to offer a bi-lingual remit. In the event, the blurring of lines between the objective and disinterested role of a national funding agency and the Arts Council's now quasi-artistic affiliation to a governmental priority was a worrying sign of things to come.

In 2004, the worst appeared to be on the horizon, with the First Minister, Rhodri Morgan, announcing his intention to redefine the relationship between the Welsh Assembly government and the Arts Council of Wales as part of a wider programme to reform public services focusing in particular on the abolition of 'quangos' (Rhydderch, 2004). A Culture Board, chaired by the Minister, would be established, in which the Arts Council, along with others, would participate. However, the crucial role of policy making would be removed from the Arts Council, and the six 'nationally' significant companies, including the English-language theatre, Clwyd Theatr Cymru, and the newly established Welsh-language theatre, Theatr Genedlaethol, would be directly funded from the National Assembly from 2006, leaving the Arts Council to develop the predominantly Lottery-funded smaller organizations. The new funding agreements would, predictably, tie the national companies in to governmental objectives, committing them to ambassadorial cultural work on behalf of the country, and a contribution to the access, participation and inclusion agendas of the Welsh Assembly. Given the same direction of travel in Scotland, it is no wonder that Christopher Frayling, the Chairman of Arts Council England, was driven to note in his 2005 annual report that '[l]ines must be drawn between elected politicians or civil servants and an independent funding body, and we are monitoring developments in Wales and Scotland with some concern' (Frayling, 2005, 2).

However, in January 2006, after 14 months of debate, and finally spurred into action by the controversial decision by the Labour-led Assembly not to renew the contract of Arts Council chairman Geraint Talfan Davies in favour of a more pro-government appointment, the leaders of the Welsh Liberal Democrats, Conservatives and Plaid Cymru demanded that the country's culture minister reverse a string of policies that they feared were seriously jeopardizing the arm's length principle, including a suspension of the decision to directly fund the six national companies and remove the policy-making remit from

ACW. Following a vote in Plenary, the Wales Arts Review was commissioned by the Minister of Culture to review the role of ACW, and the plan to directly manage the six national companies was put on hold pending the conclusions of the review. Among the report's recommendations were that a dual-strategy board should be established, in effect a partnership between ACW and the Welsh Assembly, but crucially that the six national companies should not be directly funded. The report did, however, acknowledge that the role, remit and strategic development of national companies needed addressing by the strategy board, and it also recommended the designation of 'beacon companies' among its clients, which would be allocated additional funds from a 'merit pot' on the strength of 'consistent best practice in their field, which may be art form or development based' (Stephens, 2006, 26). So, ACW, unlike the Scottish Arts Council, was to survive, but the strategic and economic prioritization of the 'national theatres' that was now in train was to have significant impact on the future of the independent theatre ecology throughout Wales, particularly in the wake of the imminent global economic crash.

Into Austerity: 2008–14 (England)

In January 2008, the McMaster review of the arts was published, a document that did much to address the tide of instrumentalism that had engulfed artistic policy throughout the previous decade. The report reinstated the notion that excellence, innovation and risk-taking must be at the heart of artistic practice, and acknowledged the need to free such practice, in the words of Culture Secretary James Purnell, 'from outdated structures and burdensome targets, which can act as millstones around the neck of creativity' (McMaster, 2008, 4). Even McMaster's references to the familiar priorities of audiences and diversity were weighted distinctly differently: advising against second-guessing what audiences wanted, and advocating a culture where audiences might be productively challenged and stressing that an understanding of diversity must go beyond race to encompass all aspects of society.

The McMaster review was undertaken in 2007 alongside a spending review which saw Arts Council England receive an above-inflationary increase in funding for the arts with the caveat of a 15 per cent reduction in administration costs that was to see its staffing reduced by 21 per cent by 2010. The spending review also heralded the

Arts Council's controversial investment strategy for the arts which proposed using the additional funding to increase the regular funding of selected Regularly Funded Organizations (RFOs) and introduce new RFOs at the expense of removing regular funding from others. Across all arts sectors, there was an increase in funding for 76 per cent of existing organizations, 81 new organizations brought into the portfolio, with 185 having their funding withdrawn. As the Arts Council chair, Christopher Frayling, expressed it, the aim was 'to champion innovation and excellence by bringing new organisations and giving others above-inflation increases rather than simply give all existing funded organisations a little more' (ACE, 2008, 2). Not only was this one of the rare occasions when a significant cull of existing arts organizations was the result of deliberate strategy and increased funding, rather than cuts, it was also spectacularly mismanaged.

There was never any public dissemination of the strategy, rationale or criteria that lay behind the decision making, leading many to doubt, as Lyn Gardner noted, 'that a genuine national strategy is being implemented. The Arts Council should immediately take steps to reassure us and prove that it really has been doing some joined-up thinking and not just been wielding the knife where it fancies' (Gardner, 2007). This was all the more vital given that, as Gardner, among others, was quick to point out, 'the RSC and National and larger regional reps seem to be sitting pretty and the main burden of the cuts appears to have fallen on smaller organisations and the independent sector' (Gardner, 2007). Raising further concerns over the lack of transparency was the decision to notify those whose grants were being cut privately, with no initial publication of gains or losses, thus shrouding the overall picture in secrecy. There were also some decisions that had been taken on astoundingly incorrect evidence, such as the decision to cut funding for the Bush on the strength of audience figures that had been miscalculated by two-thirds.

The Bush, along with the Orange Tree, the Northcott Theatre and the National Student Drama School all eventually won appeals against the original decision, but these successful appeals were rare and, probably not incidentally, 'backed by the likes of Ian McKellen, Judi Dench and Sam West' (Edwardes, 2008). Long-established theatre companies to lose their regular funding in this review were many including Compass Theatre, David Glass Ensemble, Doo Cot, Kaos, London Bubble, The People Show, Pop up theatre, Red Shift, Rejects Revenge, Sphinx and Station House Opera. Companies that quietly benefited from the debacle and were introduced to regular funding included

Punchdrunk, Ockham's Razor, Metro-Boulot-Dodo and Fevered Sleep. If there seemed to be little rationale, as Gardner had argued, in where the axe fell, there certainly seemed to be evidence, given the theatre companies benefiting, that formalistic experimentation within the independent sector of the theatre ecology was being highly prized in the new awards being made. The funding review also saw the introduction of production company Fuel to regular funding, a pioneer in the rise of the independent theatre producer that I will discuss in detail in Chapter 2. Probably not incidentally, Fuel was a staunch promoter of the type of experimental performance that also characterized most of the newly recognized companies.

The most ominous consequence of the Arts Council's mishandling of the whole affair was the hostility and distrust engendered in the arts community, demonstrated by the mass showing of disapproval at the Young Vic in January 2008 when high-profile actors and theatre artists gathered to publicly express their anger to Arts Council chief executive, Peter Hewitt. The *Evening Standard*'s theatre critic Nicholas de Jongh even argued that

> The Arts Council is an overstuffed bureaucracy. It is high time that government tried something different. Let the council be mothballed, its staff dismissed and its functions be taken over by the Department for Culture, which could draw up a diverse cultural blueprint for each art form. (de Jongh, 2008)

This was not an auspicious start for the year in which, come the crash of Lehman Brothers, everything was to change, and de Jongh might yet feel he should have been careful what he wished for.

By the summer of 2010, the arts were not only facing the worst national financial crisis in the Arts Council's history, but were dealing once again with a Tory-led government for the first time in 13 years. 'We all knew this year would be tough' the Arts Council's annual report begins, and they were not to be proved wrong (Forgan, 2010, 2). In May 2010, the Chancellor of the Exchequer, George Osborne, announced an initial round of public service cuts of £6 billion for the 2010/11 financial year. This resulted in a cut to the Arts Council's grant from the Department for Culture, Media and Sport of £19 million, in addition to the £4 million it had already cut from the coming year's budget, and on top of the previous 21 per cent reduction in Arts Council staff in line with the 2007 spending review.

The opening of the 2011 annual report was no better, beginning 'this was the year in which the whole nation, including the arts, had to face fundamental choices about where real priorities lay in the context of a severe recession and a government determined to reduce the public spending deficit' (Forgan, 2011, 4). Just three years after the strategic overhaul of 2008, there was to be another significant revision of the National Portfolio, this time out of necessity rather than choice. Again, the Arts Council resisted calls for the changes to be spread evenly across existing RFOs, and instead drew a line under all existing partnerships, requiring all organizations to apply from the outset to be taken on under the new National Portfolio agreement to take effect from 2012. Perhaps learning from previous mistakes, this was undertaken with much greater transparency, and organizations were asked to explain in their applications precisely how they expected to contribute to the realization of the Arts Council's ten-year strategy for the Arts, *Achieving Great Art for Everyone*, which focused on excellence, increased access, increased participation for young people, sustainability, leadership and diversity.

While the requirement for artists and organizations to now fit their plans to the given framework might have been transparent and equitable, it also concluded, in explicit terms and counter to the recommendations of McMaster, the inevitable trajectory set on course by New Labour, and already established in Scotland and Wales, for the artistic agenda to be set, not by artists, but by the Arts Council, which in turn was answerable to the government via the Public Service Agreement targets. The National Portfolio was to mark the point where accountability to targets would finally become the overriding concern for arts organizations in receipt of regular funding, and smaller organizations with less administrative capacity, and the greatest propensity to take artistic risks that had no certain outcome, would inevitably suffer the most. Risk-taking, it seemed, was to be supported principally by the Lottery-funded grants for the arts programme, which from this point on would be available only to artists outside of the National Portfolio, who would arguably enjoy greater freedom from the more punitive target-driven culture of the NPOs, but at the considerable cost of the insecurity and lack of sustainability of project-by-project funding.

New organizations to join the portfolio included Gecko Theatre, Red Earth Theatre, Clod Ensemble, Coney, 20 Stories High, Dreamthinkspeak, Propeller Theatre Company, NoFit State Circus, Eclipse Theatre and Slung Low. Among the existing RFO organizations who failed to win portfolio status were Action Space Mobile, Box Clever, Faulty Optic, Forkbeard Fantasy, Foursight, Nitro, Proper

Job, Quicksilver, Reckless Sleepers, Shared Experience, Third Angel, Trestle and Yellow Earth. Despite the high regard in which many of the above were held by the arts community, and the significant international profiles many enjoyed, the response was much more subdued and submissive than the unified, high-profile outcry in 2008, for a number of reasons. First, it was now the age of austerity and there was a certain degree of 'cuts fatigue' across society as a whole. Secondly, the Arts Council had approached the situation with a much greater sense of responsibility and transparency for its actions and, thirdly, the Arts Council had tried to take the brunt of the cuts to its own organization as much as was possible, limiting the cut to the budget from which it funded arts organizations to 15 per cent, rather than the 29.6 per cent cut to the Arts Council as a whole. This necessitated a further reduction in the Arts Council's own operating budget of 50 per cent by the end of the spending review in 2015 – a cut which, on top of its previous 15 per cent cut – would ultimately, by the time of writing, see the Arts Council reduced to a skeleton of its former self, with its capacity to lead on strategy, to envision and manage change for the sector, and to lobby for support seriously diminished.

Both the immediate consequences and the long-term implications of these cuts to the Arts Council were explicitly highlighted in the aftermath of the second round of NPO decisions which were announced in July 2014 for the subsequent three-year funding period. Unlike the 2011 round, where there were significant changes to the small/medium-scale theatre company sector, bringing in a number of companies that had relatively recently begun to gain high-profile attention to replace a similar number of long-standing companies from whom RFO status was withdrawn, in this round, the cuts to the independent theatre sector far outweighed the gains, with those losing 100 per cent of their NPO funding including Ridiculusmus, Dark Horse, Theatre Sans Frontieres, Whalley Range All Stars, Propeller, Big Brum, Carnesky Productions and Red Ladder. Theatre companies to be introduced to the portfolio were Chol Theatre, Third Angel, Tangle and Wired Aerial. Of these, both Chol and Third Angel had been Regularly Funded Organizations prior to the 2011 round, making their 'new' NPO status from 2015 read rather more like the reinstatement of established companies which should never have been dropped than an embrace of up-and-coming new practice. Both the contraction of the field of emergent core-funded and independently constituted theatre makers in England, and the financially necessitated reduction of the Arts Council's strategic role are, as I will now discuss, aspects of a path already well-trodden by this point north and west of the borders.

Into Austerity: 2008–14 (Scotland)

In Scotland, the proposed new organization for the arts, Creative Scotland, took an inauspiciously long time to come about. In 2007 the Joint Board of the Scottish Arts Council and Scottish Screen took over the old functions of each organization and the remit to strategically plan for the incoming Creative Scotland. But not until 2010 was the new organization clearly established and equipped to take over the funding and strategic management of the arts (other than the national organizations) – albeit within the now too familiar co-ordinates set by the Scottish Executive. As the chief executives of the outgoing SAC and Scottish Screen confirm:

> The Scottish government has given a very clear indication as to what Creative Scotland's four national priorities should be. Both Scottish Screen and the Scottish Arts Council are committed to delivering against these priorities during 2010/11 as we move towards Creative Scotland and the development of its first full corporate plan in 2011/12. (SAC, 2011, 5)

The four priorities were again focused on the combination of encouragement of artists, the necessity of improving access and participation and the raising of the international profile of Scotland; in the words of the corporate plan, 'to extend and increase the wider benefits of arts and culture, including their contribution to the promotion and development of our unique national culture and its wider place in the international sphere' (SAC, 2011, 5). The arm in the arm's length principle seemed to have undergone its final amputation with the arrival of Creative Scotland. In 2012, *Guardian* critic Charlotte Higgins noted that:

> at no point in my extensive reading about Creative Scotland have I come across an example of the organization challenging the government. The point of an arts council is to act as a buffer zone between artists and the government and at times to challenge it. Creative Scotland insists it is at 'arm's length' from the government, but if it is breaking ranks, it is happening behind the scenes. This

seems particularly important when some fear that Scottish culture is being harnessed as a semi-political tool in the branding of 'Team Scotland'. (Higgins, 2012a)

It was possibly unfortunate that Creative Scotland, having already been inauspiciously conceived, and already having suffered a difficult and prolonged birth, was finally delivered at the height of austerity. Just like its English counterpart, it had to come to terms with the fact that there might well be less grant-in-aid funding from the Executive in the future than there had been in the past. Although an additional share of Lottery money had been allocated to attempt to alleviate the cuts, and would, in fact, increase the overall total spend, this could not be used for core funding, due to the additionality clause in the original Lottery legislation. As a result, as Joyce McMillan summarizes, 'the organisation, therefore, needs to withdraw regular grant income from some arts companies, to reduce the regular element of the funding of others, and to set up some large project funds open to all comers, and it needs to make these decisions on the basis of current artistic perfor-mance' (McMillan, 2012). Not, as McMillan concluded, 'rocket science for any well-run arts agency', but Creative Scotland decided instead to announce the withdrawal of funding from the entire portfolio of flexibly funded companies, resulting in throwing 'some 49 Scottish arts organisations from a condition of modest security into a state of complete insecurity, in which they have to bargain from project to project for their right to exist' (McMillan, 2012).

One of the longest standing and most politically astute arts commen-tators in the UK, McMillan was clear where the blame for the debacle should lie, stating that 'this review raises serious questions about the board of Creative Scotland, which has knowingly appointed to key roles in Scotland's cultural life people who clearly embrace a commerce-driven ideology that Scotland in general, and its cultural community in particular, has rejected at every available opportunity' (McMillan, 2012). The '"supposedly" social-democratic SNP government' also had questions to answer about 'why it continues to preside so complacently over such needlessly controlling systems of administration, and so much insidious market-inflected corrosion of the values for which it says it stands' (McMillan, 2012).

Where previously there had been a distinction between a fairly small cohort of flexibly funded companies (core in all but name), and a much larger raft of companies which were awarded reasonably regular project funding, the revised category of flexible funding was a kind of hybrid of the two, enabling a maximum of just two year funding to previously flexibly funded companies, in addition to a number of newcomers from the old project-funded cohort including Ankar Arts, Mischief La Bas, Fire Exit, Theatre Cryptic, Vox Motus and Birds of Paradise. Foundation funding, from this point on, was targeted at buildings and programmes, leaving none of the independent theatre companies, however well established, with the capacity to plan for more than 24 months at a time.

By October 2012, the artistic community's dissatisfaction had come to a head with over 100 Scottish artists – amounting to the bulk of the Scottish arts establishment – signing an open letter to Creative Scotland's chairman, Sir Sandy Crombie, protesting against the routinely 'ill-conceived decision-making; unclear language, lack of empathy and regard for Scottish culture'. The letter continued, 'We observe an organisation with a confused and intrusive management style married to a corporate ethos that seems designed to set artist against artist and company against company' (in Higgins, 2012b). In December, the chief executive who had overseen the establishment of Creative Scotland, Andrew Dixon, resigned from his post, and Creative Scotland began the process of restoring trust with the arts community. In the annual report of 2013, Sir Sandy Crombie acknowledged that 'During the year it became clear that we were not getting everything right and that elements of the way we were working and our approach were alienating a significant proportion of the people and organisations that we are here to support' (Creative Scotland, 2013, 3). One significant change to appear in Creative Scotland's subsequent ten-year plan, published in 2014, was the restoration of three-year regular funding contracts, open to application in the summer of 2014.

Into Austerity: 2008–14 (Wales)

In 2007, plans began in earnest for the development of an English-language National Theatre for Wales, with an additional £250,000 pledged by the Welsh Assembly. In 2008 the artistic director, John McGrath, was appointed to lead an organization which, like the National Theatre of Scotland, would be a building-less company which would seek to collaborate with the existing infrastructure of theatre companies and venues to create 'a new theatre ecology for Wales' (ACW, 2007). The model of the company's launch in 2010 also echoed the NTS's strategic approach, with 12 inaugural productions taking place across Wales, beginning with *A Good Night Out in the Valleys* at Blackwood Miner's Institute in March of that year.

The year 2010 also saw, in Wales as in Scotland and England, an austerity-provoked root and branch review of its revenue funding resulting in 32 existing organizations having their funding withdrawn or significantly cut. Established theatre companies to be hit included Hijinx, Theatr Powys and Gwent Theatre. There was an inevitable outcry from those companies and communities affected by the cuts, and accusations that the decisions would cause irreparable damage to the whole arts ecology in Wales. New companies introduced to revenue funding were few, with NoFit State Circus and Theatr Ffynnon representing the theatre sector. As well as this there was a strategic injection of increased funding into a significant number of community and grass-roots organizations in some of Wales' most deprived regions.

Interestingly, there was little in the media coverage of the cuts which correspondingly emphasized the significant gains made by the national organizations; the newly established National Theatre Wales, for example, received a funding increase of £335,000 to take its annual revenue funding in 2011/12 to £1,685,000. Taken alongside the allocation to Theatr Genedlaethol Cymru, the Welsh Language National Theatre, of £1,052,942, it becomes clear that, whatever might prove to be the benefits of the two national companies established by ACW, the money that was no longer available to fund independently established and constituted companies was not inconsiderable.

Looking Ahead ...

It is notable that between 1995 and 2010, prior to the introduction of NoFit State and Ffynnon, not one independently founded, project-funded theatre company was introduced into the Welsh revenue portfolio, and none has been introduced since. Companies that were revenue funded in 1995 have been continued, folded or amalgamated to produce fewer and more centralized and building-based organiza-tions, to the detriment of a diverse independent sector. Consequently, progression opportunities towards sustainable funding contracts for young emergent companies were now seemingly non-existent, beyond theatre for children and young people, and theatre for people with disabilities, which both continue to be relatively well supported. Conversely, by 2014 Wales had no fewer than four establishment theatres funded at over £1 million, two of which had been founded by the Arts Council (National Theatre of Wales and Theatr Genedlaethol Cymru) and one of which (Sherman Cymru) was the result of a merger between formerly independent companies and a building-based theatre.

The relative absence of Welsh companies in Chapter 2 is precisely down to this deficit, and it is noticeable that since its first production in 2010, the National Theatre of Wales has worked with NoFit State and Volcano, two of the very few remaining experimental independent companies in Wales, but this number is dwarfed by partnerships with companies from across Europe, including Rimini Protokoll, and companies core funded by the English Arts Council, including Told by an Idiot, Fevered Sleep, Wildworks and Frantic Assembly. There is no lack of imagination or innovation in John McGrath's artistic direc-torship, and Welsh artists and writers feature heavily in the National Theatre of Wales' portfolio of work to date, but the innovations fostered by emergent companies sustained by regular revenue funding are simply not there for the NTW to draw on as they are sadly no longer part of the theatre ecology in Wales. Artistic innovation, it seems, is now entrusted to the national theatres which are inescapably part of the political establishment, which seriously limits the potential for Welsh theatre to mount any meaningful challenge to the Welsh 'brand' as designed and authorized by the Welsh administration in the years to come. It is ominous, for anyone who values the arm's length principle, to see in the 2013 ACW report, quite how many times the Welsh government is praised for its support, or 'applauded for its foresight', and the conclusion of the chief executive, Nick Capaldi, that 'arts and culture ... are a proper matter for our celebration, and for govern-ment's closest attention' (ACW, 2013, 10) seems to confirm the future direction of arts policy in Wales.

Despite the general sense that Creative Scotland made a welcome change of course in 2013, it is still notable in the 2014–15 annual plan that the entire ecology of independent theatre-making companies is now being funded solely from Lottery money that is still nominally reserved for 'additional' rather than 'core' spending. The implication is that, culturally, these organizations are now seen as merely 'additional' to the building-based and national organizations that are either funded from grant-in-aid or directly from the Scottish Executive, and are thus entirely dependent on the fortunes of the Lottery, as is the sector's long-term survival. This may, of course, change when the new funding regime comes into force, but it seems much more likely that what will happen is that the majority of currently flexibly funded companies will become regularly funded companies over a three-year period, in line with the National Portfolio Organizations in England. The important distinction is that much of England's independent sector remains funded by core, statutory, grant-in-aid funding, leaving the independent ecology in Scotland somewhat more vulnerable. Joyce McMillan offers some seeds of hope in her support for Scotland's Culture Secretary, Fiona Hyslop, and her cautious optimism about the 'better shape' of the institutional landscape, but she does express concern about Creative Scotland's continuing 'silence' with regard to 'addressing the question of exactly how it will make its funding decisions', noting that Scottish arts policy of recent history has

> undergone a triple challenge; first from those who rightly rejected the old, rigid canon of "great art"; then from the shock-troops of extreme individualism who wrongly argued that artistic judgment can never be anything more than individual and subjective; and finally from the purely social, economic and bureaucratic measures of the value of art that rushed in to fill the vacuum. (McMillan, 2014)

Creative Scotland's ten-year plan itself set out five priorities of experimentation, access, quality of life, a skilled workforce and, unsurprisingly given the pending referendum, the distinctiveness of Scotland as a creative nation that is connected to the wider world.

If the Arts Council of England was prescient, in 2005, to monitor 'developments in Wales and Scotland with some concern' (Frayling, 2005, 2), any hope it might have had of averting the foreseeable shortening of the arm's length, the reduction of the Arts Council's capacity for strategic leadership and the constriction of the independent theatre company ecology turned out to be short lived. The 2014 funding round confirmed the direction ACE had been heading since 2010, seeing the ecology of small companies suffer so that flagship buildings and national organizations, predominantly in London, could be sustained. Moreover, there was a further raid on Lottery funding, previously restricted under its additionality clause for project grants, to fund some NPO organizations with 100 per cent Lottery money for the first time. When the danger of this was raised with Mags Patten, the Arts Council's National Director of Communications, at a public meeting in July 2014, she responded that it had been essential to counter the government cuts in grant-in-aid funding, and so long as the Arts Council 'can be seen to be using lottery money in a distinct and transparent way', and the percentage of lottery money used for core company costs remained 'proportional', she felt that the perceived threat of it ultimately replacing grant for aid was minimal (Patten, 2014). Her subsequent assurance that the Arts Council had received 'commitment from both political parties to the principle of grant-in-aid' proved unsurprisingly less reassuring to the audience of artists whom she addressed, than it seemingly had to the Arts Council itself (Patten, 2014).

To conclude, for different ideological reasons and under different ideological administrations, the future of the independent theatre sector in the UK is looking increasingly fragile at the time of writing, and we have come a long way from the golden age of the expansion of the sector, in Scotland and England at least, under New Labour and the Scottish Parliament in the 2000s. In the following chapter I will examine in detail how this ecology grew over the period of this study, and how it has secured an artistic legacy within mainstream theatre that might yet prove, ironically, more sustainable than the independent sector itself.

Chapter 2

BRITISH THEATRE COMPANIES: 1995–2014

Liz Tomlin

PART ONE:
INFLUENCES ON THE ECOLOGY OF THE
INDEPENDENT THEATRE SECTOR

It is significantly more difficult to comprehensively chart the independent theatre ecology over this time period than in previous decades for a number of reasons. Primarily, the expansion of activity from the roll out of Lottery funding in 1995 led, not only to a proliferation of companies that far exceeds earlier periods, but also to a diversity of support for such companies that extends well beyond the traditional regular funding agreements with the Arts Councils. To look first of all at numbers of regularly funded independent theatre companies alone: for 1997/8, Brown, Brannen and Brown identify 37 English RFOs, to which we need to add five Scottish and 13 Welsh companies of comparable status, making a total of 55 (Brown et al., 2000, 383). By 2007/08, there were, at best count, 15 Scottish companies, still around 13 Welsh companies, with companies in England now numbering well over 120, making around 150 regularly funded theatre companies in total.

This activity, however, extensive though it is, remains indicative only of those organizations in receipt of regular funding from the Arts Councils, and while this might have been a reliable indicator of most significant activity in earlier periods, there are a number of reasons why this can no longer be taken to automatically apply. The advent of the Lottery, which exponentially increased the money available for project by project funding, the available funding for socially applied arts practice provided by New Labour (from both arts and social funding pots), the rise of practice-based research supported directly and indirectly by universities and via research income streams such as the Wellcome Trust, and significant levels of European funding for regeneration initiatives within designated areas of disadvantage in the UK, meant that in this period it was quite possible for companies to be established and funded for significant periods of time and make a lasting impact on the ecology of the sector, without ever having been in receipt of regular Arts Council funding agreements, although Arts Council recognition via regular project funding was usually essential and provided important leverage to obtain money from these other sources. There is no comprehensive listing of these companies, and many are short lived, but, at best estimate, drawing together project funding lists over this period, and accounting for additional companies working from university bases, or outside of arts funding programmes, as well as the Regularly Funded Organizations, I would suggest that the number has risen from the 270 identified in England at the close of the 1980s by Baz Kershaw (2004, 365) to well over 500 companies operating at any one time across the UK in the 2000s.

Creative Producers

Given the steep proliferation of emerging companies over this period, the challenge for newcomers became one of achieving visibility and profile in the eyes of Arts Council officers from among the hundreds of companies now easily able to access small project funding via the Lottery awards, but most often aspiring towards longer-term and more sustainable core-funding agreements. Battersea Arts Centre (BAC) was one of the pioneers in a growing number of small-scale venues that flourished in the early Lottery period, and offered emergent practice not only a widespread touring circuit that was new to the sector but also increasingly 'hands-on' producer support for the development of the work. BAC was among the first venues, in the 1990s, to introduce showcase platforms for 'work-in-progress', and popularized the form of the scratch night for emerging artists, which enabled a number of unknown companies to offer a 'bite-size' chunk of their work as part of an evening line-up that was designed to attract funders and promoters as well as audience members keen to play their role in the development of the work. By the 2010s, this approach had been adopted by the mainstream, and most regional theatres hosted regular work-in-progress events and had emerging artist programmes attached as a core part of their season, with even the Royal Shakespeare Company (RSC) hosting one of the regular

West Midlands 'Pilot Nights' in 2012. Programmers such as Annie Lloyd at Leeds Met Studio, and Helen Cole who established Bristol's Arnolfini Live, were among the first to not only pro-actively provide work-in-progress platforms for emerging companies whose work they wished to support, but to also become engaged in the development of the work itself, blurring the role of programmer with that of creative producer.

In this way, from the late 1990s, venue programmers were often the first to select from the wave of new companies available, those they deemed worthy of further attention by the Arts Council, thus having a significant impact on the development of particular trends within the sector as a whole. The programmers of these venues also often formed regional consortia that informally or formally co-programmed work to tour to all partners. North West venues in Lancaster, Liverpool, Manchester and Alsager were one such informal consortium in the early to mid-2000s; and in the late 2000s the more formal House consortium was established incorporating the host venue Farnham Maltings, along with Brighton Dome, Newbury Corn Exchange, New Theatre Royal Portsmouth, Oxford Playhouse, South Street Reading, The Point Eastleigh, and Watford Palace Theatre. This was good news for the companies who were introduced to such circuits, as it made touring more economically viable, and tours better marketed by the venues involved. It did, however, begin to consolidate the future of those companies, inevitably at the expense of companies who were based in those regions, or nationally, but whose work didn't 'fit' with the consortia's artistic preferences, which tended, in most cases, towards the aesthetically innovative.

Battersea Arts Centre also gave rise to the first independent production company of its kind, Fuel, which was co-founded by Louise Blackwell – a former producer with BAC – in partnership with Kate McGrath. There had, of course, been umbrella organizations prior to Fuel, principally Artsadmin (set up in 1979) which held a portfolio of client artists and companies including, during this period, DV8, Station House Opera and Getinthebackofthevan, for whom they booked tours and managed marketing and publicity, among other predominantly administrative tasks. Where Fuel was distinctly different was in its cultivation of a branded identity of its own that was designed to reflect the types of companies or artists it chose to represent. To be produced by Fuel became both a branding identification of the type of work and a hallmark of quality (for those who shared the same aesthetic values) for otherwise unknown companies or products, and could significantly short-cut the otherwise arduous journey to critical recognition for the emerging company working in isolation.

As the 2000s progressed, the pattern established by Fuel became increasingly widespread, with the emergence of creative producing companies such as China Plate and MAYK becoming particularly influential due to their alliances with venues (the directors of China Plate were also associate producers at Warwick Arts Centre) and festivals (China Plate has programmed the Pulse festival, MAYK was formed by the producers of Bristol's Mayfest). It was notable in the 2014 round of National Portfolio Organization agreements that there were as many creative production companies added to the portfolio as companies making theatre, including Creative Arts Exchange, MAYK theatre and Seachange Arts, with Kaleider both making its own practice and commissioning and producing the practice of artists external to the company. By the late 2000s, the larger regional repertory theatres were also taking a much more pivotal role in emerging artist development. Northern Stage in Newcastle, West Yorkshire Playhouse in Leeds and Birmingham Rep were among many who set up specific schemes, platforms and commissions for new work, such as Northern Stage taking over the St Stephen's venue at the Edinburgh Festival in 2013 with an entire programme of curated work by emerging artists and independent companies. So, by the end of this period, building-based theatres of all scales – via in-house creative producers or associated production companies – were often directly involved in commissioning, developing and promoting new companies, often well before any significant Arts Council investment or support had taken place. In this sense, the creative producer, building-based or independent, began to have arguably more influence than the Arts Council officers in determining which new companies would be afforded the opportunity to progress.

In addition to the creative producers noted above – both building-based and independent – who most often favoured work and companies that inhabited the experimental and live art end of the performance spectrum, there was a concurrent consolidation of the rural touring network, which was constituted as the National Rural Touring Forum (NRTF) in 1997. The NRTF provided advocacy, information and partnership-building opportunities to rural touring promoters across the country, such as Black Country Touring in the West Midlands, Creative Arts East in East Anglia and Performance Republic in South Yorkshire. Although historically rural touring was seen as a more conservative (with a small 'c') circuit, recent moves have seen a much closer alliance between the long-standing rural touring networks and the more emergent wave of creative producers, with China Plate hosting the 2012 New Directions Showcase at Warwick Arts Centre, a showcase which was designed to introduce rural touring promoters to the best of innovative new practice.

The long-term impact of such production companies on the ecology is still a little early to call, although the steep cuts to ACE's own administrative budget, which will constitute a 50 per cent reduction between 2010 and 2015, suggest that they might be a useful mechanism to counteract any further reductions of the Arts Council's capacity to assess new companies and shape the ecology of the sector from its grass roots as rigorously as it had once been able to do. One possible danger is that production companies are inevitably less accountable than Arts Council officers are for the decisions that they make, and quite legitimately select work on a purely subjective basis according to their own taste and preference. However, given that these companies and their choices are themselves subject to Arts Council scrutiny, and are funded on the basis of aims and objectives agreed and sanctioned by the Arts Council, the Arts Council still holds jurisdiction over selecting the selectors, so to speak, and can, theoretically, control the range and type of production companies funded, and thus, at one remove, the ecology that develops and expands as a result of their funding decisions.

Festivals and Showcases

Not only were producers able to facilitate tours of arts centres or rural networks of venues, they were also able to tap into the burgeoning festival circuit that was primarily targeted at showcasing new and innovative practice. The Edinburgh Fringe Festival, of course, had been in existence since 1948, but it was the 1990s that saw the beginnings of an expansion of smaller festivals across the UK that were to be far more instrumental in the promotion and profiling of experimental artists and performance companies. Glasgow's National Review of Live Art was in the vanguard of this wave, established as it was in the late 1980s, but two decades later, the UK summer season is wall to wall festivals including the Norwich and Norfolk Festival, the Brighton Festival, the Pulse Festival and SPILL (Ipswich), the Mayfest (Bristol, Glasgow), BE Festival (Birmingham), Ludus, Transform (Leeds), the Manchester International Festival, LIFT (London) and Sprint (Camden People's Theatre, London). Unlike the Edinburgh Fringe, these festivals are curated, sometimes by in-house programmers, sometimes by guest creative producers as noted above, and often contain their own showcase platforms within the wider festival itself – such as the Caravan platform at Brighton which is co-programmed by Farnham Maltings.

Although the Edinburgh Fringe was running throughout all three periods covered by this series, its impact on the professional small-scale ecology only really began to take effect in the late 1990s, due – in no small part – to the work of the British Council. Since 1997, in alternate years, the British Council has run its own showcase platform over one week of the festival, for which 20 to 30 UK productions are selected. During this week, the selected companies not only get the opportunity to showcase their work to over 200 invited international promoters, but also to network with them over breakfast meetings and other such receptions. In 2007, the British Council evaluated ten years of the showcase, reporting that '96% of theatre companies performing in the Edinburgh Showcase say that the British Council has greatly improved their international profile' (British Council, 2007). Not only did the showcase result in international touring opportunities, but also led to international collaborations that grew out of such opportunities: Grid Iron, for example, co-directed *The Story of the Death of Najib Brax* (2005) with Lebanese director Hisham Jaber; Vanishing Point collaborated on *Subway* (2007) with Etno Classic, a Kosovan band they met on tour; and Lone Twin's *Alice Bell* was co-produced by Sophiensaele, Berlin following the 2003 showcase (British Council, 2007). Although, in an interview, British Council Drama Officer Neil Webb was clear that the selection policy was to identify specific productions that answered to the remits of their international partners rather than seeking to establish and support regular clients, there are a large number of companies who reappear in the showcase with biannual regularity over a number of years. Paines Plough and Volcano were at one time the most prolific, appearing in every showcase up to and including 2009, but perhaps of more interest in terms of the British Council's influence on the sector is the frequent selection of emergent companies prior to any receipt of Arts Council regular funding. Frantic Assembly, established in 1994 and project funded by the Welsh Arts Council in 1997/98, featured in the showcase in 1997, 1999 and 2001, before finally receiving regular funding from Arts Council England in 2002/03. Suspect Culture also featured in 1997, before receiving regular funding from the Scottish Arts Council in 1998/99. Third Angel and Stan's Cafe both appeared in the showcase for the first time in 2001, to receive regular Arts Council England funding the following year.

Given that the British Council was far from averse to selecting new and emergent companies without the stamp of regular funding approval from the Arts Council, and given that, looking down the list of companies supported since 1997, very few of these have not proceeded to become regularly funded players in the UK independent sector, it becomes clear that either the British Council selectors were incredibly astute in their selection of promising good work, or that the appearance of companies in the showcase was significant in affording them the attention of the Arts Council and regular funding status. Both of these, of course, could be the case, and either way, the British Council can be seen to have played a key role in the shaping of the sector over this period. In my interview with Neil Webb, he was adamant that the British Council didn't seek to promote certain trends, but responded to the work that was being made. Such a claim might be true in part, but it is also a little disingenuous. Companies observing the type of work being selected for the showcase, and the successful international and domestic trajectories that came on the back of showcase selection, would be clearly influenced to shape their work within similar frameworks in the hope of furthering their chances of selection next time around. The emerging companies selected again and again throughout the lifetime of the showcase have been predominantly those experimenting with form. In the late 1990s, the emphasis was on physical theatre (Frantic Assembly, Volcano, Boilerhouse, The Right Size, Rejects Revenge, Ridiculusmus) and increasingly on site-specific theatre and experimental postmodern aesthetics (Suspect Culture, Theatre Cryptic, Gob Squad, Grid Iron, Improbable Theatre, Stan's Cafe, Third Angel, Unlimited Theatre). By the mid-2000s, the emphasis began to shift onto actor–audience experimentation (Quarantine, Curious, dreamthinkspeak, Tim Crouch, Action Hero, Invisible Flock). New writing in its more traditional form was still well represented up until the early 2000s by well-established companies such as Paines Plough, Out of Joint, The Bush and the Traverse – but few emergent new-writing companies featured, and none with any regularity. It is significant that such trends follow precisely the direction of travel of Arts Council support and the shape of the sector during this period, although it remains inconclusive as to whether the British Council is, as Webb claimed, merely responding to such trends, or whether it might be, as I would suggest, at the very least contributing to their formation.

In 2003, there was a significant new development that saw the influences of the independent creative producer and the British Council selection process working together for the first time to directly impact on the ecology of the independent theatre sector. The 2003 showcase included within it a mini-showcase curated by Battersea Arts Centre – the 'This Way Up Showcase' – which featured work by Gecko, Filter, Sound and Fury, and Patter. Each of these four companies gained access to the British Council Showcase for their very first piece of work through their relationship with BAC, and Gecko appeared again in the British Council Showcases of 2007 and 2009, before eventually receiving regular funding from the Arts Council from 2012. The privilege of the company's point of entry into the international showcase nine years before the Arts Council considered them significant enough to receive regular funding suggests that either the Arts Council was surprisingly slow to support the company, or that Gecko's relationship with BAC, which gained them entry to the showcase outside the application process open to other companies, won them a fast track to international promotion. This was at the expense of companies validated by the Arts Council's much more rigorous selection processes for regular funding, companies that were not working within BAC's preferred aesthetic and/or were not based in the London region and so eligible and able to access the venue's ongoing support. Although Fuel never had the same ring-fenced spot in the British Council Showcase, its client companies did continue to make up a significant aspect of the British Council Showcase programme. In 2007, Gecko, Inua Ellams, Melanie Wilson (ex-Patter) and Sound and Fury – all at one point produced by Fuel – made up 20 per cent of that year's British Council Showcase.

I would argue that the connections I have traced above between the rise of the creative producer – both building-based and independent – and the British Council Showcase can be seen to demonstrate a distinct impact on the growth of a particular type of experimental practice – focused initially on visual and physical theatre, and later on formalistic exploration primarily concerned with renegotiating audience/performer relationships. Too often the Arts Councils are seen as the sole influence in their encouragement of such trends, but in the case of the British Council Showcase I believe that there is an argument to be made for the Arts Councils responding – sometimes, it would seem, reluctantly and somewhat belatedly – to the international profiles already gained as a result of their showcase exposure by companies engaged in particular aesthetic exploration. The companies benefiting directly from these developments will be discussed in the third part of this chapter, but it is important to note that the innovations in form have also impacted on a much wider range of work in this period than that of those companies who are commonly recognized as the vanguard of experimentation. The shift towards a greater emphasis on the physical and visual aspects of theatre, the expansion of text-based theatre beyond the dramatic model, and the exploration of site and audience/performer relationships are widespread within children's and young people's theatre and the more constituency-specific models of performance that are discussed in the second part of this chapter, innovations that, furthermore, can also be seen to have transformed the broader mainstream theatre industry by the end of this period.

PART TWO: POLITICS, ACCESS AND INCLUSION

Notions of the Political

In the second volume of this series, Graham Saunders argues that the identity politics of 'constituency theatre' became 'the distinguishing feature that set the companies of the 1980s apart from their predecessors' (Saunders, 2015, 51). Baz Kershaw concurs that 'the strongest opposition to Thatcherism came in the issue-based shows produced by the growing number of community, women's, feminist, gay/queer, black and special needs groups' (Kershaw, 2004, 368–9). By this period of study, however, the identity-related politics of activist gay and feminist theatre, still evident in companies such as Gay Sweatshop and Monstrous Regiment in the early 1990s, were soon to subside, with feminist company Monstrous Regiment losing regular funding before 1995, and Gay Sweatshop having regular funding withdrawn in 1997. Duckie, just emerging around this time, was more an events collective than a company, describing itself as 'post-queer performance ... purveyors of progressive working class entertainment ... in the tradition of British illegitimate theatre that spans centuries' (Duckie website). In this sense, while retaining a strong focus on alternative sexualities, such as its LGBT youth theatre, there was a shift away from an exclusive constituency agenda and towards a wider inclusive participatory ethos in their work. The Women's Theatre Group, seeing the direction of travel, had already begun to build their new trajectory under the rebranded identity of Sphinx in 1991. This shift away from the explicitly political underpins the relative absence of companies defined by either Marxist or constituency-related identities in this period of study, with the exception of disability theatre, which saw significant expansion, and the black and Asian independent theatre sector which also grew, if a little more sporadically, throughout the 2000s. There were still women-run companies with feminist agendas, including Foursight Theatre, Sphinx, Clean Break, Stellar Quines, Kali Theatre and Vincent Dance Theatre, with Paper Birds and Rashdash two of the more recent companies to emerge. These companies, perhaps unlike previous women's theatre movements, are too diverse in their specific contexts, schools of feminism and aesthetic priorities to be considered together in any meaningful way without a depth of analysis that cannot be undertaken here, and so will be examined in the context of wider concerns throughout the chapter.

Very few high-profile companies over this period retained an identity that was allied to socialist practice, and it is probably not coincidental that the remaining two of the foremost core-funded companies who did, Red Ladder and Big Brum, had their NPO status withdrawn in the 2014 round of funding allocations. None of this is to say that this was a period without politics, but merely that the forms and vehicles taken by 'political' theatre in the 1990s and 2000s were much more amorphous, multilayered and resistant to singular definition than had been the case in previous decades. Many politically active artists in this period turned away from the corporate, market-driven model of the independent theatre company favoured by New Labour to form collectivist organizations that could engage in performative models of direct action, unencumbered by funding agreements that were underpinned by government policy. Activist arts organizations such as Platform had been around since the 1980s and they were joined in the 2000s by collectives such as the Clandestine Insurgent Rebel Clown Army, My Dad's Strip Club and the Lab of Insurrectionary Imagination, among many others, in disrupting public spaces in protest against capitalism, and in support of environmental change.

The political narratives appertaining to the independent theatre company ecology that is the focus of this study can be productively discussed under two overarching headings that will steer the direction of both remaining parts of the chapter. In this part, I will go on to discuss the range of practice that has been supported by the New Labour policies outlined in the previous chapter, policies that sought to use arts funding and artists as a key mechanism for improved social cohesion and re-engagement of disenfranchised communities through increased access to, and participation in, the arts. In the third and final part of this chapter, I will address the growing influence of postmodern theories of the political on the work of the theatre companies to emerge in and after the mid-1990s. Where applied practice and theatre addressing marginal constituencies benefited from New Labour's emphasis on access and inclusion, those companies focusing on postmodern and 'post-postmodern' experiments with theatre form benefited from the Cool Britannia emphasis on 'the new' and the Arts Councils' increasing prioritization of innovation towards the end of the 1990s. Hans-Thies Lehmann was soon to characterize much of this work as postdramatic, a term that gained greatest currency following the translation of his seminal and ground-breaking publication *Postdramatic Theatre* in 2006. In this text, Lehmann identifies a 'politics of perception' that shifts the notion of the political from the dissemination of intentionally ideological content to the notion of ideological critique (185), that is to say that the political act within a postdramatic framework was one that led the spectator to question ideological representation per se, rather than lead him or her to particular ideological conclusions. The postdramatic political has often been aligned with a critique of the dramatic model of theatre and in that sense has significantly contributed to a sustained – if not always justified – polarization of 'devised' and 'new writing' work during this period; I will explore this in the third and final part of this chapter.

Enduring Legacies

Community theatres, while on the margins of the ecology under discussion in this study, saw significant expansion under New Labour with long-established organizations such as London Bubble, Chicken Shed and Acta joined by the more recently founded Collective Encounters and Entelechy Arts. Community and youth theatre provision in this period expanded into a growing field, offering courses and often accredited professional training that was driven by New Labour's social agenda to reduce youth and long-term unemployment and social exclusion via retraining initiatives. Funding schemes for companies undertaking such work were widely available in the early-to mid-2000s, but often came with very specific requirements in terms of recognized accreditation and targets for re-employment that now replaced the broader narrative of personal empowerment, development of self-confidence, engagement with others, and growth of individual creativity and aspiration that had been at the heart of community and youth theatre historically.

Rarely did these community theatres carry with them the explicitly socialist agenda of the early alternative theatre movement, although their aims of supporting often disenfranchised or disadvantaged communities, could be seen to align with some of the key objectives, if not always the ideology, of their predecessors. Where the socialist legacies of such a tradition can be most clearly identified in the 1990s and 2000s, they are unsurprisingly found in those companies who were founded at the peak of the movement, such as Red Ladder Theatre, established in 1971, and Banner Theatre, established in 1973/74. Banner Theatre, in particular, maintains the historical trajectory of the popular theatre tradition, pioneering documentary theatre techniques and seeking out audiences that often self-identify as working-class socialists through their affiliation with the union movement, which provides one of Banner's key touring circuits, alongside community and youth centre venues.

Banner Theatre was rare in its self-conscious targeting and characterization of 'working class' audiences in this period. The mass closure of mines, steelworks and shipyards during the 1980s had led to the reconfiguration of many of the 'working class communities' in the sense that such a description was understood in the 1970s and 1980s. Where such communities had been the target audiences of the popular theatre movement, the community constituencies sought out by the political theatre companies established in the 1990s and 2000s were categorized, not by their politics or class of employment, but by their dispossession and disadvantage. Such constituencies would include the long-term unemployed (often precisely those communities who had suffered most from the annihilation of manufacturing industries in the 1980s), those suffering from mental health issues or addiction, the homeless, offenders and those at risk of offending and – increasingly in the 2000s – refugees, asylum seekers and those seen to be at risk of developing extremist sympathies with Islamic terrorism.

Although the political theatre movement of the 1970s had often invited its audience to some degree to participate in the performance, it tended to adopt the predominant model of artists making a piece of work and touring it to audiences who had, in the main, not been involved in the making of the piece. The increasing emphasis on much deeper constituency involvement in the political theatres of the 1990s and 2000s was partly in response to the necessity for more direct intervention with increasingly disempowered and disenfranchised communities and individuals. It was, however, also influenced by two key developments regarding the political currency of participation: the forum theatre of Augusto Boal and the resurgence of documentary theatre.

As Frances Babbage argues, it is reductive to credit the widespread use of forum theatre over this period solely to the practice of Boal, given the similarities of its structure to models common in the existing Theatre in Education (TIE) movement, and the psychodrama techniques developed by Jacob Moreno (Babbage, 2004, 68). Nevertheless, Boal's influence on European practice throughout the 1980s was profound, following his move to the Sorbonne in Paris in 1978 (Babbage, 2004, 22) and the publication in English of his seminal text *Theatre of the Oppressed* in 1979. As Babbage contends, the techniques Boal developed 'have been applied in every conceivable community context to address oppressions of all kinds, and have been adapted and reinvented in ways Boal could never have anticipated' (Babbage, 2004, 31). Forum theatre grew out of Boal's conviction that for a theatre to be political, 'first, the barrier between actors and spectators is destroyed: all must act, all must be protagonists in the necessary transformation of society' (Boal, 1979, Foreword). Forum theatre strategies were a significant feature of what came to be known as applied theatre in the 1990s and 2000s, and were utilized to address precisely the situations of oppression that constituencies of disadvantage were required to confront. Boal himself continued to work closely with two UK theatre companies in particular, Mind the Gap, as discussed in Chapter 3 of this volume, and Cardboard Citizens, described further below.

From Political to Applied

The broadest understanding of 'applied theatre' – including extensive use of the forum framework – would stretch to include practices that utilized theatre for personal development within corporate training programmes, such as the work undertaken by companies such as Blue Starfish for clients including Barclays and E.ON. However, given that such companies tend to be funded solely by their client revenue, rather than public funding, I will be focusing here on the sub-field of applied theatre characterized by Jonothan Neelands as 'determinedly pro-social', involving vulnerable and marginalized individuals and communities and made up of companies which 'make some political claim to be resistant to the values of new capitalism' (2007, 306–7).

Even this sub-field of applied theatre covers a wide range of practices and strategic aims, but perhaps, in the context of the legacy I am tracing from the political theatre companies of the 1960s and 1970s, the most significant aspect is the distinction that might be made between practice that explicitly upholds a resistance to capitalism in both the form and content of the work, and practice which, as Neelands suggests, might rather focus on the 'transformative' potential for the disenfranchised individual, without explicitly arguing for 'larger scale social change' (2007, 306). Neelands proposes that this latter emphasis is, in fact, in the ascendant over this recent period and that there is evidence of a realignment of applied theatre away from the politics of redistribution, a shift that reflects the therapeutic ethos of New Labour's cultural policy at the time. This ethos, I would suggest, is reflected in the increased levels of Arts Council, Lottery and other funding available for a significant tranche of companies that emerged or became established in the early 2000s with specific remits to 'affirm, include, recognise and self-actualise' (in New Labour's terms) individuals belonging to dispossessed or marginalized constituencies (Neelands, 2007, 313). Such constituencies included those from ethnic minority backgrounds, such as the black and Asian women who had suffered domestic violence and who were involved in Kali Theatre's work with Southall Black Sisters, or the predominantly Asian groups of young people supported by Peshkar Productions in Oldham and the Asian Theatre School (later Freedom Studios), under the auspices of Red Ladder in Bradford. There was also significant activity in the work undertaken by and with disabled artists and audiences, with the long-standing pioneers Graeae and Theatre Workshop joined in this period by Mind the Gap, Dark Horse (previously Full Body and the Voice), Deafinitely Theatre, Extant, Red Earth Theatre, Theatr Ffynnon, Lung Ha's, Birds of Paradise and Solar Bear.

Where the political complexities noted by Neelands become most evident, I think, is in the work undertaken with marginalized constituencies that are not categorized by fixed characteristics such as race or disability, but by actions or contextual factors that result in common, and sometimes temporary, communities of social exclusion. Such communities would include offenders, addicts, the homeless, the unemployed and those seeking asylum. Here there is a clear and long-debated ideological choice to be made as to whether such a context is viewed as predominantly the result of individual psychological frailty or predominantly the result of inequitable and oppressive social and economic structures that lie beyond the individual's control. The answer upheld by the political theatre companies of the 1970s and 1980s tended towards the latter, but there is much to suggest that New Labour was not of this way of thinking, as I will discuss further below, and given the political influence on the funding streams for applied practice at this time, it is worth asking the question about the work of companies such as Geese Theatre, Cardboard Citizens and Ice and Fire who emerged in this period as specialists within the field.

Notions of Inclusion

At the height of the New Labour government, as Sheila Preston outlines, Ruth Levitas identified three notions of inclusion: the redistributive discourse (RED), the social integration discourse (SID) and the moral underclass discourse (MUD) (Preston, 2011, 253). Levitas noted the preference of New Labour for a combination of SID, which was concerned with re-engagement through participation in economic structures, and MUD, which focused on the 'behavioural and attitudinal characteristics of the excluded and their imputed deficiencies' (Levitas et al. cited in Preston, 2011, 253). The political strategy behind the funding of applied theatre within the constituencies outlined above is, consequently, predominantly directed at changing the lifestyle or behavioural patterns of the individual, rather than addressing a redistributive discourse that might remove some of the structural barriers to their social integration. This hypothesis would explain the emphasis within many of the funding schemes on certain measurable outcomes – such as a return to employment, or evidence of a drop in reoffending rates – suggesting that the benefit to wider society is positioned as of paramount importance, as opposed to less measurable benefits to the individual, such as increased self-confidence, personal growth or levels of creativity. Not only are such benefits more difficult to measure, but they might also in some cases run counter to New Labour's perception of wider social or economic benefit, such as raised levels of political awareness of state injustice or inequity, for example. This is particularly apparent, as described in the previous chapter, in the community cohesion strategies that were part of New Labour's anti-terrorism programme PREVENT, where funds were explicitly made available to 'support' disenfranchised Muslim individuals in only one ideological direction. The other, wider, benefit of this approach, for New Labour, is that an emphasis solely on the individual's behaviour also deflects from the possibility that the contexts of these constituencies are, in great part, a result of the government's reluctance to confront growing economic disparity, as outlined in Chapter 1.

This is not to say that the companies who sign up to the funding to work with such constituencies are necessarily also signing up to the political imperatives of New Labour that underpin the Arts Council's access and participation agenda. Jonothan Neelands, drawing on widespread research undertaken during the period of this study, does, however, argue that 'increasingly the politics of AT [applied theatre] appear to be aligning themselves less with the socialism and the politics of redistribution associated with their ancestors in political theatre and more with the ambivalences of "identity politics" and philosophical communitarianism' (Neelands, 2007, 312). There are probably good grounds for this position when looking at the applied theatre sector as a whole, which grew exponentially in the wake of significant increases in government grants for this work and would include independent practitioners, institutions such as education providers and prisons, and outreach projects led by theatres and companies as an add-on to their main business. However, I will now suggest that those independent companies specializing in such practice for the most part do sustain an admirable and complex balance between the inclusion objectives of the government and funders, and their own political objectives, objectives that can be seen to be directly inherited from the Marxist-orientated theatre practice of previous decades, made fit for purpose in a twenty-first-century political landscape.

Applied Theatre Companies

Geese Theatre first received core funding from Arts Council England in 2003/04, at the height of the boom in funding allocated by New Labour to enhance their broader access, participation and social inclusion agenda. The company works primarily in prisons, and its practice is designed to support the rehabilitation of offenders back into society, through the use of theatre and workshop techniques drawn from the fields of social learning theory, cognitive behavioural theory and role theory (Baim et al., 2002, 19). Geese have become particularly renowned for the use of half-masks, which 'literalise the varying forms of evasion or self-defence that they reference' (Bottoms, 2010, 485) and enable the audience and participants to begin to analyse the social masks that they themselves adopt, and what might lie beneath them. In an analysis of the efficacy of Geese's Reconnect Programme (2005), Harkins et al. (2011) position the company's work firmly in the therapeutic field of cognitive behavioural therapy, being designed to impact on the decision-making processes and actions of the individual in order to shift previous patterns of behaviour and help to reduce the likelihood of reoffending on release from prison. The study concludes that there is evidence of the efficacy of the programme in achieving its aims, but it is clear, in the context of Neeland's analysis, that the approach here is, in the words of the researchers, to address the 'cognitive deficits' of the prisoners and not the economic or political contexts that may have played a large part in their offending (Harkins et al., 2011, 547). However, it is clear that any ideological critique of the therapeutic approach in this case would be misdirected. First, the company's constituents are not the right target audience for foregrounding the wider social structures, beyond helping each individual to better circumnavigate them, and secondly, the benefit to wider society of supporting individuals in staying out of prison is clearly aligned with the benefit to the individual of the same outcome. There are, of course, ideological minefields in psychodrama approaches, given that the onus is always on the participant/protagonist to change his or her actions regardless of the fairness, or otherwise, of the wider context in which they find themselves. But, pragmatically, for the purposes of the programme, the unfairness of the wider context is precisely what offenders are going to have to confront, and their only, if limited, capacity to change it begins with their ability to reposition themselves in a more secure position within its legal frameworks. Where appropriate, practitioners can of course make space within the work for such discussions to take place, and for the participants to critically reflect on the structures they are dealing with, as well as learning ways to better navigate them.

Stepping Out was established in 1997 in Bristol, and has never received Arts Council core funding. Working with mental health service users and their allies, they are a good example of how Lottery money in particular has enabled community theatres to flourish and professionalize without holding the status of a Regularly Funded Organization, giving them the capacity to employ permanent staff and offer high-profile and high-quality activities free of charge to participants. Under Steve Hennessy's direction, as Anna Harpin confirms, 'the company has developed from a small community arts group into an award-winning theatre company with extensive work in theatres, hostels, and psychiatric units' (Harpin, 2010, 42). Although the company delivers a range of work, including psychiatric staff training, at the heart of its practice is the mounting of large-scale productions performed by its members, who are drawn from the community of service users and those who support them. Initially these were annual performances as part of World Mental Health Day; they rapidly grew in profile and reach, and now regularly tour to other cities such as London and Cardiff, as well as supporting, in partnership, smaller community companies with similar remits, such as Chrysalis Theatre and Progress Cymru. The therapeutic impact for individuals, as in Geese's work, is clearly at the centre of the company's concerns, although Stepping Out is not, as Hennessy emphasizes in an interview with Anna Harpin, aligned with psychodrama in the same way: 'we have a greater impact by not having a structured therapeutic programme. You can't really say you have been involved in drama until you get to performance level, until you are performing in front of proper theatre audiences. The effect of that on people is just mind blowing' (Hennessy in Harpin, 2010, 43). Harpin thus concludes that Stepping Out:

> is developing in the interstices between professional theatre, community theatre, and Applied Theatre. There is a complex process of negotiation here and one that resonates with status and aspiration. A desire to be validated by an alignment with a professional (and traditional) theatre lineage is inter-cut with a desire not to be maligned with either community or therapy labels. (Harpin, 2010, 43)

The avoidance of autobiographical material, disclosure and testimony in Stepping Out's work, strategies that are common in the applied theatre field, support Hennessy's clearly articulated aim to offer a professional performance framework for the participants, and one in which they can, in a crucial sense, enjoy an empowered and applauded identity that is not aligned to narratives of either stigma or compassion. Moreover, the focus of the performance material on more epic, and often darkly comic, representations of mental health and responses to it – both institutional and social – not only enables the performers to move beyond the personal, but also enables the practice to encompass a wider ideological remit which, as Harpin argues, 'is concerned with the politics of the collective as opposed to [the] individual' (Harpin, 2010, 51). In this instance, the high production values and the touring of the company's work both serve the individual's need for recognition and validation and enable a wider audience to critically engage with the challenges posed to this constituency by the social and institutional structures around their representations and treatments.

Cardboard Citizens was founded in 1991 and in its early years it toured forum theatre work, on a Boalian model, to hostels and daycare centres for the homeless. Artistic director Adrian Jackson, previously the associate director of London Bubble and translator of many of Boal's publications, has worked closely with Boal over the company's lifetime and has developed his practice with and for homeless people since the company's conception, later widening the terms of this remit to the homeless and displaced, in response to the growing crisis of refugees and asylum seekers. In receipt of core funding from the Arts Council since 2002/3, Cardboard Citizens has been able to further develop and professionalize its activities and add larger-scale theatre productions designed for wider audiences to its portfolio, including two high-profile collaborations with the Royal Shakespeare Company: *Pericles* (2003) and *Timon of Athens* (2006), which used actors from both companies. Strategically comparable to Stepping Out, Cardboard Citizens' performers are drawn from its constituents, but given its more stable and significant funding base, it has also, since 1998, been able to pay these performers an equity-level wage, thus providing them with professional status and employment opportunities.

The company's high-profile projects have also afforded it the opportunity to address the wider inequalities of the structural system that give rise to poverty, homelessness and displacement, a strategy that complements the emphasis on personal growth and development at the heart of the grass-roots work it continues to deliver to homeless hostels in London and around the UK. While neither *Pericles* nor *Timon of Athens* was a forum theatre production, both implicitly cast the audience in roles in order to implicate the spectators in the political frameworks of the piece. Despite their predominantly negative reviews of *Pericles*, mainstream critics Dominic Cavendish and Michael Billington both expressed their unease at entering the vast Southwark warehouse to be commanded to sit at desks with an asylum application form in front of them and to listen to the real-life testimonies of their fellow-applicant performers. While unsure, for different reasons, of the artistic merits of the fusion of the Shakespeare text and the testimonies drawn from Cardboard Citizen's constituents, both reviewers were made to feel, albeit momentarily, the weight of the asylum system from the perspective of the refugee (Cavendish, 2003; Billington, 2003).

Documentary and Verbatim Performance

The use of the real-life testimonies of marginalized communities and individuals, or narratives based on their stories, became a highly popular political strategy for companies straddling the applied and professional theatre fields in the period of this study. Red Room Theatre, founded in 1995, is distinct from the other companies under discussion here in that it does not identify a specific community for its work, but seeks more broadly 'to challenge social injustice and promote human rights' (The Red Room website). As Gareth White notes, '[t]he company's involvement in advocacy for migrants and asylum seekers dates back to its earliest work, including 1996's *Coming to Land* season and the production of *The Bogus Woman* by Kay Adshead in 2000' (White, 2010, 95), and immigration continues to be a strong emphasis of the company's work throughout the 2000s. Under the artistic directorship of Lisa Goldman, the company focused primarily, though not exclusively, on the production of new writing, often, as in the case of *The Bogus Woman*, following periods of extensive documentary research. Under the subsequent directorship of Topher Campbell in 2006, this documentary approach was sustained and the form of the productions was often expanded to include testimonies of specific individuals, as in *Unstated* (2009) which utilized verbatim material as the basis for a script written by Fin Kennedy on the treatment of asylum seekers in detention centres. Unrestricted by any narrow definition of their constituency, Red Room was able to turn its attention, post-2010 in particular, to the wider consequences of the austerity politics under the coalition government, with a three-year project entitled *Poverty Project* that encompassed professional performances such as *Lost Nation* (2013), and what the company called 'platforms'. *Lost Nation* was a performance that took place in various sites in London consisting of verbatim testimonies acted by professional actors but drawn from real-life stories of poverty and dispossession in the UK. This followed the model of politically inspired documentary performance that had seen such resurgence in the wider theatre ecology, coming to characterize the work of theatres such as the Tricycle and companies such as Recorded Delivery. Where *Lost Nation* sought to raise awareness of real-life hardship not often covered by a mass media increasingly unsympathetic to poverty and those claiming welfare, the platforms that ran throughout the *Poverty Project* – the *Riot Response Platform* (2011), the *Broken Britain Platform* (2012) and the *Race and Equality Platform* (2013) – were more directly interventionist, consisting of evenings of 'conversation, live performance, music and film artists ... [for] activists, rioters, police, educators, community workers, young people, families, shopkeepers, journalists and politicians' (The Red Room website).

Similar documentary strategies and broader political aims can also be seen in the work of Ice and Fire, a company founded in 2003 to 'explore human rights stories through performance', although the structure of the company itself is very different (Ice and Fire website). Ice and Fire has a network of over 600 professional actors who are committed to offering rehearsed readings of Ice and Fire's documentary-based texts including *Close to Home: the Cuts* scripted by Annecy Hayes, *Asylum Monologues, Asylum Dialogues* and *Palestine Monologues* scripted by company founder Sonja Linden, and *Rendition Monologue, The Illegals* and *Broke* scripted by Christine Bacon. The costs for the performances of these scripts are kept to a minimum, with non-funded organizations able to book them for actors' expenses only, and donations requested from companies in receipt of funding on a sliding scale. Ice and Fire also engages members of its constituency community in performance, as seen in the work of Stepping Out and Cardboard Citizens. *Souvenirs* (2013), directed by Tamasha Theatre's co-founder Kristine Landon-Smith, was produced in collaboration with Write to Life, a long-running writing group for survivors of torture established by Sonja Linden, and comprised testimonies performed to public audiences by the participants themselves, following workshops, discussions and in-depth interviews.

A Multi-layered Political

The work undertaken by the companies detailed above, works across, and sometimes in between, forum theatre, applied theatre, documentary theatre, new writing and community theatre frame-works. All have become established under New Labour and all have been supported by the Arts Council via either core or project funding. Yet there is little sense from a comparative analysis of their working practice that what might be called the therapeutic impact of the work on the disenfranchised individuals who were enabled to participate, in any way threatened to eclipse each company's ongoing commitment to a sustained critique of the impact of the wider structures that are perceived as the root problem of the context in which their constituencies are located. Furthermore, in the work of Cardboard Citizens, The Red Room, and Ice and Fire, the structures under critique are explicitly located as belonging to a capitalist ideology in which urgent redistributive correction is required. Not only, I would argue, is the socialist commitment of the earlier political theatres sustained in this later work, but the multilayered approach that most of the companies here share demonstrates, perhaps, an even more nuanced understanding of the multifarious politics of performance than their predecessors. Not only do all of these companies evidence a commitment both to pragmatically and directly improving the life conditions of those most oppressed by the current system *and* to proselytizing on behalf of the marginalized to much wider audiences, they also show a careful attention to context and economics, as can be seen in the debating platforms of The Red Room, the professional payment structures of Cardboard Citizens, or the free-of-charge labour by professional actors in the work by Ice and Fire. The sheer scope of activity undertaken by Cardboard Citizens, for example, refutes the challenge that forum theatre may only offer 'temporary, illusory empowerment' (Babbage, 2004, 72), as it is in the wrap-around support system offered by the company's Engagement Programme, in which training, education, guidance and employment opportunities are made available, that deeper change can be instigated (Babbage, 2004, 71–2). It is thus in the 'whole' of the activity of the political companies to emerge in this period that a complex political efficacy can be read, more than in the sum of any number of their parts.

Children and Young People's Theatre

Prior to the 1990s, the Theatre in Education (TIE) movement had driven the development of theatre for children and young people, with companies funded directly by local education authorities to tour primarily to schools and undertake workshops and productions that responded to a broad educational remit. However, after the Education Reform Act 1988, one of the Thatcher government's free market initiatives, funding was transferred from local authorities to individual schools, with the result of destabilizing the TIE provision. Companies were now not only isolated from sustainable and secure funding, thus jeopardizing the quality of the work they were able to offer, but they were also increasingly required to respond to a much narrower notion of education by tailoring their programmes to fit the National Curriculum that was introduced in the same year (Bennett, 2005, 21).

The vacuum in meaningful provision for children and young people left by the decline of TIE was not immediately filled by quality provision elsewhere. In Scotland, according to Tony Reekie, director of the Imaginate International Children's Festival, 'the work [with a few exceptions] was cheap, under-produced, under-rehearsed, variations on pantomime with enough audience participation to keep the audiences from catching breath to realize what rubbish it all was' (Reekie, 2005, 38). Even by 2002, at the 'Quality of Children's Theatre' symposium in

Birmingham, *Guardian* arts critic Lyn Gardner was asking why she still saw 'far too many shows whose driving force is clearly not a passion to make theatre, but a passion to sell a product whose major selling point is the way it ties in with the National Curriculum' (Gardner, 2003, 35).

If theatre for children and young people, as Stuart Bennett suggests, can be understood historically as two branches that comprise 'theatre as an art form experience, and theatre within an educational context' (Bennett, 2005, 11), then children and young people were seemingly being failed by both in the 1990s. Yet from the very beginning of that decade, the seeds of a decidedly more auspicious future were being sown. The first ever conference on theatre for under-fives took place in the UK as early as 1989; organized by Quicksilver's Carey English, this was 'a pivotal event which galvanized many companies and individuals to go on to develop some astounding work for the age group including … Oily Cart Theatre … and … Theatre-Rites' (English, 2005, 184). The year 1990 saw the beginnings of the Imaginate Children's Festival in Scotland and a key shift in the direction of the International Association of Theatre for Children and Young People, known by its French acronym, ASSITEJ. Both of these occurrences demonstrate the vital significance of the expanding international links with Europe in the development of theatre for children and young people across this period. Imaginate, as Tony Reekie explains,

> slowly began to change the outlook of new artists coming into the area. For the first time in Scotland we could look at the best the world had to offer – work of the highest standard, that time and time again made us gasp with its passion, skill and daring … it forced artists in Scotland to raise their game, to question the how and why about their own work. (Reekie, 2005, 38–9)

The international context of Imaginate, Reekie concludes, was a decisive factor in shifting children and young people's theatre in Scotland away from the National Curriculum and towards a theatre that 'aimed to thrill, move and entertain its audience' (2005, 39). At the same time, in Stockholm, the ASSITEJ, with support and funding from the Scandinavian Centres and governments, instigated a significant change in its policy and direction away from an emphasis on education-based participatory theatre in schools to reflect their preference for a 'theatre of empowerment … characterised by collective and co-operative working, small-scale touring and a focus on children's feelings and personal needs' (Harman, 2005, 55).

These developments help to make sense of why the former TIE companies – in England and Scotland at this point – were not simply replaced by a raft of independent companies who did the same job. The political, and often explicitly socialist, objectives of the original wave of TIE companies, coupled with, in many people's minds, the reduction of the notion of educational theatre to something that expediently followed the National Curriculum, had not played well in the neoliberal climate of post-Thatcher Britain. Consequently, companies who were committed to the original vision of the TIE movement can be seen to have been steadily replaced in the ecology by companies who wanted to embrace a new vision: that of a professional theatre for children and young people that toured to theatre buildings, focused on high production values and innovations in form, and was able to look beyond local and regional impact towards building an international reputation and touring circuit, alongside the best of adult theatre. Catherine Wheels, for example, can list an extensive catalogue of international awards and platforms including the Best Production at the Shanghai International Children's Festival (2008) for *Martha*, which had been their first show in 1999; a nomination for the Drama Desk Award for Unique Theatrical Experience on Broadway (2009) for *Hansel and Gretel*; and numerous Critics' Awards for Theatre in Scotland, including, in 2011, picking up three of the ten awards available that year. As children and young people's theatre became less explicitly educational and more commercially viable, the line between core-funded subsidized companies such as Catherine Wheels and commercially independent non-core-funded companies such as Tall Stories (who held the stage rights to the best-selling children's book, *The Gruffalo*) became much more difficult to rationalize.

The distinction between theatre as an art form and theatre within an educational context is, of course, a slippery one, given that all good educational theatre is, in itself, an art form, and much of the theatre for children and young people, wherever it takes place, has educational – in the broader sense – value and often specific thematic or 'issue-based' objectives. Furthermore, as Matthew Reason notes, 'professional children's theatre companies have increasingly sought to provide schools with study guides and packs that seek to facil-itate teachers in preparing children for the performance and leading discussions or activities afterwards' (Reason, 2010, 5), and even the Imaginate International Festival has a strong commitment to 'working with teachers, developing learning partnerships with schools and the education sector' (Reason, 2010, 12). Nevertheless, I would argue that there is a distinct change in emphasis that can be seen across the sector over this period that moves the majority core-funded theatre provision for children and young people further away from school buildings and into touring circuits, festivals and purpose-built theatres, and, at the same time, further away from the explicitly educational or political objectives of the historical TIE movement.

This shift is particularly evident in the Welsh context, where the state provision of TIE was historically the strongest, as well as being sustained well into this period of study. The change in direction that followed the debacle of the Welsh Arts Council's review of TIE provision in 1999, as discussed in Chapter 1, can be seen in a brief examination of the children and young people's theatre companies that survived into the second decade of the millennium, and those that did not. Out of the seven original independent TIE providers (the eighth being building-based Theatr Clwyd YPT), Arad Goch, Cwmni'r Frân Wen, Theatr na nÓg and Theatr Iolo continue to be core funded and, while still playing to schools, also focus on small-scale theatre tours and have an overriding artistic remit. Theatr na nÓg emphasizes on its website that it 'continues to evolve from being a company that solely produces work for schools to being recognized by the Arts Council of Wales as one of their producing theatre companies' and that its association with the Wales Millennium Centre 'enables the company … to raise its profile on an international stage'. Theatr Iolo, the recipient of a Beacon Award for excellence, and a regular contributor to the Scottish Imaginate Festival, is now based at Chapter Arts Centre, renowned for its programmes of experimental practice. Conversely, Gwent Theatre which 'worked closely with schools and advisers to devise material of real educational value' (Gwent Theatre website) and Theatr Powys which was 'committed to the methodology and practice of TIE' (Theatre Wales website) have both had funding withdrawn and have consequently folded (both in 2010). Spectacle Theatre had its core funding withdrawn at the same point as Powys and Gwent and shifted emphasis to an interventionist, youth-theatre model that wasn't reliant on core arts funding. It does seem, however subjective the decision might be as to precisely where the line is drawn, that 'theatre as an art form' was substantively promoted in Wales over the 2000s, to the significant detriment of the country's historical legacy of 'theatre within an educational context'. The same direction of travel can be identified in England and Scotland over this time. In Scotland, following the 2004 Cultural Commission's definition of 'a series of cultural rights and consequent cultural entitlements', which Matthew

Reason argues underpinned the imperative to improve the provision of theatre for children and young people (Reason, 2010, 26), core funding was extended to four additional companies in 2006/7 – Catherine Wheels, Visible Fictions, Wee Stories and Giant Productions – all of which focused on the development of the art form of theatre for children and young people, above and beyond any educational remit. In England, when ACE was first able to allocate its additional spending from the New Labour government, and influenced by New Labour's drive towards access and inclusion for young people in particular, existing core-funded companies Unicorn, Polka, Oily Cart, Theatre Centre and Quicksilver were joined in the 2001/2 funding round by a whole raft of companies including Action Transport, Big Brum, Box Clever, Half Moon, M6, Open Theatre, Pegasus, Pilot Theatre, Sixth Sense Theatre, Theatre Alibi, Theatre Blah Blah Blah, Theatre Hullabulloo, Tiebreak and Travelling Light Theatre (with Theatre-Rites to come on board the following year). Many of these companies did run participatory projects with young people as part of their portfolio, but the overwhelming emphasis, with the exception of Big Brum, Box Clever and Open Theatre, was on the production of professional theatre for young audiences that could tour to theatre buildings and festivals. It might not, therefore, be insignificant to the narrative that I'm proposing, that both Open Theatre and Box Clever's core funding was withdrawn in the first round of NPO allocations in 2011, and Big Brum's in the second round in 2014. With the exception of Tiebreak, all of the others continue to enjoy NPO status.

The aesthetic developments in professional theatre produced for children and young people over this period were influenced by the same continental European performance traditions that impacted on adult theatre in the 1990s, and were evident in the visual and physically charged ensemble aesthetic that began to characterize the field. Jeremy Turner notes how the ideas of Barba and Grotowski enabled Welsh theatre-makers for the young 'to challenge conventions and expectations', identifying the fusion of a Welsh epic tale with contemporary European performance techniques as underpinning the success of Arad Goch's production of *Taliesin* (1995–9) on international stages (Turner, 2005, 33). Developments in immersive strategies, it can be argued, were also pioneered in theatre for young children well in advance of their growing popularity with practitioners more broadly. In 2002, Lyn Gardner praised the long-standing Oily Cart for its 'blurring of relationships between performer and audience and the creation of a kind of total theatre where all the senses and emotions are brought into play' (Gardner, 2003, 32–3). The sensory aspects of performance were initially developed by Oily Cart in their creation of a theatre practice specifically designed for young people with learning disabilities in 1988. Given that they could take neither sight nor hearing for granted in their audiences, as Tim Webb explains, '[o]ur theatre needed to involve the other senses, especially touch and smell, but also the kinaesthetic sense, the sense that the body has of its own movement in space' (Webb, 2005, 197). By the end of the 1990s, Webb reports, they were beginning to move away from the 'sit-down-and-watch variety' of theatre they had previously offered non-disabled audiences, to adopt immersive techniques throughout all their practice targeted at the very young (2005, 204). The importance of audience immersion and sensory stimulation beyond the verbal and visual began to underpin the majority of theatre for the very young in the 2000s and could, of course, be combined with 'sit-down-and-watch' theatre as in Giant Productions' 2006 show, *The Puzzle*, where the audience were invited to watch the adventures of the two performers from within the set, which was constructed like a soft-play area, the action complemented by interactive light, sound, scent and colourful animations.

Theatre-Rites pioneered site-specific theatre for children with its first production, *Houseworks*, a tour of an empty house in Brixton made for the 1996 LIFT festival. Such experiments are now widespread and are often produced in partnership with specialist site-specific companies, such as Pilot's 2013 collaboration with Slung Low to create *Blood and Chocolate*, a promenade performance through the streets of York. In the same year, Action Transport created *House* where the audience was led through a series of interweaving stories that took them into people's homes and hidden areas of parkland in the company's Cheshire base of Ellesmere Port, and in 2014 Grinagog Theatre performed *The Pokey Hat* from an ice cream van for the Glasgow 2014 Cultural Programme.

Developments in digital technology were also influencing the direction of theatre for children and young people throughout this period. Pilot Theatre adopted SMS text messaging and digital projection for all its shows from 2003 onwards, and produced *Sightsonic* in 2005 live on iChat between York and Amsterdam, giving simultaneous performances in both venues (Pilot Theatre website). The use of technology also became an increasingly vital platform in schools-based work, as in Visible Fictions' 2010 project, *State of Emergency*, which was a series of online dramas rolled out on the Glow network, inviting pupils to 'explore and debate the issues surrounding war' (Visible Fictions website). The 20 Stories High Company – one of the most recent theatre companies for young people to be awarded National Portfolio status – fused technological developments with documentary techniques in their 2010 scratch performance, *Tales for the MP3*, presented in its full-length version at the Edinburgh Fringe Festival in 2014. In *Tales*, teenagers performed verbatim extracts from interviews with teenagers, delivered line by line from MP3 players through headphones worn by the actors, in the manner popularized in the UK by theatre company Recorded Delivery.

It is not, of course, only in the more theatre-orientated work that such innovations in form are driving developments in the field. The kinds of interactive and participatory models developed by TIE far pre-dated similar recent experimentation in adult theatre, and companies working within schools and focusing on participatory performance rather than staged productions remain in the vanguard of how participation can best be used to engage audiences and invoke critical reflection. In her article 'The Citizenship Debate and Theatre for Young People in Contemporary Scotland', Adrienne Scullion (2008) discusses how the 'ethos of participation' that lies at the heart of the Scottish Executive's education guidelines set out in Learning and Teaching Scotland can be seen to drive TAG Theatre's 1999–2002 project, *Building the Nation*. One strand of the project, *Making Changes*, utilized role play by positioning pupils as protestors, supporters and journalists focused on the proposed erection of a mobile telephone mast, directed by the improvisations of the actors to explore how far they might go. Likewise a subsequent strand, the *Congress of Nations*, included scenario-based role play with child 'ambassadors' meeting in the chamber of the Scottish Parliament to debate what Congress might do to save the earth as a meteor hurtles towards it.

These are, necessarily, only selective examples, but a study of the timeline of work produced for children and young people across this period demonstrates clearly that the key developments of theatre as an art form seen in the work of companies to be discussed in Part Three of this chapter, such as Gecko, Shunt, Grid Iron, dreamthinkspeak and Coney, among many others, are reflected, if not sometimes prefigured, in the work of the leading theatre companies for children and young people. However, in common with the debate over the so-called marginalization of new writing also discussed in Part Three, it is far from the case that such experimentation was at the cost of new-writing developments, but often worked to enhance them. In the area of participatory TIE practice, for example, Big Brum has worked consistently with world-leading playwright Edward Bond, and Box Clever has focused on participatory programmes facilitating young people's playwriting. Theatre Centre boasts a particularly impressive track record of writer support and development, recently producing work by Ed Harris, Roy Williams, Brenda Murray, Mike Kenny, Lisa Evans, Oladipo Agboluaje, Ashmeed Sohoye, Amber Lone, Leo Butler, Noël Greig and Benjamin Zephaniah among many other renowned playwrights.

That innovations in theatre for children and young people have kept pace with, if not at times prefigured, similar developments in the wider field of theatre, offers one explanation for the degree to which companies not identified as specialists in theatre for children and young people have become increasingly involved in that provision. Punchdrunk's Enrichment Programme and Red Ladder's Freedom Studios (formerly the Asian Theatre School) are two very different examples of youth-orientated programmes run by non-specialist companies (which is not of course to say that the practitioners involved in that aspect of the company's work are not specialists in the field). Many other companies now regularly develop work for children alongside their core business, including Unlimited Theatre, Stan's Cafe, Talking Birds, Improbable Theatre, Coney and Fevered Sleep.

Whether the recent scope within children and young people's theatre to adopt and utilize innovations in form has made it a more exciting field for experimental practitioners to enter or whether such skill sets have simply lent themselves easily to enhancing the kinds of participatory engagement always at the heart of TIE models of practice is beyond the scope of this chapter to interrogate. An additional incentive for experimental practitioners to engage more widely than before in young people's theatre might also, without wishing to seem overly cynical, come down to the pragmatic fact that significant amounts of money were available to make work for this constituency across the 2000s. Given the Arts Councils' emphasis on the importance of access for children and young people, many companies might have been advised, or felt it expedient, to develop work in this priority-funded area alongside, and indeed as a way of developing, their wider experimentation in form.

Cultural Diversity

Despite repeated initiatives to address the lack of ethnic diversity in the theatre sector, from Naseem Khan's British Asian Theatre report in 1994, to the Decibel and Eclipse theatre initiatives, Arts

Council England's performance on hitting its government targets on black and Asian audience attendance and participation continued to make depressing reading. Across the three-year period set out for improvement (2005–8), the target was eventually reached for attendance, but participation rates remained lower than the baseline set in 2005 and 3 per cent off target (ACE, 2009, 57). It is notable in this context that out of the swathe of new companies admitted to the regularly funded portfolio between 2001 and 2003, around 90 in total, only two, Kali Theatre and Tiata Fahodzi, might be defined as, respectively, Asian and black. Even allowing for ambiguity around definitions, this certainly suggests that, given the 2001 census figures for England and Wales establishing a 9 per cent non-white population (BBC, 2001), the two in 90 statistic, however tentative, gets nowhere near to a representative ethnic breakdown of the new companies that were additionally supported by the significant rise in Arts Council funding made available at this time. In the late 2000s and early 2010s, perhaps in response to the failure to meet previous targets, the numbers steadily if not dramatically increased, with additions including Peshkar Productions, Freedom Studios, Nutkhut, Vayu Naidu, Zendeh, Eclipse and Tangle – although Vayu Naidu also had funding withdrawn during this period, as did Yellow Earth and Nitro.

To isolate black and Asian-led companies, as I will now proceed to do, develops the narrative of the pioneer companies described in the previous volume, but only offers a limited perspective of the contribution of black and Asian artists to the independent theatre sector during this time, given that, for example, theatre companies focusing on children and young people's theatre saw 15 companies gain regular funding over this period, many of these demonstrating a strong track record of commitment to black and Asian artists – playwrights in particular – and multicultural audiences. Likewise, many of the applied and political theatre companies discussed above will have regularly involved black and Asian artists in working with what were strongly multicultural constituencies, given the over-representation of black and Asian individuals in contexts of economic and social disadvantage.

Black British Theatre Companies

Eclipse Theatre is possibly unique in being the only independent theatre company effectively created from scratch by Arts Council England (ACE) to fulfil a particular strategic aim of the funding body.

In 2001, the Eclipse initiative was launched at a conference held at Nottingham Playhouse in partnership with ACE to address institutional racism in the theatre sector in the wake of the Macpherson Report. The Eclipse theatre initiative was subsequently established, designed to increase and support a black theatre touring network of middle-scale regional venues. In 2008, artistic director Dawn Walton was appointed to consolidate the artistic vision of what was to become, under Walton's initiative, an independently constituted company in 2009, quickly gaining NPO status by 2012. Given the evident lack of established black-led theatre companies at the time – Talawa, Nitro and the relatively new Tiata Fahodzi being the exceptions – it is perhaps not surprising that the creation of an additional new company was seen as a positive step towards addressing the lack of representation within the middle-scale independent theatre sector. However, I will argue that this cultural gap in the regional middle-scale theatre touring circuit should not necessarily be taken to reflect a lack of representation of black artists within the wider performance ecology.

Eclipse was created to plug a very particular gap, and its choice of productions reflects its target audience of mainstream theatre-goers who needed to attend in sufficient numbers to satisfy the demands of middle-scale regional theatre auditoria. Eclipse thus adopted the two-pronged cultural strategy employed to such success by Talawa on its journey from the margins to the National Theatre; the first Eclipse production was Errol John's Caribbean classic, *Moon on a Rainbow Shawl*, the second, an adaptation of Brecht's *Mother Courage* by Olapido Agboluaje. In addition to further versions of both Western and African/Caribbean classics, which were to include a new adaptation of Chekhov's *Three Sisters* by Mustapha Matura (2006) and Athol Fugard's *Sizwe Banzi is Dead* (2014), Eclipse also produced new writing by the best-known black playwright of the time, Roy Williams (2005, 2008). These were undoubtedly productions aimed primarily, albeit not exclusively, at black audiences, but the strategy otherwise mirrored mainstream programming in its preference for adaptations of the classics and the best-known names in new writing. Granted core funding at the same time as the Eclipse initiative, Tiata Fahodzi began to build its own reputation as the new-writing theatre for Africans and the African diaspora in Britain, producing primarily new texts that reflected something of the British African experience. Since 2004, Tiata have staged their annual play-reading festival, Tiata Delights, and in recent years have begun co-producing with some of the highest profile London venues. In 2012, they co-produced Bola Agbaje's *Belong* with the Royal Court, and in 2013 they co-produced Denton Chikura's *The Epic Adventure of Nhamo the Manyika Warrior and his Sexy Wife Chipo* with the Tricycle Theatre and for a subsequent national tour.

In one important sense, Eclipse and Tiata Fahodzi have adopted for their own purposes well-established models of theatre practice that, while designed to profile black voices and attract black audiences, are working within formal remits already embedded in the British independent and mainstream theatre ecology. However, running parallel to the Eclipse initiative and the rising profile of the new British African playwrights showcased by Tiata Fahodzi, a very different model of performance was emerging that had been culturally insti-gated and driven by young black artists from the start. Manchester's Contact Theatre might not have been a black-led venue in its earlier years, but John McGrath's artistic directorship provided a vital platform for young artists from the North West's diverse multicultural commu-nities to develop and establish art forms for their own generation that were destined to have a significant impact on the independent theatre ecology as a whole. Influenced by black music forms such as rap and hip hop, the rise of performance poetry (or spoken word as it increasingly became known) began to merge with the existing field of live art practice and solo performance, offering young black (and white and Asian) audiences a type of theatre that had little to do with the black theatre then touring the main stages of the regional reps or new-writing venues in London. Beth-Sarah Wright argues that, in addition to its musical roots, performance poetry has emerged as the 'ideal conduit to engage with Black performativity owing to its orality' and that the qualities of the solo act '[transform] the perfor-mance into ritual' (Wright, 2000, 272). Manchester was among the first regional cities to get fully behind the emergence of a new kind of solo performance in the 1990s that could draw on rap or dub poetry, spoken work and live art traditions. Both Contact and the Green Room Arts Centre provided early platforms for the development of a growing field of performance, with the Green Room's poetry slam session 'Speakeasy' designed to launch 'the careers and confidence of African, Caribbean and South Asian live performers of work based on the spoken word, the street lyric and underground poetry culture' (Khan, 2006, 169). This kind of practice was distinct from most of the developments in the black theatre company ecology of the time, but was increasingly supported as a vital and growing movement by regional theatres across the country, particularly in cities such as Manchester and Birmingham, with large multicultural populations.

The choice of solo spoken word over the creation of theatre companies by young black and Asian artists might be explained by a number of factors beyond the attraction of the form itself. Not least, it is worth noting that a significant majority of theatre companies to emerge over the 1990s and 2000s were formed by graduates of university drama degree programmes, and black and Asian representation on such programmes was notably low. Initiatives such as Speakeasy were specifically addressing constituencies beyond the predominantly white graduate community, and became the development ground for spoken-word artists, in the way that degree programmes were often designed to be for theatre ensembles. Perhaps foreseeing such developments in 1994, Catherine Ugwu (the then-deputy director of live art at London's ICA) claimed that '[b]lack theatre may be disappearing in one form but it is reinventing itself as live art' (Evaristo, 1994, 15, in Goddard, 2007, 154).

There was, however, one significant black theatre company that was alert to such developments and whose work began to attract this new generation of black audiences. Established in 1979 as the Black Theatre Co-operative, the company changed its name to Nitro in 1999 and reinvented itself, under the artistic directorship of Felix Cross, from a theatre that was predominantly concerned with black plays, to a theatre that had the influence of black music at its core. Speaking to Geoffrey Davis and Anne Fuchs, Cross explains that 'it suddenly occurred to me that on joining Black Theatre Coop all the most exciting Black artists, the innovative, the most original, the most dynamic ... weren't working in theatre. They were making films, they were doing rap, poetry, they were doing dance, music, especially, live art, performance artists' (Davis and Fuchs, 2006, 226). Cross set up the NITRObeat festival in the early 2000s to bring those artists into collaboration with what was to become Nitro Musical Theatre Company. By 2003, Nitro were co-producing *A Nitro at the Opera* with the Royal Opera House, which, as the *Guardian* reported 'was crammed with visitors, almost all black, almost all experiencing Covent Garden for the first time' (Higgins, 2003). If this seems a long way from Speakeasy's 'underground poetry culture', Nitro's 2004 production *Slamdunk*, co-directed with Benji Reid, grew out of a project on Manchester's Moss Side estate that produced the ingredients of hip hop, gangs and basketball, to which Cross later added the framework of *Coriolanus* (Davis and Fuchs, 2006, 220). *Slamdunk* was co-produced by Contact Theatre and Sheffield Theatres, and audiences over 25 were advised by the *Guardian* that they were not the target audience for this show (Gardner, 2004).

British Asian Theatre Companies

The first established British Asian theatre company, Tara Arts, was formed in 1977 and by the early 1990s was enjoying mainstream success playing to audiences at the National Theatre with shows such as *Tartuffe* (1992), *The Little Clay Cart* (1994) and *Cyrano* (1995) (Hingorani, 2010, 144). One aspect of the vital legacy of Tara Arts was the influence and support it offered to the British Asian theatre companies that were emerging in the 1990s, namely Tamasha Theatre, whose founder members met while working as actors for Tara Arts (Hingorani, 2010, 71), and Kali Theatre, whose 1991 tour of *Song for a Sanctuary* was originally supported by Tara Arts. Tamasha's *East is East* (1996) was a Royal Court co-commission and the first British Asian play to transfer and run at the West End, and in one important sense Tamasha could be usefully considered as extending the cultural reference points of an existing British realist tradition of new-writing companies such as Out of Joint, Paines Plough or Sgript Cymru.

The focus on new British Asian writing was also central to the work of Kali Theatre, a company which is particularly significant to this study due to the feminist agenda that underpins its work and positions the company at a telling intersection of the Asian and women's theatre movements of previous decades. This intersection can clearly be seen in the early trajectory of playwright Rukhsana Ahmad, who co-founded Kali with Rita Wolf. Ahmad had already written plays for Tara Arts in the 1980s, prior to her commission by feminist theatre company Monstrous Regiment. Although *Song for a Sanctuary* was not produced by Monstrous Regiment but went on to be the first Kali Theatre production in 1990, the influences of both of these 1980s theatre movements were already apparent.

Inspired by the murder of an Asian woman by her abusive husband, *Song for a Sanctuary* launched Kali Theatre as a writer-led company that was determined to target 'women from the Asian community in the UK, supporting them professionally and raising the profile of issues that affect them' (Ley and Dadswell, 2011, 135). In line with other women-led new-writing companies in this later period, the feminist politics were foregrounded more in the drive to give opportunities to women artists than in an overtly feminist agenda pertaining to the work itself. There were plays that addressed feminist issues directly, such as Yasmin Whittaker Khan's *Bells* (2005), which exposed the growth of courtesan, or *mujra*, clubs in Britain. However, the work produced by Kali in their 20-year history ranges from British Asian women's perspectives on the familiar diaspora themes of integration, dislocation, culture clashes and the problem of home, to the exploration of global and political events of particular interest to British Asians, such as Ahmad's *River on Fire* (2000), based on the Bombay riots of 1992, or Sonali Bhattacharyya's *A Thin Red Line* (2007) written in recognition of the sixtieth anniversary of the partition of India. Kali also continued its initial interest in supporting victims of domestic abuse and undertook sustained project work in collaboration with Southall Black Sisters, a not-for-profit organization helping black and Asian women who suffered domestic violence. Along with Sphinx and Stellar Quines, Kali have sustained a female-driven presence in the new-writing field of British theatre, ensuring that female playwrights – still woefully underrepresented in the seasons of new-writing venues and particularly vulnerable within the more traditionally patriarchal British Asian communities – continue to have platforms on which to develop their work and broaden the cultural scope of the British feminist realist tradition.

If the cultural day-to-day realities of British Asian life were reflected in much of the new writing produced by Tamasha and Kali, the Eastern influence of Bollywood spectacle also infused British Asian theatre in all its forms to varying degrees. Back in 1993, the interdisciplinary company motiroti had toured internationally with *Moti Roti, Puttli Chunni,* a piece performed in English, Hindi and Urdu that drew on the Bollywood musical form to re-create 'in minute detail all of those effects like tracking shots and close ups and the kind of interplay between screen and stage' (Khan, 2007, 97, in Hodge, 2012, 198). In 1998, Tamasha departed from their customary realist aesthetic to adapt the 1990s' Bollywood hit film *Hum Aapke Hain Koun* for the stage under the title *Fourteen Songs, Two Weddings and a Funeral,* thus neatly fusing Bollywood with the English romcom starring Hugh Grant (Hingorani, 2010, 101; see also Harvie, 2005, 175). Pravesh Kumar, who had performed in *Fourteen Songs,* went on to be the artistic director of RIFCO, the Reduced Indian Film Company – itself a clear homage to the Reduced Shakespeare Company who had recently produced their truncated version of the complete works of Shakespeare (1996). RIFCO was unashamedly populist, and was heavily influenced by the comedy revue form in its second and third shows, *Bollywood 2000* (2000) and *Bollywood – Yet Another Love Story* (2003). Nutkhut's *Bollywood Steps* was originally co-commissioned by the Greenwich and Docklands International Festival, but both the full scale version of the outdoor dance spectacle and its offshoot, *Bollywood Bites,* went on to be performed around the country including a performance at Buckingham Palace to honour the state visit by the president of the Republic of India in 2009. Although often referred to as a dance company, Nutkhut is typical of post-millennial British performance companies who comfortably move between different forms for different projects. Founded in 2003 by co-directors Simmy Gupta and Ajay Chhabra, Nutkhut defines itself as 'an ideas-led, art-focused performance company' (Nutkhut website). The artistic directors draw particular attention to the dual cultural heritage of the company, noting both their own British Asian backgrounds and the 'distinctly British comedic sensibility and eccentricity' of their work. This combination is nicely demonstrated in their 2012 production *Over the Garden Fence*, a performance that 'draws on the British love affair with all things flora and fauna' (Nutkhut website) yet features the company's Lotus Flower installation which is part of the company's *Sari Sari Nights* parade. Away from the more spectacular end of their predominantly outdoor performance, Nutkhut is also planning for 2015 to undertake a project that will map out the contribution made by South Asian soldiers to the war in Europe 'through live performance based on written and oral sources and video mapping incorporating archive film and contemporary footage' (Nutkhut website). Documentary research also featured in Freedom Studios' site-specific production, *The Mill – City of Dreams* (2011), which was based on the stories of local and migrant wool workers and located in an old textile mill in Bradford. The work of both Freedom Studios and Nutkhut is thus characterized and informed by each company's cultural heritage, but has emerged out of, and fully participates in, a contemporary British theatre ecology, drawing on the growing popularity of documentary and site-specific performance.

Beyond BAME

Twenty-first-century Britain is now inescapably multicultural in a much wider and more fluid sense than the integration of the African–Caribbean and South Asian diasporas that the term predominantly referenced in the 1980s and early 1990s. It is not surprising therefore that the UK's rich and potent artistic ecology of multiple cultural heritages begins to productively override the notion of a singular – or even dual – cultural identity for certain companies, such as ZU-UK, or Zendeh, which both emerge in this period. Zendeh's philosophy is embedded not in notions of any one cultural position, but in the recognition of the multicultural and intercultural context of global capitalism, and the need to relocate and reconfigure notions of identity, humanity and the politics of localism within such a context. Iranian myths and contemporary reference points appear in many of Zendeh's shows, reflecting the cultural heritage of artistic director Nazli Tabatabai-Khatambakhsh, but the work itself rejects realistic cultural representations in favour of a more impression-istic, physical and visual style of theatre. In this, it shares the aesthetic of other British companies such as ZU-UK, Gecko (which in light of its Arab and Jewish co-founders might also be considered further in this context) and Ockham's Razor. What becomes apparent in watching the elements of Asian choreography in Zendeh's work is the echo of the kind of intercultural performance aesthetic that is often traced back to Odin Teatret and their early experimentation with non-European forms. In an important sense, such an aesthetic now transcends both a singular non-Western origin (such as the Bollywood references noted in the work above) and the singular influence of European practice such as Barba's, but has become a genuinely intra-cultural vocabulary that permeates British physical theatre in this period, as I will now explore further in Part Three.

PART THREE:
DEVISED PERFORMANCE AND NEW WRITING

Introduction

Throughout this period of study, one of the most sustained and contested tensions within arts policy, beyond the omnipresent tussle between instrumentalism and 'art for art's sake', was the perceived distinction, in England in particular, between the growing field of devised performance and what became defined as 'new writing'. In Scotland and Wales this binary is not so prevalent, partly because the dominant 'new-writing' tradition in England was never repli-cated historically in the same way in either country. Nevertheless, the persistence and influence of the binary within a UK-wide academic context makes it a significant narrative framework in which to discuss companies and trends across all three nations; indeed, pioneering companies in both Scotland (Boilerhouse, Grid Iron) and Wales (Brith Gof, Volcano, Frantic Assembly) often anticipate the progression and expansion of site-specific and physically heightened performance in this period, as I will detail throughout Part Three.

Jacqueline Bolton describes the 1990s as a 'remarkable turnaround in the fortunes of new writing' with the proportion of new writing in the repertoires of English subsidized building-based theatres rising to 15 per cent between 1993 and 1997 (Bolton, 2012, 210). The period is well known for the emergence of the so-called 'in yer face' generation of playwrights that dominated London's new-writing venues in particular, and spread rapidly throughout new writing venues across Europe. Duška Radosavljević further reports that, following a series of ACE policy and strategy documents in the early 2000s, there was additional financial support made available for new-writing and writer-development support structures, so that by 2009 the Arts Council and British Theatre Consortium (BTC) report, Writ Large, concluded that 'new plays ma[d]e up forty two per cent of all theatre shows' (British Theatre Consortium and Rebellato, 2009, 53, cited in Radosavljević, 2013, 86). Given these figures, there is a question as to why both the BTC report and the Dunton, Nelson and Shand report (2009), as noted by Radosavljević 'found that writers felt threatened by what they perceived as the Arts Council's investment in devising over new writing' (Radosavljević, 2013, 86).

An examination of the tension between devised performance and new writing with specific reference to the independent theatre company ecology, rather than within the theatre industry as a whole, produces new insights that might help to untangle some of the reasons why this perception of the emergence of devised practice at the expense of new writing might prevail, despite the figures in the Writ Large report. I will look here at those companies who are defined by their support of new writing as a field, rather than those who work with in-house company writers. The playwright-driven practice of new writing companies can be broken down further by suggesting that there are companies where new writing is the central singular component of the company's identity, and companies with additional constituency remits, such as women; black, Asian and ethnic minorities; or children and young people.

New-Writing Companies

If we start by looking at the broader-remit new-writing companies in England, the first distinctive aspect of such companies in relation to the independent theatre ecology as a whole is their longevity as a cohort: Paines Plough dates back to 1975, Actor's Touring Company dates back to 1986, Headlong dates back to the Oxford Stage Company that can trace its own origins back to 1974, and Out of Joint, although formed in 1993, can trace its history through artistic director Max Stafford-Clark to Joint Stock Theatre which was founded in 1974. The same is found when examining those new-writing companies that have focused on rural touring: Pentabus dates back to 1974, Eastern Angles to 1982, Forest Forge to 1981 and New Perspectives to 1973. Where the political theatre companies examined earlier such as Welfare State, Red Ladder and Banner Theatre can also trace histories back to the 1960s and 1970s, none of those companies remains core funded by Arts Council England, whereas all the above-mentioned new-writing companies, excepting Forest Forge (withdrawn 2012), do. Of the devised companies that I will look at subsequently, there are no comparative examples, the People Show formed in 1966 being an isolated case, its core funding eventually cut in 2009. Furthermore, while there are a number of companies who produce new writing with a constituency or political remit introduced to ACE's portfolio in the 1990s and 2000s – such as Red Room, Kali, Yellow Earth, Tiata Fahodzi, Eclipse and Tangle – no new companies producing broad remit new writing are introduced to the portfolio over the period of this study, despite companies such as Menagerie producing nationally and internationally renowned names in new writing, including Steve Waters and Naomi Wallace, for over 15 years. The new-writing 'powerhouse' companies, it seems, have enjoyed a funding stability – and consolidation of the status quo – that is almost comparable to the new-writing 'powerhouse' venues, a stability that is very much at odds with the regular incomings and outgoings of devising companies at each of the major funding overhauls of Arts Council England over the past 40 years.

The second, and related, aspect of this cohort of companies is their ongoing interconnectedness with the new-writing establishment. Unlike the long-standing devising companies, which have generally had consistent artistic leadership that is tied intrinsically to the company identity, the new-writing companies (with the exception of Out of Joint) change artistic directors regularly, with new directors coming in from and going out to mainstream theatre venues. Max Stafford-Clark, for example, left the Traverse Theatre to found Old Joint Stock in 1974, left Old Joint Stock to become the artistic director of the Royal Court Theatre, and left the Royal Court to found Out of Joint. Dominic Dromgoole left the Oxford Stage Company in 2005 to go to the Globe Theatre, and was replaced by Rupert Goold who left the newly branded Headlong to become artistic director of the

Almeida in 2013. Theresa Heskins left Pentabus in 2006 to become the artistic director of the New Vic Theatre, Newcastle-under-Lyme, and was replaced by Orla O'Loughlin who had been international associate at the Royal Court and who left Pentabus in 2012 to take up the artistic directorship of the Traverse. Vicky Featherstone left Paines Plough in 2004 to become the first artistic director of the National Theatre of Scotland, and subsequently moved to the Royal Court. She was replaced at Paines Plough by Roxana Silbert who had been literary director at the Traverse and who went on to leave Paines Plough in 2009 to become associate director of the RSC and then artistic director of Birmingham Rep.

It is hard, given the consistency of such trajectories, and the privileged stability afforded to these companies, not to see them first and foremost as extensions of the new writing establishment, in which consecutive artistic directors are able to evidence their capabilities before moving into the venues themselves. A similar narrative can, if more hesitantly, be traced through new writing companies with an additional diversity remit, although – perhaps unsurprisingly – the trajectory of black and Asian company artistic directors into the establishment new-writing powerhouses has yet to be established with quite the same degree of conviction. Madani Younis, appointed artistic director of the Bush in 2012, and previously the director of Freedom Studios, might perhaps be the start of such a trend. It is also possibly significant, although beyond the remit of this chapter to pursue further, that artistic directors of specifically women-led theatre companies have not migrated to the mainstream, whereas female directors of new writing companies without a specific gender remit have been particularly successful in that regard, as evidenced above.

In terms of longevity, however, a very similar pattern emerges in all new-writing companies, even in the case of Sphinx Theatre which dates back to 1973 in its incarnation as the Women's Theatre Group, and which sustained core funding up until 2008. The earliest black and Asian theatre companies to be established to produce new writing, Tara Arts (founded 1977) and Talawa (founded 1985), continue to be core funded at the time of writing, as do those founded more recently and noted above. However, black and Asian companies not focusing on new writing – Black Mime Theatre (lost core funding 1998), Nitro (lost core funding 2012), Vayu Naidu Company (lost core funding 2012), motiroti and Rasa Productions (lost core funding 2014) – have not, on the whole, received the same level of continued support. One important exception to this narrative would be Yellow Earth which, despite a focus on new writing and a diversity remit of promoting East Asian artists, lost its core funding in 2012.

This alignment of new-writing companies with what is seen as the dominant field of theatre practice – in England in particular – may have focused academic attention on theatre practice that offers an alternative to a long-standing and historically dominant establishment model, rather than an examination of companies that replicate and nourish that same model. Thus, the innovations to be examined in the latter part of this chapter – from physical and visual theatre to site-specific and immersive performance to the radical reconfiguration of audiences – may have proved of more interest to an academic community historically more engaged with the alternative than the mainstream, and might, as a consequence, have been afforded much greater academic attention over recent years.

If the long-standing new-writing companies can be situated within the Arts Council portfolio, as I have suggested, as close-to-establishment clients, then the Arts Council's policy of only introducing newer companies who have an additional constituency remit can be clearly identified as part of their access and inclusion agenda. The regular incomings and outgoings of devising companies, on the other hand, can be seen to reflect the Arts Council's parallel emphasis – particularly under New Labour – on innovation and the new. For emergent new-writing companies, the constituency audiences needed to be 'new', since the aesthetic model was less so, while emergent devising companies were valued for as long as their experimentation remained 'innovative', and were replaced by other companies once the form they had pioneered became overfamiliar. This location of 'innovation' within devising practice rather than within the new-writing companies can be seen, in the late 1990s and early 2000s, to work not only against dramatic models of new writing but against text-driven work more widely, an important distinction that I will return to over the course of this final part of the chapter.

The bias against new writing as innovation can clearly be seen, for example, in the comparative absence of emergent new-writing companies in the British Council Showcase, as noted in Part One of this chapter. Furthermore, the script-based work that was selected was often explored in conjunction with physical approaches, such as the Told by an Idiot and Royal Court partnership on *Playing the Victim* in 2003. The showcase's preference for less text-based work might well have been one result of its requirement to supply an international marketplace and its consequent criterion for companies to stipulate on their application for inclusion whether their work was:

Text-based: light (very little or no text)
Text-based: medium (some text with a strong visual/physical element)
Text-based: dense (important for audiences to have a good understanding of English)

While this was a reasonable criterion in the British Council's own context, it is perhaps at least possible to speculate that the importance of the showcase to a company's development, and the benefit of a work's accessibility to non-English-speaking audiences, were key factors in the shift towards physical and visual performance in the 1990s, a topic that I will explore further below. However, the showcase's emphasis on innovation, and the types of work selected to demonstrate this commitment, helped to consolidate a growing conflation of innovation and non-text-based practice over the late 1990s and early 2000s, significantly supported in academic circles by the growing influence of Hans-Thies Lehmann's definition of postdramatic theatre.

Lehmann's groundbreaking study was influential in its claims that only a postdramatic practice could be truly political in a postmodern culture, a claim that I have interrogated and refuted elsewhere (Tomlin, 2013a and 2013b). Most significantly for this discussion, he was also clear that a postdramatic practice should not be text *driven*, but should assign 'the dominant role to elements other than dramatic logos and language' (Lehmann, 2006, 93). While many academics, and indeed Lehmann himself, have more recently reclaimed playwrights within the postdramatic rubric, one immediate consequence of Lehmann's categorization (first published in the original German in 1999) was to exacerbate the growing binary between a playwright's theatre, then declared politically ineffective, and a devising practice in which the role of text was not primary, and the political efficacy was said to be enhanced.

Lehman's rejection of drama as a potentially radical form can be seen to strengthen the narrative I have proposed above. For the 'new' writing companies to be so closely aligned with a long-standing and historically dominant establishment model suggests that they might be unable to offer either aesthetic or political renewal to the independent theatre ecology. The persistent perception of playwriting's decreasing importance, despite economic evidence to the contrary, might be, in some significant part, due to an over-emphasis on the innovation of new forms of devising practice in academic discourse. This emphasis might well have come about precisely in response to the dominant establishment position of new writing within the theatre industry as a whole, and even, as we can now see, within the sub-field of the independent theatre sector. This chapter will ultimately conclude by looking at the change in direction of text-based theatre and performance in the later 2000s and 2010s, and the resurgence of academic interest in innovations in text and new writing that were to transform the new-writing establishment itself. Most significantly, I will argue that such innovations in text-based theatre were, for the most part, not initiated either by the establishment or the new-writing powerhouse companies, but by independent companies, often engaged in ensemble devising methodologies, too often mistakenly positioned in binary opposition to text-based practice.

Physical and Visual Theatres

Deirdre Heddon and Jane Milling suggest that the 'growth and diversity of "training" for actors, dancers, mime or circus performers has multiplied exponentially since the late 1970s, and has been central to the production of this second wave of physical performance troupes' (Heddon and Milling, 2006, 160). The first wave of physical theatre companies emerging in the 1980s, predominantly influenced by the Lecoq training school in Paris, would include Théâtre de Complicité and Trestle Theatre, and the rising profile of these companies in the early 1990s, Complicite in particular, was a major factor in the growing attraction of a particular aesthetic to emerging companies of the time. Another 1980s company to provide significant inspiration to emerging practitioners in the 1990s and 2000s was DV8 (the first to explicitly use the label 'physical theatre' for their work), who have been cited as 'the first British exponents of German tanztheater, best known through the work of Pina Bausch' (Callery, 2001, 7). Heddon and Milling (2006) also identify the growing influence of non-Western performance traditions such as 'kalaripayattu, Kathakali, Noh, Kabuki' (161), and the popularization of intensive intercultural training systems developed by Grotowski and Eugenio Barba's Odin Teatret.

The best of international physical performance and training methodologies was brought to the attention of UK artists and academics by a growing network of influential workshop programmes including the Centre for Performance Research, led by Richard Gough, and the growing profile of the International Workshop Festival under Dick McCaw's directorship in the 1990s. Total Theatre, a journal produced by Total Theatre Network between 1989 and 2012, can also take significant credit for putting the growing trend of physical and visual theatre firmly on the map, not only through the journal itself, but through the Edinburgh Fringe Festival Total Theatre Awards, launched in tandem with the inaugural British Council Showcase in 1997. UK companies to feature in the awards listings include The Right Size and Fecund (1997), Ridiculusmus (1999), Spymonkey and Shunt (2000), Company F/Z and Shona Reppe Puppets (2002), Duckie (2003), Gecko, Station House Opera, Grid Iron and dreamthinkspeak (2005), Chotto Ookii (2006), Little Bulb (2008), Clod Ensemble (2009), Catherine Wheels, Ankur Productions and NoFit State Circus (2010) and Crying Out Loud (2013). Total Theatre awards also highlighted and profiled the best of international physical theatre to visit the festival, with the Russian anti-circus Derevo appearing a number of times. Derevo was just one influential example of the proliferation of the international new circus movement (including Archaos, Cirque du Soleil and Circus Oz) which had by the 1990s, as Peta Tait confirms, become recognizable in economic and artistic terms as 'an art form in its own right' (Tait, 2005, 120). In 2002, Crying Out Loud was established as a production company to develop and raise the profile of contemporary circus in the UK, both by importing the best of international practice and by supporting the growth of new practice in the UK. Crying Out Loud became an Arts Council Regularly Funded Organization in 2007 and supported the development of Ockham's Razor and Blind Summit, who were both given National Portfolio Organization status in 2012.

Although physical theatre is often seen, like the postdramatic, as a trend that represents a 'shift away from text-based theatre' (Callery, 2001, 3) such a claim is only partially borne out in a brief examination of the work of those companies to emerge in the 1990s and 2000s. It is certainly somewhat true of the physical theatre companies that derive from the non-verbal performance traditions of dance and aerial circus, such as Clod Ensemble, Boilerhouse, Scarabeus, Exponential, Company F/Z, Ockham's Razor and Upswing. It is in such models of physical theatre, where performers are predominantly trained dancers or aerialists, that the technique is most visible and the virtuosity of the aesthetic most apparent. The emphasis in most of this work, however, is not to challenge the text-based traditions of literary drama, as is the case in postdramatic theatre, but to extend the traditional disciplines of dance and circus by a fusion of physical virtuosity, visual design, text and narrative that results in interdisciplinary forms of contemporary performance. The field of theatre is, of course, likewise expanded by such interdisciplinary experimentation, but to label the majority of this work 'postdramatic' would suggest a continuing relationship with the dramatic form that seems at odds with the physical performance origins of this body of work. Both Ockham's Razor and Upswing define themselves primarily in relation to circus – Ockham's Razor as an 'aerial theatre company who combine circus and visual theatre' (Ockham's Razor website), and Upswing as 'contemporary circus infused with new writing, puppetry, stunning visuals and daring choreography' (Upswing website) – and both emphasize the importance of story-telling in their work. While text certainly plays a less significant role in the work described above than it would in a piece of dramatic theatre, it is less a shift away from text-based theatre and more a move towards a text-inclusive form of dance or aerial circus.

The 'shift away from text' is misleading in a different sense when undertaking an analysis of theatre companies working in the broad aesthetic of Lecoq, such as Told by an Idiot, Benchtours and Theatre O, where the adaptation of classic texts recurs as a frequent strategy, as indeed has been the case with Complicite. The importance of adaptation is even more pronounced in work by companies such as Kneehigh, described in detail in Duška Radosavljević's chapter in this volume, where the company's physical style of performance derives from the much wider sphere of influence of popular theatre. Mimetic replications of the language of literary texts might often be jettisoned in such work, but the original classic text still underpins the theatrical vocabularies that respond to the challenges it poses. The work is still arguably 'text-based', although the experience for the spectator is an aesthetic where the spoken text itself is less prominent among the physical and visual spectacle than it would be in a dramatic realist model of adaptation.

Volcano's long history, stretching back to their production of Berkoff's adaptation of the Oedipus myth, *Greek*, in 1987, demonstrates a more anarchic physical choreography than that which underpins the Lecoq tradition, possibly due to the Welsh lineage of Brith Gof which pioneered an almost Artaudian approach to physical performance that eschewed the formal virtuosity of specific training traditions. However, neither this legacy nor the deliberate rawness and viscerality of the company's physicality have militated against a consistent trajectory of text-based work, from classical theatre adaptations such as *Macbeth* (1999), to literary adaptations such as *A Clockwork Orange* (2012), to possibly the only theatrical adaptation ever of the Communist Manifesto (1994). The younger Welsh company Frantic Assembly, later migrating across the border to England, pioneered for the mainstream a particular conjunction of choreographed movement-based sequences created in collaboration with playwrights including Abi Morgan (*Tiny Dynamite* (2001)), Mark Ravenhill (*Pool No Water* (2006)), and Bryony Lavery (*Stockholm* (2008) and *Beautiful Burnout* (2010)), much as Complicite had pioneered a Lecoq-grounded approach to text-based theatre a decade earlier.

All of this does suggest that the 'devised' and 'playwriting' opposition was, as Jacqueline Bolton (2012) has suggested, a predominantly economic rather than aesthetic preoccupation, given that new texts were being widely developed within the field of devising throughout this period. The distinction that was causing the playwriting community consternation was, perhaps, that much of this text development, with the exception of Frantic Assembly, was being done 'in-house' as part of the company activity rather than being provided by a freelance playwright, thus leading to a perceived financial threat to those whose livelihoods depended on the traditional system of commissions. Furthermore, far from being in danger of being 'written out' of the independent theatre sector, the role of text was often vital in securing the legitimacy of certain devising practices. It might seem paradoxical, given the 'anti-text' rhetoric often applied to physical theatre, that the most successful proponents of the field – Complicite, Kneehigh, Shared Experience, Frantic Assembly – have built their reputations to a significant degree on adaptations of existing literary texts and new plays by leading playwrights, but there is much to suggest that this is the case. In the trajectories of the companies under discussion, there does seem to be evidence, as Alex Mermikides and Jackie Smart suggest, that 'mainstream venues, while they are attracted by devising as a genre, are not wholly willing to accept purely devised work' (2010, 21). The trajectory of Frantic Assembly would also bear this out. The company's first collaboration with an established playwright for *Tiny Dynamite* was accompanied by the partnership support of Paines Plough and Contact Theatre. It represented the beginning of the company's career momentum, which saw it depart from the small-scale touring circuits shared at the time with emerging companies such as Blast Theory, Third Angel, Point Blank and Unlimited Theatre, with whom they also at that point shared a much closer aesthetic than their later playwright-driven work would suggest. Likewise Mermikides and Smart observe that for those companies who do not always work with adaptation, such as Theatre O and Gecko, the point at which they have begun to make the transition from small-scale to medium-scale theatre is often marked by the adaptation of a classic text: in Theatre O's case, *Delirium* (2008) and in Gecko's, their adaptation of Gogol's *The Overcoat* (2009) (Mermikides and Smart, 2010, 21).

It was an adaptation of a very different kind that underpinned Improbable Theatre's transition from fringe to mainstream. In 1997, their collaboration with musicians The Tiger Lillies, under the creative production of Michael Morris, gave birth to *Shockheaded Peter*, which was, in the words of critic Susannah Clapp (2001), 'the most original piece of theatre of the past 10 years', touring internationally and transferring to the West End in 2001. Adapted from the macabre children's stories of Heinrich Hoffmann, where children were subject to violent acts of retribution for small misdemeanours, the production encompassed life-size puppets and white-faced actors to a soundtrack of anarchic accordion music and the 'eerie falsetto' singing of Martyn Jacques (Clapp, 2001). By the time *Shockheaded Peter* had hit the West End in 2001, the legacy of the darker side of music hall and cabaret traditions was already visible in the puppet work of Faulty Optic and Doo Cot. Whereas Doo Cot's puppets often tackled the darker side of gender and sexuality politics, Faulty Optic's work was situated in the surreal world of the macabre, from their first show, *My Pig Speaks Latin* (1988), described as 'a Punch and Judy for the Apocalyptic Age' (Alexander, 1988), to their 2006 production *Horsehead*, described as 'a series of gruesome vignettes which show the world going to hell in a handbasket' (Clapp, 2006).

Both companies, in distinctly different ways, demonstrated 'the spirit of the anarchic and the carnivalesque' that Marion Baraitser (1999, 2) identifies as intrinsic to the historical traditions of puppet theatre. The same anarchic heritage is apparent in the subsequent work of Blind Summit, although the conceptual landscape feels very distinct. Whereas Faulty Optic was situated in the modernist tradition of surrealism, Blind Summit's self-referential puppets and meta-theatrical landscapes owe much more to the conventions of postmodernism. The old man puppet in *The Table* (2013) states that he's 'getting into character' before introducing each of his puppeteers, explaining who moves what. 'I don't know what to do with you' he says to the live performer at the end of his table, 'you're dramaturgically inconsistent' (Blind Summit, 2013). After high-profile collaborations with Anthony Minghella (*Madame Butterfly* (2005)), Complicite (*Shun Kin*) and the National Theatre (*His Dark Materials* revival), Blind Summit were introduced to ACE's National Portfolio in 2012. In the same overhaul of ACE's portfolio, Faulty Optic had their funding withdrawn resulting in the company's subsequent dissolution. Doo Cot's funding had already been discontinued in 2008. Whether or not the shift from a surreal and grotesque modernist emphasis to a self-referential postmodern one, or indeed the shift, in Doo Cot's case, from a more explicitly political landscape to the mainstream high-profile collaborations of Blind Summit, had been conscious evaluations of the Arts Council's strategic development of the form, this trajectory does suggest implicit movement, at least, in that direction.

It is evident that the field of theatre that might be defined as 'physical', 'visual' or 'total' encompasses a wide diversity of practice that can be usefully, if cautiously, gathered together in light of a shared exploration of the choreographic and visual potential of performance that is generally underpinned by a level of recognized technique, be that in dance, aerial work or puppeteering. Increasingly, this aesthetic is no longer necessarily underpinned by the specialist training techniques or specific expertise of companies like Complicite, DV8 or Doo Cot. Kneehigh's work under Emma Rice, in particular, has popularized the more eclectic adoption of physical, musical and visual vocabularies, evident in the work of companies as diverse as Vanishing Point, Improbable Theatre, Reject's Revenge, Foursight Theatre, Ridiculusmus, Spike Theatre, Kiln Theatre and Little Bulb, to enhance a narrative-driven theatre practice throughout this period. Such companies, I would argue, are less accurately characterized as mounting a subversive challenge to the authority of the text, than as being committed to an aesthetic renewal of theatrical possibility, a reconfiguration of traditional modes of storytelling and the episodic style of epic theatre within the framework of an often self-referential model of contemporary performance that utilizes physical, musical and visual vocabularies and narrated text, as well as dialogue. In this sense, it is more accurately dramatic realism that seems to have fallen out of favour, rather than text-based practice, although the centrality of the spoken text within the performance as a whole differs from case to case as explored above. While I have argued that in most of the companies highlighted thus far, the rejection of the dramatic realist form of theatre is more a consequence of the influence of alternative aesthetic models, rather than the primary aim of the artists, that is arguably not the case for the work that might most closely correspond to Lehmann's definition of the postdramatic, to which I will now turn.

Legacies of the Postmodern

Before Hans-Thies Lehmann reconceptualized the notion of the postdramatic in his 1999 publication, *Postdramatisches Theater*, the influence of postmodernist discourse was already rapidly spreading from the academy to performance practice in the UK. Indeed, the proliferation of such practice across Europe and North America in the 1980s and early 1990s was precisely what necessitated Lehmann's reconceptualization of the postdramatic to offer a theatre-specific vocabulary for addressing a body of work that was actively challenging the dramatic form. In North America and continental Europe, postmodern (later postdramatic) performance was often driven by directors such as Robert Wilson, Richard Foreman, Jan Fabre and Silviu Purcarete as well as companies such as the Wooster Group or Theatergroep Victoria. In the UK, however, where the mainstream was still dominated by dramatic models of social realism at the time, it was almost exclusively the small-scale experimental companies in the 1980s and early 1990s that pioneered developments in form that would later significantly shift the aesthetics of mainstream theatre practice. Forced Entertainment, influenced in turn by Impact Theatre before them, were probably the single most significant force in shaping the landscape of postdramatic performance practice in the UK. By the late 1990s, the company's work was firmly canonized alongside the Wooster Group on undergraduate syllabi throughout the UK, and the company's increasingly familiar motifs and aesthetic frameworks begin to characterize experimental practice – for better and worse – well into the 2000s.

These motifs, identified by Sara Jane Bailes (2011) as aspects of a poetics of failure, would include the adoption of performance personae rather than dramatic characters, often resulting in representations of performers who were in some way inept, inadequate or untrustworthy attempting to construct characterizations that were utterly unconvincing. There was often a strong meta-theatrical framework that presented a performance of a performance, and dramatic conventions such as fictional character, the fourth wall or a coherent narrative were deconstructed or destabilized. Performers would address the audience directly and acknowledge the reality of the performance event, rather than construct the realist representation of a fictional world or, in Lehmann's terms, a *'fictive* cosmos' (2006, 31, original emphasis). Emerging in the 1990s, the first wave of companies to adopt and explore this aesthetic terrain would include Improbable Theatre, Stan's Cafe, Vincent Dance Theatre, Reckless Sleepers, Desperate Optimists,

Third Angel and Gobsquad, while companies of the 2000s would include Metro-Boulot-Dodo, Paper Birds, Plane Performance, Deer Park, Rash Dash, Made In China and Getinthebackofthevan, among many others.

That I have questioned the automatic alignment of the postdramatic with the political is not to suggest that the postdramatic is necessarily without potential political efficacy. Lehmann differentiates the postdramatic 'politics of perception' (2006, 185) from previous notions of political theatre, rejecting the dramatic form that consists of representational characters in recognizable real-world situations exploring explicitly political themes within a realist narrative framework. Postdramatic theatre, in its rejection of dramatic realism's mimetic representations, rather seeks to challenge the comparable constructions of illusory realities by the mass media, asking its audiences to be sceptical of anything that purports to be real or hold truth value in a world where, as the philosopher Jean Baudrillard argued, reality is no longer always distinguishable from ideological simulation. This is the political and philosophical basis of Lehman's postdramatic and Bailes's poetics of failure. If dramatic realism is thought to be inadequate in the face of the mass media's construction of reality, then the postdramatic must demonstrate this failure by its adoption of the conventions of the dramatic – realistic characterization and real-life narratives played out behind an invisible fourth wall – in order to deconstruct them as nothing more than ideological simulation. From the pastiche of Hollywood cops in Blast Theory's *Something American* (1996), the B-movie film-noir characters played in quotation marks in Third Angel's *Experiment Zero* (1997/8) and the 'rock stars' and 'air pilots' in Gobsquad's *Safe* (1999), all the way through to Paper Birds' inadequate and devious performance personae in *Others* (2010), Rash Dash's wannabe celebrities in *The Ugly Sisters* (2013) and the surreal TV executives of Little Bulb's *Squally Showers* (2013), the motif of over-theatricalized and non-credible representations of character continues to pervade an otherwise broad and disparate aesthetic field.

This postmodern scepticism of the real also raises fundamental questions about the very possibility of a singular notion of truth in the work under discussion. In Third Angel's *Parts for Machines that Do Things* (2008), the performers present what appears to be a documentary account of an air crash, which turns out to be entirely fictional, and the company tag line 'do you need to fake the world in order to understand it?' is a fitting epitaph for the company's work to date. If Third Angel most often tends to prioritize the personal, and explores a predominantly playful slippage between biography and fiction, the political potential of a postmodern scepticism is at its most acute when directly targeted at more explicitly political territory. This is seen in Desperate Optimists' *Play-boy* (1998/9), which interspersed subjective and often inaccurate accounts of Synge's *Playboy of the Western World* among a series of seemingly unrelated historical narratives presented by the two performers concerning an eighteenth century Latin American dictator called Bernardo O'Higgins; Elia Kazan, a Hollywood director called before the House Un-American Activities Committee; and the death of Leon Trotsky. The game for the spectators, as Neal Swettenham describes, is to ask of themselves how the fragmented and disparate narrative elements can best be connected and how much of it they are intended to believe. Swettenham describes 'the games and puzzles presented by such work' as 'ludic pleasure' for the audience (2005, 254), but I would hold that there is a deeper resonance due to the political undertones of the historical material selected in this instance. The questioning of received political histories and of the reliability and personal agenda of the one who narrates – in this case in the context of Irish and Latin American history, the US witch hunt of communists and the figure of Trotsky – underpins the seemingly ludic framework of *Play-boy* with a deeper political gravitas than might first appear to be the case.

From New Media to Lo-tech Theatre

The sustained interrogation or investigation of mediatized simulations of reality that persisted from the late 1990s and throughout the 2000s was often undertaken through sophisticated employment of the very technology that was at the forefront of an increasingly mediatized society. As Rosemary Klich and Edward Scheer (2012) argue, '[m]ultimedia performance, as a medium that incorporates both real and virtual, live and mediatized elements, is in a unique position to explore and investigate the effect of extensive mediatization on human sensory perception and subjectivity' (Klich and Scheer, 2012, 2). Theatre companies experimenting with early multimedia technology in the 1990s include Station House Opera, Fecund Theatre and Blast Theory. Station House Opera's 1998 production of *Roadmetal, Sweetbread*, revived in 2012, was seen as radical in its time for its fusion of live performers and their projected virtual doubles, a dramaturgical strategy that was replicated in the subsequent productions *Snakes and*

Ladders (1998), *Mare's Nest* (2001) and *How to Behave* (2003). These early explorations of the duplicity of simulation can productively be read, in one sense, as an exploration of the human in crisis or a critique of 'the impact of media technologies on contemporary culture' (Klich and Scheer, 2012, 2), given the authority and independence of the simulations that could, at key moments, undermine or eclipse the physical presence of the live performers that they doubled.

However, as the 2000s progressed and the web and digital communication landscape expanded, there are fewer examples of performance engaging in this mode of political or critical analysis. Rather, artists and companies became more interested in examining not the duplicitous virtuality of what was constructed to appear real but the new realities that were being created by the virtual. Station House Opera's later productions, *Live from Paradise* (2004), *Play on Earth* (2006) and *The Other is You* (2006) all use live video streaming to connect three different physical performance sites in different cities or countries via a fourth, shared, virtual performance space. Jem Kelly (2010) argues that *The Other is You* 'is a departure from the narrative dramatic structure of Station House Opera's earlier telematic performances as the content and aesthetic concerns of this work model, rather than represent, everyday life' (53). This move from dramatic representation to presentation of everyday life reflects, not only the wider postdramatic turn, but also what I would suggest was a shift in multimedia performance by the mid-2000s away from the imperative to critique the impact of mass media, and towards an exploration of its potential for the amelioration of social relations in an increasingly global world view. By the mid-2000s, I would argue, artists were far more interested in the new realities that a now familiar technological economy could construct and support, seeking to discover how technology might offer progressive political tools for intervention in the globally mediatized landscape. As Kelly argues, '*The Other Is You* is formed by the sense of time lived, and framed by the idea that technology can re-locate us spatially' (2010, 56); thus, here the technology is used to explore the construction of a shared reality – albeit a virtual one – in which personal connections and communications can be made across continents.

The cinematic performances of Imitating the Dog can be understood as both affirmation and critique of the political and aesthetic potential of the postmodern technological landscape. *Hotel Methuselah* (2005) establishes what is to become a signature motif of the company, restricting our view of the performers to what can be seen through a letterbox frame in the centre of a screen; our only view of the actors' heads and faces are the close-up projections that appear sporadically on the screen behind them. The dislocation of speaking heads from moving bodies and the moving bodies from the landscape they appear to be in echoes strategies utilized by avant-garde artists such as the Wooster Group to deconstruct the notion of singular and reliable identity, presence and reality. However, in both *Methuselah* (2005) and *Kellerman* (2009) such dislocation is utilized less as a means of philosophical deconstruction than as a strategy – common in the filmic tradition drawn on by Imitating the Dog – to reflect the internal, psychological dislocation of the protagonist in each case. In *Methuselah*, Harry, the hotel porter, is the classic film noir protagonist who has amnesia and is no longer sure who is he is; in *Kellerman*, the action is seen through the eyes of the eponymous protagonist's hallucinogenic state of induced hypnosis. In this sense, the company utilizes the multiperspectival modes of reality made possible by their use of technology and design to underpin and support the narrative drive of each production, although that is not to say that the questioning of the real through the eyes of their protagonists does not raise wider philosophical concerns. In *Zero Hour* (2011), however, there is a more explicit political and philosophical agenda underpinning the company's trademark cinematic motifs. This is due in part, as was the case with Desperate Optimists' *Play-boy*, to the wider political content of the piece, which follows British, Russian and German perspectives through the final moments of World War II, and due in part to the additional presence of the live camera operator and the framing of the piece as a documentary, thus supporting the reading of this piece as a questioning of mediatized constructions of history.

It is not coincidental that many of the companies specializing in multimedia experimentation in this period were aligned with academic research. Imitating the Dog's artistic direction is steered by Andrew Quick (Lancaster University) and Pete Brooks (Central Saint Martins), with many of the company's associate artists also teaching in higher education. Other important examples include Peter Petralia who worked at Manchester Metropolitan for some years while directing Proto-type Theater, Simon Jones of Bodies in Flight and Bristol University, and Andy Lavender of Lightwork and the University of Surrey. These academic connections might explain why the research element of innovative technological experimentation and its potential to enhance narrative forms and create new theatrical vocabularies is so often accompanied by a theoretically sophisticated questioning of the real itself.

It is also evident that, during this period of rapid technological expansion, initial experimentation and innovation very quickly become familiar, cheaper and easier for non-specialists to manipulate and utilize, and by the late 2000s visual digital technology can be seen as an accepted theatrical vocabulary within much of the practice discussed throughout this chapter, used as often to enhance traditional narrative forms by constructing more aesthetically rich fictions, as to engage in the kinds of deconstruction described above. The expansion of technology within live performance and its ubiquity within our everyday lives by this point in time might also explain signs of a reactive return to a deliberately lo-tech theatre, as exemplified by the growth in popularity of puppets and object manipulation, the use of live musicians and the widespread use of foley sound. In addition to the specialist work of Blind Summit described in the previous section, many younger companies are adopting strategies from the traditions of puppet theatre. Analogue Theatre has used stagehands dressed in black to manipulate objects and performers in the space; Paper Cinema's projection involves, not mediatized images, but exquisitely hand-drawn cardboard cut-outs that provide the visual narrative to accompany the live musicians in the space. These lo-tech approaches to object manipulation create an aesthetic where there is pleasure in seeing the 'deception' at work, whether that is the stagehand who 'drops' the mug in slow motion to the floor in Analogue's *Mile End* (2007), or the snapping of celery to represent the breaking of human bones in Little Earthquake's adaptation of Edgar Allen Poe's *The Tell-Tale Heart* (2013). In both cases, there is an emphasis on visible trickery that might constitute an implicit rejection – and perhaps critique – of the invisible sleight of hand of mediatized simulations of the real. There are also productions that combine both lo- and hi-tech approaches, such as Proto-type Theater's 2013 production *The Good, the God and the Guillotine*, which displays both hand-drawn graphics and digital projections, accompanied by live song and musicians who are performing music live on laptops.

Innovations in Site and Audience Configurations

In the pioneering site-specific performances of companies founded in the 1960s and 1970s, such as Welfare State and Mikron, the primary political motivation for the location of their practice was to avoid the institutional and ideological impositions of the theatre building, where any radical potential was seen to be limited by the economic and cultural systems within which the institution had to function, as Baz Kershaw has argued at length (1992; 1999). The political imperatives of this particular tradition underpin the production of much large-scale spectacular performance in this later period, such as Walk the Plank, established in the early 1990s, and Wildworks, founded in 2005 by artistic director Bill Mitchell, who had previously worked with Walk the Plank, Kneehigh and Welfare State. Mitchell is keen to stress that, despite the aesthetic potentials of what he terms 'landscape theatre', the political drive of any Wildworks production lies in its commitment to the community connected to the site, whether this be in Port Talbot, Malta or Palestine, three of the many locations to have featured in Wildworks' history thus far. He rejects the idea of a theatre company 'parachuting in' to a particular location and 'landing on people' to do a show, and believes that the quality and integrity of the company's work is due to the care and time taken to engage with the narratives of the communities in question (Mitchell, 2014, 4:30). The political resonances of this strategy are compelling. One of their earliest pieces, *A Very Old Man with Enormous Wings* (2003/5), made in partnership with Kneehigh Theatre and local arts organizations in Malta and Cyprus, required the company to get UN permission to build a village on the buffer zone between the Greek and Turkish parts of Cyprus, bringing together communities from both sides of the divide in the performance space of a derelict tavern that had been closed due to sniper fire. In 2011, in partnership with the National Theatre of Wales, Wildworks' production of *The Passion* in Port Talbot involved 1,200 members of the local community bringing contributions to the narrative and the staging of the production across the beach, steelworks and town itself, culminating in a parade that was attended by over 25,000 people. Wildworks' recognition as a National Portfolio Organization in 2012 evidences the Arts Council's support for work that continues in the community tradition of political theatre, as well as an acknowledgement of the reach that spectacular and large-scale work can attain in attracting large audiences that are not necessarily theatre-going audiences. In both senses, such work plays well with funding imperatives in the 2000s that seek to encourage greater participation both in the making of theatre and in new audience development.

Brith Gof pioneered a quite different site-specific approach in the 1980s and early 1990s, distinguished by its recognition and manipulation of the political resonances of the site itself. *Gododdin*, for example, was produced in 1988 'in the engine-shop of the enormous, disused

Rover car factory in Cardiff, itself a potent symbol of economic decline and industrial decay' (Pearson and Shanks, 2001, 103). Contemporary echoes of this aesthetic can be seen in the work of Talking Birds, a company that has been consistently engaged with sites of departure, its productions often exploring absence, disappearance and the ghosts of the past, such as *A City Grown from Worlds*, a performance installation to mark the closure of the Bishop Street Sorting Office; *Three Doctors*, which marked the closure of the Coventry & Warwickshire Hospital; and *The Last Lot*, which marked the closure of the Mart on the Barrack Street site, Kilkenny. The company dreamthinkspeak, founded in 1999, also created what it calls 'site-responsive' performances that have taken place in locations including the former Co-operative department store in Brighton, an underground abattoir in Clerkenwell and a disused paper factory in Moscow. Where Punchdrunk, emerging around the same time, constructs its own environments in buildings that, to some degree, are architectural blank canvases, dreamthinkspeak's site-responsive work selects sites that, in their own history, offer something distinctive to the performance taking place within them. *Before I Sleep* (2010), the company's adaptation of Chekhov's *The Cherry Orchard*, for example, was heightened by the melancholic air of the closed down Co-op store that perfectly complemented the themes of loss and changing political times of Chekhov's original text; a *Sunday Times* reviewer commented that 'wandering through the building there are times when you feel like the last person on earth' (dreamthinkspeak website).

Despite the above examples, explicit politics of site and content are less widespread in contemporary site-specific practice, which is as much influenced by the aesthetic as the political. Furthermore, as Fiona Wilkie suggests, site-specific performance can often be, to some degree, a predominantly strategic choice in areas of the UK – Wales, Scotland, Cornwall – where there is not a significant building-based theatre circuit for companies to utilize (Wilkie, 2002, 142–3). This would also seem to be borne out by the small-scale Scottish companies who were among the first to emerge in the most recent wave of innovative site-specific practice. Following in the footsteps of Boilerhouse, whose site-specific aerial performance was well established by the mid-1990s, Grid Iron, incorporated in 1995, gained swift international critical acclaim only two years later at the Edinburgh Fringe Festival with their adaptation of Angela Carter's *The Bloody Chamber*, which took audiences on a promenade journey of the underground vaults in Mary King's Close, with later versions of the production relocating to London Dungeon and Belfast's Lagan Weir. *The Bloody Chamber* won a host of awards, and Grid Iron continued to feature heavily in multiple awards listings for subsequent site-generic festival productions including *Decky Does a Bronco* (2000), *The Devil's Larder* (2005) and *Barflies* (2009), with *Leaving Planet Earth* (2013) produced for the Edinburgh International Festival programme and performed in the International Climbing Arena. Beyond the high profile of the Edinburgh festivals' showcases, Grid Iron also made site-specific work, such as their 2003 production *The Houghmagandie Pack*, a celebration of the life and work of Robert Burns that was made and performed in the village of Alloway, the poet's birthplace. As the company notes, the promenade performance that took the audience on a mile-long journey to exactly the places where the events of the narrative would have occurred made it 'site-specific in the truest sense' and an 'extraordinary experience' (Grid Iron website).

The rise in popularity of promenade performance, and the subsequent proliferation of performance walks in the mid/late 2000s, was significantly enhanced by new digital technologies that enabled performance text and soundtracks to be easily, and intimately, accessed by audience via headphones as they walked. In addition to the popularity of audio tours, which were often unaccompanied by any live performer, audio technology has also enhanced the possibilities of promenade performance in more theatrical contexts. Slung Low, for example, was invited by the Liverpool's Everyman Theatre in 2010 to work with seven writers on seven new plays inspired by the themes of *'Tis Pity She's a Whore*, the production that was running at the time. Audience members would arrive at the theatre and be allocated one of the seven plays to attend, following the cast out of the theatre into various locations in Liverpool, including a graveyard and cathedral. The entire text for each performance was played to the audience via headphones, giving the sense, as Lyn Gardner reports, 'that the play is unfolding inside your head and in a physical space' (Gardner, 2010).

Developments in audio technology have been at the forefront of the work of David Rosenberg, a member of the Shunt collective, whose site-specific performances in its London bases, the Arch and the Vaults, were early and pivotal factors in the growing momentum towards the acoustic and immersive potential of indoor site-specific theatre in the 2000s, also pioneered by companies such as Sound and Fury. Rosenberg's production of *Contains Violence* (2008) was commissioned by Fuel for production at the Lyric Hammersmith, and echoes the voyeuristic elements of previous Shunt performance *Amato Saltone Starring Kittens and Wade* (2005/6), which included scenes where the audience watched a man with a pig's head assaulting a woman in an upstairs room through a glass window. *Contains Violence* situates the audience on banks of seats on the terrace of the Lyric, with binoculars trained on the office block opposite in which actors perform behind closed windows. Here, as Lyn Gardner notes, it is the innermost thoughts of the characters and the amplified sounds of their actions that are relayed via headphones, an effect which Gardner finds 'extraordinarily disconcerting, as if someone else has taken up residence inside your head' (Gardner, 2008). Rosenberg explains that this is achieved by a binaural method of transmitting sounds that uses microphones planted in the ears of the person speaking, enabling the listener to hear a person and the sounds of their actions precisely as those in the same room can hear them (in Nathan, 2008). The intimacy of this technique, in conjunction with the distance of the action, is what makes the effect so unsettling. What I personally found intriguing when attending *Ring* (2012), one of Rosenberg's subsequent productions that took place in an entirely blacked-out room, was the success of the illusion that your experience was entirely individual, even though you were rationally aware that every other audience member would be having an identical experience. Because the sound appeared to be related to your own positioning in a room full of people and the narrative suggested that you were being singled out and spoken to in privacy, the suspension of disbelief was instinctive, and the fiction that the audio performance was actually being played out with only you in the role of protagonist was compelling.

The critical and academic discourse that began to emerge in tandem with the growth of site-specific work in the 2000s – both in existing spectacular outdoor locations and in specially designed immersive environments – was very much focused on the individual experience for the spectator. He or she was increasingly perceived as being no longer restricted to the seating bank viewpoint of the audience en masse, but was now being enabled to hear and see things from a unique perspective from within a site that enabled mobility and choice of positioning. This focus on the spectator's increased capacity to interact with the performance was further reflected in the growing popularity of work that sought to give the spectator an even more active role within the performance text. This was the context in which one-to-one performance proliferated, predominantly in the field of live art, but also produced periodically by many of the companies to feature in this section. Early examples include Stan's Cafe, *It's Your Film* (1998) and Third Angel's *Where Have They Hidden All the Answers* (2002), with later examples enhancing the one-to-one experience with additional sensory stimuli, such as *Olfactory* (2012) by Curious Directive which explores 'the history of perfume interwoven with perfumes created to capture the present "moment"' (Curious Directive website). There was also a proliferation of companies working interactively with audiences, requiring audience participation and input into the performance text. Pigeon Theatre's *The Rehearsal (Happy Hour)* (2005), a piece exploring the connections between the processes of rehearsal and how we deal with death, took place in a bar setting with members of the audience required to read out parts from scripts that they were handed, thus incorporating them into the processes that was the thematic core of the piece. In Action Hero's *A Western* (2009), audiences were part of the bar or 'saloon' setting of the piece, and were asked to contribute to the action at various points, including throwing a pint into the face of one of the performers and shooting down the hero with guns made with their fingers. Uninvited Guests' *Love Letters Straight from Your Heart* (2009) seated its audience around a banqueting table, asking them at certain points to stand for a soundtrack, stare into the eyes of the person opposite, and join in the final dance.

This turn towards interactive performance raises some fascinating questions around Arts Council policy and its possibly unintended consequences. Throughout this study so far, I have highlighted the emphasis in Arts Council policy under New Labour on increasing access and participation, and in the first chapter I noted that the targets for Arts Council England to raise participation rates for three priority groups – those with disabilities, those from black and minority ethnic communities and those categorized as socially excluded – had all failed to reach target by 2009, despite three years of focused initiatives to that end (ACE, 2009, 57). The Arts Council's imperative to grow new audiences and extend participation in the arts to under-represented groups was reflected in funding application forms during the 2000s. These clearly signalled the advantage, if not quite requirement, for all proposals to indicate how they would reach new audiences and/or offer opportunities for participation or new ways of working with audiences regardless of the nature of the project. For companies working in the field of applied theatre, or with children and young people, or black and Asian communities, as earlier discussed, this remit fitted comfortably with their aims and objectives. However, for the majority of companies working primarily with experimentation in theatrical form, particularly at the more innovative end of the spectrum, it was always going to be more challenging to extend their audience base beyond those that Bourdieu classifies as the first and second tiers of the avant-garde 'hierarchy of consecration', that is, the peers of the artists and producers themselves, along with arts students and graduates (Bourdieu, 1993, 136).

For such companies, one way of squaring the funding requirements with their own artistic objectives was the invention of new ways to work with their existing audiences, thus directing their experimentation with form towards an area that also made it more likely such experimentation would be funded. While this is a speculative hypothesis and needs to be read as merely one potential motivation for the growth of experimentation with audiences, alongside the influence of the postdramatic discourse and existing live art practice, it is undeniable that new audiences were indeed reached by the new forms of performance that were being popularized by companies such as Shunt, Punchdrunk and dreamthinkspeak at the beginning of the 2000s, and subsequently by a whole raft of companies including Action Hero, Uninvited Guests, Invisible Flock and Jane Packman Company, among many more. The audiences that attended such performances could be described as 'new' to the extent that they perhaps differed from traditional mainstream theatre audiences in that they were necessarily, in the words of Lyn Gardner, 'at home with experimentation, the devised, the physical and the visual and who instinctively understand the connections between a theatre tradition and a gallery tradition'. These are audiences, Gardner continues, 'who couldn't care less about plays but who care very passionately about live art' (Gardner, 2007, 15). True as this undoubtedly was, these were not the new audiences that the Arts Council's targets were aiming to capture.

There is a particular irony in the gap between the Arts Council's failure to meet the targets set for participation in any of their three priority groups and the overwhelming success of site-specific, immersive and interactive performance. Not only did this field of performance dominate the small-scale sector, encouraged by festivals such as BAC's One-on-One festival (2011) and the exclusively interactive British Council Showcase of 2011, it also began to comprehensively permeate the mainstream through its integration into the programmes of major theatrical institutions such as the Barbican, the RSC and all three Nationals. Punchdrunk's *The Drowned Man* and David Rosenberg's *The Roof*, for example, were both performed in partnership with the English National Theatre; dreamthinkspeak's *The Rest is Silence* (2012) was produced in partnership with the RSC; and the National Theatres of Scotland and Wales, as noted, have both been prolific in building partnerships with independent companies (Grid Iron [*Roam*, 2005] and Wildworks [*The Passion*, 2011] respectively) to produce site-specific work. There are huge benefits in such partnerships for the established institutions who are given access to new (and often younger) audiences, the expertise of experimental practitioners and the cultural 'edge' that site-specific work often brings with it. In return, independent companies can draw on the administrative structures, marketing reach and front-of-house support often provided by the partner institution. However, in an interview with John Nathan, who framed the endorsement of Shunt by the National Theatre's artistic director Nicholas Hytner as potentially turning 'the collective ... into the National's avant-garde wing', David Rosenberg expressed his reservation that 'having the endorsement of an institution did feel like our identity was floating away from us a little bit' (Rosenberg in Nathan, 2008).

It is clear that, although contemporary site-specific and immersive performance undoubtedly can hold political resonance as earlier noted, there no longer appears to be anything inherently radical about performing outside of theatre spaces in the way that Baz Kershaw envisaged prior to the exponential increase in such work in the mid/late 2000s. This must particularly be the case given that the institutional structures that Kershaw aligned with theatre buildings are now so often harnessed to the site-specific performances that take place outside of them.

Developments in Community Theatre

If companies engaged in formal experimentation tended in the main to reconfigure existing, if non-traditional, audiences in new ways, and community-based, site-specific productions attracted new audiences via large-scale spectacle, there were also distinctive participatory experiments in this period that are too diverse to constitute one particular strand but that are significant in the context of the wider access and participation agenda and its various manifestations. Lone Twin, who began making work in the late 1990s, are distinct from the majority of the companies discussed in this chapter in that they have purposefully resisted applying for Arts Council regular funding, despite invitations to do so (Williams and Lavery, 2011, 15), and this may be one of the reasons why their work is also able to resist any straightforward categorization in the context of the Arts Council's access and participation agenda. Outside of their work as Lone Twin

Theatre, which adopts a more familiar model of theatrical practice, Lone Twin have committed themselves to event-based work, often taking the form of journeys, such as *Totem* (1998), in which, dressed as cowboys, the two founder company members carried a telegraph pole in a direct line across the town of Colchester between two points on a map. The impact of this journey, and others they had made across the world, are described in the performative documentation of the company's work in *Nine Years* (2006). What *Nine Years* makes clear is that it is not so much the act itself that is the point, but the conversations and encounters such acts inspire along the way – both between members of the community and the company, and among the members of the community who are drawn to the spectacle. *Speeches* (2008) and *Street Dance* (2009) can be more straightforwardly read, as Williams and Lavery suggest, as 'new, more participatory forms of community-based art' (2011, 16). In these, Lone Twin works with communities on performances that construct and celebrate dances or speeches that are personal to the lives of each individual, and are performed both in the context of that community and at institutions such as Sadler's Wells. As part of the London 2012 Cultural Olympiad, Lone Twin constructed a boat that was built out of wooden objects donated by members of the public, all of which held particular stories or associations for those people. The boat was named 'Collective Spirit' and was launched on 'an epic maiden voyage covering over 600 nautical miles, visiting over 30 locations and meeting over 100,000 people throughout the summer of 2012' (The Boat Project website).

Quarantine Theatre's first show, *See-Saw*, produced at Glasgow's Tramway in 2000, involved 75 people and established the model that was to be adopted by the company in subsequent years. Quarantine's work cannot be categorized as applied, as the theatre practice is not applied by professionals to non-professionals in that sense, nor is theatre ostensibly being used to deliver outcomes other than the production itself. Neither can the work be entirely categorized as either professional experimental practice or community theatre, as the casts are deliberately made up of both professionals and non-professionals, although in some of their productions, such as *Susan and Darren* (2006), the non-professional performers (in this case Susan) also get paid. The model explored by Quarantine brings together casts that reflect the communities in the world beyond the theatre; their larger scale productions such as *Summer* (2014) ensuring the widest possible diversity of ages, ethnicities and backgrounds in their temporary communities of company members and invited experienced performers, who work alongside participants who have never done anything similar before. *Summer* involved over 30 performers, who lined up opposite the spectators watching them, and began to take their cues from a screen behind the spectators' heads. The screen prompted them through movement sequences, told them where certain performers should stand, how long to hold the audience's gaze and when to come and go, while a screen facing the spectators gave them their instructions as to how to best read what was happening before them. The audience heard fragments from individual performers about their lives, but for the most part, the performance was one of ensemble choreography, the highlight being when the 30 performers brought in suitcases and other personal items to set up a tapestry of miniature and temporary 'homes' across the wide space of the warehouse, movingly resembling both towels on a crowded tourist beach and a refugee camp.

The multiplicity of political readings of work like this – Forced Entertainment's *The Voices* (2003) and Chris Goode's *9* (2012) would be further examples – are too complex to interrogate here in any detail. On the one hand, there are questions about the 'display', or potential exoticization of the 'ordinary' which *Summer* was designed to counter in a number of ways, including the replication of the actor instruction screen for the audience, and a parallel process of getting to know the audience at the opening of the piece, before the performers were introduced. There are also questions, as with applied theatre, about where the authority lies in productions that contain power differentials between those who are experts and those who are not, and to what degree the participants are empowered to take artistic ownership of the work, rather than appearing as material within in it – a charge that I think *Summer* might find less easy to refute. However, from my own experience in leading such processes, the unique political potential can be found, above all, in the diverse communities that are formed by such projects. Unlike applied theatre, which most often maintains the shared boundaries of the constituency group and so arguably runs the inherent risk of ghettoizing the work or confirming the dominant prejudices of the participants, the Quarantine model of community theatre has the capacity to bring together people who would never otherwise engage with each other's lives, or be challenged by each other's narratives, thus creating a unique community within the event. In *Last Orders* (2006), a show I wrote and directed for Point Blank Theatre, I remember the moment of most satisfaction was seeing an insurance broker who was a veteran of amateur dramatics helping an ex-heroin addict (who went on to employment as a support worker) on his lines for the show, knowing that in no other context would this mutual comradeship and broadening of personal horizons on both sides have occurred.

Coney's work circumvents the potential risk of 'display' altogether in the company's rejection of the audience/performer binary; the productions are entirely constructed around the notion of every participant constituting a performer in a context that is closer to gaming than theatre. In *A Small Town Anywhere* (2009), created in association with Battersea Arts Centre and the National Theatre Studio, a 'playing audience' of around 30 are invited to take the parts of citizens in a small town, in a piece inspired by Clouzot's film *Le Corbeau*. The drama is contextualized by the town historian, performed by an actor with the company, and as the narrative unfolds, each participant/character has to make his or her own ethical decisions on how to act in the face of the threat to the community that is posed by the poison-pen letters circulating. Critic Lyn Gardner, allocated the part of postmistress, confesses that she not only destroyed letters accusing her of dark deeds, but also wrote her own, accusing others (Gardner, 2009). Despite the fact that, as the *Time Out* reviewer cautions, the audience's 'lack of genuine ideological investment robs it of some edge', he nevertheless concludes that 'the fraught final stages feel as complex and electrifying as any actor-based drama' with additional impact given that 'the luxury of such detachment is long gone' (Lukowski, 2009).

Developments in New Writing

The exploration of work in the above sections, broadly conceived under the heading of 'devised performance', has foregrounded a number of important factors that it is useful to highlight before concluding with a return to the role that written text has played in this period. First, the work in this field is distinct from the dominant English heritage of dramatic realism, whether that is due to its alternative disciplinary lineages such as dance or circus, or whether it is due to the artists' deliberate interrogation or rejection of certain dramatic conventions such as realist dialogue and characterization, fictional worlds, sites of performance, or actor/audience configurations. There is an increasing emphasis on the visual, physical and scenographic aspects of theatre permitted by ongoing developments in visual and aural media and new technologies, which can enhance productions in spectacular site-specific locations, or intimate or immersive artistically constructed environments. These trends have been influenced by a number of factors including the increased profile of pioneering practitioners in the 1980s, the influences of European and intercultural traditions of theatre, academic discourse on the political potentials of site-specific, postdramatic and interactive performance models and, more speculatively, the funding requirements of the Arts Council's access and participation agenda.

Although much of the experimentation outlined above begins with innovation, often aligned with academic research and so underpinned by philosophical or theoretical enquiry, the new vocabularies then increasingly become more widespread and less radical as the motifs and strategies are picked up by a wider field of practice to enhance and refresh the possibilities of theatrical narrative, rather than to deconstruct or interrogate its conventions. Indeed, Hans-Thies Lehmann himself notes in *Postdramatic Theatre* the possibility that postdramatic theatre might 'only have been a moment in which the exploration of a "beyond representation" could take place on all levels', and that postdramatic enquiry might ultimately pre-empt the return of 'narrative forms, the simple, even trivial appropriations of old stories' (2006, 144). Given that Lehmann writes this in 1999, the increasing turn away from the postmodern, fragmented and philosophically theorized experimentation of the 1990s and early 2000s towards the contemporary storytelling innovations that feature most prominently in the latter part of that decade and into the next, would suggest that Lehmann was being entirely prescient in his predictions.

Despite a resurgence in interest in text and narrative in the latter part of this period of study, artists continue to find points of departure from the broadly realist conventions of drama that characterized the new-writing companies and establishment in the 1990s but were already being abandoned by the devising practices of the time. As has been highlighted in previous sections, such a departure was particularly pronounced in the growth of spoken word and audio-based performance and the innovations of the devising companies that presented adaptations of textual source material through emphatically physical and visual vocabularies. It was also seen in the site-specific and immersive work, which often called for more direct-address narration that could acknowledge the audience who were now included in the *mise-en-scène*, and less dialogue-driven realism that excluded the audience from the fictional world of the characters.

There were also a number of devising companies in this period who were either writer-led, or who worked with a writer or writers who were core members of the company or ongoing associate artists, and it was in these companies, as might be expected, that the most explicit experimentation with textual forms can be seen. Forced Entertainment, rarely discussed in the framework of new writing, were in the vanguard of such developments, with Tim Etchells' distinctive and innovative crafting of text being every bit as vital to the company's aesthetic as the ensemble-authored theatrical vocabularies that are more commonly seen to characterize the work. A number of writers emerging in the late 1990s and early 2000s focused on developing new models of text in collaboration with an ensemble, rather than following the trajectory of the commissioned playwright within the new-writing companies and establishment. These would include, among others, David Greig working with Suspect Culture, David Leddy with Fire Exit, myself with Point Blank Theatre, Chris Thorpe and Claire Duffy with Unlimited Theatre, Chris O'Connell with Theatre Absolute, Hugh Hughes with Hoipolloi, Chris Goode with Chris Goode Company and Tim Cowbury with Made in China.

The influence of the ensemble of performers on the development of performance text manifests itself in various ways, including an awareness of the poetic and rhythmic qualities of text in performance, such as explorations of riffs on a particular theme, lists and devices of repetition pioneered by Tim Etchells and exemplified in Forced Entertainment's *Tomorrow's Parties* (2013). This aesthetic was adopted across such a significant number of performance texts over this period that the strategy ultimately became a convention that itself was held up to self-reflexive critique in Vincent Dance Theatre's *If We Go On* (2009), the list spoken by the performer concluding: 'no more clichés, including this one, and nothing stolen or borrowed or quoted … and no more lists after this one'. Despite the ubiquity of the strategy, it established a licence for wordplay as an alternative to realist dialogue, and when explored with a writer in conjunction with an ensemble, gave rise to explorations of a contemporary notion of chorus and choric text, either explicitly, as in Point Blank's *Dead Causes* (1999) which drew on the classical tragedy *Antigone*, or implicitly, in the ways in which a body of text could now be split between characters and played around with in rhythmical ways that did not mimic realist dialogue, as in Fire Exit's *Long Life the Little Knife* (2013), among many other examples. This textual strategy is particularly evident in dance-based physical theatre practice, as it rhythmically complements a choreographic approach much better than realist text, and can be seen throughout the work of DV8 and Volcano, as well as characterizing much of the text provided by playwrights Abi Morgan, Bryony Lavery and Mark Ravenhill in conjunction with the high-octane sequences of Frantic Assembly. The conjunction of devising methodologies and experimentation with text also leads to the creation of writing that might be defined as 'multimodal', in that it finds ways to move swiftly between distinctly different aesthetic models within the same piece of work, while seeking to maintain a level of aesthetic coherence. In Made In China's *Gym Party* (2013), for example, the text moved between choric audience-direct address, reflective monologues delivered by each performer, functional text in a conversational mode that was required to address results that would be different each night, and passages of abuse that one performer inflicted on the other.

Two exceptionally influential writer-led companies during this period were the Wrestling School, producing the work of playwright Howard Barker who also sometimes directed, and news from nowhere, producing the work of playwright Tim Crouch in association with artistic directors Karl James and a. smith (Andy Smith). Despite the significant influence of Howard Barker's work over a new generation of playwrights to emerge in the 1990s, including most notably Sarah Kane, the fortunes of the Wrestling School were to fare considerably worse than might have been anticipated, given the narrative of sustained support of the new-writing companies detailed at the beginning of Part Three of this chapter. Not only was Barker himself a huge name in an international academic context, a Creative Fellow at Exeter University from 2010 to 2012 with a number of monographs and edited collections published on his work, but the Wrestling School as a company also enjoyed the membership of actors and directors as significant within the wider theatre industry as Ian McDiarmid and Danny Boyle. Despite Barker's long-standing and ongoing international reputation, the Wrestling School has never been a core-funded organization and the company's application in 2007 for £40,000 project funding was turned down, leading Barker to comment that

> Given that I find it impossible to get my work staged in any major theatre in the UK, The Wrestling School was the sole means through which it could be represented to the public. In killing The Wrestling School, the Arts Council has silenced a voice, and yet further diminished the range of theatre practice when its very purpose was to extend this range. (Barker, 2007)

Despite the inevitable subjectivity of Barker's perspective, he has, perhaps inadvertently, put his finger on the very problem. If the building-based new-writing establishment in England have never supported his work to the degree that it is supported overseas, then it is not unsurprising that the Wrestling School is likewise excluded from the regularly funded cohort of independent new-writing companies that replicate the values of the establishment new-writing theatres. Yet if Barker's work was seen as too divergent from dramatic realism for the new-writing establishment, the Wrestling School's work was, conversely, too densely text-based and linguistically complex to benefit from the countertrend towards a more physical and visual theatre practice, despite the innovative choreographic and scenographic elements that have always been central to the company's work.

The trajectory of Tim Crouch and his company news from nowhere reads very differently. Rarely discussed in the context of the company identity, Crouch as an individual artist (he often also performs in the company's work) has become recognized in academic circles as one of the most innovative British playwrights of the last decade, with his 2005 multi-award-winning production *An Oak Tree* touring extensively and internationally for a number of years, and involving actors as high profile as Christopher Eccleston and Mike Myers in its many iterations. Despite Crouch being renowned predominantly as a playwright, the innovations of his work are tied intrinsically to conceptual theatrical strategies and conceits that are the result of collaborative working with directors James and Smith, along with other project-specific associate artists. *An Oak Tree*, for example, requires a second actor, different and unrehearsed for each performance, to read the part of the father who plays opposite Tim Crouch as the hypnotist, thus reflecting in form the manipulation that underpins the narrative content, whereas Crouch's previous piece, *My Arm* (2003), involves the actor's animation of objects provided by the audience at the start of each performance. Crouch's most recent productions, *What Happened to Hope at the End of the Evening* (2013) and *Adler and Gibb* (2014), have both been produced under Crouch's own name rather than as news from nowhere productions, although the same artistic team has been involved with both. This possibly reflects the fact that Crouch himself is now a much stronger brand for the work, and also that Karl James and Andy Smith are concurrently developing their own projects and trajectories. Unlike the Wrestling School, news from nowhere has proved a successful vehicle for Crouch within the UK as well as internationally, and both *The Author* (2009) and *Adler and Gibb* were co-produced by the accepted pinnacle of the new-writing establishment, the Royal Court. Nevertheless, the company itself was never core funded by the Arts Council which, when read alongside the fate of the Wrestling School and the inarguable international prestige of Barker and Crouch, does perhaps suggest there is a reluctance on the part of Arts Council England to be convinced by the playwright as artistic lead within an organization, which runs counter to the support that the Scottish Arts Council afforded Suspect Culture and the writing of David Greig, as discussed at length in Clare Wallace's chapter in this volume.

For some writers, such as Tim Crouch and Chris Thorpe, ongoing experimentation within ensembles has nourished an innovative approach to writing for performance that has enabled them to be accepted on their own unique terms within the new-writing establishment. Perhaps even more significantly, the kinds of models of new writing developed by companies such as those discussed above have begun to permeate the establishment both in terms of what it produces and the diversity of textual frameworks that commissioned writers are now permitted to explore. The Royal Court in particular has moved a very long way in recent years with two productions (in addition to Crouch's work), *The Victorian in the Wall* (2013) produced by Fuel, and *Narrative* by Anthony Nielson (2013). The latter contains all the multimodal hallmarks of new writing created within a devising process, moving from video footage of an incoherent cave-painting narrative, through scenes of dialogue underpinned by a realism that ultimately crumbles, through a seeming intervention that metatheatrically disrupts 'the show' involving a woman requesting signatures for a petition. While long-standing playwrights such as Caryl Churchill and Martin Crimp have been innovating alongside, and indeed prior to, the developments occurring in devising practice, it might also be the case that the groundswell of innovative forms of new writing from the mid-2000s onwards has helped to create a less risk-averse environment for text in the new-writing establishment in which plays produced by the Royal Court such as Churchill's *Love and Information* (2012) and Crimp's *In the Republic of Happiness* (2013) have been able to sit a little more comfortably than might previously have been the case.

Conclusion

It can be seen from the examination of the independent theatre ecology discussed in this chapter that its contributions to the wider mainstream theatre industry over the past 20 years have been extraordinarily rich. From the capacity to build diverse audiences demonstrated by companies such as Tamasha and Eclipse, to the site-specific experimentation adopted by all three National Theatres, to the innovations in multimedia technology and new forms of playwriting that have now permeated the establishment theatres, the UK has never, I would argue, enjoyed an aesthetically richer mainstream than it does at present.

This is not altogether surprising, as today's harvest was planted during the most benevolent funding regime in the Arts Council's history that lasted from the roll out of Lottery funding and New Labour's doubling of grant-in-aid at the beginning of the millennium, right up until the austerity cuts of the coalition government beginning in 2010 and set to continue. In the wake of what might yet be seen as the golden age of experimentation, the direction of Arts Council funding, as described in the previous chapter, now seems intent in all three nations on a strategy – no doubt government-driven – of consolidating the few dominant national institutions at the cost of the many small-scale and emergent companies, to the detriment of the diverse ecology of the independent sector.

Without continued investment in experimentation at this early level, the richness of the mainstream will only last as long as the current innovations remain fresh; there will be no new approaches nurtured today that could reinvigorate the theatre ecology as a whole once today's innovations grow stale. There are, of course, valid objections to current artistic policy, which I share, that are simply ideologically opposed to the current policies of protecting the privileged few at the cost of the dispensable many, but even those who believe that our flagship organizations are worth the sacrifice of the diversity of the sector as a whole might discover that what appears to be protection of the establishment today will ultimately be to the significant detriment of that same establishment in a decade's time.

There has been little space in this chapter to do justice to the innovations that hundreds of artists have contributed to the field of theatre in the UK, but I hope that it has, at the least, provided readers with a comprehensive range of starting points for further analysis of what is an extraordinary period of growth and development. For so many companies to achieve such levels of influence, sustainability and longevity while existing, for the most part, on barely adequate and short-term levels of funding is testament to the resilience and ingenuity of the sector. The following chapters enable a much more detailed examination of only six of those companies, each representing a model of practice that has seen particularly acute growth in this period, and which can hopefully illuminate, through specific case studies, patterns of political survival and aesthetic discovery that are common to the sector as a whole.

Chapter 3

MIND THE GAP

Dave Calvert

Introduction: 1988–97

Mind the Gap is best known for its work with learning disabled performers, through projects that seek to synthesize artistic quality and social engagement. The company's output ranges across three complementary strands: work with a primarily artistic focus, such as its national touring and site-sensitive productions; work with a primarily educational focus, including its innovative training programmes; and work with a primarily socio-political focus, mostly related to Mind the Gap's association with Augusto Boal and its employment of Theatre of the Oppressed techniques. Since its inception, the company's range has been diverse, with the core strands of the work augmented by innovative projects and frequent explorations of new territory that are alert to changes in the social and aesthetic climate. Its social focus has been resolute, perhaps best encapsulated in the company's mission statement, as cited by Frances Babbage, '[to] dismantle the barriers to artistic excellence so that learning disabled and non-disabled artists can perform alongside each other as equals' (Babbage, 2004, 88).

Formed in 1988 by theatre director Tim Wheeler and musician Susan Brown, Mind the Gap was established, and remains based, in Bradford, West Yorkshire. This choice of location was both strategic and cultural. At that time, Bradford was the host city of the Regional Arts Association, Yorkshire Arts, which allowed access to resources and support for the fledgling company. Described by Chris Megson (2012, 46) as one of the 'regional hubs of alternative theatre' in the 1970s, the city also had an international reputation for radical performance work. Local companies included the Bradford Art College Theatre Group, developed by Albert Hunt; the General Will Theatre Company, which saw Chris Parr, Bradford University's Fellow in Theatre, encourage the work of young political writers such as David Edgar and Howard Brenton; and Graham Devlin's Major Road Theatre Company, which relocated to the city in 1978.

If such companies were inspired by socialist politics, utilizing agitprop, carnivalesque and Brechtian tactics, Mind the Gap's aesthetics were rooted in the politics of identity rather than class. In advocating the artistic rights of people with learning disabilities, Mind the Gap inherited the practices, that had emerged in the 1970s, of organizations described by Kershaw as 'the campaign companies, which were aligned with communities of interest engaged in major social and therefore quasi-political campaigns, such as the women's and gay liberation movements and the black consciousness movement' (Kershaw, 1992, 139). Graeae, formed in 1980, arguably remains the most prominent British company of this kind engaged in disability arts, a field under-scored by a revolution in thinking about disability. The 'social model of disability' challenges the traditional 'medical model' by reformulating disability as a product of social barriers that prevent inclusion, rather than as a consequence of the functional and biological difference of the individual. Disability arts organizations accordingly viewed the exclusion of disabled performers from the industry as an outcome of the existing social structures and expectations of mainstream theatre.

Mind the Gap was among a wave of theatre companies in the 1980s (including Strathcona, Lung Ha's, the Lawnmowers and Heart 'n' Soul) to adopt the social model and extend the concern with identity politics to people with learning disabilities. These develop-ments responded to the increasing social visibility of learning disabled people, as a series of scandals led to the closure of long-stay residential hospitals. Subsequently, the Thatcher government instituted its policy of community care, an underdeveloped initiative lacking a coherent infrastructure and necessary additional finance. Community meant informal and voluntary care by the family, while the National Health Service's resistance to losing resources, along with government reduc-tions in local authority budgets, meant that the medical domination of learning disablility services remained intact (see Ryan and Thomas, 1987, 157).

Until this point, dramatic activity for people with learning disabil-ities had been mainly centred on participation in therapeutic practices, particularly dramatherapy, which, as Anna Chesner (1994, 58) observes, 'has its early origins in work with this client group'. The new companies rejected therapeutic approaches, viewing the focus on personal healing as consistent with the medical model in its presumption that any difficulty lay with the impaired individual rather than with social disadvantage. Interplay, formed in Leeds in 1970, had offered an alternative to therapeutic models, producing work with an educational focus designed for learning disabled audiences. The new companies of the 1980s, however, were not concerned with making work *for* learning disabled people but in developing opportunities in which they could collaborate as performers.

As undergraduate students at Dartington College, the company's founders, Brown and Wheeler, worked together on a project with people with learning disabilities at Occombe House, alongside musician David Ward and voice tutor Keith Yon. Although the project was initially driven by the dominant therapeutic impulse of the time, the practitioners quickly realized that the work produced by participants had artistic merit that could be distinguished from its personal value. Consequently, the founding principle of Mind the Gap was to prioritize and nurture the creative talent of learning disabled performers as an egalitarian imperative and a benefit to society as a whole, rather than as a matter of personal development. In so doing, the work pursued the same artistic and political principles underpinning Graeae's work, as outlined by co-founder Richard Tomlinson. Acting on the observation that 'disabled people have as much right as any other members of society to participate in a performing act' (Tomlinson, 1982, 9), both companies asserted this right through artistic innovation, so that non-disabled aesthetics would not restrict participation. Reconfiguring social relations was also prioritized over access to self-expression. Tomlinson (1982, 10) notes that the act of performing lends the professional disabled theatre-maker a rare degree of social status and power over the non-disabled spectator, reversing conventional relationships in which 'it is not generally accepted by society that disabled people are initiators of activities, that they are in charge, or can take command'.

While establishing such authority was already a radical project for Graeae and other companies working with actors with physical and sensory impairments, it was a far more complex matter in the case of companies engaging learning disabled artists. Leadership often remained with non-disabled practitioners such as Brown and Wheeler, necessitated by the much more entrenched barriers to full participation faced by people with learning disabilities. The complex legal, financial and administrative processes, for example, that are involved in constituting a formal company, put such schemes beyond the reach of many people with cognitive impairments. Managing the intricacies of a rehearsal and production process was also challenging for many people with learning disabilities who had little experience of theatre practice or, frequently, even independent decision making. The significant contribution of non-disabled people led to this field of work being gathered under the new umbrella term 'arts and disability', differentiating it from disability arts which refers to work that is driven by disabled people themselves. For learning disabled actors, power was concentrated on collaborative input to the devising process, and the mixture of responsibility and liberty that lent status to the onstage performer.

The third aim of disabled performance given by Tomlinson is 'education and enlightenment' through the authority and presence of a disabled person speaking about disability in his or her own name (Tomlinson, 1982, 20). This aspect, renegotiating non-disabled perceptions of disability, was perhaps more acutely urgent for the arts and disability companies than the disability arts organizations, as the former sought to address the tensions and deficiencies of an ad hoc community care scheme. Accordingly, Mind the Gap's early projects emphasized artistic exploration leading to public performances in which learning disabled performers and non-disabled audiences encountered each other, rather than the private, participatory activity that motivated therapeutic projects.

Projects such as *Shakin' Over My Bones* (1988) opened up accessible devising processes, using site-sensitive experience as a starting point. Working with members of Bramley Adult Training Centre, the project took its inspiration from Arnold Ridley's play *The Ghost Train* (1925), drawing further stimulus from collective trips and performative encounters on the Worth Valley Railway, a local steam-train service. A subsequent project, *How Does Your Garden Grow?* (1990), was developed in a residency at Bradford University's Theatre in the Mill, and led to the establishment of the Drama Club, a weekly group held at the venue for learning disabled adults with an interest in acting. Situating the projects in theatre venues was crucial to the status of the work, raising the expectations of the audiences and the aspirations of the actors.

The development of performance skills that was engendered by the Drama Club led to the company's first national tour in 1993. *Wake Up!* took its ironic title from Prime Minister John Major's rallying cry to the country, and, in a scenario reminiscent of Beckett's *Happy Days* (1961), mixed tenderness and monotony in following the daily awakening of a woman who lives inside a ramp (a perennial symbol of disability). The two actors, performing alongside non-disabled musician Nick

Wiltshire, were Andrew Kenningham and Susan Middleton, regular attendees of the Drama Club. Another member, Neil Heslop, joined them for subsequent national tours of *The Plot* (1994) and *Harry Heads for Las Vegas* (1995).

Between 1995 and 1998 there was a hiatus in Mind the Gap's national touring work with learning disabled adults, as the company turned to working with different communities. *Keeping Mum* (1996) developed work with users and survivors of mental health services, and led to the formation of Leeds-based company One in Four, while *Change of Mind* (1997) was a collaboration with playwright Peter Spafford that explored the difficulties of early-onset Alzheimer's disease. In 1997, the company refocused and strengthened its core work with people with learning disabilities, as part of a wider company expansion. Subsequently, formal training opportunities for learning disabled actors were established, along with a more extensive outreach programme. New collaborations were also initiated, some of which led to long-term associations, and the combination of these initiatives saw major developments in Mind the Gap's national touring programme. The significant and substantial output of this period is the focus of the remainder of this chapter.

History of the Company's Development: 1997–2014

Mind the Gap's reasserted focus on learning disabled theatre coincided with a national expansion of the field, as a second wave of companies emerged including The Shysters, Full Body and the Voice, No Limits and Blue Apple. This growth resulted in part from the outreach work of the first-wave companies, inspiring and fostering accessible opportunities and initiatives in new areas of the country. Where the first-wave companies were reacting to the social difficulties presented by an inadequate policy of community care, the second wave were operating in a much more politically supportive context. Social inclusion was a central tenet of Tony Blair's newly elected government in 1997, informing arts and educational policy as discussed in Chapter 1 of this volume. Theatre companies experienced in developing work with learning disabled practitioners were well placed, and consequently encouraged, to begin to address the social marginalization of this constituency.

Social inclusion was driven as much by economic integration as a sense of egalitarian justice, a context which resonated with the desire of arts and disability companies to see learning disabled theatre-makers recognized and rewarded as professional actors. For disabled people, the drive towards social inclusion was legislatively underpinned by the 1995 Disability Discrimination Act, which saw certain legal rights established over a phased period. Employment rights, along with the rights to access goods, services and facilities, came into force in December 1996.

Mind the Gap's national touring work had also been concerned with the economic independence of people with learning disabilities. The 1995 production of *Harry Heads for Las Vegas* explored the title character's fantasy of winning untold wealth. The first touring show of this period, *The Big Picture* (1998), written by Wheeler and directed by Antony Haddon, teamed Kenningham, Middleton and Heslop for the final time in a suspenseful comedy that explored the trials and anxieties of three learning disabled employees in an independent cinema. Significantly, this was the first national touring production by the company that was performed entirely by learning disabled actors. Kenningham retired from performing following the tour, and the next production, *Neville's Advocate* (1999) centred on Heslop and Middleton as bank robbers in an Ealing-esque crime caper. Wheeler returned to directing duties for this show, which was the company's first collaboration with two particular artists: non-disabled playwright Mike Kenny was commissioned to write the script, which emerged from a devising process with Wheeler and the actors; and Nottingham-based Jez Colborne, a singer-songwriter with Williams syndrome,[1] composed and performed a live musical score.

To date, *Neville's Advocate* is the last original dramatic work produced by Mind the Gap for a national tour. The next production was an adaptation of John Steinbeck's novella *Of Mice and Men*, written by Kenny, and with Colborne taking on his first acting role in the part of George. This heralded a new direction for Mind the Gap's professional shows, with the majority of subsequent touring productions either adapting or taking inspiration from classic texts: *Dr Jekyll and Mr Hyde* (2001); *Pygmalion* (2002); *Don Quixote* (2003), a collaboration with Northern Stage Ensemble; *Cyrano* (2004); *Boo* (2009), inspired by characters from Harper Lee's *To Kill a Mockingbird*; *Stig of the Dump* (2011); and *Treasure Island* (2013). Wheeler explains that these adaptations allowed the company to explore 'a canon of work with trace elements of questions and connections and potentials … *Pygmalion*, for example, has a really interesting thing about how much you can craft and create image, and that opens up a sense of performativity and disability' (Wheeler, 2014). Each of the adaptations was written by Kenny and directed by Wheeler, with Colborne taking the lead role in each production up to *Cyrano*.

As the transition from the early projects to the national tours raised the company's profile, it also presented increasing technical and formal challenges to the actors, intersecting with debates about learning disabled aesthetics that were emerging at this time. Jon Palmer and Richard Hayhow (former Artistic Directors of Full Body and the Voice and The Shysters respectively) place learning disabled performance within a theatrical 'quest to unearth the remnants of authentic behaviour beneath the strata of social and psychological impositions' (Palmer and Hayhow, 2008, 34). Tracing a line from the work of André Breton and the Surrealist movement's 'attempts to expose the machinations … of socialisation on the human mind' (Palmer and Hayhow, 2008, 36), they argue that authentic behaviour as a pre-socialized impulse is more available to learning disabled actors since a 'lack of highly sophisticated and fully assimilated social behaviours' is characteristic of learning disability (Palmer and Hayhow, 2008, 41). Accordingly, they propose a learning disabled theatre which is predominantly physical and improvisatory to limit mediation by non-disabled structures in favour of 'the theatrical forms that come most readily to the actors' (Palmer and Hayhow, 2008, 55).

Wheeler recalls that Mind the Gap's early work inclined quite heavily towards the surreal, but views this as a reflection of the historical circumstances in which learning disabled people were allowed little access to education, rather than an essential element which imagines them as 'the true Surrealists':

> I think we learn very early on how to sequence, or not. I think it's a socially developed skill and we learn that through language acquisition, and reading and writing. If we don't have those areas of our lives stimulated and developed, I think our sense of narrative is different … What we were observing [in Mind the Gap's early work] was the effects of what it was like to not have that level of educational input early on, that people's incongruity was the fact that they'd been ignored, they'd been left and actually I think [learning disabled people] can acquire those skills. (Wheeler, 2014)

The national tours, shaped by directorial and authorial choices, challenge the actors to repeat a performance 'night after night after night and try and attempt to approach it in the same authentic way'

(Wheeler, 2014). Theatrical authenticity relies here on what Richard Schechner terms 'restored behavior', the repetition of consciously or unconsciously selected strategies based in experience, and in which the 'original "truth" or "source" of the behavior may be lost, ignored or contradicted – even while this truth or source is apparently being honoured and observed' (Schechner, 1985, 35). Actors with learning disabilities are authenticated *as actors* by the discipline of effectively and theatrically harnessing 'restored behavior'.

Mind the Gap still engages in occasional forays into the surreal as a means of refreshing its own sense of free play. *Chicken Coup* (2010), for example, is a largely improvised street theatre performance, comprised of giant chickens engaged in clowning, visual comedy and audience interaction. Other strands of the work have also explored new artistic territory. Following *Cyrano*, a series of high-profile projects began which centred on the versatile talents of Colborne. *On the Verge* (2005) departed from the usual dramatic structures employed by the company, featuring Colborne in a solo show about his experiences travelling along Route 66 as a pillion passenger on Wheeler's Harley Davidson. The production combined footage of the road trip filmed by Jonathan Bentley with original songs and cover versions performed by Colborne, who also recounted and re-enacted elements of the trip scripted by Mike Kenny.

The necessary editing of *On the Verge* omitted several episodes of the road trip, and one of these, Colborne's encounter with the sound of warning sirens, became the starting point for a subsequent site-sensitive project, *Irresistible* (2010), performed in a range of non-theatre venues. Involving actors and singers from other wings of the company's work alongside Colborne, the show followed the lone travels of a modern-day Odysseus through a hostile urban landscape, linking the term 'sirens' with its origins in Greek myth. These projects opened up international opportunities for Colborne and the company, with performances in China, Switzerland and Germany.

Although an increasingly central figure in Mind the Gap's theatre output, Colborne's transition from singer-songwriter to actor was an unplanned one that came about following a casual remark. In 1999, Colborne was chatting with another company member, Kevin Pringle, when Marketing Manager Sally Bailey commented that they resembled George and Lennie, the central characters in *Of Mice and Men*. Wheeler had a long-held ambition to produce a version of the story with a learning disabled actor in the role of Lennie, arguably the best-known learning disabled character in literature. The fortuitous pairing of the two actors led to the realization of this ambition.

Pringle, an actor with Down's syndrome and former member of the Drama Club, was training at this time on the company's three-year apprenticeship programme, Making Waves (1998–2001). Twelve learning disabled apprentices on the programme were led through formal education in the performance, production, marketing and administration processes involved in making theatre. The project followed Wheeler's recognition that the company's touring actors required a more solid grounding in performance skills and professional development than the Drama Club allowed. In the absence of any existing in-depth training schemes that could – or would – accommodate such students within mainstream education, Mind the Gap decided to establish its own.

This attended to a specific aspect of the social inclusion agenda, which focused on Inclusive Education, following a commissioned report of the same name by Professor John Tomlinson that investigated the provision of Further Education for learning disabled adults. Education was not covered by the Disability Discrimination Act until the introduction of the Special Educational Needs and Disability Act 2001. In the interim, the influential Tomlinson Report sought to 'avoid a viewpoint which locates the difficulty or deficit with the student and focus instead on the capacity of the educational institution to understand and respond to the individual learner's requirement' (Tomlinson, 1996, 4). This social model approach led to the radical recommendation of 'redesigning the very processes of learning, assessment and organisation so as to fit the objectives and learning styles of the students' (Tomlinson, 1996, 4).

Making Waves adopted these principles to offer training that would compare with the equivalent vocational training in mainstream adult education. The purpose was not only to establish a pool of trained performers for the company's own work and the wider industry, but to equip the apprentices with the range of backstage skills that might enable them to establish their own company. Following the three years of training, six of the graduates formed the company SFX, which delivered a series of projects in collaboration with Mind the Gap.

Perhaps the most significant of these projects was In*clue*do which looked at the development of learning disabled audiences in regional theatres, through a mixture of research, consultation and training. The centrepiece of the project was *Never Again!*, a Forum Theatre production. The members of SFX were familiar with the practice of Forum Theatre, which had formed a staple element of Making Waves. As the Honorary Company Adviser, and a friend and mentor to

Wheeler, Augusto Boal worked on several occasions with Mind the Gap, and the company continues to employ Theatre of the Oppressed techniques for both practical and political reasons. Much of Boal's early work was developed in contexts where literacy skills were limited, and so explores ideas primarily through physical and visual means. Such techniques as Image Theatre allow for complex engagement and a multiplicity of readings without the barriers presented by literacy, making them accessible for people with learning disabilities. Moreover, while Boal's European techniques in *The Rainbow of Desire* turned towards therapeutic practices based on the notion of an internalized cop-in-the-head, Forum Theatre observes the social model of disability by addressing external forms of oppression that still need challenging. In terms of the education and training programmes, developing short Forum Theatre anti-models gently introduced the students to cause-and-effect sequences intrinsic to dramatic narrative and allowed them to deepen their political understanding of learning disability as a fundamental component of their own practice. Finally, as Babbage (2004, 89) notes, 'the spirit of playful competition in which Forum ideally operates can prove particularly liberating for participants with learning difficulties'.

After the completion of Making Waves, the training wing was reimagined as a one-year opportunity called Making Theatre. This continues to run as a rolling programme, introducing new members to the company and allowing continuing professional development for existing members. Between 2004 and 2008, Mind the Gap also co-ordinated a new training programme called Staging Change. While Making Waves and Making Theatre operated on a conventional three-term model, Staging Change involved a series of intensive residencies over the course of a year. Some of these residencies took place in high-profile drama schools, such as Mountview Academy, Guildford School of Acting, Arts Educational Schools London and the Oxford School of Drama, where participants worked with tutors and students from the host school on developing specific skills, such as performing to the camera and exploring Shakespeare's text.

Having initiated comprehensive opportunities for high-level training and professional performance work within the core activity, Mind the Gap also strengthened the points of entry into, and exit from, the company to connect this work with wider social structures. After disbanding the Drama Club in 2000, engagement with 'special' schools across the region increased and the outreach activities expanded to include weekend residencies and summer schools, bringing potential new performers into contact with the company. In recent years, outreach projects have also pursued a social agenda dealing particularly with a rise in 'hate crime', in which learning disabled people are the victims of abuse by non-disabled people. The core focus remains artistic, however, with the outreach work serving to engage and nurture an increasing pool of talented artists with learning disabilities.

As productions featuring skilled learning disabled actors became more widespread, mainstream opportunities also began to increase. In June 2008, Mind the Gap established its own actors' agency to manage, advise and offer specialist guidance on professional contracts to both the actor and the industry. This guidance draws from the company's expertise in the legal, structural and practical matters associated with learning disability, rather than with strictly artistic criteria. Such areas include the value, function and provision of necessary pastoral support, advice on accessible practice in terms of production processes, and information regarding relevant legislation on employment.

The company's work has, therefore, established a potential route for an enthusiastic performer with learning disabilities to develop from an informal experience of theatre practice through specialized formal training to professional recognition and engagements within the mainstream industry. This advance in the status of people with learning disabilities is considerable compared to the situation in the mid-twentieth century when, as Tomlinson (1996, 2) describes, they 'were deemed ineducable and never offered any formal educational opportunity or stimulus'. If the growth in Mind the Gap's range of work since 1997 has promoted, facilitated and secured greater opportunities for learning disabled artists in line with its original aim, it has also required a solidifying of the company's own structure.

Company Structure and Funding

Mind the Gap was formally incorporated as a company limited by guarantee in 1989 and became registered as a charity later in the same year. Responsibility for the company lies ultimately with the voluntary Board of Directors, which meets periodically and appoints the senior managerial employees of the organization to lead the day-to-day activities. Following the departure of Susan Brown in 1994, Tim Wheeler continued to manage the company as Artistic Director. In 1997, Julia Skelton was appointed as Administrative Director, establishing a partnership of joint senior officers that continued until Wheeler's departure in 2014. Both officers worked in close negotiation with each other, determining the strategic direction of the company in consultation with the Board of Directors. Wheeler took lead responsibility for the artistic and educational outputs of the company, while Skelton managed the operational infrastructure, secured the resource base and co-ordinated the advancement of the company's profile through business and marketing activities.

By 1997 Mind the Gap was a Regularly Funded Organization of the Arts Council of England, receiving annual funding towards core costs. *Change of Mind*, a project exploring the impact of early-onset Alzheimer's disease, had also brought in additional revenue that enabled Skelton's appointment. The complementary skills of the two directors assured the company's future fortunes, aided at the time by a conducive funding climate. In 1996, Virginia Bottomley, then Secretary of State for National Heritage, relaxed the rules on Lottery funding, which had hitherto been restricted to subsidy for capital projects. The newly introduced Arts for Everyone scheme had a core focus on widening participation, explicitly foregrounded in its title, which anticipated New Labour's commitment to social inclusion. Mind the Gap secured £300,000 of funding from the National Lottery over three years to deliver Making Waves.

The company's geographical base was also significant, presenting an opportunity to apply to the European Social Fund for match funding for Making Waves. This source was concerned with local regeneration, and targeted particular urban areas. As a city whose rejuvenation was long overdue after its industrial heyday had diminished, Bradford was ripe for attracting such subsidy. In keeping with the requirements of these key funders, recruitment for the training programme was mainly focused on learning disabled people from West Yorkshire aged between 18 and 30.

In addition to core revenue funding from the Arts Council and Bradford Metropolitan District Council, Mind the Gap's central activity has been predominantly supported through several sources. The high-profile productions have been principally subsidized by the Arts Council's National Touring Scheme. The establishment of Learning and Skills Councils (LSC) in 2001/2, as regional boards of a centralized agency charged with co-ordinating adult and vocational education, allowed for ongoing support of the company's education and training programmes. The Dance and Drama Awards (originally funded through the Department for Education and Skills, and subsequently transferred to the LSC) included a flexible provision strand designed to encourage the training of disabled performers. This scheme enabled the delivery of Staging Change, which recruited students nationally. The European Social Fund also continued to offer valuable sources of revenue, particularly in support of work that was locally engaged. Occasional funding opportunities from other sources allowed for unique performance and outreach projects to take place.

Combined, these funding streams supported a substantial increase in the company's project-based work over this period, which was further underwritten by an uplift in the core funding from the Arts Council. Between 2001 and 2004, the annual grant stepped up incrementally from £20,000 to £80,000, rising in further stages to £144,000 in the financial year 2011/12. The advance in core and project funding since 1997 also allowed the company to expand its operational team, introducing new roles in marketing, theatre development, production management and administrative support, as well as managerial posts with responsibility for the training programmes and outreach projects. The company's central commitment to artists with learning disabilities also required specialized staff with responsibility for the pastoral care of actors, students and participants, offering individual and collective support to ensure that opportunities were accessible, and engaging with wider support networks. After a period of working towards independence, SFX undertook a full review with Mind the Gap's staff and Board of Directors, and all parties agreed that the separate companies should combine as a single organization. SFX was reintegrated as the Acting Company, forming a core element of Mind the Gap's artistic team, employed in accordance with the Department for Work and Pensions' rules on permitted work for people in receipt of disability benefits.

Aside from its prolific artistic output and the growth of its infrastructure, Mind the Gap's other major project in recent years has been the establishment of a permanent home. Following extensive development and feasibility studies, the company successfully attracted a combination of funding from the National Lottery's capital scheme, introduced in 2001, and the European Regional Development Fund, to convert the Silk Warehouse, part of the Manningham Mills complex in Bradford, into purpose-built offices and studio spaces. The building is designed to reflect the central principles of Mind the Gap's work. Its stylish design is aligned with impressive technological facilities to present a highly contemporary environment, foregrounding the company's identity as a successful professional organization with an acutely artistic agenda. At the same time, Mind the Gap's social commitment is announced through the building's total accessibility, achieved by integrating advanced technology with carefully co-ordinated architecture.

The financial crisis that broke in 2008 has had an adverse impact on the arts sector in general, and Mind the Gap has sought to utilize the building as a means of raising additional revenue through hosting unique events and hiring out space. Nevertheless, the company has had to scale back its core operation as a result of decreases in available funding. The Staging Change programme was ended, as the LSC's flexible funding provision was withdrawn. This loss, along with the harsh economic climate, meant that Mind the Gap was compelled to reduce its core team in 2009, losing the managerial posts of Director of Learning and Skills and Director of Outreach. As a result, there is now greater dependency on freelance artists and contributors, a focus on a more concentrated range of activities, and a necessity to fix longer-term plans, rather than simply respond to short-term or unexpected opportunities. The company achieved National Portfolio Organization (NPO) status in Arts Council England's restructure of its funding operation in 2011, which saw an apparent increase in core funding to approximately £205,000 annually for three years, although this new grant incorporates the costs of national touring which were previously funded through separate streams that NPOs can no longer access. The company retained National Portfolio Organization status from 2015, with standstill funding allocated until 2018. While this funding, along with ongoing support from Bradford Metropolitan District Council, allows at least short-term security in terms of core revenue, dwindling opportunities for further subsidy in the current economic climate mean the company is increasingly exploring new avenues of funding through private forms of sponsorship such as crowd-funding projects and cultural philanthropy.

Key Projects

Of Mice and Men *(2000)*

Mind the Gap's touring version of *Of Mice and Men* was the first professional production to feature a learning disabled actor in the role of Lennie. The challenge differed from the company's later adaptations of existing texts, which aimed to open up resonances in work that was not directly concerned with learning disability. In tackling Steinbeck's depiction of Lennie, Mind the Gap sought to complicate, extend and deepen the audience's engagement with learning disability. At the same time, it aimed for a faithful theatricalization of the novella's themes, atmosphere and tragic intensity.

The casting of Jez Colborne and Kevin Pringle as George and Lennie was visually resonant. The mutual dependency of the two characters is suggested by their physicality, and the contrast between the wiry Colborne and the heavily set Pringle echoed Steinbeck's construction of the pair functioning collectively as a single force of intellectual and physical strength. There are other differences between the actors that further underscored the complementary relationship between the characters. Colborne, as a musician, singer and songwriter, has a developed ear and a wide vocabulary, so the demands of a highly verbal text and an American accent presented little problem. Pringle, by contrast, has comparatively little verbal communication. Kenny accordingly wrote specifically for the actors, and the text for Lennie comprised only a handful of words, foregrounding gesture, action and Pringle's physically expressive range, which drove the emotional intensity of the play.

Pringle's Down's syndrome thus explicitly informed the aesthetic choices on both verbal and visual levels, adding dimensions to the character that disrupted simple allegorical readings and avoided the conventional representations of an archetypal innocent. Lennie here was volatile as well as vulnerable, perceptive and calculating, as well as gullible and trusting. Kenny's adaptation accentuated this by drawing out the sexual intensity of the narrative in the mutual and dangerous desire between Lennie and Curley's wife, the woman he murders. Subsequently, George's 'final act of despatching Lennie from a cruel and uncaring world' was here a tragic torment rather than 'an act of kindness in much the same way that Carlson shooting Candy's decrepit old dog is seen as an act of mercy' (Kempe, 2013, 23). This atmosphere of sexual difficulty, coupled with the physical and verbal presence of Pringle, presented Lennie as a much more complicated, conflicted character, whose murder was greatly problematized.

The question of authenticity is pertinent in assessing the significance of a learning disabled actor undertaking this role. Wheeler (2014) observes that Lennie has 'a canny intellect ... that's just frustrated by a verbal communication issue'. Pringle, he notes, shares this characteristic, allowing him to bring particular embodied insights to the role as written by Kenny. Palmer and Hayhow (2008, 37) are wary of the imposition of linguistic structures on learning disabled performance, commending

Artaud's recognition that 'the "tyranny of words" betrays a deeper, more immediate reality'. Yet it is through Pringle's embodied difficulties set against the demands of the text that his own impairment made Lennie's more complex and immediate. The audience, in direct proximity to Pringle's physical presence and his verbal wrestling with Kenny's script, 'felt endangered near Kevin, though he was the mildest person you could encounter … And all of the same things that Lennie was facing in that story, Kevin faced: that concern about whether there was any predatory sexual threat' (Wheeler, 2014). Pringle's physical and emotional power accords with Palmer and Hayhow's notion of the authentic as something beyond articulation that is only ever present in its live embodiment by a given actor. In this instance, however, the performer's authenticity lent affective impact to a fictional character within a traditional dramatic structure. It was only through negotiating the fixed text that this correspondence between actor and character was realized.

The production explored sexual tensions further in a framing device introduced by Wheeler and Kenny, in which George, after the murder of Lennie, revisits the prostitute Suzy (played in the original production by Ysabel Collyer), a minor character from the novella, and recounts the narrative which is then enacted as a series of flashbacks. This device allowed the story to retain a close focus on the unfolding tragedy that engulfs Lennie and George, while Colborne and Collyer could also double as other characters. This three-handed version of the text toured twice in 2000, attracting new audiences to Mind the Gap's work through the dual status of Steinbeck's text as both a canonical novella and a staple fixture of the National Curriculum.

The production was subsequently revived twice in adapted versions. A 2005 tour increased the cast members from three to five, with Alan Clay and Donna Lavin (graduates of Making Waves and Making Theatre respectively) joining Pringle and Colborne. The role of Crooks, the black stablehand, was also expanded and performed by Glen Wilson, a black actor and the only cast member without a disability, restoring the novella's exploration of racial identities alongside disability and gender politics.

The next revival in 2011 returned to the original three-hander, refocusing on the dramatic intensity rather than the thematic breadth of the original novella, with Colborne again reprising the role of George. By this time Pringle had left the Acting Company, and a Staging Change graduate, Robert Ewens, took over the role of Lennie. Ewens has greater verbal articulacy than Pringle, and Kenny updated the script to employ and reflect this fluency. The addition of original songs composed by Colborne and a redesigned set that incorporated digital projection refreshed the earlier versions, and allowed for greater thematic exploration. The overall effect, however, was more crafted and literary. Ewens's interpretation of Lennie had a more markedly representational aspect than Pringle's, resulting in a constructed version of learning disability that was closer to Steinbeck's than his own. While a polished and intelligent performance, the audience's encounter with learning disability in Ewens's characterization was, in some ways, more easily assimilated and carried fewer of the troublesome contradictions that Pringle brought to the role.

Incluedo (2000–1)

Incluedo attended to the ongoing efforts of the theatre industry to attract new audiences, promoting the right of people with learning disabilities to experience theatre as spectators rather than performers. Helen Jermyn (2001, 2) points to the Arts Council's distinction between social inclusion, which addresses the potential to make a full productive or economic contribution to society, and access to artistic activity, which has always been a wider project allowing people to engage in, and benefit from, the cultural life of that society. Incluedo is focused on access in this wider sense.

As such, the project is underpinned by the social model of disability, seeking to identify and eliminate the barriers to cultural participation that arise as a result of the infrastructure, design and operational systems of theatre venues. Towards the tail end of the Making Waves programme, a number of apprentices engaged in exploratory workshops on a theme of theatre-going, alongside non-disabled young people. This was followed by covert visits to theatre venues to identify specific barriers and points of difficulty; these informed the creation of a Forum Theatre anti-model, *Never Again!*, later developed by Mind the Gap and SFX in collaboration with playwright Peter Spafford. The central protagonist, Anna (played by SFX member Anna-Marie Heslop), is thwarted in her desire to enjoy a visit to the theatre by her family's apathy, audience hostility, off-putting architecture, inaccessible signage, poorly devised systems and the impatient attitudes of Front of House staff.

The production toured to special schools and colleges as a further stage of research and consultation, using the audience interventions to gather potential solutions to the access difficulties. This combined process of investigation and consultation fed into the final stages of the project, in which the results were presented to the regional theatre industry through a conference, run in conjunction with disability arts consultancy ADA Inc (Access, Disability and Inclusion), and the production of a subsequent CD ROM, including an animated version of *Never Again!* for training use by venues. For arts organizations, there were multiple benefits in attending to these areas. Suitable adjustments would help organizations to realize their obligations under the terms of the Disability Discrimination Act, and allow them to attract new audiences. Adopting inclusive practices, as the Tomlinson Report had demonstrated, not only caters for people with learning disabilities but also improves accessibility for a much wider range of people.

In her analysis of *Never Again!*, Frances Babbage (2004, 97) notes that 'In*clue*do aims to create bridges between arts organizations and potential audiences. It is recognized that both parties may have to change their past practices to some degree for this to happen'. The use of Forum Theatre in this process shifts some of the foundational ground of the form. Boal contends that, strictly speaking:

> only spect-actors who are victims of the same oppression as the character (by identity or analogy) can replace the oppressed protagonist to find new approaches or new forms of liberation …
>
> If a spect-actor who is not experiencing the same oppression wants to replace the oppressed protagonist, we manifestly fall into the theatre of advice: one person showing another what to do. (Boal, 2002, 269)

The employment of Forum Theatre in In*clue*do, by contrast, resists the antagonisms which are intrinsic to early Theatre of the Oppressed structures, and takes a wider dialogical view. When the research findings are presented to a non-disabled audience for consideration, the fixed boundaries between protagonist and antagonist, oppressed and oppressor, soften. The oppressor is credited with a desire as well as an obligation to resolve the difficulties experienced by the oppressed, and invited to act on that desire. At the same time, the related opposition between the social and medical models loses some rigidity too. By inviting both parties to consider their responsibilities within the scenario of *Never Again!*, rather than simply challenging non-disabled society to look to itself, the production, along with its associated research and training processes, approaches disability access as a negotiation between impairment and societal structures.

Making Theatre (2001–Present)

Making Theatre was introduced in 2001 as a new one-year course, replacing Making Waves. All students were expected to engage in performance work, and could also specialize in one of the additional areas of production, marketing or administration. The course content involved training sessions in accessible practice and equal opportunities, as well as performance work and vocal skills. Each student undertook an appropriate work placement in a local arts organization, widening their understanding of professional contexts, establishing valuable contacts and alerting potential employers to the contributions that could be made by learning disabled workers.

The students received qualifications through accrediting body the Open College Network, and both the training and the evidencing of student achievements demanded accessible strategies without any essential reliance on literacy. For the most part, the course was vocationally focused and demonstrated achievement through the production of theatre work in a range of public contexts. Twelve students enrolled on the first run of Making Theatre in 2001/2, producing three devised performances: *Citizen Chain* (2001), a Forum Theatre project that toured locally to special schools; *Dig Deeper* (2002), an interactive performance devised for Bradford Festival; and *Stranger in a Stranger Land* (2002), a conventional theatre performance at the Studio Theatre in the Bradford Alhambra.

Productions were crafted, refined and learned in the rehearsal room. Where needed, scripts would be available in a range of formats, including conventionally printed texts and audio recordings. Learning Support Workers, with an understanding of both theatre practice and learning disability, implemented accessible strategies for the development and recording of student achievement as well as overseeing pastoral care. The students built up comprehensive portfolios, which included the documentation of performance and related work, copies of finished materials and recorded interviews to demonstrate cognitive understanding as well as practical ability.

Forum Theatre was employed in Making Theatre for its educational value as well as its socio-political purposes. *Citizen Chain* followed the difficulty of the learning disabled protagonist in pursuing an intimate relationship with his partner while being literally manacled to a support worker. The spect-actors were challenged to find ways to remove the manacles and acquire the desired degrees of independence and intimacy. In preparing the play, the students had to explore the social issues at stake in the story (which drew from their own experiences) while also meeting the aesthetic requirements of the production. Forum Theatre always demands two approaches to performance: understanding of the internal logic of the scripted anti-model as it is established through the mechanisms of situation, narrative and character; and the ability to retain this understanding during improvised responses to spect-actor interventions.

If the form places certain demands on the performers, then style can also be used to develop artistic ability. Boal (2002, 242) has observed that the anti-model 'can be performed in any genre (realism, symbolism, expressionism, etc.) except surrealism or the irrational. The style doesn't matter, as long as the objective is to discuss concrete situations (through the medium of theatre)'. The symbolic motif of the manacles in *Citizen Chain* gave rise to a primarily comic framework that explored slapstick, physical clowning and caricature. The aesthetics in these productions steered away from naturalistic representation, as many of the students were already familiar with such tropes.

The following production, *Dig Deeper*, was a devised show that exploited a contemporary enthusiasm for archaeology. The performance was based around three archaeological tents that formed a courtyard in Bradford's Centenary Square. The assembled audience watched episodes from a medieval story in the outdoor courtyard, interspersed with visits in smaller groups to the archaeological activity in the tents. The students played the medieval characters and archaeologists, with non-disabled performers in the supporting role of 'tour guides', managing the audience's journeys. The final production, *Stranger in a Stranger Land*, borrowed its structure from *Gulliver's Travels*, following Stranger, an everyman figure with a learning disability, who finds himself repeatedly outcast from imaginary and fantastical lands. This central structure offers a familiar narrative pattern while allowing for a flexible devising process in which the students give theatrical shape to social critique and reflections on loss, desire and alienation.

The overarching development of the three productions saw a gradual decrease in non-disabled support during the performances. The non-disabled Joker of the Forum Theatre production retained the power to intervene and manage the performance at any point; the tour guides of *Dig Deeper* had a circumscribed set of responsibilities, and the performers possessed the greater degree of autonomy; while in the final performance, the learning disabled students held total responsibility for the onstage action. The course structure therefore echoed the development of the company as a whole towards increased autonomy for learning disabled actors.

Supported by Bradford Metropolitan District Council, and taking between eight and 14 students each year, Making Theatre continues to form the core training opportunity within Mind the Gap's suite of projects. The programme of activities varies annually, as the students' training and accreditation is increasingly integrated into the core activities of the company's work. The Making Theatre students, for example, appeared alongside Jez Colborne and the Acting Company in the various versions of the final project for discussion, *Irresistible*.

Irresistible *(2012)*

Irresistible centres on Jez Colborne, who combines roles as lead-actor, composer and musician (mentored by sound designer, producer and musician Si McGrath) and adds an additional credit as co-director, working alongside Tim Wheeler. Along with members of the Acting Company and Making Theatre students, the show also features percussionist Billy Hickling, two backing singers and an integrated sign-language interpreter. The soundtrack is punctuated with a variety of warning sirens, which, for Colborne (as for the heroes of classical mythology) contain a compulsive mixture of pain and beauty, attraction and fear:

> I felt that as a musician – even though it might be harsh for my ears – there are loads of tones to them and they all have their own voice; just really loud, like an opera singer. I started listening to them as musical instruments, my fear went away and I started to be more and more interested in them. (Mind the Gap, 2014a)

Instead of following the autobiographical journey of *On the Verge*, Colborne here travels through a fictional landscape that is sparse and hostile. The narrative is told through a song cycle, linked by percussive interludes. The visual aesthetics, reminiscent of Hollywood's familiar visions of a post-apocalyptic world, complement the American influences that thread through Colborne's songwriting. The ensemble is divided into two collectives of urban misfits, the antagonistic 'Crew' and the antagonized 'Hobos', while Colborne's character appears as a redemptive stranger in the tradition of the film Western.

These filmic influences are overlaid on a retelling of Homer's *The Odyssey*, exploiting the double meanings within the central motif of the sirens. The backing singers perform a jazz-influenced version of their Greek ancestors whose seductive voices lured sailors into peril. Odysseus' hard-fought resistance to them is claimed, in some versions of the myth, to have led to their deaths. In telling Colborne's own story through a reference back to this parallel original myth, the mundanity of the contemporary warning-siren, and its encounter with learning disability, is invested with heroic grandeur. This is reinforced by the setting and design for the performance, which has been continually refreshed and adapted as the piece has occupied various sites. One version performed at dusk in Bradford City Park (2013) featured the addition of a flaming car, with the singing sirens being raised and lowered on a giant cherry-picker crane under a colourful and spectacular lighting state.

Irresistible was originally designed in 2010 to be performed at the Cow and Calf Rocks on Ilkley Moor in North Yorkshire, an open-air space that is at once magnificent and intimate. The necessary journey on foot to reach the rocks sets up the homage to *The Odyssey* and anticipates the wandering hero. The performance redefines the space, however, as the characters carry a sense of broken urbanity that both complements and disturbs the rural environment.[2]

Commissioned by the Unlimited programme, which funded and co-ordinated a showcase of Deaf and disabled artists as part of the Cultural Olympiad, the production had further revivals at the Southbank Centre, the National Theatre's Watch This Space Festival and Olympic Park in London in September 2012. These performances redefined their respective spaces in the opposite direction to the original production, as an atmosphere of untouchable desolation inserted itself into the bustling urban environments that accompanied the Paralympics, arresting the audience through its spectacular mixture of visual and aural elements.

Irresistible has set in train a new direction for Mind the Gap, with Colborne being commissioned to lead two new projects: *Trickster*, as part of the Ignite scheme in Ireland, a devised piece with emerging artists in Galway; and *Gift*, which 'uses a shipping container as a musical instrument and performance arena' (Mind the Gap, 2014b). Both of these productions take further inspiration from resonant episodes found in *The Odyssey*: the image of the Cyclops and the story of the wooden horse respectively.

Critical Reception

Learning disabled theatre has received relatively little attention as a field, and, consequently, Mind the Gap has perhaps been afforded less critical consideration than other companies of a similar size, longevity and output. In addition to Babbage's case study of *Never Again!*, Matt Hargrave has considered the aesthetics and reception of *On the Verge* (Hargrave, 2009) and *Boo* (Hargrave, 2010), and, with Emma Gee, has co-authored an article on the politics of training learning disabled performers (Gee and Hargrave, 2011). He draws attention to an entrenched tendency in which 'performers with intellectual disabilities are always placed (negatively) in relation to a perceived ideal and judged accordingly' (Hargrave, 2009, 42).

This difficulty in reconciling a learning disabled actor with perceived ideals perhaps accounts for the limited press attention, as well as academic consideration, of the company's work. Critics may lack a vocabulary for appreciating the ways in which actors with learning disabilities may deviate from convention, or the supposedly inherent characteristics of a given text. Furthermore, the long-standing perception that learning disabled people are essentially vulnerable adults requiring care, protection and charity may frame such work as socially worthy and deter critics from offering negative appraisals, however valuable. Perhaps for this reason, reviews tend to be motivated by a rounded appreciation of the work as both a social and artistic project.

The Stage and Television Today has been consistently attentive. Its critic Kevin Berry has reviewed national touring productions and written articles on company projects and members. His review of *Of Mice and Men* acknowledged that '[n]othing less than a frank and honest review will do for the Mind the Gap company's actors' and reflected that the production 'significantly redefines what is possible in a theatre' (Berry, 2000, 15). His reviews of *Boo* and *On the Verge* were equally favourable, describing the former as 'a landmark production' (Berry, 2009) and the latter as 'laced with delicious irony and irreverent humour' for which 'the Arts Council has got its money's worth' (Berry, 2005).

In his analysis of Colborne's performance in *On the Verge*, Hargrave (2009, 42) identifies what he calls 'the eloquence of *dis-precision*' as the performer's gaze, pacing and consistency, judged against Kenny's text and Wheeler's direction, differ from the spectator's expectations of a 'traditionally trained actor':

These are little tear marks in the performance where the audience is able to see the joins created in rehearsal; the blocking that has been learned through repetition. 'Seeing the join', a continuous decon-struction of the performer and the text, felt alien: none of it felt quite 'natural'. (Hargrave, 2009, 42)

This opens up a third possible relation between the authentic presence of the actor and the performance text. As with Pringle's performance in *Of Mice and Men*, this is less the liberation of a pre-socialized self than the immediacy of the actor's struggle to realize the text. If Pringle's embodied presence extends and substantiates Kenny's script, however, Colborne's authenticity emerges in those surplus charac-teristics that resist directorial or authorial structures. The resultant fractures between actor and text disturb their synthesis, rendering each more visible to an audience. Such tear marks thus expose perceived ideals, making them objects of critical suspicion in themselves. Berry's review of *Of Mice and Men* is, perhaps, best understood through this lens. The political impact of learning disabled performance is no longer restricted to Graeae's early observance of disability rights, redressing a power imbalance and educating non-disabled audiences. By exposing performance conventions as limited and frustrating, actors with learning disabilities produce and demand the restless redefinition of theatrical – and, by extension, social – possibilities.

Nevertheless, a commitment to theatrical ideals still troubles the industry recognition of learning disabled performers as well as the critical reception, limiting opportunities for professional employment. Mind the Gap is aware that overturning preconceived notions of inferiority requires a long-term approach. I have described elsewhere (Calvert, 2009, 77) how the concerted efforts of theatre and learning-disability companies over this period have succeeded in establishing 'a first generation of professional learning disabled performers that can meet mainstream expectations', citing the casting of Making Theatre graduate Jonathan Lewis in the radio play *Coming Down the Mountain* (2003). Lewis allayed the anxieties of BBC executives through a 'balance of technical ability, creative power, vocal authenticity and professional attitude' (Calvert, 2009, 77). Other graduates from Mind the Gap's training programmes have also found occasional employment within the industry. Alan Clay toured nationally in Benchmark's production of *The First to Go* (2008), by Nabil Shaban, the co-founder of Graeae, while television roles have been secured by Anna-Marie Heslop (*Rhinoceros* (1999), *The Bill* (2002) and *Doctors* (2006)) and Edmund Davies (*Cold*

Blood (2007) and *Holby City* (2011)). Heslop and Davies also appeared in Radio 4's *Walter Now* (2009), in which Ian McKellen reprised his earlier television role as Walter, a learning disabled character.

Many of these television and radio opportunities are in single-episode dramas and are usually concerned directly with disability-related issues, especially medical provision. One notable exception is *The Pursuits of Darleen Fyles*, a Radio 4 drama featuring Edmund Davies along with another Making Theatre graduate, Donna Lavin, in the title role. The drama, written by Esther Wilson, has completed several radio series and a television special since 2008. This longevity demonstrates the capacity of the two lead actors to sustain and develop complex characters, as well as to explore the roles in rounded and dramatic ways beyond their narrower identities as learning disabled people.

Nonetheless, such inroads are only the first stages towards full equality, and constitute the exception rather than the rule. Fourteen years after Mind the Gap's first adaptation, for example, a production of *Of Mice and Men* at the West Yorkshire Playhouse (2014) cast a non-disabled actor in the role of Lennie. Wheeler draws attention to the ongoing discrepancies in the politics of casting disabled parts as opposed to other identity-based roles:

> it's still not occurring to directors that we've moved significantly on from Shakespearean times when there were only men on stage ... [Black actors] started appearing on our stages not just because the plot needed them but because there were some brilliant actors. But we're still stuck in this time bubble around disability, particularly around learning disability. (Wheeler, 2014)

If the slow pace of change reflects dominant social expectations regarding learning disability, it may also be bound up with prevalent expectations about theatre aesthetics. The limited tendency to cast learning disabled actors in appropriate roles often remains motivated by their unique capacity to bring aspects of realism, or authenticity, to the part rather than an acknowledgement of their rights or artistic abilities as professional performers.

As Mind the Gap continues to lobby and lay the groundwork for wider industry recognition, it pursues new opportunities and artistic directions for learning disabled performers. The diversity of styles, forms and tones across the company's work refuses to presuppose a natural and singular approach that comes most readily or advanta-geously to learning disabled actors. Taken as a whole, Mind the Gap's body of work negotiates the ever-changing historical, social and artistic landscape encountered by artists with learning disabilities. Its contribution to the development of theatre reflects, explores and reshapes that landscape in this period by introducing both the conventional and the unique contributions of previously overlooked performers.

Acknowledgements

I would like to acknowledge a debt of thanks to Tim Wheeler and Julia Skelton at Mind the Gap, for generously giving their time and support to the development of this chapter.

Productions 1995–2014

Harry Heads for Las Vegas by Mick Martin, 1995, Bradford (national tour)

Keeping Mum by Mary Cooper, 1996, Leeds

Change of Mind by Peter Spafford, 1996, Bradford (national tour)

The Big Picture by Tim Wheeler, 1998, Bradford (national tour)

A Damn Good Show, 1998, Bradford

The Art of Democracy, 1999, Bradford

Neville's Advocate by Mike Kenny, 1999, Bradford (national tour)

Open Art Surgery, 1999, Bradford

Of Mice and Men by Mike Kenny, 2000, Bradford (national tour)

Chilli Out 2000!, 2000, Bradford (regional tour)

Keep it in the Family, 2000, Bradford

Let the Stars Decide by Dave Calvert and Neil Murfin, 2000, Bradford (regional tour)

Hitting the Streets, 2000, Bradford

Dr Jekyll and Mr Hyde by Mike Kenny, 2001, Bradford (national tour)

The Pied Piper by Mike Kenny, 2001, Bradford

Citizen Chain, 2001, Bradford

Pygmalion by George Bernard Shaw (adapted by Mike Kenny), 2002, Bradford (national tour)

Stranger in a Stranger Land, 2002, Bradford

Dig Deeper, 2002, Bradford

Stranger in Paradise, 2002, Bradford

Don Quixote by Mike Kenny (collaboration with Northern Stage Ensemble), 2003, Newcastle upon Tyne (national tour)

When Will I Be Seamus?, 2003, Bradford
Emperor's New Clothes by Mike Kenny, 2003, Bradford
Never Again! by Peter Spafford, 2003, Bradford (regional tour)
Cyrano by Mike Kenny, 2004, Bradford (national tour)
Ellie Billyot, 2004, Bradford
Icarus, 2004, Bradford
On the Verge by Mike Kenny, 2005, Bradford (international tour)
Animal Farm by Mike Kenny, 2005, Bradford
Taming of the Shrew, 2005, Bradford
Phoenix, 2006, Bradford and Croydon
I'm with Stupid, 2008, Leeds
Boo by Mike Kenny, 2009, Bradford (national tour)
Real Voices Real Lives, 2009, Bradford
Shadow People, 2009, Bradford
Chicken Coup!, 2010, Bradford (international tour)
Irresistible, 2010, Ilkley
Stig of the Dump by Mike Kenny, 2011, Bradford (national tour)
Immovable, 2012, Barnsley and York
Treasure Island by Mike Kenny, 2013, Bradford (national tour)
Gift, 2014, Bradford (New Music Biennial 2014, national tour)
Trickster, 2014, Galway

Chapter 4

KNEEHIGH THEATRE

Duška Radosavljević

From its beginnings in 1980 as a small-scale rural troupe based in Cornwall, Kneehigh Theatre has certainly had an unusual career journey. Since the early 2000s, the company has gradually acquired increased national and international prominence under the leadership of director Emma Rice, before eventually reaching the West End and Broadway. By most accounts, this would be seen as a major success story for the artists concerned. However, from the perspective of alternative theatre history, one might anticipate a slightly uncomfortable question as to whether the company's success might be seen as an instance of capitulation to consumerist capitalism and therefore inherent disloyalty to their own founding principles. Kate Dorney notes, for example, that '[f]or some, [Kneehigh's] move to a national and international platform is seen as a betrayal of their local roots' (in Dorney and Merkin, 2010, 119–22).

In political terms, the company's genealogy spans several interesting periods: emerging as an example of what Sandy Craig (1980) defined as 'alternative theatre', surviving Thatcher and then Blair on its own terms, and eventually absorbing into its fabric some international influences too. Since its inception, Kneehigh has relished defining itself in terms of its relationship to the community, and in this respect it shares many features of the 1980s community theatre as defined retrospectively by Baz Kershaw in 1992, which 'aimed to combine art and action, aesthetics and pragmatics' that 'were shaped by the culture of their audience's community' (Kershaw, 1992, 5). But, as Kershaw himself noted, rather than being driven by a coherent ideology, the 'rural community theatre movement' to which Kneehigh can be seen to have belonged, operated within a political spectrum ranging from those companies that were reinforcing the status quo, 'through traditional forms of entertainment', to those that mounted a radical critique of particular policies (Kershaw, 1992, 4). Kneehigh's method, as this chapter will show, was at neither end of this scale, as the company opted for subversive populism over explicit radicalism.

More significantly for the purpose of our study here, the 1990s were a time when the principles of community theatre underlying Kneehigh's existence up until that point began to experience a crisis. In 1999, Kershaw revisited the terms of 'political theatre' and 'radical performance', observing that, as a result of the 'collapse of communism', 'old notions of political theatre were falling into intellectual disrepute' (Kershaw, 1999, 5). Likewise, the term 'community' itself had fallen out of vogue, and Kershaw traced this to the radical liberalism of postmodernism (Kershaw, 1999, 18).

Diagnosing a new 'promiscuity of the political' – as the radical can be claimed by both the Left and the Right – Kershaw went on to argue that 'political theatre' per se had become untenable as institutional, building-based theatre was, by definition, subject to disciplinary mechanisms of consumerism and commodification. He took Raymond Williams's definition of the 'radical' as simultaneously non-dogmatic and demanding of a fundamental change (Kershaw, 1999, 18), and then analysed the radical potential of various types of performance which took place beyond the theatre space, including protests, street theatre, prison drama, reminiscence theatre and outdoor spectacles, as well as postmodern, immersive and maze performances. However, at the core of his argument is the notion that the real democratizing power of performance is situated in those practices which transform the spectator into a participant (Kershaw, 1999, 24). Interestingly, the book's references to 'community theatre' are, by this point, restricted to historical examples of Ann Jellicoe's work in the 1970s or the EMMA theatre company in the 1980s.

The kind of performance that Kershaw advocated – such as outdoor spectacles – had been precisely the staple of Kneehigh's own activity throughout the 1980s and 1990s, but this practice remained largely invisible to audiences outside of Cornwall, as the company ended up forging its national and international profile on the basis of its building-based work. Radical more in the sense of being non-dogmatic and resistant to the dominant ideology rather than openly revolutionary or transgressive, Kneehigh's brand of community theatre has survived into the 2000s by keeping the audience involved. The form of audience participation the company deploys is implicitly reflected in its choice to focus on well-known, commercially successful adaptations of classics. Appealing to the sense of community sought by the individual members of the audience, rather than any ideas of community imposed from above, Kneehigh Theatre therefore creates an opportunity for Jean-Luc Nancy's idea of a community in the sense of 'being together' (1991). Heather Lilley recognizes this mechanism specifically in Kneehigh's use of fairy-tales which, according to her, aids the formation of an 'interpretive community' among the audience by enhancing their sense of 'collective interpretation' (Lilley, 2010, 46). Similarly, the company's choice, at times, to focus on screen-to-stage adaptations, taps into community spirit through potential 'ritual re-enactment of shared popular myths' (Hesse, 2009, 145).

In the Epilogue to *The Radical in Performance*, Kershaw offers a representative example of what he sees as an ideal of 'democratised performance' whereby 'a community of people [was] constructing a sense of identity through the production of a culture that could potentially enhance their collective agency, self-determination and responsibility to each other' (Kershaw, 1999, 219). Shown as part of a variety programme for family audiences in the commuter village of Kenton in Devon, the performance described by Kershaw was a solo number by an awkward agricultural labourer, Roy. It consisted of a rendition of *The Blue Danube* on a hand-held percussion instrument made of bones. Although the performance initially met with an unfriendly reception from younger audience members, Roy's personal conviction, investment and persistence – he repeated the performance four times in order to sway the audience – did eventually produce a desired effect. Kershaw sees this as an example of 'radical performance' because it was '*more* than resistant to the normative values that may be seen as constraints to democracy' – instead it '*transcended* those normative values and, at least for the time it was happening, created a space and time beyond the dominant' (Kershaw, 1999, 219, original emphasis).

In this chapter, I will argue that despite its apparent pragmatic alignment with the mainstream – or Kershaw's 'disciplinary' theatre – Kneehigh never really relinquished the inherent political and aesthetic values that underlie the entire body of the company's work, whether building-based or not. Focusing on some of its most high-profile productions – *Cymbeline* at the Royal Shakespeare Company (RSC), (2006), *A Matter of Life and Death* at the National Theatre (2007) and *Brief Encounter* in the West End (2008) – I will look for the ways in which their permeation of the mainstream was, in its nature, a continuous political act that has provoked and challenged some estab-lished modes of theatre viewing in Britain, and eventually changed the terms on which Kneehigh's work has been received. In other words, analogous to Kershaw's example above, I would like to ask: could those three productions be seen as a process of 'transcending the normative values' through personal conviction and persistence and, ultimately, as a means of democratizing the theatre-going experience?

In the sections that follow, I will first of all chart the development of the company's body of work and working methodologies throughout the 1980s and 1990s, with reference to some primary materials and conversations with Mike Shepherd and Emma Rice. This will outline the most significant aspects of the context within which the company's work was initially produced and received, as well as helping to define the company's artistic policy at the beginning of the 2000s. The second half of the chapter will focus on three key productions from the 2000s, with specific reference to their critical reception, charting some recurring ways in which the work confronted and subverted pre-existing attitudes. In this case, critical reception will be understood as a mechanism through which Kneehigh's work is assessed by reference to a set of inherent normative values. This process is made particularly acute by the fact that the three chosen productions – and indeed most of Kneehigh's output in the 2000s – are also adaptations of important classics. The inherent normative values in those cases are not solely restricted to the politics of theatre-making and theatre-going, but also to the relationship between the 'original' and the 'adaptation', and, especially in the case of *Cymbeline*, the relationship between (Shakespearean) 'text' and performance.

History of Kneehigh

There is a lovingly handwritten little black notebook in Box 73 of Kneehigh Theatre's archive at the University College Falmouth library. In it, Mike Shepherd undertook the difficult task of recording a history of the company that he founded in 1980 and that blossomed two decades later. Its roots go back even further, however, into Shepherd's own childhood memories, and a particular instance of thwarted heroism whereby his attempt to rescue a school friend's confiscated teddy bear led to his own shameful punishment. This pattern, he claims, influenced his theatre endeavours. After experiencing disillusionment with pursuing an acting career in London, Shepherd returned to teaching in his native Cornwall in the late 1970s, and started 'playing around' with non-professional actors, creating outdoor spectacles after work hours. In his notebook, he offers this succinct explanation of his creative impulse: 'An over-heightened sensitivity to injustice, coupled with innate naughtiness, led me to start Kneehigh' (Shepherd, Notebook, n.d., 3).

The innate naughtiness manifested itself in Kneehigh Theatre's first show – an outdoors family spectacle, *The Adventures of Awful Knawful* (1980), featuring stuntman and athlete John Mergler and ending in Shepherd's arrest for performing without a licence (Cavendish, 2010). This was, nevertheless, followed by more rousing work for children and families over the coming years. Besides the company's obvious passion for somewhat subversive populist theatre, the first decade of Kneehigh's work can also be seen as being part of the then prevalent trend of Theatre in Education (TIE), and this too was laced with certain political urges. Another of Shepherd's notebooks from the mid-1980s notes that a tour of schools the company conducted in 1983 'was seen very much as "fighting a cause" for TIE as, unfortunately, the attitude that theatre visits are nothing more than an end of term, pantomime-style treat, still pervades throughout Cornwall' (Shepherd, Notebook, n.d., 2).

In an interview I conducted with Shepherd, he stated that one of the first significant moments for Kneehigh was their collaboration in 1983 with the already renowned community and TIE practitioner, Jon Oram, who was sent to them by South West Arts as an animateur but who ended up being cast in their production of *Jungle Book*. In 1985, Oram went on to devise and direct *Tregeagle – A Cornish Faust* for the company, a production described by Shepherd as a 'key show for Kneehigh's development [which] launched the company nationally to touring departments and venues' (Shepherd, Notebook, n.d.1). This production introduced both live music and a more visual vocabulary of mime and masks into the company's way of working and it marked the first time that it obtained Arts Council funding. An important additional factor for Kneehigh's success at the time was the fact that in 1984 another major Cornish company that had operated in the area since 1971 – Footsbarn Travelling Theatre – left the UK to tour internationally. Shepherd has freely admitted that, although Kneehigh's work was perceived as inferior, it did inherit Footsbarn's audience, and the pressure of expectation forced it to improve (see Gardner, 2004). This was fortuitous and even crucial for the company's survival as it still relied on box office takings rather than Arts Council funding.

Shepherd's openness to other influences, as well as his eagerness to co-opt interesting people into his ranks – and even give them the reins of his company – can be seen, perhaps, as the secret of Kneehigh's longevity. Significant collaborators from this point on included writer John Downie with whom the company created a highly acclaimed version of *Woyzeck* entitled *Cyborg – A Folk Tale for the Future* (1988); writer Nick Darke who was originally from Cornwall and who returned to the area in the late 1980s/early 1990s; and designer Bill Mitchell, who had previously worked with Welfare State International but also settled in Cornwall at the turn of the decade. The 1990s could therefore be seen to represent another distinctive phase in the company's development, which Shepherd summarizes as follows:

> [A]t that point we had two different sorts of work. There was the outdoor work which is non-text based, and then we worked for a decade with Nick Darke. And that started to get us back into the cities because rightly or wrongly people recognised a script. (Radosavljević, 2012)

Nevertheless, these two strands were often intertwined. Between 1990 and 1992, Bill Mitchell began directing for the company. A significant production was his version of Nick Darke's *Ting Tang Mine* (1990), which had originally premiered with a stellar cast at the National Theatre in 1987, but which left Darke dissatisfied. The Cornish production was a way of 'reclaiming' it for him (Shepherd, Notebook, n.d.1). In the same period, Mitchell created an outdoors version of Ibsen's *Peer Gynt* (1991), which toured nationally and internationally, and 'heralded Bill Mitchell's golden era of directing, designing and shared Artistic Directorship' (Shepherd, Notebook, n.d.1). Successful collaborations between Nick Darke, Bill Mitchell and Mike Shepherd continued throughout the 1990s, and the company also had a pool of regular performers/makers, including former Welfare State International member Sue Hill, as well as long-term Kneehigh regulars Dave Mynne, Giles King, Jim Carey, Tristan Sturrock, Bec Applebee (who joined for *Peer Gynt*) and Emma Rice (who played Cinderella in *Ashmaid* in 1994/95). Another latter day regular, Carl Grose, joined as an apprentice on the production of *King of Prussia* in 1996, which marked the company's breakthrough into London. The show was sold out at the Donmar Warehouse, which was at the time run by Sam Mendes, and the company attracted the attention of Trevor Nunn and Richard Eyre (the then Artistic Director of the National Theatre). This led to a co-production with the National of a new play by Nick Darke, *The Riot*, in 1999. According to Lyn Gardner, although critics 'admired [the production's] exuberance' on that occasion, they also 'branded

Kneehigh folksy and parochial' (Gardner 2004). Unfortunately, because of the habitual institutional emphasis on the text in British theatre, the production caused tension between the writer and the company, and it marked the end of their long-term collaboration.

At this point it was the turn of Kneehigh performer Emma Rice to inject new blood into the company. In 1999, encouraged by Mitchell and Shepherd, Rice created a 'dark, sexy and distinctive' (Shepherd, Notebook, n.d.1) version of Thomas Middleton and William Rowley's *The Changeling*, which toured indoor and outdoor venues. However, an unprecedented breakthrough for Rice as director and for the company as a whole arrived with her second production, *Red Shoes*, in 2000, which also won her the Best Director Award in the Barclays TMA Awards in 2002.

Rice took over as the Artistic Director from Bill Mitchell in 2005, and her leadership can be seen to have been crucial in placing Kneehigh on the international map as a major British theatre company. However, Rice has not broken from the company's past in order to make her mark. There is a strong sense of continuity of both ethical and aesthetic values, although she has brought to the company some methodological rigour, as well as an interest in commercial enterprise. The notion of adaptation is discernible not only as a feature of the company's programming but also as its method of survival.

The focus on adaptations in its programming has allowed the company to hone and assert its own theatrical language and maintain a relationship with the audience. As I have written elsewhere, Kneehigh's 1980s alternative theatre origins have given the company a very open and inclusive audience rapport, as well as a set of distinctive aesthetic tools (Radosavljević, 2013b, 73). Kate Dorney has qualified the company style as combining 'physical robustness with live music and songs', and as 'a kind of rough theatre' (Dorney and Merkin, 2010, 118). Given the company's longevity, it has also been tempting to follow patterns of self-reflexivity in Kneehigh's work, subtle ways in which certain characteristic leitmotifs reappear, for example, the motif of lovers being elevated or suspended in mid-air featuring in *Tristan and Yseult* (2003), *Rapunzel* (2006), *A Matter of Life and Death* (2007) and *Brief Encounter* (2008), or the ways in which Stu Barker's music might sound consistently recognizable whatever the genre of the particular show.

Since Emma Rice's directorial debut and gradual takeover of the company, a noticeable development of the company's style has occurred. Dave Mynne, a founder member who returned to appear in *Don John* notes:

We used to joke about the 'Kneehigh school of pointing, shouting and running': if in doubt, fill the space and make a noise. Emma has added a lot of the elements that we always wanted to have there: the darkness, the stillness. (Costa, 2008)

A potentially significant area of influence on the company's work is Emma Rice's brief stint as an actor with the Polish Gardzienice Theatre Association.[1] In an interview I conducted with Rice, she commented that 'as a performer [she] felt cracked open by Gardzienice in a way that three years at Drama School had not touched [her]!' (Radosavljević, 2013a, 106), and that 'Poland was simply the most influential thing that happened to [her]' (2013a, 105).

It is worth noting here that the emphasis on training was always at the heart of Kneehigh's working ethos. The company has a defined rehearsal process (described in detail in Radosavljević, 2013a, 101–3 and 2013b, 75), which, as Shepherd frequently stresses, is subject to periodic reinvention and continuous company retraining.[2] The company's values are written in large letters on the wall of their rehearsal barn in Gorran Haven, and the biggest word, according to him, has always been 'generosity'. In 2012 Shepherd still believed in the same values the company had honed over the years, underlining a few more related words: 'wonder, play, anarchy, ambition, naughtiness – there's a good word! – glee' (Radosavljević, 2012).

Rice's testimony above – which goes on to elaborate on her acceptance of her own roots following the Polish experience – also points to an interesting act of cultural adaptation. Rather than attempting to repeat and transpose unaltered the ways of working she had learned in Poland, Rice instead acquired a deep understanding of the underlying principles, and found her own cultural equivalents (Radosavljević, 2013a, 106). A similar method of relating to an external stimulus through faithfulness towards personal 'emotional memory' and one's own artistic idiom is discernible in her approach to the adaptation of classics too: 'When I decide to do a story, I do not tend to go and read or watch it, I tend to work on what my cultural memory of it is, because that's my truth' (Radosavljević, 2010, 93). The aim is not, therefore, to replicate the original, but to render it through one's own means of expression – a practice that, as Rice rightly points out, was frequently deployed throughout the history of theatre, including by Shakespeare and Brecht themselves. This is also a method that can be seen as 'transcending the normative values' of many mainstream theatre-making practices in Britain, bound by notions of fidelity towards the original text, as will be discussed later.

Funding and financial partnerships

The advent of the New Labour government in 1997 changed things for Kneehigh but, perhaps surprisingly, the 'bonanza time for everyone' (Radosavljević, 2012) was not necessarily a major cause for celebration. Kneehigh had learned to survive without relying on the Arts Council throughout the 1980s and 1990s through a combination of educational work, business sponsorship and box-office takings. Even their 1999 co-production of *The Riot* with the National Theatre was only made possible thanks to a benefit concert given in Cornwall by The Who's Pete Townsend on the company's behalf, which according to *The Stage* raised £20,000 (Smurthwaite, 1999).

Shepherd also cites the benefits yielded by the Enterprise Allowance Scheme which was brought in by Thatcher's government in an attempt to tackle unemployment:

> So if you had an idea for a business you'd be put on the Enterprise Allowance Scheme, but for us it was actually rather good because I think we got £40 a week which back then was probably like getting about £200 a week now and then whatever you earned, there were no questions asked. So ironically, we were out of the radar more easily with the Conservative government. (Radosavljević, 2012)

With the arrival of New Labour, there was more emphasis on accountability. In Shepherd's view, funding was dependent on meeting particular criteria and on ticking the right boxes. In effect, New Labour's cultural policy seemed to require a greater level of conformity – a condition that was sharply at odds with Kneehigh's ethos of subversiveness.

This view is echoed by Michael McKinnie's analysis of New Labour's arts policy, as also discussed in Chapter 1 of this volume. In McKinnie's view, New Labour 'assume[d] that the paramount function of the arts [was] to confirm or reproduce dominant social ideals', and '[did] not acknowledge that art might be critical, subversive, or socially dissonant' (McKinnie, 2004, 188). Although there might have been useful synergies between New Labour's and Kneehigh's own interest in the community, the key difference could be seen to have resided in their respective attitudes towards 'the potential for the art to provoke a rebellious subjectivity that [was] unwelcome in New Labour's Britain' (McKinnie, 2004, 190). The theme of 'rebellious subjectivity' could be easily traced in Kneehigh's oeuvre – from *Red Shoes* (2000) to *Don John* (2008) – throughout the New Labour era, but this was effectively masked behind the company's ever-increasing popularity with audiences, co-producers and funding bodies throughout the 2000s. Kate Dorney notes the way in which Kneehigh's own brand seemed to have coincided with the priorities of the funding bodies in the 2000s – 'touring, accessibility, working with children and the local community, co-producing with regional reps, even their physical style' (Dorney, 2010, 118). However, it is significant that these values within the company's work preceded the advent of New Labour, and placed the company in a fortuitous position without them having to sacrifice any of their ideals or subscribe to a new ideology.

Following a major international tour of *Red Shoes* with the British Council in 2001, Kneehigh embarked on a string of co-productions with major regional and national venues. Initial collaborations included a retelling of the Lulu story, *Pandora's Box* (2002), in collaboration with the Northern Stage Ensemble in Newcastle, and *The Bacchae* (2004) and *The Wooden Frock* (2004) in co-production with the West Yorkshire Playhouse in Leeds. This eventually led to the National Theatre programming Kneehigh's earlier production of *Tristan and Yseult* in 2005 and commissioning, in 2007, an adaptation of the Powell and Pressburger classic film *A Matter of Life and Death*. In 2006 Kneehigh was commissioned by the RSC to do a production of *Cymbeline* for their year-long Complete Works Festival. Since then, the company has returned to Shakespeare's birthplace with a production of *Don John*, based on Mozart's opera, in 2008, and Tanika Gupta's play *The Empress*, directed by Emma Rice at the RSC in 2013. In 2008, in co-production with the West End impresario David Pugh and Nottingham Playhouse, the company presented one of their biggest hits, an adaptation of Noël Coward's *Brief Encounter*, at the Haymarket Cinema, while further West End productions included *The Umbrellas of Cherbourg*, directed by Rice in 2011, and *Wah! Wah! Girls* by Tanika Gupta at Sadler's Wells as part of World Stages London in 2012. Throughout this time, the company continued to tour its work both nationally and internationally.

In 2004, as a result of the Theatre Review 2000 (also known as the Boyden Report), the company's funding 'increased by 40 per cent [...] rising to £185,000' (Annual Review 2004, 29). In 2012/13, Kneehigh received £352,628 from the Arts Council as a National Portfolio Organization, £86,364 from sponsorship and donations, £29,265 from Council grants, and the largest part of their revenue – £768,816 – was earned income (Kneehigh Facts and Figures). In the 2014 funding round they secured National Portfolio standstill funding for the next three years in the context of heavy cuts to the Arts Council budget. Kneehigh is a registered charity, and in 2012/13 the company's work was seen by over 120,000 people in the UK and abroad. Interestingly, despite a growth in capital projects for building-based theatres under New Labour, Kneehigh remains a non-building-based company. They do have a rehearsal space in Cornwall and, as of 2010, have been touring with their own purpose-built tent, The Asylum – another testament to their nomadic roots, their working ethos and their freedom to be 'naughty'.

Critical Reception

As already mentioned, the ultimate purpose of this chapter will be to examine closely the ways in which Kneehigh's more recent and commercially successful work, from the late 2000s, retained the underlying political ethos of the company's founding principles by confronting and challenging the expectations of the critical establishment in the UK. Contextually, it might be helpful to provide some detail on how the company's work was received by the London press in the late 1990s on the occasions of their largely successful runs of *The King of Prussia* (1996) at the Donmar Warehouse and *The Riot* (1999) at the National Theatre.

The terms most often used by critics to describe the company's work have included irreverent, enthusiastic, racy, exuberant, jokey, energetic and boisterous. The company's acting skills, ensemble spirit, delight in storytelling and inventiveness are often highly praised, although some critics struggle to accept the possibility that the company's work can have deeper significance and at the same time be populist and entertaining. *The King of Prussia* – Nick Darke's short play about an eighteenth-century Cornish brandy smuggler – elicited some explicit metropolitan snobbery against 'community' work. For example, Paul Taylor noted: 'There are metropolitan sophisticates for whom the idea of community theatre has about as much appeal as a plate of Yorkshire pudding would have had for Proust' (Taylor, 1996). Sheridan Morley saw the piece as an example of regional theatre that had 'more enthusiasm than expertise' (Morley, 1996), while Nicholas de Jongh, clearly unimpressed, invoked the qualifiers of 'smoothly respectable agit-prop' and 'student dramatics at the Edinburgh Festival Fringe' (de Jongh, 1996). Similarly, Robert Butler (1996) speculated that perhaps one needed to be 'local' in order to appreciate the more 'substantial' content of the piece; although, interestingly, Sarah Hemming had no trouble in seeing the piece as a 'critique of capitalism [which] raises questions about the points where justice, conscience and the law part company' (Hemming, 1996).

Michael Billington also admired the inherent political value of 'a real company at work in London's West End'; he compared their efforts on this occasion to Peter Cheeseman's Stoke-on-Trent musical documentaries of the 1960s (Billington, 1996). Three years later, when the company collaborated with the National Theatre on *The Riot*, Billington positioned Kneehigh within the lineage of 7:84, Shared Experience and Complicite on the strength of their 'inventive panache'. He found *The Riot* 'dazzling' and the acting 'outstanding', the only problem being the weight of content, which made it difficult to work out the production's 'political stance' (Billington, 1999). With many more reviewers flocking to this show, what is also discernible is a distinction between those reviewers who were new to Kneehigh and those who had experienced the company's previous work (such as Michael Billington, Charles Spencer, Benedict Nightingale and Robert Butler). The latter group displays a certain loyalty towards, and growing expertise in reading, the company's specific performance idiom, which inclines them to be forgiving of the fact that this production can be perceived as merely 'enjoyable', where previous productions were perhaps more exhilarating. The newcomers, on the other hand, are once again offended by a 'slight plot' (Curtis, 1999), the fact that the work is 'too flippant to take seriously' (Brown, 1999) and – more tellingly, as *The Times Literary Supplement* would have it – the fact that 'pit-a-pat dialogue' and the 'distractingly comic' acting 'frustrates our attempt to seek emotional sympathy with any one character or action' (Waywell, 1999). This latter comment encapsulates particularly well a literary bias internalized as a normative value by much of the critical establishment. For a company like Kneehigh, whose own primary values have been concerned with other aspects of theatre-making, such as storytelling and community engagement, such a bias was indeed going to pose a serious challenge. And this underlying problem would certainly come to a head some years later.

Key Works

The second half of this chapter examines in some detail three of Kneehigh's productions from the late 2000s, highlighting the ways in which they 'transcend the normative values' and 'create a space and time beyond the dominant' (Kershaw, 1999, 219). It is worth noting here that Kneehigh's work began to receive academic attention at about the same time, particularly in the field of adaptation studies. Aside from Hesse (2009) and Lilley (2010) mentioned earlier, another more recent study by Claudia Georgi has focused specifically on the company's 'dialogic' adaptation of *Brief Encounter* as an instance of the company 'asserting its own adaptation of history' (Georgi, 2013, 67). The following analyses are therefore concerned with both the company's means of production – specifically the subversiveness of their adaptation method – and the ways in which this effected changes in the reception of their work.

Kneehigh's Cymbeline: *A Take Off*

In 2006, the Royal Shakespeare Company, under the Artistic Directorship of Michael Boyd, embarked on a year-long international festival, the purpose of which was to showcase all of Shakespeare's 38 plays. Boyd's leadership could be seen as distinct from many of his predecessors, in his desire to embrace variety and innovation over the preservation of traditionalist approaches to Shakespeare as a British cultural icon. As a director whose formative influences included the Edinburgh Festival Fringe and an apprenticeship to the Soviet theatre director Anatoly Efros, Boyd was a staunch believer in the ensemble way of working, and the notion of community per se (see Radosavljević, 2013a, 33–41), which would have given him a natural affinity with Kneehigh's own working ethos. However, neither Boyd nor Kneehigh could necessarily count on an all-encompassing enthusiastic embrace of their values, especially not among the guardians of tradition in Stratford-upon-Avon (see Edmondson, 2010).

According to Shepherd's 'History' document, although *Cymbeline* was commissioned by the RSC, it was rehearsed in Cornwall and, in typical Kneehigh fashion, it was originally performed as an outdoors event in Rufford Abbey. The adaptation, which uses Shakespeare's text very sparingly, is credited to Emma Rice and Carl Grose, who also played the Queen and Posthumus respectively. Shepherd doubled up as King Cymbeline and the drag act, Joan Puttock, supposedly returning from Spain to offer a prologue for our benefit:

> JOAN Bloody complicated, innit? It's like a Shakespeare play!

> Everyone is either miserable or dead! I rather wished I'd stayed
> in the Costa del Sol!
>
> (Rice and Grose, 2007, 14)

This sets the scene for the rest of the show, which is similarly peppered with tactics designed to keep the audience engaged in a story that is often perceived as overly convoluted, problematic and inaccessible. Róbert Lučkay's Iachimo is conceived as a charming Italian playboy, while Hayley Carmichael's vulnerable yet feisty Imogen provides one of the most memorable moments in the play, as she delivers a Shakespeare-parodying gag contained in a letter from Posthumus:

> IMOGEN *(Reading.)* Dear Pisanio, Thy mistress hath played the
>   trumpet in my bed—
> *(To* PISANIO.*)* I can't even PLAY the trumpet!
> PISANIO   Strumpet!
>
> (Rice and Grose, 2007, 43)

Although humour and irreverence are the most often noted features of this version, also threaded through the narrative is a series of rap numbers set to Stu Barker's melancholy urban score, and performed with verve by Dominic Lawton, one of a group of musicians seamlessly integrated into the dramaturgy of the piece. Other notable aspects of the production included Michael Vale's vertical set made of metal bars that provided several levels on which the action could be played, and the inherent physicality of the piece which came with Kneehigh's customary emphasis on the corporeal.

When Kneehigh's production of *Cymbeline* eventually arrived in Stratford in September 2006, it did not meet with everyone's approval. Peter Kirwan's review for the *Shakespeare Bulletin* (2012) records at least two waves of walkouts on the night of his attendance, while numerous anecdotal accounts testify to angry protestations at the RSC box office that 'this was not Shakespeare'. At the same time, the show did frequently receive standing ovations from the members of the audience who stayed.

These reactions were mirrored in the critical reception of the piece, although interestingly, those who enjoyed the show in Stratford, such as Dominic Cavendish (2006) and Paul Taylor (2006), for example, felt obliged to warn purists about the version's shortcomings. Despite his past admiration for the company, the *Guardian*'s Michael Billington dismissed the Kneehigh 'paraphrase' as a 'cop-out [which] ducks the real challenge of making Shakespeare live through his language' (Billington, 2006, 1054). Perhaps predictably, when it came to safeguarding the normative values concerning the staging of Shakespeare, Billington's literary bias outweighed any political considerations.

The contentious relationship between text and performance is a subject of my monograph, *Theatre-Making* (2013), which provides more detail on Kneehigh's *Cymbeline* and its critical reception in this respect. Particularly pertinent here is the finding that by abandoning Shakespeare's text (except for some 200 quoted lines) – in an act that could perhaps be seen as 'naughty' – Kneehigh appears to have presented the critical establishment with a different set of terms on which it required the work to be received. As noted by several reviewers of this production – including notably the Arden editor of the play, Valery Wayne, who incidentally contested Billington's claim that we were being asked to 'celebrate Kneehigh's cleverness rather than Shakespeare's genius' (Wayne, 2007, 231) – the company ultimately engaged with the spirit rather than the word of the original and, in the process, brought popularity to one of the lesser-known plays by Shakespeare.

Interestingly, however, by the time the production reached London, following a regional tour, it met with a largely enthusiastic response. Outside of Stratford, critics were perhaps more able and willing to read the production in the context of the company's own values rather than those of a Shakespearean literary heritage. *Metro*'s Claire Allfree decidedly shunned any potentially purist responses on the grounds that 'this lewd bastardisation gets to the heart of the original as powerfully as any slavishly faithful revival' (Allfree, 2007a, 52), while Sarah Hemming, who continued to see the show in the context of the company's previous output, praised it for being 'fun' and because 'it [found] a clear narrative route through this knotty drama' (Hemming, 2007, 52). A comment in Patrick Marmion's review came particularly close to pinpointing the key principle of Kneehigh's adaptation method:

> what Shakespeare covers in two pages of verse is often rendered with a visual image instead. This might mean Posthumus setting sail in a toy boat in a fog of dry ice or the miming of the dastardly ravishing of sleeping Imogen. (Marmion, 2007, 52)

The process of 'transcend[ing] the normative values' and 'creat[ing] a space and time beyond the dominant' (Kershaw, 1999, 219) ultimately occurred on two levels in the case of Kneehigh's *Cymbeline* – in the company's approach to the classical text, and in the way in which they might be perceived to have achieved a greater democratization of the play's reception. In the aftermath of the production, Emma Rice said 'I hate theatre that excludes the audience by making them feel inferior', and 'We simply made a difficult text accessible, rather than tacitly collude in this bizarre cultural notion that if you don't understand something, there's something wrong with you' (Rice in Allfree, 2007b). However, Kneehigh's other important achievement in its Stratford debut was that the company's work, through its own artistic integrity, was able to elicit critical evaluation on its own terms, rather than according to the values of the critical establishment. Additionally, having injected the Bard into the body politic of the company, Kneehigh appeared to have compounded its status as an important British theatre company, and this marked a new chapter in the company's career, perhaps even the beginning of its Golden Age.

The Upward Struggle

It is the nature of classic texts to be able to uphold the diverse ideologies projected onto them, and this is precisely why *A Matter of Life and Death* was still able to work in a Britain increasingly tired of its American allegiance during the Iraq war, 60 years after the film's original release.[3] According to Harper and Porter (1989), the film was originally commissioned as a means of reconciling the British public to the Americans, who had been previously perceived as annoyingly 'overpaid, over-sexed and over here'. In Kneehigh's 2007 version at the National Theatre, adaptors Tom Morris and Emma Rice made a series of interventions to the original ideological framework, while foregrounding a more explicit anti-war message than the original had been able to do. They also took the more sobering view that – however powerful love may be – the matter of life and death is determined by chance.

In addition to the community-building potential of ritualized audience participation, Beatrix Hesse isolates three more ingredients in her proposed model of a successful screen-to-stage adaptation. They include a familiar plot, the notion of 'surplus value' (such as live singing and dancing or, conversely, a Grotowskian renunciation of technology and a focus on the actor), and 'some inherent criticism of the source film' (Hesse, 2009, 147). She uses Kneehigh's *A Matter of Life and Death* as an explicit example of the latter function of screen-to-stage adaptation, which therefore invites the audience 'to view the film in a new light' (Hesse, 2009, 147). While pinpointing the ways in which

Kneehigh offered a critical perspective on the source film, it is also worth highlighting some methods by which this version 'transcended the normative values' of screen-to-stage adaptation, in favour of the 'surplus value' of stagecraft. Thus, a purely incidental use of a bicycle in the film, for example, becomes a major theatrical device here, with a chorus of nurses pedalling up and down the stage. The more radical interventions, mostly concerning the plot, were particularly apparent in the second half of the show. Re-appropriating the film's passing reference to Shakespeare's *A Midsummer Night's Dream*, Morris and Rice moved this notion of magical light relief into the military hospital where the protagonist Peter would be operated on. Mike Shepherd's Bottom the Weaver, with his ears made of hospital slippers and a garland of flowers on his head, would stay by Peter's side until the end. In a major deviation from the screenplay, Peter would then face his father and William Shakespeare at the prosecutor's bench in heaven, Shakespeare being a replacement for a reference to Walter Raleigh in the film. Rice explains:

> I really like the work to be accessible, we were trying to work out the cultural references that would translate and Shakespeare is the best-known poet. So at one point in that trial we did have Sir Walter Raleigh turning up, but basically it didn't mean anything to anybody. Whereas Shakespeare turns up, and everybody in the country, every child will know who Shakespeare is. (Radosavljević, 2010, 94)

This reconceptualization of the trial becomes even more cogent once we understand Peter's ordeal as being a matter of his own conscience, a nightmarish trial between a soldier, a poet, a son, a clown and a lover within himself. There was a particularly poignant moment when Peter's troubled mind confronts us with the chorus of Dresden and Coventry widows, but this is completely surpassed in poignancy by June's desperate bid for her beloved's life, which in Kneehigh's adaptation has her climbing from one precariously suspended bed to another one above, to replicate a scene in which she runs up the giant stairway to heaven in order to offer up her own life in exchange for Peter's.

It is significant that a key contextual circumstance of Kneehigh's production was the intensely unpopular British and American involvement in the war in Iraq. Seemingly questioning the notion of the film's 'happy ending', the fate of Peter and June's love is literally decided here by the flip of a coin tossed by a random audience member. Although in Kneehigh's conception of the event we are actively cast to replace the audience of soldiers and nurses in the celestial court, in conclusion to this piece we are simply told that there is no democracy in matters of life and death.

The reception of Kneehigh's version of *A Matter of Life and Death* was, notoriously, so hostile that it prompted Nick Hytner to publicly denounce the critical establishment as consisting of purist and woman-hating 'dead-white males' (Hytner, 2007), as once again female critics were much kinder. Complaints lodged by the 'dead white males' had ranged from 'why mess around with a masterpiece' (Spencer, 2007, 574) to a disapproval of the company's penchant for 'silly acrobatics' (de Jongh, 2007, 575) and of their use of rap, which is seen as potentially trying to pander to younger audiences (Edge, 2007, 577).

However, those – mainly female – reviewers who managed to see past this adaptation's potential flaws usually celebrated the piece for the power of its theatrical imagery. This is particularly well captured by Rachel Halliburton's theatrically literate observation that this version 'avoided the trap of most stage adaptations of films by evolving its own playful visual language which can turn the flaring of a match into an exploding universe, or a swinging hospital bed into an image of ecstatic romance' (Halliburton, 2007, 578). This kind of lyrical and visual metonymy is also recognizable as an element of the company's methodology, although Kneehigh's artistic idiom is possibly eclipsed on this occasion by the desire to make its political stance explicit, rather than, as the case might have been previously, quietly subversive. Given the direct political engagement of the audience, this particular adaptation is classifiable not only as an instance of 'democratised' but perhaps even overtly 'radical' performance, in Kershaw's terms. For this reason, Kneehigh's *A Matter of Life and Death* appears to be a less typical example of the company's distinct style. In replacing trademark naughtiness with a more activist stance, it might perhaps even be argued that this departure from the company's usual way of relating with the audience has in fact resulted in a less politically effective piece of theatre.

Soaring among Gilded Chandeliers

It is no wonder that Kneehigh's production of *Brief Encounter* was antic-ipated with both trepidation and excitement. Its underlying conceptual approach and Kneehigh-style reflexivity was already apparent in the producers' choice of venue – the Haymarket Cinema – which was origi-nally built as a theatre, but which screened the premiere of David Lean's 1945 film. The genealogy of Kneehigh's version – which they cautiously, or perhaps provocatively, billed as *Noël Coward's Brief Encounter* – is also more complicated on this occasion, as the film that has become a much-loved classic is itself an adaptation of Coward's pre-existing stage play *Still Life*.

Once again, the reasons for many decisions made in relation to this particular adaptation can be traced back to the company's theatrical idiom. Having flirted with the use of video projections in *Pandora's Box* in 2002 and *Cry Wolf* in 2003,[4] Rice finally got the chance to make a projection screen a centrepiece of a Kneehigh production. The show's opening – rather ingeniously – has the protagonists of this story of doomed love sitting among us in the cinema auditorium, which is peppered with cast members dressed as 1940s ushers. On the screen we see crackly black-and-white footage of Laura's pipe-smoking husband sitting in his lounge and pleading with her to return to him, prompting her in turn to run out of her seat and onto the stage where – in a reversal of the technique used in Woody Allen's film *The Purple Rose of Cairo* (1985) where a lead character escapes the screen to enter real life – she literally enters her life on the screen.

This particular moment is significant on a number of levels. Apart from confronting the normative critical 'why mess with the master-piece' stance, it positions the audience right in the middle of the world being created, and it turns the screen into a theatrical device. Thus the screen would be used to metaphorically delve into Laura's inner feelings (as well as facilitating the running of 'real' trains through this stage version). In addition, the opening moment is a reversal of the opening of the film where exhausted Laura is sitting with her husband in the drawing room, and beginning to experience a flashback to her tumultuous affair. On the stage, the ushers in pillbox hats swiftly follow in the unfortunate heroine's footsteps and assume their positions as an on-stage band.

Following the experience with *A Matter of Life and Death*, Rice must have been well aware of the risks she faced with the critical estab-lishment in deciding to create a stage adaptation of this film. Adrian Turner charts the changing status of *Brief Encounter* as a cinematic classic since its premiere in 1945 when it was seen as a realistic depiction of the emotional restraint of the British middle class, via the sexual liberation of the 1960s that turned it into an object of derision, to the present day when it is not just a much-loved film but can even be seen as the 'British *Casablanca*' (Turner, 2000). While reminiscing about the early stages of developing her idea, which included listening to Noël Coward's songs, Rice confides:

[W]orking alongside those discoveries of the breadth of his words and his work, was me thinking 'I'm putting one of the most loved films ever on stage, I want it to be really honouring cinema and really honouring theatre.' That is why I wanted the cinema screen but I also wanted the front-cloths – the front-cloths are one of the most ancient theatre traditions. (Radosavljević, 2010, 93)

Thus, Rice is acknowledging that an expectation of 'fidelity' will be held against her and will involve no other hierarchy but the audience's sentimental relationship to the film. In response to a challenge like this, she can only resort to her own method as a theatre-maker – one based on fidelity to her own 'emotional memory'. However, this is intertwined with a desire for authorial authenticity, as Rice claims: 'I always try and think – "what is unusual?", "how can I make this into a piece that is mine, not somebody else's".' (Radosavljević, 2010, 93)

What, therefore, appears to make this adaptation particularly successful is the fact that, as the adaptors, Rice and Kneehigh position themselves and their set of performance-making tools very clearly in relation not only to the text or, as Rice prefers to say, the 'story' that forms the departure point, but also in relation to their audience, which will have a set of expectations from Kneehigh as a company, and in relation to the platform, their first West End gig. Hence, the ultimate 'authority' is devolved to the audience, and the notion of 'democratisation' becomes part of the company's authorship mechanism and adaptation methodology regardless of the site of performance. Even when it uses the features of a West End musical in its production, for example, Kneehigh is able to filter them through its own recognizable performance idiom, once again using Stu Barker's musical signature.

Rice, therefore, opts for an intertextual approach that allows her to utilize Noël Coward's songs as a stage equivalent of a 'cut to', alongside lashings of Rachmaninov's *Piano Concerto No. 2* taken from the film. This is potentially justified by the fact that the company is also revisiting Coward's play *Still Life* on which the film is based. In this way, they destabilize their source text and its 'authority' by treating it as only an adaptation in itself (albeit an adaptation which has acquired a superior status to its source text). Claudia Georgi has provided a helpful analysis of this version's relationship to the stage play and the film (Georgi, 2013, 67–73), but the company's key strategy is actually contained in subjecting both source texts to its ensemble way of working, thus allowing two other love stories in addition to Laura and Alec's to come to the fore. This creates many additional conceptual layers within

Kneehigh's adaptation, and an opportunity to skilfully deflect the issue of 'fidelity'. But the ultimate achievement of this production is that 'fidelity' itself is made present through its apparent absence. And what better tribute could there be to fidelity when the text in question is the nation's best-loved cinematic apology for marital infidelity?

Foregrounding the company style, therefore, typical Kneehigh moments in this production include the use of puppets as Laura's children, a watering can and a tin bath conjuring up rain, and the smitten lovers hanging off a posh restaurant's chandelier. The latter – although it represents a Kneehigh leitmotif seen in several productions – was the only moment some of the critics condemned as possibly excessive. Otherwise the production was almost unanimously deemed a 'delight'.

'Far from being the crude hatchet job I'd feared,' wrote Charles Spencer, 'the show largely proves a witty and sympathetic homage to Coward's unforgettable portrayal of English reserve and romance' (Spencer, 2008, 175). Meanwhile, de Jongh praised the fact that 'Miss Rice's adaptation never mocks or caricatures the would-be, guilty lovers or the inherent improbability of their frustrated romance' (de Jongh, 2008, 175). Most usefully, Paul Taylor provided a point of comparison with another West End version of the film from eight years previously, which he considered an 'act of conscious sabotage designed to show that what works in one medium can fall flat on its face in another'; however, his verdict here is that 'this *Brief Encounter* manages to have the best of several worlds in an experience that is still the more effective for artfully straddling stage and screen' (Taylor, 2008, 176).

Conclusion

The secret of Kneehigh's success has been its ability to straddle much more than just the art of stage and screen. Unafraid of fusing the traditions of classical and community theatre, text-based and physical performance, and rap and Rachmaninov, it has managed to find ways of engaging the audience and the critical establishment through its own performance idiom, on its own terms. By managing to demonstrate that bringing Shakespeare closer to the audience was more important than fulfilling the pre-existing critical expectations about how the Bard should be honoured, Kneehigh can be seen to have achieved a greater democratization of the cultural capital. This is a process that continued with its tackling of significant film classics whereby, in testing different models of political theatre, the company refined and perfected its own unique brand of aesthetic irreverence. In this way, it has successfully created a time and space beyond the dominant normative values; whether challenging or appearing to meet the standards of the mainstream, the company has ultimately retained its political subversiveness even at a time when its way of working seemed to become representative of government policy. But above all, what Kneehigh's Golden Age highlighted is the model of theatre authorship based on staying faithful to one's own political history, company values and emotional memory, regardless of how far one gets in life.

Acknowledgements

The author wishes to thank Chloe Rickard for her prompt and tireless help with numerous queries in the course of this research, as well as Mike Shepherd and Emma Rice for their time and generosity. Additional thanks to Archive Services at Falmouth Exeter Plus.

Key Productions in this Period

The King of Prussia – 1996 – Donmar Warehouse
Written by Nick Darke; designed by Bill Mitchell; directed by Mike Shepherd

Strange Cargo – 1998 – outdoors production, national tour, including National Theatre

The Riot – 1999 – National Theatre, national tour
Written by Nick Darke; designed by Bill Mitchell; directed by Mike Shepherd

The Itch – 1999
Adapted by Emma Rice from *The Changeling* by Middleton & Rowley; designed by Bill Mitchell; directed by Emma Rice

Red Shoes – 2000/2001 – international tour
Adapted from Andersen by Emma Rice; designed by Bill Mitchell; directed by Emma Rice
TMA Award for Best Director for Emma Rice 2002

Tristan & Yseult – 2003 – originally an outdoors production, national and international tour
Written by Carl Grose and Anna Marie Murphy; adapted and directed by Emma Rice; designed by Bill Mitchell

The Bacchae – 2004 – West Yorkshire Playhouse co-production, national tour
Written by Carl Grose and Anna Marie Murphy; designed by Bill Mitchell; directed by Emma Rice
TMA Award for Best Touring Production in 2005

Cymbeline – 2006 – commissioned by the RSC as part of the Complete Works Festival / national tour
Adapted by Emma Rice; written by Carl Grose; designed by Michael Vale; directed by Emma Rice

A Matter of Life and Death – 2007 – National Theatre
Written by Tom Morris; designed by Bill Mitchell; directed by Emma Rice

Brief Encounter – 2007/8 – co-produced by David Pugh; originally a middle-scale touring production before opening at the Haymarket Cinema in 2008; national and international tour
Adapted and directed by Emma Rice; designed by Neil Murray
Four Olivier Nominations: Best Director, Best Set Design, Best Entertainment; Best Sound Design 2009
Off Broadway Awards for Best Design and Music 2010
Two Nominations for Tony Awards; Best Sound Design of a Play and Best Performance by a Leading Actress in a Play

Don John – 2008 – RSC commission, national tour
Directed and adapted by Emma Rice; designed by Vicki Mortimer

The Umbrellas of Cherbourg – 2011 – Gielgud Theatre, West End
Directed and adapted by Emma Rice

The Wild Bride – 2011 – family show, national and international tour
Directed and adapted by Emma Rice

Steptoe and Son – 2012 – co-production with the West Yorkshire Playhouse
Directed and adapted by Emma Rice; designed by Neil Murray

Chapter 5

SUSPECT CULTURE

Clare Wallace

Introduction

During its lifetime Suspect Culture was regularly identified as one of
Scotland's most innovative theatre groups; it was the first (1998/9) –
and for some years the only – Scottish theatre company to be revenue
funded that had contemporary formal innovation at its core. In 2000,
journalist Neil Cooper was to assert that '[n]o company in Britain
captured that state of pre-millennial ennui and ontological flux better
than the Glasgow-based Suspect Culture' (Cooper, 2000). However,
such enthusiasm is somewhat offset by the scarcity of scholarly critical
response to their work and its relative invisibility in publications on
contemporary British theatre to date. One aspect of this disjunction
has been the success of playwright David Greig, one of the company's
founders, which has tended to occlude assessments of Suspect Culture
in its own right. Another has been the company's acceptance of the
ephemeral nature of performance; on the whole, their works were not
conceived of as texts for publication and, while recordings of shows
exist, they are not publicly available. This situation has been partly
remedied by the company's website, and by *The Suspect Culture Book*,
an anthology of articles, interviews and scripts edited by Graham
Eatough and Dan Rebellato published in August 2013. Both sources
are conscious attempts to archive and preserve some traces of Suspect
Culture's history.

One of the most interesting features of Suspect Culture's work was
the effort to navigate between the poles of devised performance and
playwriting. As their website declares, the company was seeded in a
desire to merge new writing with experimental dramaturgy: 'The idea
at the outset was to develop a style of theatre that combined the best of
English and European traditions, working with high quality writing but

giving equal weight to visual and musical elements' (Suspect Culture, 2013). That concept was to take more distinct shape later but, at least initially, both Eatough and Greig were processing the influences of work they had encountered at university while attempting to carve out their own roles as theatre-makers on a minimal budget. With Greig providing the writing energy and Eatough as performer, their first project, *A Savage Reminiscence*, was presented in Bristol in 1990 and then at the Edinburgh Festival Fringe in 1991. It was a pattern repeated the following year when they took a cluster of shows to the festival, including *The Garden*, *And the Opera House Remained Unbuilt* and *Stalinland* (all 1992), all penned by Greig. By 1993, the company's Scottish base had been established, with both Eatough and Greig resident in Glasgow. The reasons for the nascent company's preference for a Scottish home were a blend of personal and professional, not least among them the fact that the Edinburgh Festival Fringe had provided a valuable locus for their early theatre experience. Moreover, Greig has since described how he felt strongly that he needed to be in Scotland to develop as a writer and that as a theatre-maker it was a Scottish audience he first and foremost hoped to address (Fisher, 2011, 17).

The confluence of location and artistic influence is vital to the trajectory Suspect Culture began to take. Orientated not towards the theatre culture of London or the prevailing traditions of British theatre writing, but towards Europe, Suspect Culture gravitated towards Scotland where few other companies were working with such a blend of devising and text, and where cosmopolitan affiliations have habitually been somewhat more welcome, partly as a consequence of the Edinburgh Festival. In retrospect it becomes clear how little they looked to England as a place for their work. Only three of their many shows – *Timeless*, *Mainstream* and *Static* – were taken to London, while a number of others travelled to several cities in the UK as part of tours. This choice only becomes more meaningful with Scottish devolution in the late 1990s and the pro-European momentum of Scottish culture since. Hence, if Suspect Culture's cosmopolitanism was both physical and metaphysical, it was, simultaneously, always deeply rooted in Scotland. There, the company reaped the benefits of the developments in performance spaces in Glasgow – the new Tramway Theatre which had hosted Peter Brook, Robert Lepage and the Wooster Group, and the Arches, a club and performance venue – and developed strong ties with Edinburgh's Traverse Theatre.

This dovetails with the artistic impulses that moved Greig and Eatough in those early years. In various sources, both cite their interest in the work of Bertolt Brecht and, in particular, Howard Barker. During their studies in Bristol, Eatough and Greig, along with Sarah Kane and others, had performed in a production of Barker's play *Victory*. As Eatough puts it, that stimulus appears markedly in Suspect Culture's own early work, having an influence:

> not just on the writing but on what the shows were setting out to achieve, politically and intellectually. What Barker does, whether or not the plays are successful, [is] he scouts out the possibilities for alternative theatre. He neither points towards a mainstream theatre style but nor is he swept up in current avant-garde movements ... And for those who didn't want to leave playwriting behind, Barker was a model for something that could still be radical, which I think was important for David. (Rebellato and Eatough, 2013, 9)

For Greig, as an emerging writer, this came to involve a refusal of English realism and a reaching towards a 'European sensibility' that he found in writers like Barker and Brecht (Billingham, 2007, 79). Less widely documented, but of comparable significance to Eatough's sense of the performing body, was the impact of seeing German choreographer and dancer Pina Bausch's *Café Müller* at the Edinburgh Festival in 1992. Eatough describes how, for him as an actor and later as an artistic director, that show was an epiphany: 'it suddenly opened up different possibilities about what bodies on stage could be and how powerful very simple gestural performance can be' (Rebellato and Eatough, 2013, 12).

Those founding influences set Suspect Culture at odds with the dominant qualities of mainstream British theatre and the preponderance of provocative new plays staged during the 1990s. As Eatough remarks, they 'were always inside and outside' the 'New Writing' category so popularized and endorsed by institutions like the Royal Court Theatre and beyond the UK, the latter often with the aid of the British Council (Eatough, 2013). Less predictably, they also positioned themselves at variance with physical work that dispensed with text altogether. This preservation of a textual point of reference, together with an exploration of the physical resources of performance, became the key to an aesthetic Suspect Culture began to investigate and develop, involving the merging of various elements: music, movement, design and text in a manner described by Dan Rebellato as 'intellectual' and 'minimalist'– qualities that have earned their work both admiration and censure (Rebellato, 2003, 62).

History of Artistic Development and Working Methodologies

Suspect Culture began when Greig and Eatough, both of whom had been students of English and drama at Bristol University, began to make shows together. In that early phase, Greig saw his contribution as devising/directing rather than playwriting, while Eatough was focused on acting. By 1992, however, they had begun to consciously consider the shape their company might take. For Eatough, as already mentioned, this was in terms of an approach to performing while for Greig the positive reception of *Stalinland* at the Edinburgh Festival Fringe – the show won a Fringe First – meant that he gradually began to see himself more in the role of writer.

Following their relocation to Glasgow, Eatough and Greig worked on raising funds for further projects. The first of these was a double-bill titled *Europe*, developed in 1993 and staged at the Arches Theatre in Glasgow in mid-1994. One of the shows, *Stations on the Border* was a devised piece; the other, *Petra's Explanation*, was a play written by Greig that he later revised for TAG (Theatre About Glasgow is the branch of the Citizens Theatre in Glasgow that produces work for young people). The focus upon the changing political geography of Europe that was explored throughout these productions was to gain sharper resolution in their next project, *One Way Street* (1995), a one-man show performed by Eatough. It is at this point that Suspect Culture as a theatre company was professionally established. For Eatough, *One Way Street* launched their 'internationalist agenda' (Rebellato and Eatough, 2013, 14). It was certainly part of a preliminary exploration of a set of interests that is threaded through much of their subsequent work, as well as also being a first step towards recognition and more regular funding.

It is at this point too that the core creative team grew to include designer Ian Scott and composer Nick Powell (who had previously worked on *The Garden* (1992) and *Europe* and whom Greig and Eatough had known at university). They were to collaborate on all Suspect Culture's shows for the next five years, and more intermittently over the years up to 2007. Structurally, the company remained strongly collective throughout its existence. Activities of the main creative group were supported by a small team of administrators who also actively participated in decision making. So, for instance, Pamela Carter worked as Research Associate and Projects Officer between 1998 and 2002, contributing to the creation of *Casanova* (2001) and organizing the Strange Behaviour symposia. Patrick Macklin similarly had a long-term involvement; from 1998 onwards he designed much of the company's production artwork and its website. Nonetheless, it was Eatough, as artistic director from 1995/6 onwards, who was increasingly the public representative for the company as a whole.

Touring was to become a central pillar of their development and practice. They went on to work not only in Scotland, Germany, Italy and Spain, but also in Bulgaria, Brazil, the Czech Republic, Croatia, Canada, England, Greece and Ireland. The topicality of post-Berlin Wall European identities led to British Council support for a tour of *One Way Street* in several cities in former East Germany, and then a workshop in Madrid. As a result of these opportunities the group developed a network of creative associates and collaborators, initially chiefly in Spain and Italy. Important among these were Andrés Lima, Maurício Paroni de Castro, Renato Gabrielli and Sergio Romano. Projects with international associates not only brought experience of non-Anglophone dramaturgies and exchanges of performance practices, but also propagated work that explored communication across cultures and languages: in *Airport* the cast mixed Spanish/ Italian and English; in *The Golden Ass* the protagonist is Portuguese; *A Different Language* is a two-hander in Italian and English.

In tandem with this international cooperation, the company also forged relationships closer to home. In the years up to 2002, a group of performers were regularly involved, including Louise Ludgate, Callum Cuthbertson, Kate Dickie, Paul Thomas Hickey and, later, Paul Blair and Selina Boyack. These actors were instrumental in the devised and non-naturalistic physical vocabularies that became a characteristic of the Suspect Culture performance style and, as Eatough states, they 'became an essential part of the company' (Rebellato and Eatough, 2013, 21). Through Nick Powell, musician Lucy Wilkins was also enlisted as an artistic associate and performer in *Timeless* and *Candide 2000*.

A final facet of the company's distinctive profile was the Strange Behaviour symposia, a sequence of seven that took place between 1998 and 2007. These one-day events drew together an eclectic mixture of participants and speakers, and consisted of workshops, talks and presentations themed around diverse subjects ranging from geography, divinity and mathematics to economics. They proved to be a strategic subsidiary space for the testing of ideas through interdisciplinary debate, at points incorporating participation from some international associates. One of the clear outcomes of Strange Behaviour is the way playwright and scholar, Dan Rebellato (who had known Greig and Eatough at Bristol University), crossed into Suspect Culture space, first through participation in several of the symposia, then as a scholarly interpreter of their work and, finally, as a creative collaborator and artistic associate.

Although not all members of the core team had participated in the bi-lingual project, *The Golden Ass*, in late 2000, a reorientation of the company began in earnest in 2003. In August that year, Greig's play *San Diego* premiered at the Edinburgh International Festival, while Eatough created a devised, music-based show titled *One Two*, with Powell's band OSKAR and Scott's design, for the Fringe Festival at the Traverse. In his process diary on the piece, available on the company's website, Eatough remarks how '[i]t's been an ongoing project to fully integrate music, often played live, into our shows. Despite this ambition it's sometimes frustrating to see it gradually sidelined as a show develops [...]. Here the music is firmly at the centre of the show which balances somewhere between a play and a gig' (Suspect Culture, 2013). Although Greig and Eatough were quick to discount any personal animosity, a divergence in creative direction is readily apparent. Indeed, Eatough's interest in devised performance and visual art becomes pronounced in his later projects such as the installation *Killing Time* (2007), the film *Missing* (2007), and *Stage Fright*, the company's closing exhibition event in 2009. Greig, Eatough, Powell and Scott temporarily regrouped to produce *8000m* (2004), a physical show about climbing Lhotse, the world's fourth highest mountain, a piece that involved performers scaling the Brook Wall at the Tramway. Notwithstanding *8000m*, the competing career currents of each of the four members were now evident. Although Ian Scott continued to contribute to Suspect Culture's stage and lighting design, he had always simultaneously worked widely on many other theatre productions. Nick Powell was busy as a musician, composer and sound designer for companies such as Paines Plough, Improbable and the National Theatre of Scotland. And, by 2004, Greig's growing commitments as a playwright had also tugged him away from the everyday workings of the company. Apart from *Futurology* in 2007, for which he produced the text with Dan Rebellato, Greig's direct involvement with the company ceased at this stage. The remaining shows produced by the company involved other writers: Renato Gabrielli was involved in *A Different Language* (2005), Simon Bent in *The Escapologist* (2006) and Rebellato in *Static* (co-produced by Graeae in 2008). Meanwhile, Suspect Culture's work evolved in an increasingly interdisciplinary fashion beyond theatre. Eatough joined visual artist Graham Fagan to produce *Killing Time*, an event that combined video projections and stage sets inviting viewers to explore ideas on performance, reality and participation. He also wrote and directed his first short film, *Missing*. Pertinently, the company's farewell work, the installation/exhibition *Stage Fright* at Glasgow's Centre for Contemporary Art, also crossed between media to investigate lines of connection between visual art and theatre and notions of 'authenticity, reproduction and the position of the viewer in relation to the work' (Suspect Culture, 2013). Since the dissolution of the company, Eatough's work has continued to move in this direction.

Clearly, what had defined the company at the height of its success was 'a fluid collaborative ethos' among the core creative team, the performers and, periodically, a floating team of associated artists throughout the development process (Eatough, 2013). Work never commenced from a play text or a completed project proposal; instead, brainstorming retreats, workshops and rehearsals were used to develop ideas around themes and images. Sometimes initial workshops took place abroad within the context of a tour; for instance, early ideas for *Casanova* emerged from a workshop organized in Prague while the company was touring *Mainstream*. Similarly, Simon Bent, who was to develop the text for *The Escapologist*, first met Eatough while Suspect Culture was doing a workshop at the National Theatre Studio in London. Accordingly, as Pamela Carter remembers in the process diary on *Mainstream*, 'the development of [...] work is better described as negotiative rather than navigational. The process is digressive and liable to wander, it is informed by a number of voices, and ideas accrue over time in conversation, in workshops and discussions' (Suspect Culture, 2013). That process they came to call the Suspect Culture method, but it remained deliberately loose and flexible.

Following a period of ideas exchange, workshops and exploratory exercises, each of the members of the team would develop his ideas for the show's design, music, physical language or text. With regard to his role, Greig commented that the writing itself was not collaborative: 'What I found was that I liked to work with the actors in the rehearsal room and then I would go away and write at night – I didn't want their words, I wanted them to help me to try to find the right situation' (Billingham, 2007, 74). The same principle applied to the roles of Powell, Scott and Eatough. They then reassembled and revised until the show fell into shape. As Eatough observes, devising continued right up to, and sometimes even after, a show opened (Eatough, 2013). Credit was shared; their interest in the existence of the work as performance, not merely as text, is indicated by the fact that during the company's first phase, only *One Way Street* and *Casanova* appeared in print, the former with no author's name, the latter, titled awkwardly, as 'a David Greig text Suspect Culture's *Casanova*'. Later, during its final phase, and indicative of the changing creative configuration of the company, this contour of its practice was to change with the publication of *The Escapologist*, attributed to Simon Bent but also described on the cover as 'a Suspect Culture stage play', with *Static* more simply credited to Rebellato with the Graeae and Suspect Culture logos.

Static, in particular, is a useful marker of the company's development and endgame. A quirky and clever homage to the resonances of pop music, how it moulds our impressions of the world, generates identities and, perhaps most importantly, makes and releases memories, this play may be correlated with the company's enduring fascination with experiential and emotional soundscapes, as well as with the language of gesture and splintered communication. Written by Rebellato, *Static* was co-directed by Eatough and Jenny Sealey of the London-based company Graeae, whom Eatough had first met back in 2003 and with whom Ian Scott had previously worked on numerous occasions. Graeae's remit, as stated on their website, is to produce performances accessible to people with disabilities and to provide a space for disabled performers. The cooperation between Eatough and Sealey led them to emphasize a shared 'ethos' in using physicality, emotional intensity and simple, yet metaphorically charged, design to draw out the qualities of the script (Graeae Theatre Company, 2013). Consequently, at the hub of the production is an intricate interweaving of spoken and sign language. In an interview with with Maxwell McCarthy, prefacing the published text, Eatough stresses the elements of continuity with Suspect Culture's preceding projects, highlighting the shared themes of loss, communication across languages and the physical idiom the company had developed, which he likens to the aesthetics of sign language (McCarthy, 2008, 11). To a degree, *Static* shares the design minimalism and some of the emotional texture of shows like *Timeless*, *Mainstream* and *Lament*. It is also somewhat reminiscent of the experimental music-narrative fusion of *One Two*. Yet certain details distinguish it as contiguous with the ongoing realignment of the company since 2004. Of the original creative team, only Eatough and Scott remained, although patently Eatough was the guiding force, which had also been the case with *The Escapologist* and, to a lesser extent, *A Different Language*. Perhaps incidentally, Sealey was the first female directorial collaborator (as opposed to performer or musician) to work with the company. Music remains a significant element but, in contrast to *One Two*, *Static*'s soundtrack is a medley of recorded songs around which the stage narrative revolves, rather than an original composition. And finally, while Suspect Culture's work had regularly probed the possibilities of postdramatic or experimentally deconstructed performance, the episodic scenes in *Static* are anchored in a coherent, and arguably quite traditional, sense of character and narrative that unite the action and dialogue, even though at times the alternation between sign and speech in performance presented a challenge to comprehension. *Static* opened in February 2008, and was, like *A Different Language* and *The Escapologist*, successful, although moderately so. However, in March/April 2008 the company's application for Arts Council funding was rejected, so the question as to whether these shows signalled a diminution of the company's energies or a new chapter in its identity was foreclosed.

Funding and Structure

Suspect Culture clearly benefited from the reorganization of the Arts Council of Great Britain which resulted in the establishment of an autonomous Scottish Arts Council (SAC) in April 1994, with a specific remit to develop and sustain the arts nationally. The company was first awarded funding by the SAC in 1995. Their shows between 1995 and 1998 were also enabled through a mixture of commissions, cooperative associations abroad and British Council support – such as tours to Germany, Spain and Italy. The perception of Suspect Culture as flourishing, young and Scottish, yet with international reach and appeal, all key to the strategic priorities of SAC at this point in time, along with the emphasis placed on touring, were among the factors that led to SAC fixed-term funding for four years in 1998. At the time, this generated some disgruntlement, since amid intense competition for resources, established, and overtly political, companies such as Wildcat had their funding cut. Suspect Culture continued to receive funding from the SAC, including a renewal of core funding in 2004/5, signalling a continued commitment to the company's role in the national theatre culture (Scottish Arts Council, 2010). Yet already it was clear that a considerable shortfall in available funding implied that cuts were imminent. Originally, in early 2004, the Council informed the eight non-building-based companies (among them Suspect Culture) that their core grants could only be guaranteed until 2005, rather than 2006 as planned, before managing to supplement the expected deficit with unallocated funds. In 2006 plans for Creative Scotland, a new body that would replace the SAC and Screen Scotland in 2010, were announced giving rise to considerable debate about the future of arts support. Despite this institutional and financial turbulence, Suspect Culture continued to be supported by the SAC-administered National Lottery Distribution Fund until the end of 2008, and received grant support for *Stage Fright*. Throughout its existence, Suspect Culture used a co-production model for all its work, depending on partnerships and sponsorships that extended beyond the support base provided by SAC funds.

As is to be expected after more than a decade of interaction with funding bodies including the British Council and the SAC, by 2008 Suspect Culture's artistic policy had settled into a cluster of clearly expressed principal values. Four branches of this policy had grown through practice from the company's early years including: a commitment to collaboration, internationalism, interdisciplinarity and interpretation. As has already been discussed, these values had a direct and ongoing impact on the company's working methodologies, even before they came to be articulated so precisely.

To some extent it might be asserted that the company evolved in response to the requirements of funding bodies to combine inter-nationalism with community-orientated projects, and to extend the framework of activities beyond the performance itself. That impetus can be seen in the participation of young people in works such as *Local* (1998) and *Candide 2000* (discussed below). *Local* was produced in collaboration with the Tramway and Castlemilk Video Workshop, and supported by Barclays PLC. It involved 11 workshops with teenagers who helped to devise and perform a show about their experiences of Glasgow. Similarly, *The Golden Ass* was produced in association with the Tron Theatre and the Gorbals Initiative, and involved workshops with eight people from the James Shields Project for young homeless people in Glasgow. All three projects were positively received. The significance of such outreach activities is also manifest in the discursive and workshop events surrounding the National Theatre of Scotland's co-production of *Futurology* (to be discussed further below) and *Static*, which was supported by Arts Council England.

SAC evaluations of *One Two* (2003), *8000m* (2004), *A Different Language* (2005), *Futurology* (2007) and *Static* (2008) provide some insights into the perceived effectiveness of these projects and their realization – audits were generally positive, with the marked exception of *Futurology*. The unfavourable assessment of *Futurology* had a strong impact on the company's application for Flexible Funding in November

2007. Notably, the lead officer advising on the application had also been one of the evaluators of *Futurology*. While the assessors' report on the request acknowledged the strength of the company's 'artistic vision, effective governance, a commitment to engagement via its Interpretation Programme and [that it] has developed its financial planning and management' (Scottish Arts Council, 2008, 1), it listed a number of reservations. First, the report notes that, despite the vibrancy of its interdisciplinarity, the proposed project with visual artist Graham Fagan would not qualify for funding under the scheme. Second, it expressed concerns about future partnerships that were largely in negotiation or unspecified. In addition, it was felt that the proposal lacked strong marketing ideas. Third and perhaps most significant, were doubts about the quality and reach of the proposed work in the light of the company's past record: 'It was felt that the work of the company had been variable in quality. The company was in danger of becoming repetitive. Some thought that there was a gap between what the company promised and what it achieved on stage. Some of the work lacks the intellectual depth and rigour that it aspires to' (Scottish Arts Council, 2008, 2). In conclusion, the assessors intimated that perhaps the company had run its course and that Eatough's artistic work would have space to grow in other environments. Yet, as Trish Reid shrewdly observes, other less immediately visible factors were involved (Reid, 2008, 401). In her view, Suspect Culture finally fell victim to changing tastes and priorities. In the fierce competition for shrinking funds, the National Theatre of Scotland now occupied pride of place in the exporting of Scottish theatre, in the fostering of international cooperation and in the queue for national funding.

Key Works

One Way Street *(1995)*

One Way Street was inspired by the confluence of Greig and Eatough's interest in psychogeography, in particular in Walter Benjamin's *One Way Street* (1928) and *A Berlin Chronicle* (1932), by the transformative energies of post-Communist Europe, and by Greig's experience of interrailing on the continent in the early 1990s. Greig describes how he and Eatough had 'become seduced by Walter Benjamin's idea of "drawing a map of your life" and [...] wanted to make a play which somehow was both a map and theatre at the same time' (Greig and

Eatough, 1998, 227). Performed first at the Traverse in Edinburgh, with Eatough in the role of the protagonist John Flannery, *One Way Street* is a seminal work in Suspect Culture's development, because of the ways in which it unites these points of reference with a gestural language and a methodology they would hone in the years to come. In a prefacing note on the text, Greig emphasizes that the play is not his work, but rather the outcome of a month of collaborative exploration followed by a period of writing and then a month of rehearsal during which the text was shaped around the performance. In consequence, he stresses that *One Way Street* is 'a piece of theatre first, and a text second' (Greig and Eatough, 1998, 227).

'Psychogeography is', as Merlin Coverly suggests, 'the point at which psychology and geography collide, a means of exploring the behavioural impact of urban place' (Coverly, 2006, 10), and following this line, *One Way Street* explores 'personal history as geography' (Suspect Culture, 2013). Flannery, an Englishman in Berlin, has been commissioned to produce a tourist guide, 'Ten Short Walks in the Former East', but finds himself continuously transgressing. He is distracted by quintessentially psychogeographical preoccupations: urban wandering, remembering and mapping the personal and historical associations of location. The result is that, despite the very specific locations listed for the proposed walks ranging from Prenzlauerberg to Alexanderplatz, the identity of place is destabilized and chronology is distorted in the stream of consciousness flow of observations and memories. The history of Berlin becomes contiguous with his youth in the UK and experiences in the German capital, creating a palimpsest of private and public histories. Walter Benjamin's idea of the map of life is ironically hailed as Flannery, after a night of drinking, contemplates a pool of his own vomit:

> My sick has made a little puke map of my life. [...] That's home, all warm, all pink in the potato hills of Lancashire ... a little carroty college, German language and literature department to the south ... a bile dribbling line of the route to Berlin. And there she is. The black stout splash is Greta's flat ... (Greig and Eatough, 1998, 246)

The nature of what Mauricio Paroni de Castro describes as *One Way Street*'s attempted 'emotional cartography' is comically obvious here (Paroni de Castro, 2013, 58). Place is experientially portrayed as a mixture of layered and mingled realities, past and present, rather than a stable, objectively known setting to be rationally navigated.

Displacement is a key quality to *One Way Street*'s approach;

repeatedly Flannery asks 'Where are we? [...] How did we get here?' (Greig and Eatough, 1998, 235). The performance is divided into ten sections corresponding to the proposed tourist guide, and in each Flannery is shown in the process of researching the project, interacting with Berliners and with his own past, as well as incorporating his editor's displeasure at the result. On the stage floor, a huge road sign marks out different routes, an image used also for the show's posters.

The layering of history, memory and emotion is paired with the idea of possible routes not only through a place, but also through life, and is underscored by Eatough's performance of the multiple voices in the piece. The force of these themes, the minimal stage design and Eatough's work with stylized, repeated movement led *Scotsman* reviewer Joyce McMillan to conclude that, with *One Way Street*, the company

> had found the intellectual and emotional content to match [their] style: the political geography of a new Europe that was unifying, converging, removing barriers to movement and communication; and – most importantly – the emerging emotional geography of a world where a new intensity of communication, and similarity of urban experience across the globe, did not seem to deliver love, fulfilment, or a true sense of connection with other people. (McMillan, 2013, 44)

As a company, Suspect Culture had begun to stake out its identity.

Airport *(1996/7)*

Although, unsurprisingly, Suspect Culture's interest in the changing territory of the new Europe diminished after the mid-1990s, displacement, situation and the emotional geography of place remained a source of inspiration and experiment. As Greig has remarked in interview, '*Airport* was almost the archetypal transnational play. It contains ... all the themes ... that Suspect Culture went back to' (Fisher, 2011, 14). It is also an 'archetypal' Suspect Culture work in the sense that it developed from the international context in which they found themselves, and from their interest in communication within such contexts. Greig goes on to assert that '[a] play like *Airport* only exists because we went to Spain and decided to try and create a play in two languages and set it in an airport. [...] We were inter-ested in the strangeness that two people from so far apart could be so similar in their middle-class cosmopolitanism' while, at the same time, 'adopt[ing] the surface clichés of their identities in these moments of meeting' (Fisher, 2011, 19–20).

Airport itself is the product of a moment of meeting, though of a less transient nature. Begun in Madrid as a result of workshops at the Cuarta Pared and at the Fundación Olivar de Castillejo where the group explored questions of identity, performance practices and language barriers, the show initiated many of Suspect Culture's transnational, creative relationships. Three of the Spanish actors who had participated in the workshop in Madrid performed in the opening run at the Tramway in Glasgow. Later, following a further workshop led by Eatough, the play was presented at the British Council-sponsored Scotfest in Milan, with Italian performers.

Airport unpacks experiences of identity in a globalized world; its characters encounter each other in an airport and try to communicate in either the language of uncannily shared memories or in the language of clichéd national stereotypes. As Eatough remembers, they found themselves 'drawn to the spaces that you'd associate with global economies: retail spaces, entertainment spaces, travel spaces' (Rebellato and Eatough, 2013, 15). In his 2003 essay on Suspect Culture, Rebellato persuasively views this aspect of their work through the lens of anthropologist Marc Augé's seminal work on 'non-places.' For Augé, 'non-places' are disconnected from the usual co-ordinates that make locations meaningful; they are places through which one moves, not places where one settles or resides. Consequently 'a person entering the space of non-place is relieved of his usual determinants. He becomes no more than what he does or experiences in the role of passenger, customer or driver' (Augé, 1995, 103). Above all, these are places where personal identity is loosened but where behaviour, nevertheless, is scripted. A consciousness of this is physically rendered in *Airport* through the use of choreographed movements repeated by the performers.

The potential sterility of the non-place is signalled by the minimalism of Scott's stage design for the show, which is dominated by two conveyor belts, a tiled floor and strip lighting. The natural world and memories of it in the shape of the moon, a sunset and a tree intervene in this mechanized space, through the use of projection upstage between the conveyor belts. Similarly, the exchanges between performers suggest a dissonance between, as Marilena Zaroulia notes, 'mobility and belonging', but also between solitude and similitude (Zaroulia, 2013a, 48). *Airport* probes spaces of possibility where the behavioural scripts of the non-place are deconstructed and the default settings of commodified identities therein are tested, even when communication within them is flawed or failed. Whereas the exchange of national stereotypes signals the empty interactions acceptable and expected in this mechanized space, the fact that several of the characters fail to move appropriately through it to some destination (one perpetually misses his flight home, for instance) points to a human flaw in the mechanism. As Eatough describes, 'what these environments give you dramatically is the antagonist, in a sense; they are environments in which it's very difficult to get a meaningful human exchange, or maybe you do in unexpected, slightly perverse … or comic ways' (Rebellato and Eatough, 2013, 15). And it is this sense of possibility, indeterminate as it may be, that underwrites Rebellato's claim that Suspect Culture's work is characterized by a utopian dimension (Rebellato, 2003, 61–80).

Timeless *(1997)*

That utopianism is still more palpable in their next project, *Timeless*, which was commissioned by Brian McMaster for the Edinburgh International Festival and was first performed at the Gateway Theatre in Edinburgh and later at the Tramway in Glasgow and the Donmar Warehouse in London. Following *One Way Street* and *Airport*, Suspect Culture's work moves away from the conventions of character and plot, and towards figures and scenarios derived from the experiences of the group explored through devising and workshopping. If self in *Airport* is disjunctive, oscillating between the broadest of national stereotypes and shared human emotions, generic and specific, then, with *Timeless*, the company continues with a postdramatic exploration of the effacement of character, dispersed impressions of self in performance, and a turn towards a theatre of states rather than action, in which music plays a central role.

As Eatough recalls, the catalyst for *Timeless* was formal experiment and 'the basic idea was to structure three acts around three movements in a piece of music and to integrate the action with the music rather than just have it as a kind of accompaniment' (Rebellato and Eatough, 2013, 16). The three main strands in the process of the work's development were physical, musical and textual. Eatough worked with choreographer Nisha Kumar; Powell with violinist Lucy Wilkins, and musicians Ruth Gottlieb, Rebecca Ware and Jo Richards; and Greig with the text. Uniting these elements was 'the idea of four characters that mirrored the four musicians in the quartet' (Rebellato and Eatough, 2013, 16).

Described enthusiastically by Neil Cooper as 'a late twentieth-century *fin-de-siècle* epic about friendship and all the littler epiphanies that bind people', *Timeless*, then, melds music and memory, nostalgia and speculation, melancholy and longing (Cooper, 2013, 51). The piece presents four friends, Ian, Martin, Veronica and Stella, at three moments in their relationship, labelled present, past and future. They are drawn together by shared moments in the past that they describe as 'timeless'. Primary among these experiences is one that gradually gathers epiphanic significance for all four – an evening picnic on a beach, which may or may not have happened as they remember it. Their story is a slight one with neither climax nor progress; their characters are elliptical, disturbingly needy, hesitant and incomplete. Echoing the string quartet's role in chamber music, the playing and replaying of versions of this story is contained in three movements, the versions taking on different meanings, acquiring alternate nuances. Thus, in each act each character interacts with the others, sometimes as a group, sometimes in pairs, but also performs a monologue solo. 'Throughout, certain motifs lend a sense of poetic unity and continuity where the usual dramatic signposts are lacking – the repetition of the words 'poignant', 'serene,' 'inevitable', 'pornographic'; images of birds in flight, lungs contracting, skin shedding; and phrases that signal a shared, personal language. These are twinned by physical motifs – each of the four performers repeats particular gestures and expressions across the different scenarios – and key images – sitting together or alone at a bar table, lighting candles, checking reflections – that develop the show's evocative yet elliptical texture.

The question of whether any of this adds up to anything hovers above the exchanges even from the first act: as Ian says '[e]ven pictures that don't come out capture something'; by contrast, Veronica questions whether framing a failed photo merely results in 'a frame around nothing' (Rebellato and Eatough, 2013, 143). In the third act, a projection into the future, each character individually imagines an idealized reunion with the others and in doing so they betray both their insecurities and their fantasies. A nagging sense of absence and insufficiency curls through these scenarios. The longing to 'say the perfect thing' brings forth a banal substitute 'Blah, blah, blah' (Rebellato and Eatough, 2013, 174), vividly suggesting the utopian impossibility of pinning down that ideal communication. The movement of the closing scene of *Timeless* comes to orbit a shared imagined perfect moment, despite the ruins of fantasy scattered about:

The beach we went to that one time.
We bought pakora from the shop.
Got pissed and watched the sun go down.
And even though it was just some fucking picnic,
Something happened to us all.

(Rebellato and Eatough, 2013, 182)

This refrain is laced through the characters' speeches, repeated five times in choral unison becoming a stable theme amidst the uncertainties, failures and speculative projections that make up the piece. *Timeless* experiments with displacing plot and character in favour of musical movements along the lines of the allegro, minuet and rondo sequence for classical string quartet compositions, as well as the structural use of polyphony and counterpoint; the result is character as instrument, plot as musical form and speech shot through with poetic textual effects (Wallace, 2013, 25).

Candide 2000 *(2000)*

In some respects *Candide 2000* revisits Suspect Culture's exploration of the non-place but on a grander scale: 'We were very interested in the juxtaposition of the surface of modern life and modern environments with the humanity inside them: what people want to achieve, what they are able to achieve, what isn't permitted in these environments', Eatough explains (Rebellato and Eatough, 2013, 15). This is overtly and provocatively realized in their postmodern version of Voltaire's classic picaresque satire on the philosophy of optimism that again used onstage musicians to craft a soundscape, amplifying the satire and aurally signalling prolepsis and ellipsis, jumps forward and gaps in the action. Candide's world-roaming adventure is transplanted to the precincts of a shopping centre, a contemporary consumer paradise, which contains the world condensed in simulated forms. Colin, an employee in one of the fast food chains there, is the modern day Candide who encounters other revamped characters from the novel. The passivity of Candide's oft-repeated motto in Voltaire's novella that he exists in 'the best of all possible worlds' becomes the equally docile acquiescence of the twenty-first century consumer.

Two aspects of *Candide 2000* make it noteworthy in the company's development. The first is that it was their first large project with non-professional actors. Though obviously the text of *Candide 2000* is constructed with reference to the schema provided by Voltaire, a further inspiration, for Eatough in particular, was the work of Belgian theatre-maker Alain Platel, who controversially mixes professional and non-professional performers on stage. Platel provided Eatough with a model that 'challenged you to do work that was *better* because it had the involvement of these young, non-professional actors' (Rebellato and Eatough, 2013, 22). As already mentioned, in 1998 the company had made *Local*, a devised show with young people from Glasgow; *Candide 2000* constituted a more concerted and ambitious attempt to integrate this type of outreach with their work to date. In the eight months before opening, the company worked with groups of young people from each of the tour cities (Glasgow, Newcastle, Aberdeen, Inverness and Edinburgh) to develop the show and to recruit a cast for the teen chorus that would perform with five professional actors in the final work; the resulting production was generally well received and deemed a success.

The second striking aspect of the piece is the unambivalently critical attitude towards the values and codes of behaviour authorized and encouraged within the confines of the consumerist non-place. As Rebellato observes, throughout *Candide 2000* the utopia of consumerism is ruthlessly satirized (Rebellato, 2003, 75–6). While previously the company had concealed such value judgements and the political positioning they imply, here there is little doubt. 'To think the world is not as it should be, to be angry, is to start to think politically', Greig remarks in an essay on the show titled 'Optimism' (Suspect Culture, 2013). While the issue of political engagement is one Greig has pondered a great deal in his solo work, it only sporadically makes such open appearances in Suspect Culture's projects.

Lament *(2002)*

According to Eatough, *Lament* arose from the company's 'desire to do a political show' (Rebellato and Eatough, 2013, 26), yet there are few similarities with the openly sardonic tone and loosely narrative progression of *Candide 2000*. Formally, with its episodic arrangement of fragments of dreamed, projected and remembered selves, it follows on from *Mainstream* (1999), which played extensively on physical and verbal repetition. The space of the exploration is 'between the personal and the political', but also between the present and the absent and 'the heartfelt nostalgia we feel today for a world that perhaps never existed', as stated on the company's website (Suspect Culture, 2013).

Suspect Culture's conscious presentation of *Lament* as 'a poem for the theatre' invites reflection upon the nature of the poetics of the performance. Drawing on the textual, musical and spoken dimensions of lament, the show attempted to accommodate its various resonances, from the expression of grief, to complaint, anger and petition. It did so using music, a chorus of voices and a web of associations charting the process of lamentation from knowingly naïve remembrances to melancholy regret to keen anguish, while raising the question of the mutation, transformation and disappearance of such cultural patterns in a contemporary context.

Juxtaposition, metaphor, metonymy, synecdoche, cadence and cacophony are among the prominent structuring devices used. Nick Powell has described the soundscape for the show as composed of contrasting and opposing elements: 'I wanted the technical side to sound very electronic and in your face, like a barrage of technology. But the piano music is very simple to express something sad and true. In the end the piano music is quite bittersweet and emotional' (McMillan, 2002a). The opening collage of material presented on video provides the motifs that are played and replayed throughout. In the subsequent 'maelstrom' section, a rapid juxtaposition of fragmented scenes and images swirls and builds to a crescendo finally halted by a prayerful silence. In the next phase of the performance, each motif expands into its own stanza-scenario. Repetition intermittently provides a cadence between the 16 stanzas: a discussion of apricots recurs in different scenarios, mutating from a central part of a humble primitive community's diet to a fad food in a TV comedy, to the focus for bitter nostalgia in a war-ravaged country. Similarly, the scent and taste of ripe tomatoes recurs as a sensory metonym for lost plenitude and communion with nature. Conjoining these image nodes is a multifaceted thematic of loss expressed through a series of contexts that metaphorically point towards a broad critique of contemporary globalized society: primitive communities invaded by Western consumerism, languages on the verge of extinction, endangered species, exploitative tourism and war. These major political issues are interleaved with intensely personal experiences of alienation, longing and grief. The effect is to collapse any neat space of judgement or safe objectivity.

In *Lament*, memory and nostalgia are ambushed by sentimentality and inarticulacy. The performers cannot fully conjure up the idyllic organic communities and stable values of the past. The representation of lost or dying traditions – be they farming, hunting or storytelling – is frequently arrested by the absence of sufficient vocabulary, gaps that may be the result of the erosion of memory or the imperfections of fantasy. The consciously flawed expression of personal, philosophical and political despair functions as an act of necessarily incomplete public validation of that which has been lost and is being lost. The use of mixed media, personal narration seeded in the performers' experiences, fragments of cultural reference and episodic structure make *Lament* an ambivalent and contradictory project that, on the one hand, enacts an implicitly political resistance to comfortable dramatic resolution, while on the other, threatens to get lost in its own mournful frustration (Wallace, 2013, 28–30).

Futurology *(2007)*

Some of the issues that fed into *Futurology* had been percolating through the Strange Behaviour symposia since 2004: money, geography, futures thinking and theatre. As Eatough notes, he was motivated by 'an ambition that we would involve all of the company's many artistic associates … and we'd find a form that could involve them all' (Rebellato and Eatough, 2013, 29). Gradually, after a number of workshops first in Florence, then in Glasgow, in 2006 the company had produced an outline of a show and invited contributions from their nine international associates. Throughout 2006, three further workshops took place concluding with the planned structure and script co-written by Greig and Rebellato.

Produced in cooperation with the National Theatre of Scotland and the Brighton Festival, *Futurology* expanded into a major project (Suspect Culture's biggest), embracing politics in a much more direct manner that departed from the company's previously dominant postdramatic aesthetic. Expectations of the production ran high, boosted by the launch of a blog on futurology in 2006 and publicity by the National Theatre of Scotland. Workshops with Jennifer Edgar and Gareth Nicholls in each of the cities in the run, a lengthy information pack and a filmed interview with Graham Eatough supplemented the show itself. Replacing the melancholic and personal dimensions of *Lament*, *Futurology: A Global Revue* opted for comedy and cabaret to explore the global problem of climate change. The show was structured around the premise of a conference on climate crisis, and incorporated an international cast of performers as world leaders and regional representatives who deliver speeches, songs, dance, contortionist tricks and sketches. What it attempted to capture is the absurdity of human lack of action on our rapidly changing environment. *Futurology* shares something of the spirit of raucous satire that typified *Candide 2000*. However, the scale and variety of the revue format, along with the range of ideas that had emerged over the development process, meant that it struggled with its own polymorphousness, and the company's practice of devising right up to and after the opening of a show proved much less feasible. Two independent assessments for the SAC remarked upon the weakness of the script and how the potential of the subject matter was diminished by the stereotypical characters, the slapstick humour and an overly ambitious mixture of styles that failed to cohere (Lumsden, 2007; Patience, 2007). *Futurology* played at conference centres in Glasgow, Edinburgh and Aberdeen in April 2007 before continuing to the Brighton Festival. As both Eatough and Greig have noted, the tour venues proved to be a serious stumbling block (Eatough, 2013; Fisher, 2011, 28). Initially, they had been 'interested in the arid and inhumane nature of the conference centre' for use in the performance, but the fact that such spaces (arguably again, non-spaces) were 'not made for emotional connection' was detrimental once the show took a revue format (Eatough, 2013). While acknowledging its flaws, Eatough remains convinced of the tone of the piece, arguing that the 'overwhelming sense of political frustration that we'd looked at in other shows was maybe never better expressed' (Rebellato and Eatough, 2013, 31). Greig is more candid about his sense of failure and went on to write a miniature play, *Kyoto* (2009), in an effort to redeem some of its subject matter (Wallace, 2013, 68–9).

Critical Reception

Reception of Suspect Culture's work falls into two spheres that will be discussed separately here: reviews and articles in the media, and scholarly work. Surveying the former, it becomes clear that although there is much agreement about the value of Suspect Culture as one of Scotland's main experimental companies in the 1990s and 2000s, responses to their shows consistently ranged across a broad spectrum from laudatory to ambivalent.

While, understandably, the company's website archive cites positive reviews of each show, further scrutiny reveals more mixed, at times starkly polarized, reactions. A vivid case in point can be found in the reviews for *Lament*. For *Guardian* reviewer Elisabeth Mahoney, '*Lament* is another example of Suspect Culture's ability to discard many dramatic clichés to access a raw emotional landscape we rarely see in contemporary theatre' (Mahoney, 2002). Joyce McMillan flagged the show's political orientation, suggesting that, even though some may perceive the work as not political enough or even as self-indulgent, it 'begins to mark out a whole new slice of postmodern space, both in Suspect Culture's work and in Scottish theatre' (McMillan, 2002b). However, these are counterpointed by much more negative impressions: Thelma Good for the *Edinburgh Guide* was deeply unimpressed, finding the show confusing and unconvincing and betrayed by a 'lack of solid purpose' (2002), while Canadian reviewer Rebecca Caldwell felt that although 'terrifically ambitious', ultimately *Lament* was 'a triumph of style over substance' (2003). Similarly, the SAC assessments of *8000m* by Magdalena Schamberger and Jon Pope were strongly positive (both 2004), and Mark Brown in the *Sunday Herald* described it as a 'coup de théâtre' (2004). By contrast Mark Fisher, a critic usually much more sympathetic to Suspect Culture than Brown, found it banal and literal (2004). Responses to *The Escapologist* also ranged from dismissive to moderately positive. British Theatre Guide reviewer Ged Quayle felt that the connections between Freud and Houdini were laboured, and dismissed it with 'a half-hearted shrug' (2006). Mark Fisher in the *Guardian*, Steve Cramer in *The List* and Sarah Jones in the *Independent* (all 2006) were all modestly generous in their assessments. At the other end of the spectrum, confirmed Suspect Culture advocate Neil Cooper found that '[b]eyond the text's initial understated banality ... lies a brooding, slow burning meditation on the truths and illusions of self-definition' that becomes 'thrillingly expansive' (2006). With *Futurology*, such critical discord reached a higher pitch. Both Mark Fisher (2007) and Joyce McMillan (2007) offered qualified praise largely on the grounds of intention and effort. The evaluations by the Arts Council representatives Jaine Lumsden and Alexandria Patience were, however, very critical of the gap between the potential of the project and the quality of the outcome (Lumsden, 2007; Patience, 2007). Less restrained still was Mark Brown's review in the *Telegraph* which slated the show's lack of coherence and concluded that *Futurology* was 'simply a lumbering, predictable, desperately unfunny white elephant of a production' (2007). Finally, *Static* was commended for the strength of the soundtrack and inclusive agenda, but faulted on characterization. Andrew Haydon's positive evaluation in the *Financial Times* (2008) was matched by Mark Brown's panning of the play in the *Telegraph* (2008). An issue that emerged in several reviews concerned the intelligibility of the performance with its mix of sign, speech and music. In the *Scotsman*, Joyce McMillan, who was typically quite supportive of the company's work, was lukewarm: 'The plays swithers between looking at loss, deafness as a metaphor for death, and music as a metaphor for life, ending up saying not much about any of them. Technically interesting for its use of movement, but flawed' (McMillan, 2008).

What emerges from even such a partial overview is the active and predominantly astute appraisal of the company's work, in particular in the Scottish media, by critics such as Joyce McMillan, Neil Cooper, Thelma Good and Mark Fisher. While convinced of Suspect Culture's importance to Scottish theatre, reviewers generally maintained a sense of judgement, and critical dissonance was a consistent characteristic of this aspect of the company's reception. Moreover, this is not necessarily something the company shied away from. As suggested by Graham Eatough himself, most of the company's work 'intentionally sought out a complicated response' (Eatough, 2013) and by and large this is precisely what it generated.

The scholarly reactions to Suspect Culture's work have been much more intermittent. While there has been a growing interest in David Greig as a playwright, there has been a dearth of work that has focused on Suspect Culture. Dan Rebellato was the first to provide a detailed, theoretically inflected analysis of the company's projects in an article titled '"And I Will Reach Out my Hand with a Kind of Infinite Slowness and Say the Perfect Thing": The Utopian Theatre of Suspect Culture' published in 2003. In that article he described the company's approach as utopian, finely tracing the influence of German philosopher, Theodor Adorno's writings, in particular *Negative Dialectics* (1966), on Greig and Eatough's thinking. Rebellato's evaluation of Suspect Culture concentrates on the political reverberations of the work, an issue he continues to explore within the broader spectrum of his research on globalization and the ways it has changed what it might mean to write politically. As Eatough has remarked, 'We felt a lack of confidence about making seemingly straightforward political statements in theatre and simple political statements in general at that time. They didn't seem to ring true anymore' (Rebellato and Eatough, 2013, 16). Yet, Rebellato vigorously refutes the charge that Suspect Culture's work up to 2002 was somehow apolitical or apathetic, arguing that they emerged at what is now perceived as a point of transition, away from older modes of bringing theatre and politics into relation (Rebellato, 2003, 61–80).

In a chapter on Suspect Culture in my study of David Greig's theatre, I framed their projects with reference to Hans-Thies Lehmann's understanding of the aesthetic of the postdramatic (Wallace, 2013, 16–30). Lehmann delineates an aesthetic that offers many tools for understanding the deconstruction of dramatic conventions often found in contemporary theatre, specifically in its attitudes to performance, text, space, time, the body and media. Suspect Culture's work with repetition, fragmentation, sound and image are richly illustrative of some aspects of the tendencies Lehmann describes, and again aligns the company with more continental attitudes to theatre and performance. Perhaps most critically evocative is the way Lehmann outlines this aesthetic in contemporary theatre as engaging with 'a politics of perception', an analysis that I would suggest might further expand Rebellato's interpretation of Suspect Culture's political achievements (Lehmann, 2006, 185).

Other scholars have occasionally highlighted elements of specific works. Peter Zenzinger (2005) treats *One Way Street* in terms of European identities, but more problematically identifies the play as simply the work of David Greig. Marilena Zaroulia's work on mobility and globalization considers *One Way Street*'s 'way of representing human interaction beyond culture and nations, thus indicating how small, lived experiences might offer a way of transgressing – even momentarily – the most enduring ideological, socio-political and cultural borders' (Zaroulia, 2013b, 193). Transnational experience also guides Anja Müller's (2011) reflections on the ethics of identity and the workings of cosmopolitanism in *Casanova*. The characteristic that unites, but also limits, these various analyses (my own included) is that they tend to be subordinated to considerations of Greig's work as a playwright, rather than attempts to position Suspect Culture as a collaborative creative venture.

In addition to these publications, a concise descriptive overview of the company's work and methods is provided by Kristen A. Crouch in the *Columbia Encyclopedia of Modern Drama* (2007, 1308–9); also brief, though more illuminating, is an interview with Greig in *Trans-global Readings: Crossing Theatrical Boundaries*, which gives an account of the company's practices (Wright, 2003, 157–160). Responding to news of the termination of the company's funding, Trish Reid gave an energetic defence of their achievements in the 'Backpages' of *Contemporary Theatre Review* (Reid, 2008, 398–401). That said, the most potentially enriching contribution to the scant discourse surrounding the company is the volume edited by Graham Eatough and Dan Rebellato titled *The Suspect Culture Book* (2013). This book, in a sustained act of self-presentation, collects not only the texts of *Mainstream*, *Timeless* and *Lament*, but also a selection of contributions principally from the members and artistic associates of the company. The extended interview with Eatough, remarkably the first of its kind in print, offers many valuable insights into his perception of the company's identity and progress. The anthology closes with an essay by Rebellato providing a detailed historical overview of the company. Built upon his earlier work concerning politics and utopianism, he goes on with characteristic acuity to analyse the later works through to *Stage Fright*. The only drawback is that his multiple roles as critic, collaborator and chronicler ultimately leave him with the unenviable task of accounting for and assessing his own contributions to the company's oeuvre. Nevertheless, in conjunction with the company's website, these resources may finally catalyse greater recognition and further exploration of the role played by Suspect Culture within British theatre and performance culture in the 1990s and 2000s.

List of Productions

1990 *Savage Reminiscence*
Text: David Greig
Bristol University

1991 *And the Opera House Remained Unbuilt*
Text: David Greig
Bristol University

1992 *The Garden*
Text: David Greig
Bristol University

1992 *Stalinland*
Direction and Text: David Greig
Theatre Zoo, Edinburgh

1993 *An Audience with Satan* based on Tony Parker's *Life After Life*
Performers: Graham Eatough and Alan Wilkins

1994 *Europe* double bill:
Stations on the Border devised by company
Petra's Explanation
Text: David Greig
The Arches, Glasgow

1995 *One Way Street*
Direction and Text: David Greig
Performer: Graham Eatough
Traverse Theatre, Edinburgh

1996/7 *Airport*
Direction: David Greig and Graham Eatough
Text: David Greig
Edinburgh (co-commission Tramway, Glasgow and Traverse Edinburgh)

1997 *Timeless*
Direction: Graham Eatough
Text: David Greig
Tramway, Glasgow

1998 *Local*
Direction: Graham Eatough
Text: David Greig
Tramway, Glasgow

1999 *Mainstream*
Direction: Graham Eatough
Text: David Greig
MacRobert, Stirling

2000 *Candide 2000*
Direction: Graham Eatough
Text: David Greig
Fruitmarket and Royal Lyceum, Edinburgh

2000 *The Golden Ass*
Direction: Mauricio Paroni di Castro and Graham Eatough
Text: Mauricio Paroni di Castro
Tron, Glasgow

2001 *Casanova*
Direction: Graham Eatough
Text: David Greig
Tron, Glasgow

2002 *Lament*
Direction: Graham Eatough
Text: David Greig
Tron, Glasgow

2003 *One Two*
Direction and Text: Graham Eatough
Traverse, Edinburgh

2004 *8000m*
Direction: Graham Eatough
Text: David Greig
Tramway, Glasgow

2005 *A Different Language*
Direction: Graham Eatough
Text: Renato Gabrielli
Tron, Glasgow

2006 *The Escapologist*
Direction: Graham Eatough
Text: Simon Bent
Tramway, Glasgow

2007 *Killing Time*
Event/Installation: Graham Eatough and Graham Fagan
Curation: Katrina Brown
Dundee Contemporary Arts

2007 *Futurology*
Direction: Graham Eatough
Text: David Greig and Dan Rebellato
SECC, Glasgow

2007 *Missing*
Film
Direction and Text: Graham Eatough

2008 *Static*
Direction: Graham Eatough and Jenny Sealey (Graeae theatre company,
London)
Text: Dan Rebellato
Tron, Glasgow

2009 *Stage Fright*
Exhibition
Contributors: Luke Collins, Graham Eatough, David Greig, Patrick
Macklin, Sharon Smith and Felicity Croydon (Max Factory), Nick
Powell and Jonny Dawe (OSKAR) and Dan Rebellato
Centre of Contemporary Arts, Glasgow

Chapter 6

STAN'S CAFE

Marissia Fragkou

Since the early 1990s, the prolific Birmingham-based theatre group Stan's Cafe has built a reputation for artistic innovation that stretches beyond UK borders. Its projects range across theatre, film and live art, and have been presented in a wide range of spaces, with inventive and critical uses of scenography and technology. While articulating a strong interest in global concerns, its work is often underpinned by a local remit; this dual focus on the local and the global chimes with its environmental ethic, visible in its practice and process. The group has also produced an extensive educational portfolio, working closely with children, adolescents and university students.

Stan's Cafe's 'brandless brand' (Yarker, 2008a) ethos resists the ways in which the theatre industry and the academy categorize artistic work, and this can partly account for the sporadic academic attention it has so far received. Through mapping the company's diverse working practices and aesthetics, this chapter aspires to bridge this gap, drawing attention to Stan's Cafe's uncompromised style and innovative methods, as well as its international reach. It will further examine how the company's stylistic experiments and uses of theatricality match an often explicit political engagement with contemporary reality, encompassing concerns about 'home' and the global.

History of the Company's Artistic Development and Methodology

Stan's Cafe is a non-profit theatre company founded in 1991 by James Yarker and Graeme Rose (both graduates of Lancaster University), which operates under Yarker's artistic directorship. In 1995, Rose formed another theatre company, The Resurrectionists, but has maintained his affiliation to Stan's Cafe as an associate artist and leader in education projects. Craig Stephens, the company's associate director, has also performed in most of their shows. The company employs a number of freelance staff, including actors, composers, photographers and technicians; long-term devisers and performers include Amanda Hadingue, Heather Burton, Gerald Bell, Bernadette Russell, Sarah Archdeacon and Jake Oldershaw. It also has a general manager, Charlotte Martin, and an advisory producer, Nick Sweeting,[1] as well as a Board of Directors chaired by Alan James.

Stan's Cafe (pronounced Caff) was named after a restaurant off Brick Lane: 'Stan's Cafe the place was somewhere people were welcome, but gave them things they needed like food and warmth at a low price and where they had a chance to dream a little' (Tushingham, n.d.). The company's press releases and theatre programmes always highlight the correct pronunciation of its name to mark the fact that Stan's Cafe aims at engaging wider – rather than elite – audiences: 'In Britain a Caff is a place workers go to drink big mugs of tea and eat unhealthy fried breakfasts of bacon, egg, sausage, tomato, etc. A Café, pronounced with the 'e', is a delicate and pretentious place, not somewhere we feel so comfortable' (Stan's Cafe, n.d.a.).

The decision to choose Birmingham as its base was primarily underpinned by practical reasons, such as the fact that it was 'cheap to live and easy to tour from', but also due to circumstance, as, at the time, the city was undergoing major restructuring that benefited the arts (Stan's Cafe, n.d.b.). Throughout the years, Stan's Cafe's work has been embraced by a number of enthusiastic supporters who have offered the company the opportunity to perform at local and international level. During its early stages of development, the group toured its small-scale productions *Perry Como's Christmas Cracker* (1991) and *Memoirs of an Amnesiac* (1992) without any public funding, while rehearsing in various spaces such as schools, community halls and mac birmingham (then Midlands Arts Centre). Its site-specific *Canute the King* (1993), presented in Moseley Baths, Birmingham, helped to raise the company's profile in the city (Yarker, 2007a). In 1994 Stan's Cafe received its first grant from the Arts Council of England (ACE) for *Bingo in the House of Babel*, while in 1996 it won the Barclays New Stages Award for *Ocean of Storms* which was performed at the Royal Court Upstairs.[2] Since the mid-1990s, the group has been regularly supported by ACE and other organizations, and commissioned by international theatres, which has allowed it to constantly push its artistic portfolio in different directions and attract more audiences across the globe.

As a local arts company, Stan's Cafe has been closely associated with mac Birmingham (mac), one of the city's best-known theatre venues for commissioning new work, and served as one of its resident companies between 1997 and 2001. Dorothy Wilson, mac's director of programming in the 1990s and later chair of the Board of Stan's Cafe, booked its first two pieces and later offered the company space to rehearse (Yarker, 2007b). Alan James, another early advocate of Stan's Cafe, also commissioned projects such as *The Black Maze* in his capacity as programme manager of Birmingham City Council's Forward Festival and programmer for mac.

By 1994, Stan's Cafe had secured its first international gig with *Bingo*, performed at Théâtre 95 in the outskirts of Paris (Cergy), yet its work only began to receive sustained international attention after 2000, when it started touring *It's Your Film* (2003). The piece was performed in a number of international festivals under the auspices of the late Marie Zimmermann, the renowned German theatre producer and artistic director of the Vienna Festival (Wiener Festwochen). Zimmermann later commissioned the world version of *Of All the People in All the World*, which premiered in Stuttgart in 2005, and *The Cleansing of Constance Brown* presented at the Vienna Festival in 2007. More commissions came from Frankfurt's Mousonturm Künstlerhaus for *Be Proud of Me* (2003), from Los Angeles' Skirball Cultural Centre for *Exodus Steps* (2013) and from Montpellier's Domaine d'O for *Apollo Steps* (2010) and *The Cardinals* (2011).[3] *Of All the People* has so far been performed across more than 50 cities around the world, while other shows, such as *The Black Maze* and *The Cleansing*, have toured widely within and outside the UK. This international recognition has inspired a heightening of the company's national profile: in 2012, it received a commission for *Golden Steps*, presented as part of London's 2012 Cultural Olympiad. *Golden Steps* created a designated route for visitors travelling from Euston Station to St Pancras along prints that commemorate 12 golden International Olympic medals, and forms part of the company's *Steps Series* whereby audiences are invited to 'plot their own way around a set of vinyl footprints, handprints and script fragments' (Yarker, 2007a).

Stan's Cafe's commitment to 'home' and the 'local' is mirrored in its support of Birmingham's arts scene; it has been nominated for, and won, a number of awards, such as the Creative City Award (Creative Industries Awards 2008) and the Invisible City Award (2010) in recognition of its ongoing contribution to the city's arts sector. In 2008, the company used a vacated space in the premises of A. E. Harris & Co. (Birmingham) Ltd, located in Birmingham's Jewellery Quarter, to stage the UK premiere of the 'world version' of

Of All the People and secured the space full-time between 2009–13.[4] During this time, A. E. Harris became not only a home for Stan's Cafe's shows, but also a hub of creative activity for Birmingham and the West Midlands; it has been used as a rehearsal and performance space for artists and local companies such as Kindle (now Kiln), Little Earthquake, ARK Theatre, The Happiness Patrol and Untied Artists. A. E. Harris has also hosted showcasing events such as Pilot Nights, and an early edition of China Plate's Bite Size festival.[5] Most significantly, the company was instrumental in founding and hosting the acclaimed annual BE Festival, a theatre festival that brings together emerging European artists with the aim of forging artistic networks, and increasing the exposure of Birmingham audiences to cutting-edge European work.

Stan's Cafe has developed highly original and versatile vocabularies that cut across a range of artistic techniques. Its body of work includes site-specific, immersive and durational performance, non-text-based and scripted projects, and the frequent use of music in place of text. By refusing to adhere to a predominant aesthetic, the company problematizes labels such as 'physical theatre' or 'visual performance' (Stan's Cafe, n.d.c), and mixes different genres, such as puppet theatre (*The Cardinals*, 2011), docudrama (*Home of the Wriggler*, 2006), dark thriller (*Be Proud of Me*, 2001), sound installation (*Broadway Hertz*, 1993) and radio show (*Tuning Out with Radio Z*, 2010); on other occasions, it invents new styles such as in the case of *Lurid and Insane* (2001), presented in the form of a live concert and described as 'performance obituary'.

A common denominator in Stan's Cafe's artistic portfolio is the choice to eschew mimetic representation, and its attempt to 'convince someone about something which is blatantly untrue' (Yarker, 1996). This critique is mirrored in the group's DIY aesthetic, including simple costumes and sets made from recycled material, and an array of anti-mimetic and self-reflexive stylistic vocabularies also encountered in work produced by other theatre companies working in the 1990s, such as Forced Entertainment, Reckless Sleepers and Third Angel: fragmented characterization and storytelling; heightened theatricality; critique of grand narratives and interrogation of the 'real'. Performers often embody a range of different characters within the same piece, commenting on the failure to 'represent' or to 'perform' by trying 'to get the story right'. This critique of representational practices can be read in the light of Sara J. Bailes's study of contemporary performance companies and, specifically, her notion of 'the poetics of failure', which seek to undermine 'the cultural dominance of instrumental rationality' and offer 'an opening into several ... other ways of doing that counter the authority of a singular or "correct" outcome' (Bailes, 2011, 2). For example, in Stan's Cafe's *Good and True* (2000), questions around common sense, representation and authority are explored in the form of self-reflexive exercises and misunderstandings rehearsed in the guise of a pseudo-interrogation scene and slapstick role-playing, where false or unreliable evidence is presented (for example, a child's drawing) to 'prove' the culpability of the person in the hot seat. *The Cardinals* (2011), where three cardinals seek to narrate the history of the world through the Bible, is also replete with slapstick moments of mismanagement and 'accidents' or 'misfires' on stage that undermine the 'authenticity' of the story being told. Moments such as a Handel piece played on an old-fashioned tape recorder being unexpectedly interrupted by Prodigy's 'Smack My Bitch Up', overwritten 'by mistake', disrupt the scene's flow and reverential tone.

Rupturing mimetic representation and the illusion of reality is further achieved by an emphasis on theatricality, often illustrated by revealing 'the act of acting' (Heddon and Milling, 2006, 209). This does not involve the adoption of performance personae such as in the case of Forced Entertainment; rather, Stan's Cafe tackles character largely through an exploration of Brechtian *Gestus* which, according to Patrice Pavis, 'radically cleaves the performance in two blocks: the shown (the said) and the showing (the saying)' (1982, 45). In a number of the company's productions, the distinction between character and actor is rendered visible through devices that draw attention to the performer's physical effort as a commentary about the story being told (*Home*, *The Cardinals*), and by foregrounding the theatre frame (*The Just Price of Flowers*).

In the context of postmodern performance, scholars such as Philip Auslander (1997, 60) and Dee Heddon and Jane Milling (2006, 204) have located the 'political' in the ways in which contemporary theatre companies challenge representational frames and grand narratives that construct 'reality' and dictate singularity of meaning. Lehmann's 'politics of perception' (Lehmann, 2006, 175–87) in postdramatic theatre further draws attention to theatre's potentiality to invoke a 'response-ability' that might overcome the desensitization of audiences towards current political issues. Stan's Cafe's engagement with the political is manifest in different ways across the company's trajectory: while its earlier work was mostly interested in identity (Yarker, 2008b), it later shifted attention to the exploration of new relationships with the audience, and articulated a more explicit political commentary that is uncommon in much of the performance work that shares a comparable postmodern aesthetic. In its negotiation of the relationship between form and content, the group's millennial work asks crucial questions regarding local and global inequalities, (neoliberal) capitalism, ecology, power and the war on terror, and invites 'other' ways of seeing and imagining the world. Further, the company toys with the concepts of space and place by borrowing elements from the traditions of site-specific art and digital technologies to examine the impact of global realities and 'space and time compression' (Harvey, 1990, 284) on notions of identity, home and the 'local'.

Stan's Cafe devises collaboratively and stresses the importance of shared ownership, although Yarker maintains a leadership role within the group, initiating projects and doing most of the writing, directing and dramaturgy.

> As artistic director I tend to bring the core ideas to the table for each new project. These may well have been influenced by discussions with other company members, they may arise out of previous shows we have worked on or common lines of thought, but I tend to set the agenda first off. (cited in Heddon and Milling, 2006, 213)

The devising process continues after the premiere, with Yarker swiftly responding to comments with further edits and improvements.

Stan's Cafe's starting points range from found objects (such as two cans of beer – *Voodoo City*), design concepts (*The Cleansing*), real people (Eric Satie – *Memoirs*) and events (the closure of the Longbridge Rover factory – *Home*), while further inspiration is drawn from the visual arts. Additional material derives from various sources such as biography, newspaper cuttings and phrasebooks. Improvisation is key to the creation of the work and the consolidation of its aesthetic; the company's devising process is also bound to a set of 'rules' which either precede the development of a piece or are discovered throughout. For example, the silent *Simple Maths* (1997) was rooted in a struc-tural principle resembling musical chairs, while *Be Proud of Me* was based on the idea of using slides and foreign language phrasebooks. Nevertheless, in some cases, those initial rules have been selectively broken: for *Tuning out with Radio Z*, another largely improvisatory theatre piece in the form of a radio show, the company had initially agreed that the radio station would be set somewhere specific (a hospital, the FBI headquarters), but in the end decided against setting it in a fictional place, and presented it in the event of the performance (Yarker, 2013).

Two significant aspects of the group's working method are uses of set and technology. Scenography is integral to the conceptual framing of its pieces, such as in the case of *The Cleansing* where the use of a glass pane generated ideas for the shaping of the whole piece. Nevertheless, the company has not always collaborated with professional set designers:

> With set design so often wrapped up in the conception of Stan's Cafe shows there often doesn't seem an obvious point at which [to] bring a designer in, especially as devising often advances in unpredictable leaps often away from rehearsals regardless of timetabled meetings. With the logic of performance bound up with the rules of the set this is a sensitive area to invite strangers into, so usually we don't. (Yarker, 2007c)

Both digital and more traditional technologies have contributed to the aesthetic and conceptual shaping of the company's projects, often borrowing from cinematic, radio and optical illusion techniques. Nevertheless, Yarker has been quite critical of what he terms 'the banal, push-button, Prozac primate stimulation' promoted by digital realms that stultify participation and connection with others (Yarker, 2008c). It is for this reason that Stan's Cafe avoids placing technology 'centre stage as the main attraction', or 'fetishising "the new" for the sake of its novelty' (Yarker, 2004), and often explores ways of using technical equipment that facilitates audience engagement. For example, *Tuning Out* is played live to two audiences, as it is broadcast digitally while also including direct audience participation in the live performance, inviting emails and texts from both audiences to be incorporated in the show. On the contrary, in *Home*, technical equipment draws attention to the impact of wasting resources: stage lighting is generated by the performers with the aid of '[a]n exercise bike and twelve speed racer [which] have been customised with dynamos and switches to run seven lights, a kettle and a home-made turntable' (Stan's Cafe, 2006b).

Experimentation with ways to engage audiences is a chief concern, and viewing is regarded as a 'participatory and creative act' (Yarker, 2001a). As Yarker argues, one of their fundamental artistic principles is to treat audiences as 'collaborators', reflecting Howard Barker's idea of 'honouring' the audience as 'a partner' (Yarker, 2001a). In this light, spectatorial engagement is facilitated by offering 'provocative material to work with and space to do that work', and inviting 'the creation of personal poetic links between passages, motifs and ideas' (Yarker, 2001a). This does not exclude more direct participation, as a number of projects invite various means of audience contribution; for example, *Lurid and Insane*, which adopted the form of a music gig, included live interaction with the audience in the form of mini-interviews.

The company's interest in finding forms that match the content of its work (Yarker, 2013) underpins its intention to 'promot[e] the possibility of alternative ways of looking at the world and alternative value systems' (Yarker, 2008b). This emphasis on the 'alternative' mirrors an opposition to the hegemony of the neoliberal market that permeates contemporary art. Yarker exemplified the company's vision in the context of its Future Arts Symposia, a festival Stan's Cafe organized in 2000 in collaboration with a range of individual artists and arts organizations, which sought to explore 'New Art for the New Century' and to build audiences for new work:

> Our art is trying to promote the possibility of an alternative worldview: not a specific ideology but the possibility of something that is outside of the market, outside sporting competition, outside conventional consumerism, an alternative way of thinking, a glimpse into some other world. (Yarker in Stan's Cafe, 2001, 28)

The above critique of consumerist ethos and commodified art is further made palpable not only in the questions that Stan's Cafe asks in the body of its work, but also through its diverse artistic approaches and resistance to branding, combined with a belief in 'the freedom of not-theatre' (Yarker, 2007a). While allowing the group to experiment with style, space, set and performer/audience relationships and to engage with local and global communities, this freedom has produced certain challenges, working against basic business principles that would enable them to become more recognizable:

> [g]ood business sense would be to knock out at frequent, predictable intervals, shows which, though different from each other, are consistent in their form and tone. Instead we pursue whatever ideas interest us in whatever directions they lead us, regardless of what art form they may wander into and whether they are "the kind of thing we do". (Yarker in Stan's Cafe, 2001, 28)

The lack of an apparently consistent identity in Stan's Cafe's portfolio requires that each piece is promoted from scratch, which renders the loyalty of venues hard to sustain, as promoters find it difficult to be confident of what they are booking and to frame it appropriately within their programme. This was the case for *Of All the People*, which was not initially accepted as part of the 2004 Edinburgh Showcase because the festival originally labelled it 'live art' rather than a piece of theatre (Arts Council England, 'Stan's Cafe', 13).

Another significant dimension of Stan's Cafe's work is its educational remit, which so far translates into more than 30 collaborations with schools and university students on projects closely attached to its creative work and methods. These range from devised pieces, to video projects and installations following the 'principles of individual expression, ensemble playing and active hands-on learning' (Yarker, 2006). A salient example of such practice is *Plague Nation* (2004), created with schools in Birmingham, Bristol and Nottingham. The project stemmed from the rationale of *Of All the People* and aimed to explore statistics on epidemics such as AIDS and the history of vaccination. As Simon Parry notes, students that participated in the project 'saw and reflected on how they were situated in relation to other people in the world' (Parry, 2010, 328). Stan's Cafe is adamant that its education work cannot be classified as TIE, but rather views it as 'an important investment in audience development and the future prosperity of the theatrical form' (Stan's Cafe, n.d.c.), as well as a means of aiding participants to 'gain the creative confidence and skills they will require to fend for themselves successfully in the future' (Yarker, 2008b).

Stan's Cafe continues to produce new work while touring other repertory shows across the UK and abroad; in 2013, the company presented its adaptation of Robert Burton's *The Anatomy of Melancholy* at Warwick Arts Centre and the Birmingham Rep, and *The Cardinals* at London's Mime Festival and the Edinburgh Fringe Festival. *Of All the People* reached Perth, Australia and was later brought back to Birmingham, celebrating the show's tenth anniversary.

Funding

Originally self-funded, Stan's Cafe started receiving small project grants (up to £5,000) from West Midlands Arts, the Arts Council of England (between 1994–2002), Birmingham City Council (until 2010), and mac (Stan's Cafe, n.d.c.). The company benefited from the New Labour government's support for the arts; in the wake of the 1999 Theatre Review that looked to invest additional money across the theatre sector, it was included in the ACE's portfolio of independent, regularly funded West Midlands theatre companies, together with Coventry-based Talking Birds and Theatre Absolute. It secured Key Regional Organization status (KRO) in 2002 before switching to Regularly Funded Organization status (RFO) in 2007 (Gagen, 2013). This first stable funding was crucial for its further development, as it was used 'to supplement an income generated through performances, education projects, speaking engagements and the hire of high end video gear … acquired through a capital arts lottery bid in 1996' (Stan's Cafe, n.d.d.). It further supported Stan's Cafe's investment in 1,000 kg of rice for its performance installation, *Of All the People*, a risk worth taking as this project single-handedly increased the group's public funding sufficiently to enable it to appoint a full-time administrator and a production manager, and to gain greater access to 'European funding streams' (Arts Council England, 'Stan's Cafe', 15). The growth of its turnover was positively acknowledged by ACE as evidence that Stan's Cafe offered 'excellent value' which, in turn, helped to increase its funding throughout the years, reaching £100,000 in 2008/9 (Stan's Cafe, n.d.c.). At the time of writing, Stan's Cafe is included in the ACE's National Portfolio scheme, which from April 2012 replaced the previous regular funding programmes, having secured £461,192 funding for the period 2012–15 and £470,594 for 2015–18.

According to Alison Gagen, Arts Council Relationship Manager for Theatre in the Midlands and a long-time advocate for the company, the success of Stan's Cafe's application is largely due to its strong international profile, educational remit and digital engagement, which fulfil key objectives set by ACE's National Portfolio funding programme (Gagen, 2013). ACE has also recognized the company's generosity in sharing A. E. Harris with emerging and more well-known artists and companies; in 2010 it was awarded a two-year £60,000 subsidy (2010–12) under the ACE's 'Grants for the Arts' scheme, to support the running of the venue as a space for creative activity in the region.

The company has received further support from the British Council to showcase *It's Your Film*, *Of All the People*, *The Cleansing*, *The Cardinals* and *Home* in international festivals and venues in cities such as Edinburgh, Tokyo, Bucharest, Buenos Aires and Beijing. In 2004, it also secured a grant from the Wellcome Trust's 'Pulse' scheme for *Plague Nation*. Another regular funding supporter has been Birmingham City Council, which has acknowledged Stan's Cafe's work with the community and contribution to the city's cultural life (Blackaby, 2008; Woolman, 2010). Due to cuts made by the government to Birmingham City Council's budgets in 2010, Stan's Cafe has now lost this source of revenue, yet Yarker admits that the company is in 'a fairly strong position' as a result of the income generated from its international touring: '[b]eing independent, we can be flexible, innovative and light on our feet. So hopefully that means we will be able to absorb most of the blows. Saying that, these are still very scary times' (cited in Jackson, 2010).

Key Work Produced in this Period and its Impact

It's Your Film (1998)

It's Your Film is the most widely performed Stan's Cafe project (4,500 shows) to date; it is a silent, four-minute piece, with a film noir aesthetic, performed to one audience member. It was originally commissioned by Birmingham's Bond Gallery in 1998, which liberated Stan's Cafe 'not just from the conventional finances and architecture of a theatrical institution, but ... from all the baggage that a theatre show made for a theatre has placed upon it' (Yarker, 2007a). The company here experiments with illusion and presence using a cinematic vocabulary of 'long shots, close ups, exteriors, interiors, cuts' (Stan's Cafe, n.d.a., 2) and simple technological devices (video projector, lighting and a glass pane to produce a Pepper's Ghost effect) that merge film and theatre in innovative ways.

'By pretending to be a film and then doing a thing film cannot do but theatre can' (Stan's Cafe, n.d.a., 7), *It's Your Film* toys with notions of witnessing and action, illusion and the real, producing, in Liz Tomlin's words, 'a self-aware experiment in simulation' (Tomlin, 2004, 509). Audience members enter a photo booth alone and, through a small rectangle glass that serves as screen, they watch the actions of two characters (a private eye and someone in search of his lover) whose images fade into each other.[6] Action is performed live behind the booth, thus the cinematic illusion is often ruptured by the sound produced by the performers' bodies and their direct eye contact with the spectator (Yarker, 2013). The reflexive merging of cinematic and theatrical devices then collapses the distinction between the two media, while opening up a space in-between. The displacement of both artistic boundaries has a further impact on practices of viewing and perceiving. In the final scene, the spectator becomes the lead protagonist in the story as he or she ends up 'looking at [his/her] own reflection, travelling by car through a city at night' (Stan's Cafe, n.d.a., 4). This symbolic 'entrance' in the cinematic frame foregrounds his/her involvement as 'witness and protagonist in their own live action film' (Yarker, 2008b). At the same time, in his/her effort to experience the different layers that the piece offers, the spectator 'undergoes', as Sarah Gorman observes, 'a kind of physiological disorientation' (Gorman, 2010, 273) that chimes with the experience of displacement brought by 'space and time compressions' (Harvey, 1990, 284).

Despite its short duration, *It's Your Film* has enjoyed wide success on its international tour; it is one of the earliest examples of one-to-one performance, well before the rapid growth of the genre in the mid/late 2000s, and also significantly differs in approach from many subsequent models: instead of placing emphasis on the physical presence and proximity between performer and audience, their connection is mediated through the use of different technological devices and framing.

Of All the People in All the World *(2003)*

Of All the People or 'The Rice Show' is Stan's Cafe's most renowned project to date. The piece is a performance installation that opened at Warwick Arts Centre, and was later showcased in the context of the inaugural Informal European Theatre Meeting (IETM) held in Birmingham for the first time in 2003 (Arts Council England, n.d., 11). This paved the way for the first international commission of the piece's world version by Theater der Welt in Stuttgart and the Edinburgh Fringe in 2005, prior to its numerous productions across Europe, the US, Canada, Asia and Australia.[7]

As the company admits, its various travels across different cities created a sense of 'being on the lip of a vast landmass' which had to be probed further (Yarker, 2005). The project grew out of the need to explore how we experience place and the world at large and to understand the number of people we share the planet with. *Of All the People* scales down the world, and creates new global geographies, using rice as a metonymy for human life. Rice was chosen due to its durability, texture, size, cheap price and its 'humanoid' shape (Stan's Cafe, 2003). Upon entry, each member of the audience is given a single grain to represent him/herself. Piles of rice of variable sizes are placed across the space, labelled and grouped together to suggest a particular narrative; the number of grains on each pile is determined by statistical data that represent facts about populations of the city and/or country in which the show is being performed, sourced by the company and in consultation with audiences. Performers, dressed in plain factory clothes, weigh rice quantities using scales, conduct research, print labels and reshape the installation landscape by adding more piles as the show progresses.

The company applies a reflexive dramaturgy to represent space, place and asymmetrical power structures through statistics, and promotes a critical spectatorial engagement. According to Nicola Shaughnessy, the piece invites 'an embodied perceptual experience in which we are both critically and creatively engaged. Our affective understanding is created through embodied spectatorship (and we might argue critical empathy)' (Shaughnessy, 2012, 127). The spatial arrangements of the piles carry poignant political significations, unpacking, among other ideas, issues about life, death, health, mobility and precarity. The piles also include contrasting statistics such as the Twitter followers of Kylie Minogue or the people who watched the Eurovision Song Contest. The organic continuity across the project's different reincarnations is evidenced by each show's engagement with the local community: statistics relevant to the place where the piece is staged (historical facts, population data) are included, some of which are carried through in subsequent showings. Comparisons are often drawn across the global and the local, facilitating a clearer understanding of the evidence; for example, in the exhibition held in the Royal Shakespeare Theatre, Stratford-upon-Avon, for the 2012 World Shakespeare Festival (part of the 2012 Cultural Olympiad), the number of people who left their homes due to the violence in Syria was compared with the population of Birmingham. Other shows comment on the implications of the uneven distribution of wealth globally and in the planet's overpopulated areas. In Perth, Australia, the company used statistics that commented on food waste: for example, a huge pile represented the amount of food wasted in China each day, while each grain stood for a person who could live on that food. The performative power of such a dramaturgy further rests, as Parry suggests, in 'the spectacular visual impact of the size of the piles and the totality of the installation' (Parry, 2010, 326), which reverses the alienating impact of numbers. As Yarker observes:

> It's quite difficult to understand what it means when you hear that two million children will die this year from diseases for which a vaccination exists but when you see two million grains of rice and a piece of paper, suddenly that becomes a very shocking, powerful statistic. (Yarker, cited in Parry, 2010, 325)

In reconfiguring the world, and engaging the participants in an 'embodied perceptual experience', this work forges new readings of world ecologies, interconnectedness and social responsibility towards local/global cultures of waste. The piece's political ecology is further illustrated by the ways in which Stan's Cafe disposes of the rice: the company owns one ton of rice which is reused for UK shows, while elsewhere promoters are responsible for supplying and disposing of it either by returning it to the supplier for washing and resale, or by donating it to charity or for animal feed (Parry, 2010, 325).

The world version commissioned by Theater der Welt's Marie Zimmermann in Stuttgart attracted the attention of international promoters to the company's other work, and resulted in more commissions from venues in Europe and beyond, such as Toronto (2009), Tokyo (2010) and Washington, D.C. (2010). The piece was used as a springboard to create educational projects in schools, such as *Plague Nation* (2004) and its subsequent incarnation *Smartie Mission* (2009), led by Year 5 Birmingham students who were asked to represent different facts, from the world's tallest buildings to the victims in Gaza, using food material (Stan's Cafe, 2009d).

Home of the Wriggler *(2006)*

Home is another project that encapsulates Stan's Cafe's ongoing ecological concerns, and its commitment to finding forms that match the political content of its work. Funded by Birmingham City Council's Arts Programme, it opened at mac in 2006 and subsequently at A. E. Harris in 2009, followed by a regional tour and a British Council showcase in Beijing. The show stems from two opposing stimuli: the threatening of Birmingham's car industry, and global warming. It is set in an underground shelter in the year 3006 where four performers (Heather Burton, Amanda Hadingue, Bernadette Russell and Craig Stephens) take turns in narrating stories of people who used to live in Birmingham between the 1960s and the early 2000s.

Due to its setting, DIY aesthetic and factual content, the piece is described as 'lo-fi sci-fi docudrama' (Stan's Cafe, 2006a), inspired by the threatened closure of the Rover car plant in Longbridge, Birmingham, the world's largest car manufacturer in the 1960s, which finally shut down in 2005. Based on a collage of fragments from 'interviews, anecdotes, personal experiences and documents about living, working, growing-up, falling in love, making/buying/selling/driving/sitting in cars in Birmingham' (Stan's Cafe, 2006a), the piece is not a documentary about the factory; rather, it traces connections across the stories of the people who were remotely or intimately connected to it. As Yarker points out, *Home* is not intended to talk solely about the factory workers, but 'the whole community: the people behind the motor industry and finding out who made the sandwiches, cleaned the clothes, cut the hair and taught the kids of those who shaped the parts, that made the cars, that filled the Midlands' roads' (Yarker, 2010a). The narration of the stories is non-linear, while sources have been 'mixed, mashed and re-imagined so that any resemblance to any characters living or dead should be considered un/happy chance' (Stan's Cafe, 2006a). Stan's Cafe utilizes a 'reporting' and 'presentational modality' common in documentary theatre, through the third-person narration that puts on display its 'means of persuasion' (Paget, 2009, 228), creating a distance between performer and character. Ultimately, the piece becomes a collage of individual voices that progressively forms a large imagined community of people who are connected to each other.

Home was also inspired by the imminent birth of Yarker's daughter, who was described as 'wriggling' in the womb (Yarker, 2010a); as Yarker admits, this transfused the piece with a deep concern over the planet the young generation would inherit (Yarker, 2010a). In *Home*, baby Chloe's birth is placed against the backdrop of precarious environmental and other conditions that disrupt traffic, cause damage and deaths: 'a huge wave hit thousands of miles of coastline', 'an earthquake shook the East', '80,000 people died. No reason was given' (Stan's Cafe, 2006b, 33). The focus on global warming is further enhanced by the bleak perspective from which the performers narrate those stories. In this post-apocalyptic setting, cast members generate the power required for lighting the set using minimal technical equipment.[8] This choice draws attention to the performer's physical labour, foregrounding the mechanization of factory work, while also punctuating the piece's anti-mimetic registers. It also exemplifies the company's ethical stance towards environmental issues, as all material was taken from 'recycled/ scavenged waste sites' (Yarker, 2010b). As Yarker admits, the process shaped the company's environmental awareness of energy waste (such as trying to boil a kettle using pedal power) (Yarker, 2010a). The significance of ecology was further enhanced by an emphasis on inter-connectedness, also evident in the set's backdrop, a diagram picturing part of a car's engine that illustrates how all parts fit together. Here, these parts have been replaced by names of characters used in the piece to trace connections across the diegetic community that represents the whole of humanity.

The Cleansing of Constance Brown *(2007)*

This 70-minute piece, co-commissioned by Wiener Festwochen and the West Midlands' Fierce! Festival, premiered at Warwick Arts Centre. It was included in the British Council's 2007 showcase in Edinburgh and has since received a number of international productions. It was performed to a limited audience by seven cast members who play over 68 characters, and was 'set-driven', the main original stimulus being to scale up the set of *It's Your Film*:

> Whilst performing *It's Your Film* we started speculating on what its sequel might look like. The obvious approach was to scale up the Pepper's Ghost mechanism so a larger audience could watch. Imagining the largest piece of glass you could sensibly tour with, led us to consider a set just two meters wide but very deep. (Yarker, 2007c)

The set was then shaped as a long corridor which generated further ideas and became a metaphor for 'what lies outside the frame'. The concept of 'corridors of power' became central in thinking about 'the difference between who is and is not allowed in the room', and 'whether the negotiations would happen in the room or in the corridor' (Yarker, 2013), which further led Yarker to consider a way of narrating what has happened offstage (Yarker, 2013). This process also determined the acting style adopted. As Yarker explains:

> From the first day on a mock-up set it was clear the shape of the playing space would heavily influence the performers' acting style, how the show was blocked and how focus would be moved around. As expected, the corridor set led us to throw focus off stage. Actions on stage were contrived so as to generate readings as to what was happening in fictional spaces immediately off stage. (Yarker, 2007c)

Despite the detail in costume and props, the piece limits any potentially empathetic response to character, and its focus lies rather on visual and aural aspects, such as the use of a loud music soundscape to substitute text.

The Cleansing toys with the doubleness of 'cleansing', which, for Yarker, is one of the most loaded words, encompassing contradictory ideas such as purification and genocide (Yarker, 2013). The piece's voyeuristic frame is placed against the backdrop of women and power, prompted by Yarker's personal interest in feminism and the position of women in society (Yarker, 2008b). *The Cleansing* offers glimpses of a fragmented and fleeting image of a controversial woman 'who appears to have lived in all ages, both here and around the globe' (Stan's Cafe, 2007), and the audience has to work hard to puzzle the pieces together, and to imagine the action that has taken place inside the rooms. The piece both celebrates and problematizes (female) power through numerous references to iconic figures, from Elizabeth I and Florence Nightingale to Lynddie England, the US soldier convicted for abusing Iraqi prisoners in Abu Ghraib prison, who are all portrayed through evocative tableaux and a range of improvised stories.

Scenes intercut and blend into each other making connections across time and space; the only text used ('I can see you') deflects the audience's gaze, shattering the illusion of empowerment evoked through our peeping from the end of a corridor into the characters' personal lives. After the end of each performance, spectators were invited to leave their own individual symbolic trace by walking down the corridor to examine the off-stage spaces; the quantity of costumes as well as the detailed instruction boards marking all entrances and exits drew attention to the performers' physical and mental labour, revealing the theatre-making process.

The Just Price of Flowers *(2009)*

The Just Price of Flowers, also known as Stan's Cafe's 'austerity production', premiered at A. E. Harris in 2009 and is the company's most explicitly political piece to date. Placed against the backdrop of the Netherlands of the seventeenth century and the first 'financial bubble', it urgently engages with its historical and political context, the 2008 financial breakdown, examining its causes and implications. As explained by the company, 'tulipomania' was caused by a growing passion for tulips imported from the East that led to a rise in their price and 'the possibility of making profit through speculative buying. For a brief time certain tulip bulbs were sold for prices equivalent to those of a house, or three years of a craftsman's wage' (Stan's Cafe, 2009b).

By pointing to the differences between human needs and commodity fetishism, and through interrogating notions of injustice and responsibility in a capitalist system, the piece proffers a clear position towards the economic recession. This commentary is conveyed through a simple yet resonant story of a young lower-middle-class farming couple, the Van Leasings, who are rapidly drawn to the fashion of collecting tulips, resulting in a substantial amount of debt, the mortgaging of their property and, ultimately, the loss of everything. Central characters in the plotline are Van Eek (the old money/the bond credit rating), Van Hire (the banker), Van Tage (the financier) and Van Drive (the servant who loses his pension despite his refusal to invest in tulips), who appear in short vignettes signposted by titles written on pieces of paper that foreshadow the financial devices discussed (for example, 'Credit', 'Credit Default Swap', 'Short Selling'). The piece also involves a narrator who introduces each scene by playing the accordion and offering brief references to fictional and factual stories from the present (for example, 'Sean gets his car repossessed and can no longer get to work', 'Ralph Cioffi and Matthew Tannin are put on trial for insider trading and later acquitted').

The Just Price is an explicit homage to Brecht, as the use of various *Verfremdungseffekt* devices of historicization, songs (written by Craig Stephens), episodic structure and the use of placards clearly suggests. Form is inextricably linked to content, further pronouncing the company's ethics, ecological processes and material conditions of production. It was written and rehearsed in 11 days, and performed by local actors who worked on reduced wages and shared box-office and bar sales (Stan's Cafe, 2009c). It also included recycled materials used in previous shows which further reinforced its 'austerity' aesthetic. Objects of value, such as tulips and a peacock, as well as bits of costume, were made of paper to serve as an index for the disproportionate relationship between an object's exchange and use value. The company incorporated the origami skills of its music director Brian Duffy who created the props, and the suggestion of Hadingue (who also co-directed with Stephens and Yarker) to adopt a Rembrandt aesthetic which became manifest in the series of tableaux created (Yarker, 2013).

The Cardinals *(2011)*

The Cardinals was commissioned by Domaine d'O (where it also premiered) and Warwick Arts Centre. Similar to *The Cleansing*, the piece is primarily non-text based (with the exception of a little text in Latin) and furthers the company's experimentation with storytelling and form. Three cardinals dressed in crimson robes (Rose, Stephens and Gerard Bell), and their female Muslim stage manager (Rochi Rampal), attempt to narrate a biblical version of the story of the world through a series of vignettes presented in the form of a puppet show. Set design consists of a puppet stage with scenery resembling a modern diorama manipulated by the actors; surrounded by a paraphernalia of props, costumes, ladders and a light console, the actors also perform as (oversized) puppets.

By drawing attention to what is happening within and outside the frame of the Cardinals' performance, the meta-theatrical function of the puppet stage teases out some crucial questions regarding artifice and reality in the context of the narration of history and the ideology of religion, but also of theatre itself. The frantic atmosphere 'offstage', with performers bumping into each other while struggling (and often failing) to swiftly handle the numerous pieces of props and set, is juxta-posed with the reverential music and tableaux representing various key moments from the Old Testament to the Crusades, finally reaching the dawn of the twentieth-first century to end with the apocalypse.

Such techniques, which dismantle the theatrical apparatus, chime with the overarching theme of belief which, according to Yarker, is pertinent in both religion and the theatre: '[t]he Cardinals ask us to "believe" whilst classically the theatre asks us to "suspend our disbelief"' (Stan's Cafe, 2009b). In its attempt to 'clumsily' represent the history of the world with reference to the cornerstone of western civilization, *The Cardinals* articulates a political commentary about the power relation-ships endemic between the West and the East, Christianity and Islam. This is accentuated by an additional ironic narrative thread about the clash between different faiths and genders, which is illustrated by the struggles deployed 'offstage': one of the Cardinals objects to the fact that their stage manager is a Muslim female and continuously criticizes her work; however, the Cardinals' control over the final performance product is put at risk when she takes a short break for prayer, leaving them clueless as to how to operate the technology.

The piece was originally meant to be focused on the Crusades, but this ultimately formed only one section of the show. Nevertheless, the reference to the Crusades holds a central position in the piece's politics, drawing a link with the violence inflicted in contemporary Palestine. This is further supported by numerous devices (the diorama stage design, reprises of images with different costume and scenery) that sketch Jerusalem as a palimpsest of different civilizations, histories and architectures and, as such, a space subject to the repetition of violent historical cycles.

Critical Reception

Stan's Cafe has been positively received by the press; although the majority of national newspapers have had little to say about its work, the *Guardian*'s Lyn Gardner has expressed her support for the company since discovering it through *Of All the People* in 2008, proclaiming it the 'most interesting company working in the UK today' (Gardner, 2009). The regional daily newspaper the *Birmingham Post* has also acted as Stan's Cafe's advocate often featuring articles on the company's achievements and sometimes serving as a platform to express their views, such as on the ideological underpinning of the arts cuts (Jackson, 2010) and the need for 'a return to creativity' (Yarker, 2008c).

In brief, the productions receiving most positive coverage so far are *Of All the People*, *The Cardinals* and *The Cleansing*, which have all gained more visibility due to their international tours and London productions. The *Telegraph*'s Dominic Cavendish described *Of All the People* as 'ingenious' (Cavendish, 2008), while other international reviews have also commended the company for the ideas behind its work. Germany's *Süddeutsche Zeitung* praised *Of All the People* for the wealth of the 'astonishing knowledge' it contains (cited in Stan's Cafe, 2003), and *Der Zeit* praised its inspiring symbolism (Kümmel, 2005), while France's *Les Trois Coups* found *The Cleansing* to be a fascinating 'tour de force' with a particularly British composure and sense of irony (*flegme*) (Harant, 2009).

A common note of praise encountered in reviews by critics and industry professionals concerns innovation. David Tushingham, dramaturg and curator for the Salzburg Festival and the Duesseldorfer Schauspielhaus, celebrates the group's ability to create original experimental work: '[i]n a world where all artists have to claim they are innovative, Stan's Cafe are the real thing' (Tushingham, n.d.). Similarly, Gardner found *The Cleansing* to be a 'fascinating and exhilarating piece of work from a company of real artistic innovators who always have new things to say and new ways of saying them' (Gardner, 2011). Apart from possessing an originality of style, Stan's Cafe's projects have also been acknowledged as thought-provoking and moving. *Of All the People*'s tour has generated a wealth of comments from audiences that demonstrate an impact on a personal level.[9] Negative responses have overall been sporadic and focused on two pieces: *The Cardinals* and *The Anatomy of Melancholy*. Gardner conceived the former mostly as 'an exercise in style rather than a provocative examination of the nature of faith' (Gardner, 2013a), while Cavendish read it as 'a case not so much of breaking boundaries as dragging us across the threshold of patience into new realms of tedium' (2013). Similarly, Gardner critiqued *The Anatomy* for being 'illustrative, repetitive, dusty and dry' (Gardner, 2013b).

Despite the growing body of publications on contemporary performance practice, academic notice with regard to Stan's Cafe's body of work has so far been limited. Extant work revolves around examples such as *Of All the People* (Parry, 2010; Shaughnessy, 2012), *It's Your Film* (Gorman, 2010; Tomlin, 2004) and the revival of Impact Theatre's *The Carrier Frequency* (Babbage, 2000; Jürs-Munby, 2006; Tomlin, 2004) while others mention these in passing. Parry (2009) and Shaughnessy (2012) both offer a more detailed account of the process underpinning *Plague Nation* and *Of All the People*, placing them within a rigorous discussion. While Heddon and Milling (2006) refer briefly to Yarker's role as artistic director and dramaturg, Adam Ledger (2013) considers Stan's Cafe's ensemble ethos more closely, with reference to *Good and True*, *The Cleansing*, *No Walls Just Doors* and *Adult Child/Dead Child*. With the exception of Ledger, no other existing publication has yet paid close attention to the company's material contexts of production, and there is no study, prior to this one, that examines the company's diverse aesthetic approaches, international reach and politics.

As shown, Stan's Cafe's portfolio, impressive in its range, eclecticism and mix of performance forms, suggests a commitment to innovative artistic practice. The company experimented with styles such as one-to-one and immersive performance before these became common topos in other performance work. Stan's Cafe's interest in exploring ways of attracting new audiences to innovative art is inextricably linked to its commitment to the local Birmingham arts scene; this dual perspective is mirrored in the company's numerous involvements in the West Midlands community, by invitation or through its own initiative under different capacities. Stan's Cafe's absence from most theatre studies curricula, and the difficulties incurred in promoting its work can be attributed to the lack of a consistent and recognizable style, which resists the academy's and industry's tendency to pigeonhole artistic work according to specific theoretical and stylistic vocabularies. However, none of this has compromised the company's artistic and business ethic: it still maintains a DIY aesthetic, ecological remit, low ticket prices and an ongoing dedication to the creation of thought-provoking and oppositional work in both form and content.

Acknowledgements

I am grateful to James Yarker and Alison Gagen for providing clarifications and useful information.

List of Key Productions by the Company

Canute the King (site-specific)
Premiered: Birmingham (Moseley Baths, 1993)
Tour (second version) included: London (I.C.A.), Lancaster (Nuffield Studio)

Bingo in the House of Babel
Premiered: Birmingham (mac, 1994)
Tour included: London (BAC), Liverpool (BlueCoat Arts Centre), Cergy-Pontoise (Theatre 95)

Ocean of Storms
Premiered: Birmingham (mac, 1996)
Tour included: London (Royal Court Upstairs), Bradford (Theatre in the Mill), Southsea (Portsmouth Arts Theatre)

Simple Maths
Premiered: Coventry (Belgrade Theatre Studio, 1997)
Tour included: Manchester (The Green Room), Birmingham (mac), Oxford (Pegasus)

It's Your Film
Premiered: Birmingham (Bond Gallery, 1998)
Tour included: Manchester (The Green Room), Hannover (Theatre Formen Festival), Galway (Galway International Arts Festival), Rio de Janeiro (Rio Cena Contemporanea), Leipzig, Germany (Euroscene)

The Carrier Frequency
Premiered: Birmingham (Crescent, 1999)

Good and True
Premiered: Birmingham (mac, 2000)
Tour included: Leeds (Studio Theatre), London (Royal Opera House and Lyric Hammersmith)

The Black Maze (sensory art installation)
Premiered: Nottingham (Freefall and Now Festival, 2000)
Tour included: Sheffield (Site Gallery), London (National Theatre).
International tour included: Noisel (La Ferme du Buisson), Montpellier
(Domaine d'O), Thessaloniki (Edinburgh in Thessaloniki Festival)

Be Proud of Me
Premiered: Frankfurt (Mousunturm, 2001)
Tour included: Birmingham (mac), Belfast (The Old Museum Arts
Centre), Warwick (Warwick Arts Centre), London (Lyric Theatre
Studio), Cergy-Pontoise (Theatre 95)

Lurid and Insane
Premiered: Lancaster (a barn near Nuffield Theatre, 2001)
Toured in: Leeds (a cellar bar), Birmingham (a gig venue), Edinburgh
(Bongo Club, Edinburgh Fringe)

Of All the People in the All the World (installation)
Premiered: Warwick (Warwick Arts Centre, 2003)
Tour included: Birmingham (A. E. Harris), Mainz (No Strings Attached
Festival), Perth (Perth International Arts Festival), Buenos Aires (Palais
de Glace), Tokyo (Setagaya Public Theatre)

Home of the Wriggler
Premiered: Birmingham (mac, 2006)
Tour included: London (BAC), Beijing (Theatre 9)

The Cleansing of Constance Brown
Premiered: Warwick (Warwick Arts Centre, 2007)
Tour included: Vienna (Wiener Festwochen), Edinburgh (British
Council Showcase), Toronto (Harbourfront Centre), Montpellier
(Domaine d'O), Bucharest (Festivalul National de Teatru).

The Just Price of Flowers
Premiered: Birmingham (A. E. Harris, 2010)
Toured in: Warwick (Warwick Arts Centre), Southwold (Latitude)

Tuning out with Radio Z
Premiered: Birmingham (mac, 2010)
Tour included: Bristol (Tobacco factory), Chichester (Studio Theatre),
Oxford (Oxford Playhouse)

The Cardinals
Premiered: Montpellier (Domaine d'O, 2011)
Tour included: Plymouth (The Drum, Theatre Royal), London (Roundhouse, International Mime Festival), Edinburgh Fringe 2013

The Anatomy of Melancholy
Premiered: Warwick (Warwick Arts Centre, 2013)
Tour included: Birmingham (Birmingham Rep), London (Ovalhouse)

Chapter 7

BLAST THEORY

Maria Chatzichristodoulou

Introduction

Blast Theory is an internationally renowned, award-winning British company based in Brighton, UK. Founded in 1991, the company chose its name from an anarchist fanzine that had, in turn, appropriated it from British painter and editor of Vorticist magazine *BLAST*, Percy Wyndham Lewis (Blast Theory, 2004, 8). The phrase that so impressed the young graduates at the time was 'Blast Theory, Bless Practice'. Finding themselves against the backdrop of postmodernism and a post-Thatcherite recession, the group was keen to set about taking action rather than dissecting ideas (Blast Theory, 2004, 8). The company's core membership shifted during the first few years but has been stable since 1994; Matt Adams, Ju Row Farr and Nick Tandavanitj have led the company ever since.

Although this volume considers Blast Theory as part of a theatrical tradition, the company is not, strictly speaking, a theatre company. None of Blast Theory's founding members is trained as a theatre practitioner: Adams developed an early passion for theatre and has a background as a performer and director, but his studies are in English literature and film; Farr trained as a dancer and fine artist in textiles; and Tandavanitj, the most technologically adept member of the group, studied arts and social context. The result is an interdisciplinary team that develops work as much through collaboration and convergence as it does through the differences that arise from the members' divergent disciplinary viewpoints. Adams, Farr and Tandavanitj collaborate with a range of associate artists who also come from diverse backgrounds, such as drama, theatre and performance, dance and choreography, visual arts and communication design. Moreover, the company works closely with partners in academia and the industry; those collaborations have provided the expertise, know-how and resources that have supported and often triggered the company's strong technological outlook.

Blast Theory has an ambivalent relationship with any kind of genre classification (Adams, 2007). Although Adams perceives the company's work as situated within a theatrical lineage, he considers it as 'incredibly divergent' from what he calls 'traditional theatre' (Adams, 2007). Perhaps more significantly, in a period when rejection of theatrical tradition is increasingly common, he sees the company's early work as originating from a position of 'tremendous naivety about experimental practice'; consequently, Blast Theory has never comfortably fitted within the context of live art either (Adams, 2007). It is not a coincidence, says Adams, that most of the seminal moments of live art history, such as the National Review of Live Art (1980–2010), do not include Blast Theory (Adams, 2007). The company tends to discuss its practice not in terms of genres, but in terms of character-istics. For example, although members resist defining their practice as theatre, performance, live art or new media art, they do describe it as 'performative'.

Performative elements are more prominent in some works than they are in others but can be traced throughout the company's trajectory. For example, Adams discusses aspects of *Day of the Figurines* (2006) as an improvisational theatrical process, whereby participants 'are invited to create characters, represent those characters and act out with other people interactive improvisational narratives' (Adams, 2007). He does not consider the piece to be a theatrical performance, but suggests that it has a 'strong theatrical position'. This applies to several of the company's projects that use formats immediately recognizable to anyone who is familiar with contemporary live art practice. So, although Blast Theory might not define itself as a performance company, its members are 'incredibly engaged with the idea of performance, the idea of a performer and an audience member having a live exchange or inter-action in a particular moment in time and place' (Adams, 2007). This, says Adams, is 'the animating principle' behind much of the work they make (Adams, 2007).

By resisting the pigeonholing of its practice within a single disci-plinary stronghold, Blast Theory 'weave[s] in and out of other disciplines and other modes of practice', learning from different methodological paradigms (Adams, 2007). Indeed, several of its artworks fall within categories other than performance: from the very beginning, the company engaged with video work and has made several video art and installation projects, such as *TRUCOLD* (2002). In more recent years, Blast Theory has also made interactive installations and games, sometimes for educational purposes (such as the *Energy Gallery* installation at the Science Museum (2004)). In Blast Theory's practice, threads of creative process often result in more than one artistic output of different types. For example, *TRUCOLD*, a traditional video installation, is based on footage that was shot partly by accident while the company was working on a live project in Germany and that had previously been used in the performance project *10 Backwards* (1999).

Whether seen as a theatre or performance group, an art ensemble that uses different methodological approaches including live performance, or a new media art company that creates works informed by cutting-edge technology, from the very outset Blast Theory has actively questioned, challenged and transgressed disciplinary boundaries, merging theatre, performance, interactive arts and gaming. Through its artistic practice, the company innovates by developing new models for active audience participation: using emergent technologies and interactive media in ways that have shaped the contemporary British and international cultural landscapes; exploring formats that merge practices and approaches; situating its work in unconventional or unexpected contexts; confronting audiences with tough questions and challenging demands; and, above all, being prepared to take risks. Though refusing to be defined as a theatre company, Blast Theory has certainly helped shape the contemporary theatre landscape in Britain and internationally by inspiring companies to experiment with participative practices, locative media, mobile interfaces, pervasive gaming and the creation of complex and layered immersive experiences. Its influence can be perceived in explorations by artists such as interactive theatre company Coney, multidisciplinary ensemble Proto-type Theatre, artist-led collective Active Ingredient, immersive theatre company Punchdrunk, social games festival Hide and Seek, and the Atom-r collective among others. Its influence is also palpable in contexts as different as dreamthinkspeak's ambitious large-scale performance/film/installation projects on the one hand, and Hannah Jane Walker and Chris Thorpe's intimate interactive work on the other. Furthermore, as the company is frequently presented as part of undergraduate curricula in theatre and performance, it is influencing new generations of performance makers wishing to experiment with non-linear, participatory, interdisciplinary or immersive theatre practices.

Company Development and Artistic Methodologies

The group came together in 1991 as a hybrid collective founded by Matt Adams, Ju Row Farr and Will Kittow, artists who happened to be working at the same cinema as ushers, cashiers and bar staff (Adams with Rieser, 2011, 401). The multidisciplinary nature of the group meant that, from early on, its members had to establish a basic language for talking about their practice with each other, as well as to the wider public. An intense engagement with technology was central to the group's interests from the early stages of its practice. Influenced by club (sub-)cultures and intent on questioning and reinventing its dominant aesthetic languages, the company used projection and computers in the very first piece that it made, *Gunmen Kill Three* (1991), to explore issues of 'presentation and representation through the image' (Adams, 2007). *Gunmen* featured an early live 'video stream' in a scene where someone with a shoulder-held camera chased someone else; the scene was projected live via a radio link (Adams, 2007). The integration of the recording device and live video feed meant that the chase was not only a live occurrence within the performance space, but also a screen-based representation of a particular viewpoint of the action. The technology, far from being sleek or intuitive, was in fact cumbersome and temperamental; the company depended on a massive, old video projector that kept breaking down, requiring a devoted engineer who travelled with the company in order to operate the machine (Adams, 2007). Despite the technical challenges, the company was able to launch its artistic trajectory with an immersive experience, where multiple actions and stimuli unfolded simultaneously, competing with each other for the audience's attention. *Gunmen Kill Three* asks questions about reality and representation, power and control, access and social responsibility, all in relation to digital technology – questions that have been central to Blast Theory's work ever since. As the company's first ever piece, it is already indicative of Blast Theory's aims, intentions and artistic vision, offering a glimpse of how these might develop in the future.

Blast Theory's structure as a collective means that its core members (Adams, Farr and Tandavanitj) share equal responsibility for all artistic and managerial decisions. Each member's role differs, reflecting his/her individual strengths. Adams is seen as the person who directs the vision of the company and generates the networks with various partners. Farr translates the bigger picture into smaller, concrete steps by developing detailed plans for every project; she also nurtures relations between the company and its audiences, the company and its partners, as well as between the company's members, staff and associate artists. Tandavanitj is the technical brain of the company; he writes the code for several of the works and tests out materials and software (Dekker with Somers-Miles, 2011, 19). Despite these differences in roles, all Blast Theory members are of equal ranking, and none of them undertakes to 'direct' the others. Because Adams often acts as the spokesperson of the group, he is sometimes mistakenly regarded as Blast Theory's leader; however, he is keen to stress the evenness of the group's tripartite structure whereby decisions are taken collaboratively, and all core members have equal input (Adams, 2007). This is not always a smooth process: Adams, Farr and Tandavanitj often argue over contrasting views of how the work should develop. Blast Theory's creative process is based on lengthy discussions, arguments, and continuous challenging of each member, until they are all satisfied that each and every project is separate from any single person, representing all the different strands they each bring to the mix (Adams, 2007). In this way, Blast Theory has developed a working method whereby internal differences of opinion are used to safeguard the development of robust concepts and projects (Dekker with Somers-Miles, 2011, 20). Although the company's core is collaborative and non-hierarchical, Blast Theory can have clearly defined, hierarchical relationships with their associate artists and other collaborators. According to Dekker, the group can be rather 'rigidly structured in their adherence to the integrity of Blast Theory's artistic voice' (Dekker with Somers-Miles, 2011, 20).

The company operates both within and beyond artistic contexts. Individual company members hold professional roles in education (Adams, for example, is a Visiting Professor at the Central School of Speech and Drama, University of London). Some of the company's early works were developed with young people in formal or informal education settings. *The Gilt Remake* (1995) was created with students at De Monfort University and *Ultrapure* (1996) was a collaboration between Blast Theory and the Royal Court Young People's Theatre, among other partners. Since 2009, Blast Theory has taken responsibility for actively supporting and nurturing a new generation of artists through an international residency programme for artists, scientists and theorists working in the areas of pervasive gaming, interactive media, mobile devices in artistic practice, games design and theory, interdisciplinary and live art practice (Blast Theory website). The residency programme – based at the company's studios in Portslade, near Brighton, UK – offers mentoring, advice and insights into Blast Theory's practice, working methods and research activities, and has hosted artists such as Andy Field (2009), Sheila Ghelani (2010), Natasha Davis (2010) and Francesca da Rimini (2012). Establishing the mentoring of emerging artists as a major strand of the company's educational and social activity, Blast Theory demonstrates a desire to use its own experience to support and nurture a growing artistic community. Through hosting artists, scientists and theorists working in relevant fields, the company aspires to 'create an interdisciplinary community of international significance' (Dekker with Somers-Miles, 2011, 20).

Moreover, Blast Theory has been involved in various types of research-informed or research-related practice from early on. The company's first research collaboration was with the Mixed Reality Laboratory (MRL) at the University of Nottingham for the eRENA (Electronic Arenas for Culture, Performance, Arts and Entertainment) research and development project in 1997. MRL brings together over 50 academic staff and research students from the fields of computer science, psychology, sociology, engineering, architecture and the arts aiming to 'explore the potential of ubiquitous, mobile and mixed reality technologies to shape everyday life' (Mixed Reality Laboratory website). The first public output of this collaboration was Blast Theory's seminal work *Desert Rain* (1999), a response to the first Gulf War. Branded as 'possibly the most technologically ambitious art instal-lation ever made' (*The Times*, 2000) and nominated for a BAFTA award in Interactive Arts (2000), *Desert Rain* marked the beginning of one of the longest-lasting collaborations between an art group and a research laboratory, and impacted on Blast Theory's increasing interest in the use of new technologies in its artistic practice. Adams acknowledges that the group's 'exploration, project-related research and use of technology' could never have developed so strongly without its partnership with MRL, which has resulted in some of the company's major works such as *Can You See Me Now?* (2001), *I Like Frank* (2004) and *Rider Spoke* (2007) (Dekker with Somers-Miles, 2011, 22). These projects explore the possibilities of interactivity in mobile devices and pervasive gaming and demonstrate the potency of art–science collabo-rations in 'addressing technology problems that have social outcomes' (Blast Theory, 2004, 15).

Indeed, the company has been instrumental in paving the way for art–science collaborations that develop on an equal footing and that advocate artistic methodologies as productive resources in the shaping of robust research processes. Blast Theory's input has led Beaver, Gaver and Benford to argue for the benefits of ambiguity, often 'considered anathema in Human Computer Interaction', as a resource for design 'that can be used to encourage close personal engagement with systems' (Beaver et al., 2003, 233). As ICT (Information and Communications Technology) is becoming integral to our daily lives, changing the nature of both social space and social interaction, sophisticated art and technology collaborations such as those between Blast Theory and MRL are becoming increasingly important, as they have the capacity to 'stimulate novel solutions to challenges in technology and society and provide a new conceptual base for innovation narratives' (Foden, 2012, 2). Other artist and scientist collaborators have also argued that artistic perspectives can challenge scientists to think creatively and with more freedom, question rigid rules and stimulate new ideas (Wright and Linney, 2009). D'Inverno and Prophet have gone so far as to suggest that it is the very gaps in one's knowledge of a specific discipline that, in interdisciplinary collaborative contexts, can be harnessed to enable creativity and generate out-of-the-box thinking (d'Inverno and Prophet, 2004, 268).

Blast Theory stresses the importance of such thinking in its account of the collaborative development of games such as *I Like Frank in Adelaide*: the game relies on understanding the position of players in the city, which would traditionally have been achieved through GPS. However, the technical problems encountered in urban environments, where tall buildings obscure satellites, led to a creative solution: audiences were asked to indicate their own position by clicking a button marked 'I Am Here' on a 3G phone (Blast Theory, 2004, 9). Allowing players to manually self-input their location removed the need for location-based hardware. When MRL came to analyse the results of this technique, however, conclusions showed that some participants understood and exploited it by inaccurately reporting their position. By sidestepping what would have been the 'traditional' route of computer science – that is, to improve the performance of the technology – and 'inverting' the problem, Blast Theory came up with a quick and cheap solution that enhanced player experience (Blast Theory, 2004, 15). While curious and excited about the possibilities and affordances (Gaver, 1991) of technological innovation, Blast Theory also develops work that critically reflects upon the social impact of technology. Works such as *I Like Frank*, *Day of the Figurines* and *You Get Me* (2008) research the social implications of mobile communication technologies, examining the technologies' capacities and limitations, and considering the extent to which these can help bridge social divides. In *You Get Me*, for example, the technologies were used to create connections between young people at Mile End Park and audiences at the Royal Opera House in Covent Garden.

Although the company creates work that results in different types of artistic outputs, such as videos and installations, its live practice always aims to situate audiences at the centre. Furthermore, audiences are never present as witnesses – they are asked to immerse themselves in an experience, take an active part in the development of a piece by performing certain actions, making choices, playing a game, making decisions that will shape their own and others' experience of the work, solving problems, competing with each other and undertaking various challenges. Adams explains how the company developed the format of their early works (mostly promenade pieces) from a wish to invite audiences to each create their own version of the performance experience offered. Fully immersing them in rich environments where a plethora of stimuli compete for their attention, ensures that individual audience members can make their own choices about where and how to position their body, where to turn, what to look at and which stimulus to follow at each point in time, co-creating a performance experience unique to them as a result (Adams in Chatzichristodoulou, 2009a, 108). The same desire to bombard audiences with competing stimuli and immerse them in complex, layered environments also led Blast Theory to adopt the use of digital technology from the very beginning of their practice.

Blast Theory's audiences do not, in general, get an 'easy ride': taking part in the company's work can be both a rewarding and a challenging experience. As an audience member you could be asked to exert yourself physically and take actual risks (by cycling in busy city streets while also trying to 'hide' secrets in specific locations, as in the case of *Rider Spoke*), or to commit yourself to demanding emotional undertakings (by making yourself available to emotionally support a stranger over the period of one year, as in *Uncle Roy All Around You* [2003]). Alternatively, you could be confronted with tricky dilemmas that demand that you make tough decisions (as in *Day of the Figurines*, where participants' characters are placed in increasingly challenging situations that call for difficult decision making); you could be asked to share intimate information with strangers (as in *Rider Spoke*); or you could find that you have become part of the show, your actions and responses being recorded and exposed to other audience members to witness – and judge, as in *Safehouse* (1997) and *Ulrike and Eamon Compliant* (2009).

Funding Streams and Partnerships

Blast Theory successfully attracts funding and support from a range of sources. The company's main funding comes from the arts: Blast Theory has received core funding from Arts Council England (ACE) since 1994 (Walwin, 2003). Specifically, the company received approximately £140,000 per annum from ACE South East for the years 2012/13, 2013/14 and 2014/15 (Arts Council England website), and remains as a National Portfolio Organization set to receive £402,472 over the period 2015–18. It has also received several ACE National Touring Programme Awards, and other arts funding such as research and development and production awards. Moreover, the company receives fees for presenting its work throughout Europe, the Americas, Asia, the Middle East and Australia, and in prestigious contexts such as the ICC Museum in Tokyo (Japan), the Chicago Museum of Contemporary Art (USA), the Sydney Biennale (Australia), the National Palace Museum in Taipei (Taiwan), the Hebbel Theatre in Berlin (Germany) and the Sónar Festival in Barcelona (Spain). Blast Theory's income streams are not restricted to the arts, however, as a substantial part of the company's income stems from its research collaborations, which ensure access to technological innovation and resources that would otherwise be out of bounds for an arts company. MRL is its most important partner, providing in-kind research and technical support for the company's most influential projects, including *Desert Rain*, *Can You See Me Now?*, *Uncle Roy All Around You*, *Day of the Figurines*, *Rider Spoke* and *Ulrike and Eamon Compliant* (Blast Theory website).

Following the success of *Desert Rain*, Blast Theory has been involved in major research projects that bring together academic and industry partners, such as IPerG (Integrated Project on Pervasive Gaming, 2004–8), an EU project with partners including Sony Net Services, Nokia and the Swedish Institute of Computer Science. Feeding on Blast Theory's experience with developing pervasive games that expand in time and space, such as *Uncle Roy All Around You*, IPerG aimed to 'create entirely new game experiences ... tightly interwoven with our everyday lives through the objects, devices and people that surround us and the places we inhabit' (Blast Theory, 2004, 15). The project also aimed to develop new tools for pervasive gaming, and research new markets. Blast Theory pieces, such as *Day of the Figurines* and *Rider Spoke*, were informed by the research undertaken through IPerG and were considered 'exemplary' by EU reviewers (Blast Theory, 2004, 15). IPerG was followed by the Participate research project (2006–8), which also featured major industry partners such as the BBC, British Telecom and Microsoft Research, and 'explored convergence in pervasive, online and broadcast media to create new kinds of mass-participatory events' (Participate project website). These research projects have not only informed Blast Theory's artistic outputs, but have also shifted the company's profile towards a more research-focused, creative-industries-related agenda. The company's probing of issues around gaming, mobile platforms, mixed media, mixed reality, interactivity, engagement and participation has also led to its increasing reputation within the cultural industries as games innovators. Since winning the Maverick Award at the Games Developers Conference (2005) the company has been represented by the Creative Artists Agency in Los Angeles in relation to game design, and has been invited to contribute to 'debates about the development of games as an artform that can be conceptually, intellectually and emotionally demanding while also engaging a wide audience' (Blast Theory website). Blast Theory and individual company members also receive fees for services to the education and creative industries sectors (for example, through running workshops, or through production partnerships with the BBC and Channel 4).

Blast Theory's general attraction for funders and partners results not only from its creative use of emerging technologies within widely accessible performance and interactive contexts, but also from the company's sophisticated approach to the marketing and documentation of its work. Its usage of video documentation, in particular, is explorative and creative, resulting in videos that serve not only as documents, but also as promotional materials. They document the atmosphere and general ambience of a piece, rather than the concrete detail of what occurs in the unfolding of the work, preserving tacit knowledge (that is, forms of knowledge that cannot be transferred through linguistic representation, such as sensory information) (Dekker with Somers-Miles, 2011, 30). The company's diversification of income streams demonstrates an energetic and ambitious entrepreneurial spirit that, arguably, provides a model for a sustainable approach to arts funding that emergent artists could aspire to follow. Since 2009/10, several European countries have found themselves in the process of re-examining approaches to cultural policy and practice, as a response to an international economic crisis that has – so some argue – rendered reductions in public spending on the arts and culture inevitable (CultureWatchEurope, 2010). In times when arts funding is under threat in Britain and internationally, Blast Theory's business model could be put forward as a successful alternative to many artistic companies' complete dependence on arts funding avenues. However, despite its international profile and its skilful approach to accessing a wide range of funding, and regardless of numerous attempts, Blast Theory has rarely succeeded in attracting corporate sponsorship; the company puts this down to its 'lack of ability to speak the language of corporate professionals' (Dekker with Somers-Miles, 2011, 26).

Key Works

Gunmen Kill Three *(1991)*

Blast Theory's first project was made over the summer of 1991 by Matt Adams, Lorraine Hall, Niki Jewett, Will Kittow and Ju Row Farr, and was indicative of what was to come. *Gunmen* was a thematically daring work inspired by current affairs: the title was appropriated from a newspaper headline story that described the shooting of three people by the Irish Republican Army (IRA) in a shop situated within a Republican area. *Gunmen* launched the company's career trajectory through the challenging political issues of terrorism, nationalism, religion and violence. This difficult-to-classify piece integrated live performance with audience participation, live wireless video projections, an installation, live DJs and a bar run by the artists. Despite a lack of means, the artists embraced technology by integrating a live video feed in the performance. The work was structured around a re-enactment of the shooting, and took the form of a promenade performance. This entailed audience immersion as, inevitably, audiences became implicated in the happenings. Wishing to test the boundaries between performers and audiences even further, the artists handed a paintball gun to an audience member, inviting him/her to fire up to three shots at two performers who were in their underwear. By placing a gun in the hands of an audience member, Blast Theory confronted its audiences with a challenging dilemma: they could either accept the offer to participate and engage in the performance through committing an act of violence on the vulnerable, semi-naked performers, or decline it, making the ethical choice of resisting the act of violence proposed to them, but potentially stalling the work's development. That difficult choice indicated the way that participation would develop in Blast Theory's works, where it would always be bound up with challenging ethical and moral choices, and loaded with responsibility. It confronted audiences with questions that, whatever their choice in that particular moment, were likely to linger in their minds and continue to trouble them long after they had left the performance space. *Gunmen* was presented at the Union Chapel in London, the Sheffield Independent Film Festival and Bournemouth Polytechnic, environments that demonstrate Blast Theory's non-conventional venue choices, as well as their early engagement with the creative industries (film) and educational sector. Other promenade pieces that followed were: *Chemical Wedding* (1992), a piece commissioned by the ICA to deal with the subject of HIV/AIDS, and *Stampede* (1994), which explored questions of crowd behaviour and rioting, asking what could induce people to take to the streets.

Kidnap *(1998)*

In 1997 Blast Theory was offered a nine-month residency at Künstlerhaus Bethanien in Berlin with a proposed performance called *Succumbing*. Though *Succumbing* never materialized, the company produced the live installation *Safehouse*, which formed part of the research for its piece *Kidnap*. The work 'used an interview format to explore the presence that kidnapping has in the life of each visitor, whether as a concept, a political tool, a media construct or in their own experience' (Blast Theory website). For this piece, Blast Theory invited visitors to consent to being video-recorded while being interviewed; afterwards, visitors were offered the opportunity to browse through footage of other interviewees and watch their recordings. The practice of inviting audience responses to challenging questions, which first emerged in *Safehouse*, runs as a common thread in Blast Theory's work, as does the idea of collecting intimate (one-to-one) testimonies that are recorded and made available to all participants to browse through. As a result, the very act of participating in Blast Theory's work makes one a member of a community of people who might have never met face to face, but who have witnessed each other's intimate testimonies. The Künstlerhaus Bethanien residency and the production of *Safehouse* led to *Kidnap*, one of Blast Theory's seminal and most influential artworks.

Kidnap does what it says in its title by inviting audiences to be kidnapped. It was preceded by *Kidnap Blipvert* (1997), a 45-second video that was screened in cinemas around the UK. *Blipvert* carried a Freephone number, which allowed people to register their interest in being kidnapped. Blast Theory chose at random ten finalists from England and Wales who were put under surveillance for one month. Participants were given no clues as to the nature of the secret location or of the kidnapping experience; they were, nonetheless, reassured that they would not be harmed in any way, and were offered the chance to 'walk out' of the project by quoting a 'safeword'. On 15 July 1998, as announced in advance, two out of the ten people under surveillance were kidnapped and taken to a secret location where they were held for 48 hours. They were Debra Burgess, an Australian 27-year-old temping in the UK, and Russell Ward, a 19-year-old who worked at a convenience store. The whole process was broadcast live on the internet; indeed, this was one of the first performance projects developed for live broadcasting.[1] Visitors to the Institute of Contemporary Arts (London) and Green Room (Manchester) could interact with the work online by controlling the camera inside the safehouse and communicating live with the artists/kidnappers via dedicated web terminals.

Adams has described *Kidnap* as a piece concerned with the notion of giving up control. It asks in what ways we, as audience members, give up control to the performers on stage, and why do we do that. The work explores the process of relinquishing control within a performative setting as an experience that might illuminate surrendering control in other aspects of our lives, such as when getting angry, drunk or high on drugs, through politics, or by following religious leaders. 'Clearly', says Adams, 'there is something about giving up control that we actually like, that we are drawn to. And this is so counter to the Westernised notion of the agency of the individual. [...] Why do we leach so much agency away from ourselves?' Inviting audience members themselves to become the protagonists of the work was the 'ultimate destination of that process of enquiry' (Adams, 2007). *Kidnap* captured the zeitgeist of its times, predating *Big Brother* which was launched a year later in 1999, by interrogating issues of surveillance and control in a poignant, challenging and daring manner. A unique piece of work, it was bound to generate both strong responses and some numbness. James Rampton of the *Independent* asked the (ever-present) question, 'but is it art?' while trying to understand what might induce audience members to pay an entry fee of £10 for the privilege of being spied upon, abducted, imprisoned and 'generally abused for two days' (Rampton, 1998). In the same paper, Judith Palmer repeatedly compared *Kidnap* to an S&M experiment, focusing on Debra who, (apparently 'chin quavering') responded to the press straight after her experience that, though Blast Theory were performing, for her 'it was real' (Palmer, 1998). *Kidnap* was a daring piece of work that raised potent political questions about issues of agency and control, responsibility and surveillance. In many ways *Kidnap* was ahead of its time, predating several artistic practices that have since used surveillance and live broadcasting in different ways, including works that use surveillance technology to subvert its dominant practices, known as 'surveillance art' (see McGrath, 2010 and Dixon, 2007, 437–56).

Desert Rain *(1999)*

Kidnap was followed by another seminal work, *Desert Rain*, only a year later. A milestone in the company's developmental trajectory, *Desert Rain* was created in collaboration with MRL, and was Blast Theory's most technologically ambitious work to that date. A hybrid between a game, an installation and a live performance, the piece remained consistent with Blast Theory's practice of merging formats and disciplines. In *Desert Rain*, participants were grouped in teams of six and were each asked to find their 'target' – a person they were given a photograph of – and to achieve their mission within 20 minutes. Though each person was sent to his/her adventure alone, participants were asked to work together as a team to find the exit and leave the world once they had achieved their individual missions; indeed, the group's success depended on group members escaping together. The piece was a response to the first Gulf War, and confronted participants with relevant fragments of information. Some of these were clearly related to the Gulf War, such as extracts from interviews with people whose lives had been affected by it: a journalist, a soldier, a peace worker, an actor, a tourist and a consumer of media coverage. Others pointed to the war more loosely, for example, through a virtual space that contained a floating field of numbers, all of which were estimates of Iraqi casualties; participants had to physically push their way through those numbers to reach the exit. On leaving, participants collected their coats and bags (which they had previously left with the artists) to discover, at a later point, a small bag of sand concealed in their belongings. The bag contained approximately 100,000 grains of sand, a reference to a speech by General Colin Powell who infamously responded to a question regarding estimates of Iraqis killed during the US invasion: 'It's really a number I'm not terribly interested in' (Powell in Dixon, 2007, 616). *Desert Rain* was influenced by Jean Baudrillard's article 'The Gulf War did not take place' first published in *Libération* on 29 March 1991. In this article, the philosopher suggested that the Gulf War, though very real in terms of direct casualties, was in fact virtual – or attained a virtual nature – due to its mediatization. Drawing on Baudrillard, Blast Theory explain that,

> Whilst remaining deeply suspicious of this kind of theoretical position [we] recognise that this idea touches upon a crucial shift in our perception and understanding of the world around us. It asserts that the role of the media, advertising and of the entertainment industries in the presentation of events is casually misleading at best and perniciously deceptive at worst. ... while televisual information claims to provide immediate access to real events, in fact what it does is produce information events which stand in for the real ... (Blast Theory website)

By confronting audiences with a mixed reality environment that appropriated elements of the Gulf War, while also constantly blurring the boundaries between reality and fiction, *Desert Rain* aimed to bring a 'new understanding of ... the role of the mass media in distorting our appraisal of the world' (Blast Theory website), raising awareness of the 'virtual' nature of all media news gathering and presentation. For that reason, Adams suggests that *Desert Rain* perhaps represents the most profound level the company has reached in trying to make sense of the world 'when we are so overwhelmed with different sources of information, and when there is such a fluid boundary between fact and fiction' (Adams, 2007). As the first public output of the ongoing collaboration between Blast Theory and MRL, *Desert Rain* marked a shift in the work of the company. From this point onwards, Blast Theory's work became more technologically complex, being situated at the forefront of ICT research and innovation.

Desert Rain was a technologically ambitious piece that incorporated a collaborative virtual reality environment (CVE) and 'a physically permeable mixed reality boundary' (Shaw et al., 2000), aiming to foster new relationships between performers and participants, as well as between the participants themselves. The piece also employed various interactive and gaming practices, projections on water screens that operated as (literally) fluid interfaces between the real and the virtual, as well as live physical performances. Blast Theory rightly argues that *Desert Rain* 'has become a significant work in the world of performance and new media' (Giannachi, 2007, 52). Indeed, the work has been described as 'a seminal experimental production fusing the technological complexity of hard science skills with a truly original artistic vision' (Dixon, 2007, 616), and as 'one of the most complex and powerful responses to the first Gulf War to be produced within the sphere of theatrical practice' (Giannachi, 2007, 52). The piece was nominated for an Interactive Arts BAFTA Award (2000), won an

Honorary Mention at the transmediale Awards, Berlin (2001), and received wide critical acclaim in the UK and Europe.

Can You See Me Now? *(2001)*

Although, by the turn of the millennium, Blast Theory was already known in the UK and Europe as an innovative performance and media art company, *Can You See Me Now?* (*CYSMN?*) was instrumental in establishing the company's international reputation. Another MRL collaboration that is seminal in the company's trajectory, *CYSMN?* was Blast Theory's first pervasive performance-game project. The piece, which 'draws upon the near ubiquity of handheld electronic devices in many developed countries' (Blast Theory website), employed cutting-edge mobile technologies and locative media to create a mixed reality in which boundaries between real and virtual space were blurred. Structured on a traditional chase game, *CYSMN?* unfolded both in the streets of a real city and online, within a virtual simulation of that same city. In fact, the project took place in several cities; it has been presented in the UK, the Netherlands, Germany, Austria, Spain, Ireland, Denmark, the USA, Canada, Japan and Brazil, over a period of nine years. Online players, based (almost) anywhere in the world, were pitched against Blast Theory members called 'runners', who were based in the real urban environment. Using GPS tracking, the runners' positions in the real city were identified and 'translated' into the virtual simulation of the same city, in relation to the online players. The runners chased the online players using handheld computers that displayed the players' positions within the simulated world. With up to 100 people playing online at any one time, the multiplayer aspect of the game allowed players to collaborate and exchange tactics. Players could also 'eavesdrop' on the runners' discussions through an audio stream running from their walkie-talkies. *CYSMN?* examined the distortion of the boundaries between public and private space as mobile telephony has encouraged users to broadcast private conversations into public arenas, rendering passers-by the inadvertent audiences (or eaves-droppers) to their personal dramas (Blast Theory website).

In each *CYSMN?* performance-game, two cities, a 'real' and a virtual, would meet and merge into one hybrid city built from overlapping layers of physical and digital space-time, each with different qualities and behaviours. As Blast Theory puts it, 'the virtual city … has an elastic relationship to the real city. At times the two cities seem identical … At other times the two cities diverge and appear very remote from one another' (Blast Theory website). Each time two cities merged and then were torn apart, a new space was produced. This was neither exclusively physical nor exclusively virtual; it was, instead, a hybrid space created from the players' interactions with each other, which pertained to the interstices between physical and virtual. This hybrid city was shaped by the relations developed between the different layers of space-time and the people who 'inhabited' them. As I discuss elsewhere (Chatzichristodoulou, 2009b), *CYSMN?* used the overlay of this emergent city to explore ideas of distributed presence and absence, and of the grey areas in between. For example, the online players were both present (in the hybrid city) and absent (in a corporeal form, from the physical city); the runners were also present (in the hybrid city) and absent (in the proximity of the players). Finally, when a player was caught, the runners took photos of the exact physical location where each player was 'spotted'. These photos, called 'sightings', were then uploaded to the website, functioning as an abstract but poignant documentation of each game. As players became mapped onto the physical terrain they had abandoned, the sightings functioned as poetic acts, interweaving the digital, virtual city into the physical, tangible one, while augmenting real space with yet another layer of relationality. Through their weaving of the physical and the digital, these sightings linked the player to a fragment of cityscape that, possibly, s/he might have never visited. The work's visceral nature, which resulted from the intensely physical activity of the runners battling against natural elements, hostile urban environments and the limitations of their own bodies, kept juxtaposing itself against the smoothness of the virtual realm the players occupied, not only through the sightings, but also through the runners' walkie-talkies. Blast Theory succeeded in creating a rare hybrid: a computer game that invited real life to burst into the virtual realm, 'contaminating' it with its unexpected, messy and often paradoxical essence.

In developing *CYSMN?* the company posed the question, 'when games, the internet and mobile phones converge what new possibilities arise?' (Blast Theory website). This focus on convergence media proved to be particularly pertinent at the time, and an area of fruitful investigation for successive works, such as the research project, *Participate* (2006–8). *CYSMN?* won Blast Theory's first major award, the Golden Nica for Interactive Art at Prix Ars Electronica (Linz, Austria), among several others. It launched a series of important live gaming projects, such as *Uncle Roy All Around You* (2003), also a mixed reality game that unfolded simultaneously within a virtual and a real city, and *I*

Like Frank (2004), which (according to Blast Theory) was the world's first 3G mixed reality game. *CYSMN?* also opened the way for the development of the company's locative media practice, which has not always been dependent on gaming structures. Locative media pieces that do not function as games include *Rider Spoke, Ulrike and Eamon Compliant* and the locative cinema piece *A Machine to See With* (2010).

Day of the Figurines *(2006)*

Blast Theory's first 'game' that unfolds over short message service (SMS), *Day of the Figurines* (*DoF*), was a durational piece that invited players to engage with it over a period of 24 days, each of which represented an hour of the figurines' time. Like previous work, *DoF* merged different layers of space-time, bringing together the physical and virtual to create mixed experiences. In this case, the physical space was an actual installation of a vast model town (the piece opened at the Lighthouse in Brighton, where the model was installed), inhabited by 1,000 plastic figurines. Each figurine was moved by hand once every hour for the duration of the game. To take part in the game, players had to physically visit the installation and register their own figurine, by naming it, answering questions about its past (for example, describing a place in the fictional character's childhood), and considering how the figurine would like to be remembered, 'invoking feelings of mortality and legacy' (Adams and Delahunta, 2006, 149). The figurine was then placed in the town and, from that point onwards, the game unfolded via SMS.

According to the game's background story, all figurines were refugees who had just arrived in a British city, where they had to learn how to survive. Like all of Blast Theory's works that employ gaming structures, and unlike most commercial games, *DoF* had no clear objective or set of rules. Players were told that their main goal was to help others, while they all tried to survive within a fictional town that shifted 'from the mundane to the cataclysmic' (Blast Theory website). Players received at least one text per day that updated them on the progress of their figurine and invited them to make certain decisions about its actions. Figurines' 'health' levels could decrease or improve according to their actions and objects acquired (such as food and drink). Players received communications of 'events' via authored messages that provided the underlying narrative of the game; 'dilemmas', which were 'events that demanded a multiple choice response' and which impacted upon the figurines' health levels; and 'missions' which were more complex structures that combined 'multiple events, dilemmas, destinations and objects' (Flintham et al., 2007). Players could become increasingly ill and eventually die if they responded wrongly to dilemmas or failed missions. As the day became increasingly challenging for the refugees, culminating with the appearance of an occupying army in the town's High Street, players were faced with more complex moral dilemmas, such as how to respond to abusive soldiers, and whether to help other people survive. As a result, players had to make some difficult decisions about the fate of their figurine, its relation to and impact on other refugees and the town as a whole, and the responsibility – and risk – their character was prepared to undertake. Furthering issues raised by previous works, *DoF* 'continue[d] Blast Theory's enquiry into the nature of public participation within artworks and electronic spaces' (Flintham et al., 2007), raising concerns about social awareness, engagement and responsibility, and testing ideas relating to 'trust, community and democracy' (Adams and Delahunta, 2006, 151). Although previous works had engaged participants through the use of visually rich virtual environments, *DoF* was almost an exercise in minimalism: once they had registered their character, participants were invited to engage via the narrow channel of SMS messaging. Therefore, the restriction placed upon the mode of joining the game (through visiting the real space installation) was important in providing 'a rich and stimulating aesthetic experience at the outset to imprint the geography of the town into the minds of the players' (Adams and Delahunta, 2006, 150). At the same time, says Adams, this real-space encounter undergone by the players with a tangible representation of the fictional city, their own figurine and other players, helped retain 'a performative aspect', as players saw each other joining the game and witnessed the moving of their figurine for the first time (Adams and Delahunta, 2006, 150). From this point onwards, the low-tech nature and durational aspect of the piece set a dynamic that was distinct to it: Blast Theory attempted to create work that was 'situated within players' daily lives and c[ould] be accessed at any time' (Blast Theory website). Adams suggests that the long duration of the piece 'add[ed] to the sense that the game is personalized' as the information provided by each specific player is processed and addressed back to him/her (Adams and Delahunta, 2006, 149). Though players were not required to return to the board after having registered their figurine, some did occasionally do so to observe the changes in the town from close up. A website also allowed players to stay abreast with developments in the town and 'current affairs'. As is often the case in Blast Theory's work, *DoF* operated on different levels of player engagement, to create a layered narrative: not only did players co-author, to some extent, the narrative of their figurine through their actions and choices (and also, as a result, the narrative of the whole town), but visitors to the venue where the installation was exhibited were able to follow the game on a meta-narrative level, as observers, via video displays. Developed with MRL, Sony Net Services and the Fraunhofer Institute as part of the European research project IPerG, *DoF* was a complex and demanding piece to produce and orchestrate, and was only performed in Britain twice, in Brighton and Birmingham (Blast Theory website). It was followed by *Ivy4Evr*, another piece that used SMS to target a teenage audience, inviting them to engage in discussions on issues such as sex and drugs, by going to 'places that other dramas can't go – onto your phone and into your pocket' (Blast Theory website).

Ulrike and Eamon Compliant *(2009)*

This is one of Blast Theory's few pieces (along with *Desert Rain*) that has sought to explicitly engage with actual political events, posing profound questions such as: 'What are our obligations to act on our political beliefs? And what are the consequences of taking those actions?' (Blast Theory website). Building on previous locative media projects, Blast Theory invited participants to walk through the city of Venice (the piece was commissioned by the De La Warr Pavilion for the Venice Biennale), while receiving instructions on their mobile phones. The locative media aspect of the work was low-tech and depended on the participants' mobile phones, with no specialist gear required (as in *Rider Spoke*), rendering the work widely accessible.

    Ulrike drew on the lives of Ulrike Meinhof, leading member of the Red Army Faction,[2] and Eamon Collins, member of the Irish Republican Army.[3] It asked participants to assume the role of either Ulrike or Eamon, thus placing them as the main protagonists at the centre of a convoluted, treacherous and morally contentious world. The format of the work furthered dramaturgical and stylistic threads that had developed in pieces such as *Safehouse* and *Desert Rain*, where participants were invited to observe live interviews with others, without knowing that they would themselves become the subject of observation at a different point within the piece. In the case of *Ulrike*, interviews were layered; participants first watched the video of a live interview, then they were interviewed themselves and, finally, they were led to the realization that their interview was being watched, as they were invited to watch someone else being interviewed through a two-way mirror. Through this layering of surveying and being surveyed, Blast Theory exposed our willingness to sit back and witness others being challenged, while feeling secure in the shaded anonymity that the role of audience can provide. Once more, the company denied its spectators any comfort, not only through 'turning the tables' on them to make every single one a protagonist of the work for a brief passage of time (although they were not addressed as such, when interviewed participants assumed the roles of Ulrike or Eamon), but also through inviting them to watch others respond to challenging questions. The interviews invited participants to engage with the contentious ideas of political conflict and terrorism, and to consider aspects of their character with which they might not previously have been confronted. For example, they were asked what they would fight for, whether they would kill, and what they would do if people came into their area and killed their friends and neighbours (Blast Theory website). Blast Theory consciously probed for inconsistencies in people's stances, looking for 'the gap between [their] ideas of social engagement and the reality of [their] lifestyle' (Blast Theory website). *Ulrike* sought to reposition terrorism, often viewed through the prism of Islam and other racial, linguistic and religious divides, as a 'home grown' phenomenon, examining it as the corruption of a noble purpose. The work tested the participants' ethical stance towards terrorism by confronting them with difficult moral dilemmas to highlight the consequences of their imagined actions, asking 'what are the norms and bounds of fairness and justice?' (Blast Theory website). The locative film project *A Machine to See With* (2010) followed *Ulrike*, using similar technologies in inviting participants on a guided walk through the city using their mobile phones.

Conclusion

There is little doubt that Blast Theory has been one of the most influential art and performance groups operating in Britain before and after the turn of the millennium. The group's innovative, groundbreaking practice, which fuses disciplinary contexts, questions conventional understandings of theatre and pushes both technological and artistic boundaries, naturally lends itself to analysis, turning Blast Theory into the darlings of the academic establishment. As might be expected, the extended list of bibliographic references to the company's work originates from different disciplinary areas, primarily, drama and theatre studies, human–computer interaction (HCI) and game studies. The company's long-term collaboration with MRL at the University of Nottingham further ensures the critical reception of its work, as its artistic projects constitute research in their own right. Blast Theory's work has been discussed in relation to its use of locative media (see Gordon and Souza e Silva, 2011), urban, mobile and pervasive gaming (see Crogan, 2011), the design of interactive experiences (see Adams and O'Grady, 2011), and the performance of mixed reality (see Benford and Giannachi, 2011) among other issues, as well as in numerous overviews studying new media art and digital performance. The nature of the company's work – complex but accessible – also means that Blast Theory is studied in many drama and theatre departments in the UK as a successful example of a company engaged in interactive and participative theatre practice, and invested in the use of digital technology in contemporary performance.

Though highly respected in the academic world, Blast Theory is not always well received by theatre critics, who tend to approach the company's unconventional performances with some scepticism, and to be critical of the technology's shortcomings. Howard Loxton found *Rider Spoke* 'insufferably slow', and criticized Blast Theory for having made 'no attempt to construct a narrative or to give the experience a dramatic structure' (2007), while Simon Tait comments in relation to Blast Theory's *I'd Hide You* (2012) among other digital performance projects, 'I've seen the future of theatre … and it doesn't work' (2014). This is in contrast to the reception accorded by games journalists such as Keith Stuart, who describes the company's works as 'astonishing' (2011) and Liat Clark who, unlike Tait, enjoyed *I'd Hide You*: 'Blast Theory and Sheffield Doc/Fest are making interactivity what it should be: really, really fun' (2014).

Although acclaimed within artistic circles and studied in academia, Blast Theory has always been inspired by and concerned with popular culture. The company is unique in creating work that is conceptually sophisticated, thematically challenging, mentally, emotionally and physically demanding, while being accessible and indeed attractive to a vast range of audiences, crossing boundaries of nationality, age, gender and class. Blast Theory's engagement with popular culture is key to its success. The company confronts its audiences with challenging social and political questions, which emerge through familiar formats and settings such as club nights, computer games or one's mobile phone. This strategy lures audiences into the work with the promise of playful entertainment, averting the danger of alienating them by its conceptual complexity, technological mindset or political content. It is my belief that the company's virtuosic merging of the sophisticated, innovative and challenging with the everyday, familiar and popular is the cause of its wide appeal in many different circles, including those audiences described as 'hard to reach'. Blast Theory also owes its success to its use of digital and mobile telecommunication technologies, balancing technological innovation with user-friendly and intuitive low-tech solutions. Unconcerned with 'showing off' technological competences, Blast Theory uses emerging technology to focus on the art. As Rohan Gunatillake suggests, 'It's about time we gave the arts the chance to influence digital technology as much as the other way round' (Gunatillake, 2013). Blast Theory succeeds in employing technological innovation to advance art and social interaction and influence the way technology itself is being developed and applied. Gunatillake further argues that 'we need more art that takes digital tools and digital thinking and uses it to express and curate beauty, meaning and debate' (Gunatillake, 2013). To achieve this, we need more companies like Blast Theory.

Key Works

Gunmen Kill Three, 1991, London
Chemical Wedding, 1992, Hull
Stampede, 1993, Cambridge
Invisible Bullets, 1994, London
The Gilt Remake, 1995, Leicester
Ultrapure, 1996, London
Blipvert, 1997 (video)
Safehouse, 1997, Berlin
Kidnap, 1998, Manchester
10 Backwards, 1999, Bristol
Desert Rain, 1999, London
Can You See Me Now?, 2001, Sheffield
TRUCOLD, 2002, Venice (video)
Uncle Roy All around You, 2003, London
I Like Frank, 2004, Adelaide
Integrated Project on Pervasive Gaming (IPerG), 2005–8 (research)
Day of the Figurines, 2006, Brighton
Participate, 2006 (research)
Rider Spoke, 2007, London

You Get Me, 2008, London
Ulrike and Eamon Compliant, 2009, Venice
Ivy4Evr, 2010 (SMS drama)
A Machine to See With, 2010, San Jose
I'd Hide You, 2012, Sheffield

Chapter 8

PUNCHDRUNK

Josephine Machon

What shall we call this company? What is it, when you punch someone, they're reeling, that dazed expression? Punchdrunk. (Barrett, 2013b)

Punchdrunk is renowned for having pioneered a radical approach to immersive theatre. With a signature Punchdrunk event, audiences of up to 600 per night (with entrances staggered over a three-hour run) are thrust into densely designed theatrical worlds inspired by classic sources and staged within vast, abandoned sites. Individuals roam free to explore the intricate installations and discover intoxicating performance encounters. Punchdrunk's practice is unique within the British landscape of theatre in its particular aesthetic and the way that it shifts the lines between space, design, performer and audience member. Although perceived as a rapid rise from the fringe to the mainstream (from *Sleep No More* in 2003 to *The Drowned Man: A Hollywood Fable* in 2014), the vision and practice of Felix Barrett, founder and Artistic Director of Punchdrunk, evolved across a number of years prior to this decade.

My analysis of Punchdrunk's practice is intentionally personal, a feature that results from the decidedly individual nature of audience reception that arises from immersive practice in general, and Punchdrunk's work in particular. The purpose of this chapter is to chart the hitherto unpublished history of Punchdrunk's practice. It starts with Barrett's childhood inventions, which evolved into theatrical form across his student years. Consequently, this discussion offers new insights to the mission and methodology of Punchdrunk, from its inception to the way in which the company is known today.

Prehistory

> Dens have been there since year dot, according to mum. (Barrett, 2012)

Barrett spent his youth transforming his bedroom into otherworldly abodes with fictional facades, fake entrances that subverted expectation for those lucky enough to be invited in. Barrett's home, a Victorian terrace in South London, offered a variety of architectural features within which he could play, enabling him to pinpoint spaces he found ominous and those that were 'pockets of absolute safety' (Barrett, 2012). These imaginative hideouts were scaled up around the age of 12 when he discovered the attic: 'anybody or anything could be around the myriad corners ... so much shadow, you couldn't just flick a light on and see everything. It was filled with detritus ... strange objects that were from a foreign time' (Barrett, 2012). Here Barrett became aware of how elements of architectural space could ignite the imagination and how the histories bound up in objects might become mythical narratives. Barrett recalls de-cluttering the attic, building a secret labyrinth and carefully replacing each item, a theatrical event that was only ever experienced by himself and his best friend Alex.

Barrett's first defining theatre experience, aged seven, was ('it pains me to say it') Andrew Lloyd Webber's musical *Cats*. Barrett remembers the set spilling out into the audience, the blackout:

> live music started, it makes me tingle now to think about it. I felt it was out of control because cast were moving behind us, it was so far away from what my perception of theatre was ... I was on the back corner of the stalls and one of them brushed my shoulders, looked me in the eye, all of which happened in a moment. (Barrett, 2012)

Barrett acknowledges that this alerted him to the potency of intimate interaction, the power of *the moment* for an individual audience member. Barrett was so inspired by this encounter he wanted to relive it through the soundtrack, 'I got it for Christmas and we put it on and as soon as it started playing I cried, because the experience came back again, was utterly visible' (Barrett, 2012). This experiential recall was crucial for Barrett, even at this young age. More than the evocation of the spectacle, overwhelmingly it was the bodily reiteration of 'that beat of tactile intimacy' that was important, 'one moment that only two of us shared' (Barrett, 2012).

Barrett's years on a scholarship at Alleyn's School, Dulwich further nurtured his theatrical imagination. Drama teachers Matthew Grant and Geoff Tonkin concentrated on 'the outer reaches of theatrical practice', both influenced by the Romanian director, Silviu Purcărete (Barrett, 2012). Barrett was enthralled by accounts of rehearsal techniques that Purcărete would employ; meeting with his company to explore Aeschylus' *Les Danaïdes* in an old aircraft hangar, putting them into couples, giving each pair a candle, and instructing them to find a space in which to improvise the wedding night of Hypermnestra and Lynceus. For Barrett, these techniques foregrounded the power of theatre as *experience*. The use of the candles encapsulated how duration as much as event could become meaningful. It was the concept of 'the narrative being woven into the flicker of a flame' and the framing of moments, 'the unseen as much as the seen', that proved significant, expanding the possibilities of what might be uncovered within the source text and communicated through performance (Barrett, 2012). Subsequent visits to Benjamin Britten's *Peter Grimes* and Béla Bartók's *Bluebeard's Castle* at the English National Opera became deeply influential, as did Barrett's studies into the work of Edward Gordon Craig. Alongside the visual sweep of Craig's designs, Barrett was drawn to his theories regarding the delivery of text on the edge of the breath, 'that quality of *felt* experience' (Barrett, 2012).

During his final A level year, Barrett opted for directing as a specialism. His assessment piece, a post-apocalyptic imagining, involved remixing 'the orchestral crescendo of [The Beatles] *A Day in the Life*, the peak of which dropped into a dance track … [t]he audience were sat on sand, I got a lot of old white goods and junk from skips, to create a world that [they] were within' (Barrett, 2012). This installation performance demonstrated Barrett's sophisticated, interdisciplinary approach to the theatrical medium. It was inspired by a profound and defining event in his artistic development. In 1995, Barrett visited Robert Wilson and Hans Peter Kuhn's installation, *H.G.* (at Clink Street Vaults, London). Following that, 'everything changed' (Barrett, 2012):

it was densely atmospheric with huge, implied narrative but you *never* came across performers who were telling that story … The first time I experienced it was with very few audience members. It was the room to breathe, the amount of space your imagination had to fill in the gaps, which was totally seductive. (in Machon, 2013, 164, emphasis original)

His second experience of *H.G.*, returning a week later with his family, was crucial in the honing of his own method. Now 'packed with audience', for Barrett, the 'spell was broken'. The overwhelming presence of 'other people and other people's readings and responses to it somehow dirtied the experience' (in Machon, 2013, 164). It was the probing of this problem that was fundamental to the next phase of Barrett's practice and that produced the signature forms and techniques for which Punchdrunk would become famous.

From 1997 to 1999, Exeter University Drama Department offered fertile ground for Barrett's ingenuity, a result of the investigative approach taken across the undergraduate course. This approach was project-led rather than curriculum-led and focused on 'practice and experimentation and getting things wrong', culminating in a practical essay in the final year (Barrett, 2012). For Barrett, it was like being up in the attic again, 'eight hours a day of nothing but making' (Barrett, 2012). Crucial to Barrett's aesthetic was the fact that he was encouraged by his tutor Stephen Hodge to explore installation as a theatrical form. Developing a knack for uncovering an experiential concept within classic source material, in his final year Barrett used a monologue from *Faust* to explore his interest in urban mythology. Fellow student Joel Scott performed this on a main road – forest either side, cars zooming past – between midnight and 1.00 a.m. The audience, unbeknownst to them, were the drivers of the cars tearing past. Barrett's overriding concern was the blurring of art and life, making drivers believe they had seen something real, 'it was a scary, windy night, autumn term, so magic was in the air' (Barrett, 2012). The significance of his findings through this investigation, a cornerstone of Barrett's mission to uncover what a theatrical experience might be for an audience member, lay in 'the flash, the beat of the moment' (Barrett, 2012). Rekindling that flicker of the candle flame, these moments are not as much about what is seen but rather about what is *felt*, the thrill and trepidation of the imagination filling in the gaps.

It was in his final production, with the remit that it must be directed in a found space, that the Punchdrunk methodology for large-scale productions was formed. Barrett directed Georg Büchner's *Woyzeck* in an old Territorial Army barracks. This was the origin of what was to become Punchdrunk's classic loop structure. Inspired by the fragmentary nature of the text, Barrett deconstructed a version of the play, and looped this 20-minute edit on repeat for three hours. The audience arrived at the site to receive instructions from a ringmaster on the gate. They were ritualistically masked and individually invited into the fairground to encounter Woyzeck's world, 'as much art gallery inspired by the text as it was theatre show' (Barrett, 2012). Three weeks before the opening night, Barrett had realized that the challenge of the audience getting in the way or assuming 'that the fellow audience member is a performer' remained, a problem that had bothered him since his second experience of *H.G.*: 'I've had two eureka moments in my life and that was one; *if we mask them they become invisible* ... I knew immediately it should be a neutral mask – we'd played with them throughout university – because that way an audience member could become anything' (Barrett, 2012, emphasis original). The experimentation in *Woyzeck*, from the loop structure to the audience masks to the scenographic detail (including taxidermy, scents and real human hair collected from barbers), established what was to become the signature Punchdrunk aesthetic.

Early Punchdrunk

[I]t was the mask that was the real turning point ... we spent the next five shows pushing the mask and seeing which iterations worked. (Barrett, 2012)

Punchdrunk was founded by Barrett with fellow graduates Joel Scott and Sally Gibson (since, Scott), now both of Goat and Monkey, supported by a collective from Exeter including Pete Higgin, Euan Maybank (both still core members) and Becky Smith.[1] The fledgling company, which Higgin recalls as 'informal – friends working on projects' (Higgin, 2013a), benefited from the backing of the university, which supported this experimentation by providing access to lighting kit, space and technical capability. Barrett was keen to pursue the pace and practice of 'churning stuff out ... to keep up that momentum ... The last thing I wanted to do was spend a year hypothesising' (Barrett, 2013a). The first four Punchdrunk shows explored different forms and shapes, beginning with *The Cherry Orchard* (2000), conceived and directed by Barrett to exploit forms initiated in *Woyzeck* within the intimacy of a town house.

Here, Punchdrunk experimented with unexpected performance intervention among the audience, with the intention of further blurring boundaries between the real and the fictional. It was also the first point at which there was an aesthetic fusion of film with theatre to reflect related concerns of the narrative. Beginning in the safety of a domestic space, the audience watched the daughter's drowning in Nicolas Roeg's film *Don't Look Now* (1973) as a reference to Raynevskya's drowned son. Collecting the mask in this house, the audience were then led to another where a performer, planted on the street, intervened by asking for money as a device to destabilize the audience. This worked most effectively for some American tourists who, thinking they had booked for *The Cherry Orchard* at Exeter's Northcote Theatre, were completely taken in, and consequently more receptive to the whole experience.

When Scott and Gibson left to travel the world, Barrett took charge and experimented with *The Moonslave* (2000), *Johnny Formidable: Mystery at the Pink Flamingo* (2001), *The Tempest* (2001) and *The House of Oedipus* (2002) before making the move to London. *The Moonslave* (involving a headphone journey, crumbling mansion, evocative installations and lone audience member cast as protagonist) became the paradigm for a uniquely Punchdrunk experience whereby the active audience-participant becomes intimately involved with an epic event. Other Exeter experiments pointed up problems and solutions for the evolving method. Barrett gained insight from misapplying *The Moonslave* form to *Johnny Formidable*. The principle of the headset failed when employed in a studio space for multiple audience members, as opposed to one at a time, chiefly because they read it as a theatrical experience rather than an event that was invading 'real life' (Barrett, 2013a). *The Tempest* at Buckland Abbey offered valuable lessons in style, as the experiential form and lengthy Shakespearean monologues seemed at odds, leading Barrett to recognize that he had to find alternatives to the traditional delivery of speech. *The House of Oedipus* provided Barrett with his second eureka moment:

> Outdoors, daytime, six hour durational, masks. Didn't work. Because of the natural light. Punchdrunk is about curiosity, exploration and discovery of those beats of wonder. If you can see in the distance what you're going to discover in five minutes time, once you actually get there, it invalidates it; there's no reveal. You need the reveal. The reveal is crucial. (Barrett, 2013a)

Darkness and secrecy in the lighting design became an imperative: 'you need an atmosphere to be thick with the crackle of distant magic' (Barrett, 2013a).

These Exeter projects, followed by initial experiments in London, were crucial, 'finding strategies and ways' artistically and technically 'to realise the vision' (Higgin, 2013a). The space hunting, the loop structure, the mask were all vital from *Woyzeck* onwards, and are illustrated by Punchdrunk's current production at the time of writing, *The Drowned Man: A Hollywood Fable* (2013–14). The potency of one-on-ones, explored through Barrett's student installations and *The Moonslave*, remains the Punchdrunk ideal audience experience. The desire to explore physical performance that grew out of *The Tempest* was to be first realized when Barrett collaborated with Maxine Doyle on *Sleep No More* (2003). The intervention technique, used in *The Cherry Orchard*, has been employed on various projects, most recently adding unsettling texture to Punchdrunk's one-on-one theatrical journey, *The Borough* (2013).

The importance of placing the audience at the centre of the experience, the fundamental criterion of the company's policy, has existed from Barrett's childhood dens onwards. Site that tells stories, dressed space and chiaroscuro light; the breathing and whispering of text; the physical presence of a living performer who is there, then gone; the creation of 'moments' for individual audience members; the excavation of the essence of a source, rather than a narrative rendition of a classical text; in total, the exploitation of the sensuality of an event to establish *an experience*; all of these constitute Barrett's aesthetic, finely honed from a young age. His artistic mission and methodology, the foundations of which were laid during his time as undergraduate-practitioner, have been coloured and pushed further by Barrett's collaborations with a range of artists within the company since 2001. This long-standing core creative team includes Stephen Dobbie, Sound and Graphic Designer since 2002; Maxine Doyle, Choreographer and Associate Director since 2003; Peter Higgin, founding company member and Enrichment Director; Colin Marsh, Producer and Manager from 2003 to 2011, now Strategic Associate; Euan Maybank, founding member and Technical Associate; Colin Nightingale, member of the core team since 2002, now Senior Producer; Livi Vaughan and Beatrice Minns, Design Associates since 2005; and Griselda Yorke, Executive Producer since December 2011. Supported by a strong band of associate artists nurtured since 2003, the team refer to a shared sensibility, what Nightingale calls 'a shorthand' (Nightingale, 2013a). Doyle argues that 'Felix' vision is so epic … it allows everyone else their own space and their own voice', thus emphasizing how the nature and scale of Punchdrunk's work requires a comparable vision and voice from all collaborators (Doyle, 2013).

Punchdrunk has evolved from a nomadic, project-led collective of artists to a subsidized company with a trading subsidiary, led by Barrett as Artistic Director. In bringing Barrett and Doyle together,

Marsh's role was crucial in galvanizing the unique style of practice that is thought of as the trademark Punchdrunk aesthetic. Early large-scale projects were ambitious, despite being produced under budget constraints. Multi-tasking has been an attribute of the working practice of the team from the start, as all members had to be involved across the creation, production and performance of the work, as well as undertaking technical and administrative tasks. Now Punchdrunk's infrastructure defines specialist roles to realize the complex projects. Barrett 'sets parameters' and company members 'get on with it', without any feeling of being constrained (Nightingale, 2013a). Jennifer Hoy, on the administrative team since 2008 and now General Manager, believes the collaborative and 'radical' way in which Barrett 'shares his vision with his fellow creatives' is key to the success of the company (Hoy, 2013).

Evolving Structures, Evolving Forms: Artistic Policy and Working Methodology

> The physical freedom to explore the sensory and imaginative world of a Punchdrunk show without compulsion or explicit direction sets it apart from the standard practice of viewing theatre in unconventional locations. (Punchdrunk, 2013)

Punchdrunk has, since the mid-2000s, described its practice as 'immersive' (see Machon, 2013). Punchdrunk's signature masked events follow a unique methodology that is modified for smaller-scale work. Each project establishes a method that is bespoke to the needs of a concept, fashioned with high production values involving close collaboration among the creative team, and an overriding commitment to the experience of the individual audience member.

Barrett is responsible for the initial concept, which he fixes once space is finalized. He steers this throughout the whole production, developing it with Doyle in the rehearsal space, and working closely with Dobbie, Minns and Vaughan to realize it on site. First and foremost a site is assured, and only then can the rest of the process continue: 'With each project we go into, I know how much of a player the building is; it becomes a battle to try and match it. That's what marks Punchdrunk out among other companies that do site work; so often the site or building dominates and the show doesn't do anything in it' (Doyle, 2013). In Punchdrunk events, it is the space that unlocks and underscores the challenges of the concept in theme, narrative and form.

Barrett and Doyle together spend a long time casting, which supports or shifts the vision of the piece, the concept evolving through their discussion and debate. Alongside the casting, a storyboarding exercise occurs, initially between Barrett and Doyle, then shared among the core creative team, imagining potential experiences for the audience within the space. From the outset, there is no hierarchy of performance elements; each is as vital as the other. This is 'the most intense part' of the Barrett/Doyle collaboration because 'it's about the thinking behind it, we commit to these characters, we create their arcs and their stories ... we're looking at the space, the site, trying to work out how the building needs to work, where people need to be so that the building is animated and alive' (Doyle, 2013). Concurrently, the site is made safe and the design team, led by Vaughan and Minns, and overseen by Barrett, enter the space to begin the painting, building and dressing, an activity that resonates with Barrett's creation of labyrinths in the attic. Lighting is explored once each space is dressed: 'The way Felix works with his design team ... dovetails with the development of the narrative, different texts and inspirations that he uses feed into a series of different narratives and loops' (Yorke, 2013). Sound sets the atmosphere and tone, extending beyond the emotional to the visceral. The sound 'is a hugely defining characteristic with regard to the world and the atmosphere of the show', carefully designed to shift 'perception and experience' (Dobbie, 2013). Barrett and Dobbie's development of the sound-score in response to the space encourages the audience to become highly attuned to sound, where it exists and is absent, firing the imagination to culminate in a whole-body experience. The sound world supports an entire environment, on a micro level, in terms of the demands of each room, and on a macro scale, in terms of the world of the event. Sound is omnipresent, even where designed to bleed into a non-sound-scored room from another locale, and is logistically and harmonically complex. Sound-design develops organically alongside other aspects of the show to accompany the audience on its journey, as both sonic architecture and an individual 'cinematic experience':

> every layer is supported with the right score ... if they've felt that resonance and those vibrations, the ups and downs and fluctuations in emotions ... without necessarily noticing where and how and why those things happened then that's the goal ... to let them piece it together for themselves, often subconsciously. (Dobbie, 2013)

Punchdrunk has built up a core ensemble of dancers who share a movement vocabulary and methodology. While the design team overhaul the space, Doyle focuses on the performers, developing the choreography in studio rehearsals. This is playtime, where the movement language begins in an abstract manner in a safe and warm environment, 'where the floors are soft' and dancers are nurtured. Barrett and Doyle 'bombard' performers with information related to the production, including visual, audio and literary stimuli, using the classical text as source and structure for the work to ensure 'everyone is on the same page for the creative frame' (Doyle, 2013). This establishes 'a concentrate' of the movement language that will be translated to the space (Doyle, 2013). Barrett is in and out of the studio, in constant consultation with Doyle. Exploration with music during rehearsals feeds Dobbie's sound design. His process thus traverses the dance composition and the site in construction, attuning one to the other organically. Scoring large choreographed scenes alongside intimate, individual moments, he ensures the situated sound supports or contrasts with the choreography. Doyle and the performers work with instinct on long improvisations, shifting music and adding props, to foster a movement form and dynamic that will be responsive to, and effective in, the space.

When the ensemble enters the building, Barrett initially takes control. His childhood pockets of threat and safety directly relate to the lead exercise that he sets up for the performers in the space: a game where they must seek out safe spaces and discover where the threats lie, to explore the performance potential of each. This 'offers the performers the opportunity to engage with the space as individuals, to pick up on its atmospheres, to be excited by it, challenged by it, frightened by it' (Doyle, 2013). Barrett and Doyle then embark on a combination of facilitating, editing and creating with the performers and designers, to rework the material and effects in the space. Emphasis is placed on the performers working on their own journeys through the space, crafted and guided by the directors and those carefully constructed storyboards. 'Each scene has a treatment' that occurs in a particular space; 'when we enter the building each character has a strong sense of where they're going, who they're going to meet, what their arc is, what that scene is about' (Doyle, 2013). The focus becomes the lead narrative loops, the backbone for every character's story, while 'the space offers an immediate context to work within'. As a consequence, the choreography needs to do 'less work', because the space is telling stories and offering emotional possibilities for audience and performer (Doyle, 2013).

Finally, the audience comes into that space and shifts the production as a whole to the extent that, during preview runs – vital to the Punchdrunk process, routes, levels, lighting and so on have to be changed to ensure the audience are enabled to 'find what we want them to find' (Doyle, 2013). Sound design, in league with the scenography, signposts where to head on the journey; echoes of sound at a distance in the building tantalize and indicate where important or incidental action occurs. The dance vocabulary in set sequences, as opposed to long speeches, allows for a fluidity of expression in performance that supports individual journeys; there is no need to hang around and wait for the scene to play itself out in order to get its gist. Furthermore, pleasure can be gained from observing the cycle repeat itself, altered each time by the effects of the dancers' ongoing toil, alongside different responses and positionings of new audience members. Performers have to develop the capacity to respond instinctively to the presence of the audience, 'becoming really skilled in changing the movement language in response to other bodies and other bodies in space', turning the choreographic volume up to get attention (Doyle and Machon, 2007). Timings shift, characters may have to meet characters with whom they had not previously interacted. The audience involvement produces 'a whole new layer of improvisation … within the process of previews and by the end of the previews that improvisation is then set' (Doyle, 2013).

The mask is a critical device in the audience involvement, shifting status and encouraging active engagement in various ways. The overriding intention is 'to remove the rest of the audience members *being the audience* from the picture … if they're part of the scenography then they're either excluded from, or a complementary addition to, your reading of the work' (Barrett in Machon, 2013, 164, emphasis original). The impact of the mask differs for each audience member. It can liberate, invite a sense of playfulness through role play, grant permission to be curious, enable the audience member to become part of the otherworldliness or simply sit back and be. The effect is that audience merges with the mise-en-scène, eerily present witnesses, like spectres in the shadows.

Punchdrunk's process highlights its central artistic mission: creating myriad ways in which the audience is placed at the heart of the live experience within a complex and rigorously designed immersive world. Smaller-scale projects such as *It Felt Like A Kiss* (2009), *The Crash of the Elysium* (2011) or *The Borough* do not employ dance or masks, as the audience are given a specific role to play; 'there's no need for a mask as their status has already shifted' (Barrett in Machon, 2013,

161). Correspondingly, Enrichment projects also involve alternative approaches in concept and to performer/audience interaction.

Enrichment Projects

[I]t all comes back to making sure that whatever you do, whatever you create, it makes an individual feel 'punchdrunk' … we get to develop that … 'now that we've actually got somebody feeling punchdrunk, how do we use that, how can that be a positive force for change?' (Higgin, 2011)

Punchdrunk's Enrichment arm produces much of its small-scale work. These projects are designed to reach out to children, young people and the wider non-theatre community, as well as to nurture individuals and creativity from within the company as part of this process. The intimate structure of Enrichment productions offers models for performance and audience engagement that directly impact communities while also uncovering methodologies (creative and strategic) for how new concepts and large-scale projects can be managed. Enrichment was the brainchild of Higgin, who had specialized in Applied Theatre at Exeter and worked as a teacher in secondary schools. Higgin had witnessed a newfound sophistication in his A level-students' discussions and practical work following visits to *Sleep No More* (2003) and *The Firebird Ball* (2005) that demonstrated the 'potential for transformative engagement' within the parameters of the form (Higgin, 2012). Higgin's belief in this was cemented when he witnessed the participatory work during the collaboration with Battersea Arts Centre (BAC) in 2008.

The principles of Enrichment were inherent early on in the volunteering opportunities offered by Punchdrunk: 'an engagement ethos always existed in the company … it creates community, it enthuses people in the ambition of the work, the idea of transforming space' (Higgin, 2013b). Funding from the Paul Hamlyn Foundation in 2008 enabled Punchdrunk's outward-facing approach to be formalized as the Enrichment arm. Enrichment projects endeavour to offer the Punchdrunk experience at a community level on bespoke projects addressing the needs and space of the host community. With its work in schools, the overriding aim is to raise standards in literacy and attainment through experiential engagement. Each project is centred on an installation – a narrative and a world created within the school to address educational needs, as well as creating 'a buzz' across the site, uniting staff and pupils (Higgin, 2013b). Enrichment projects have inspired teachers to rethink learning in the context of INSET training, and supported them in setting up ways to create their own immersive projects. For Higgin, this taps into the sensibilities of teachers 'who were doing this type of all-encompassing, whole school activity, teacher-in-role work back in the seventies and eighties, which is less employed nowadays', empowering children to experience learning 'as an adventure' and promoting heuristic ideals of 'ownership through discovery and curiosity' that is the premise of the signature mask work (Higgin, 2013b).

Beyond schools, Punchdrunk has produced outreach projects that have received critical acclaim, such as *The Uncommercial Traveller*, originally created in 2011 with Arcola Theatre's 60+ group in Hackney, and since adapted across a diversity of international communities including Cape Town, Karachi, Melbourne, Penang and Singapore, as part of the British Council's 'Dickens 2012' Programme. Punchdrunk's work aimed to reinvigorate the participants' relationship with the urban life and history of their cities. Enrichment projects are 'always about modes of facilitation' (Higgin, 2013b), creating a dialogue and process that allows Punchdrunk to be civically responsive while still pushing the forms and potential of the practice.

Funding and Supporting Partnerships

Punchdrunk began by producing work thriftily, out of Barrett's own pocket and by his ability to charm various people into lending space or objects. Since 2008, the company has been an Arts Council England Regularly Funded Organization (RFO) and in receipt of backing from The Esmée Fairbairn Foundation and Bloomberg. In each case, the funds given have acknowledged innovative practice and supported the company's artistic policy, which has impacted on the way in which company members, as much as the wider public, perceive Punchdrunk's achievements. Arts Council funding supports the core operation of the company and, consequently, enables Punchdrunk to explore a range of artistic ideas effectively with the status of a not-for-profit organization. This, alongside financial recognition by the Nesta Trust for technology-enhanced interactive investigations within *Sleep No More*, New York (2011–) affirms Punchdrunk as pioneers.

Punchdrunk's structures operate according to the principles of many medium-scale arts organizations, which are funded as charities, with investment schemes for supporters. An additional producing challenge for Punchdrunk is the sourcing and obtaining of permission to use huge sites, involving complex negotiations. The creative team's process is also unique, 'the scale of it is the biggest difference … it's like designing and directing a 200 scene play'. Yorke's job is to find 'the right partners and financing for the vision of the project' (Yorke, 2013). Collaborations and co-productions with the likes of the National Theatre, Manchester International Festival and BAC have been fundamental in supporting the ambition of Punchdrunk's ventures. A long-term aim is to have infrastructure in place allowing Punchdrunk to function on its own behalf. For Barrett, the significance of financial support is the shared desire to achieve the vision: 'it's about someone saying, alright this is ambitious, it's going to cost a lot of money, there are problems, but let's try and do it' (Barrett, 2013a).

Branded support, alongside Nesta funds, has provided the resources to test out creative ideas through research and development projects. For instance, a network of chauffeured journeys across intimate locations in East London was explored in the Stella Artois-financed *The Black Diamond* (2011), and an investigation of how audience member becomes player/protagonist in a performance-meets-gaming context was undertaken in … *And Darkness Descended* (2011), funded by Sony Playstation. Punchdrunk has been criticized for 'selling out' on commercial projects, including collaborations with Louis Vuitton, Bacardi, W Hotels, Alexander McQueen, Xbox and Virgin Media (see Gillinson, 2012; Silvestre, 2012). Connie Harrison, Punchdrunk's Brand Partnerships Director since 2011, defends this approach to funding, arguing that 'selling-out implies personal gain whereas actually every single penny goes back into the company' (2013). Although ancillary to Punchdrunk's work, these exercises allow ideas to be piloted and offer opportunities to budding artists, producers and managers from within the company. They expose the company to new audiences, while generating an income that directly feeds into Punchdrunk Enrichment projects, securing buildings and subsidizing ticket prices. Yorke emphasizes the challenges of funding Punchdrunk's wider ideals of reach and impact: '[W]hen people snipe at us for doing corporate work it grates a bit … if you're going to run a business, and a charity is a business, then you're going to have to be able to resource it' (Yorke, 2013). The 'snipes' highlight the implication that there is a different agenda attached to the giving and receiving of private rather than public funding, that public awards are politically or philanthropically motivated and are related to recognition of practice that offers something back to the society in which the work is produced, whereas commercial funding establishes only a money-making relationship where there is a misappropriation of the profile, pleasures and potential of the art. Adam Alston provides an interesting analysis of this by considering the impact of branding within Punchdrunk immersive events, and proposing that combined public/private funding approaches might be consistent with the 'neoliberal' consumerist society in which Punchdrunk operates (see Alston, 2012, 2013).

The collaboration with Emursive on *Sleep No More*, NY shifted Punchdrunk's experience of commercial relationships. As much as Punchdrunk was solely responsible for the artistic concept and execution (there was no franchise-model 'how-to' manual for jobbing directors and designers; instead, the core team created the bespoke production for a one-off building), Emursive incorporated money-making ventures, such as the selling of masks and related memorabilia, in order to make the production costs viable and maintain the show's run. This required careful collaboration and negotiated compromise in terms of Punchdrunk maintaining the artistic integrity of the project. That said, this production has been transformational in terms of how Punchdrunk considers itself, as much as in how it is perceived globally. At the time of writing, *Sleep No More*, NY is in its third year and continuing to sell out performances, playing every night of the week. It has shown that signature productions offer a business model that works financially while upholding high standards in process and delivery.

Punchdrunk has only recently begun to benefit financially from *Sleep No More*, NY, and any profit is immediately invested in the running of the company and its smaller-scale projects. Although the quality of production may suggest otherwise, Punchdrunk is not yet in the position where it can attract a level of corporate sponsorship that could replace subsidy. The recent 'premium ticket', offering private experiences to the holder, for *The Drowned Man*, is an illustration of the finance required to realize its scale:

> the more professional we've become as a company, the more expensive it's become. People have to be paid properly ... there's not a massive profit to be made between the expenses versus the income so we have to look for ways to generate greater income so that we can afford to do these projects. (Doyle, 2013)

A significant strategy related to funding, structure and operation that enables the company to function and achieve its artistic vision is the use of volunteers on the large-scale productions. Punchdrunk has recently introduced an internship programme, through openly advertised positions, that pays a group of interns a London living wage, as well as establishing mentoring opportunities during the internship. Such opportunities, ingrained in company policy, serve as a training ground for a new generation of artists, technicians and administrators.

From the Fringe to the Mainstream: Defining Productions

It's always, always, always about the audience. (Barrett, 2013a)

In order to convey the experiential quality that is central to Punchdrunk's work, this following section intentionally adopts a reflective style, ranging across tenses and first and third person analysis, in an attempt to communicate the specific tone of each production and to convey some sense of the immediacy of each immersive experience from the audience-participant's perspective.

The Moonslave

The Moonslave was a 40-minute one-on-one show, presented across four nights only, where the lone audience-participant was immersed in the world via a headphone experience. Jane Milling, a tutor at Exeter, was one of only four audience members to experience the work. It began pretending to be a conventional performance. Alone, you enter a village hall with a classic proscenium-arch stage, programmes on every seat, an old telephone on a rickety table centre stage. Phone rings, no one answers; it must be for you. The caller instructs you to go outside and get in the car. The masked and gloved chauffeur, head to toe in white, provides an alarm that you can hit if you want the performance to stop. He places you on the back seat, and silently drives you into the countryside. A sound-score begins via the car stereo system; Igor Stravinsky's *Firebird Suite* overlaid with narration telling of a castle and a princess who was forbidden to dance. During this prologue the car turns onto a dirt track and pulls up at a ruined mansion, one lit window at the very top. Your chauffeur disembarks, opens the door, puts the headset on you, gets back in the car and speeds off. You are alone. The soundtrack continues; one night, Viola breaks free from the palace, follows the path into the forest. There is a burning torch lighting your path; all you can do is follow this, like a moth drawn to the flame. Milling recalls, 'part of me thinks this is lovely, part of me thinks if somebody wanted to attack me this would be the moment to do it' (Milling, 2013).

This was an era before iPods. Walkmans were used alongside old mobile telephones and a very basic transmitting device ('a car battery and a radio transmitter') worked by Barrett and Smith who were following at a distance, changing tracks manually and transmitting them to the headset; 'lo-fi but it worked' (Barrett, 2013a). As Viola, in the story, reaches a gate, so do you, and gradually you realize you are becoming the protagonist. The next full moon, Viola returns, missing her engagement party; as you turn a corner, suddenly you see a banqueting table laid out for 20 people, coffee still steaming, cigarettes still smouldering. On you go, through one environmental installation after another, evocations of the narrative. The night before her wedding, dusk falls and Viola bursts out of the palace, in her haste forgetting her shoes, cutting her feet as she runs to the clearing. She calls to the moon and her music plays more powerfully than ever before. But it is the night of the lunar eclipse. As she dances the eclipse occurs and *'suddenly she was no longer dancing alone'*. You have been alone for 30 minutes, firelight ensuring you cannot see beyond your immediate vicinity; 'at the point of that italicised sentence the music swells', a marine flare shoots into the sky turning everything for 15 miles bright red and revealing 200 scarecrows, 'the biggest reveal achievable on £200', to suggest those that have danced with the devil before (Barrett, 2013a). Milling remembers 'having a sense of "oh how marvellous that's what I needed to see now, dramaturgically and scenographically"' (Milling, 2013). A second flare, you are blinded by floodlights from 50 metres away which reveal a figure moving towards you, through the scarecrows: your chauffeur. He takes you by the hand, leads you through the scarecrows, removes your headset and returns you to the car. Here the epilogue plays; her fiancé finds the blood trail from her feet leading to the clearing, her footprints in the sand alongside another set of footprints, these with a cloven hoof. At that point, as the participant is driven through the country lanes, Joel Scott is lurking in the shadows, ready to look at the vehicle so that each of the audience-participants might see only the flash of his face looking intently at them as they drive by: 'Out of the four audience members, two of them were sitting on the wrong side of the car; he was out there for hours for a total of twelve seconds performance ... it's all about the moment, the punctuation' (Barrett, 2013a). Founding members consider *The Moonslave* as 'the ultimate Punchdrunk experience'

(Higgin, 2013a). Audience-participants were pivotal and progressively aware that they were simultaneously voyeur and protagonist. Sensual installations took them through each stage of the story. The location and journeying was integral to narrative, theme and orientation into another world, blurring boundaries between the real and imagined. The use of fairy tale and the gothic surroundings heightened and layered the experience. The 'final reveal' was a spine-tingling crescendo, visually, aurally and conceptually. *The Borough* 'picks up that baton' (Barrett, 2013a), supported by technologies that have caught up with the ideas. The 'headphone experience offers so much more than the large-scale shows, the craft that needs to go into it needs to be so much more precise and refined, because the sound is right in-between their ears … transforming the world the participant is in' (Dobbie, 2013). Here, sound accompanies the participants in an immediate, intimate fashion, enabling them to attune to the environment and their place within it.

With *The Moonslave*, the influence of *H.G.* is clear, yet the audience member walked in search of where the performers might be, slowly becoming aware that he or she was also the performer. Milling 'was glad there were no people in it … there was nothing to disrupt the game that you were having with your imagination, with the narrative and with the excellent acting that the environment was doing' (Milling, 2013).

Faust *(October 2006–March 2007)*

Sleep No More (2003) and *The Firebird Ball* were the first productions where there were funds, albeit limited, to pay the core team. With both productions, Doyle's choreography had added a new performance language to the mix that was intimate, immediate and visceral, meeting the aesthetic of the work and proving that Punchdrunk's immersive form was made more powerful by the use of dance. *Sleep No More* gained critical recognition from Lyn Gardner (Gardner, 2003), which meant that *The Firebird Ball* was on the radar, attracting the interest of Tom Morris, then Artistic Director of BAC, who returned to the show taking Nicholas Hytner with him. This resulted in the support of the National Theatre for what was to become Punchdrunk's grandest production to date, *Faust*.

Punchdrunk's *Faust* was an adaptation of Goethe's classic text, reimagined in 1950s Deep South, small-town America. In a vast disused warehouse, *Faust* fused the aesthetic of Edward Hopper paintings with the imagery, and accompanying Angelo Badalamenti soundtracks, of David Lynch's work. The journey to the anonymous building on a menacingly deserted road that was a walk from an end-of-the-line Dockland's Light Railway station became a readying device before entering the threatening world. Eventually locating the entrance hidden behind a 'Dangerous Structure–Keep Out' sign, you were masked and guided into an archaic freight elevator. An unnerving operator hinted at what might be awaiting you on the other side, before ejecting you on a floor of his choosing, physically and figuratively transporting you to this intoxicating world.

Faust unpacked the narratives and themes of the sources. Characters that only have brief moments in the original extended these in a three-hour loop. The masked audience-participants shaped and discovered their own through-lines, during which it was possible to encounter clandestine one-on-ones, where the audience-immersant would be unmasked, for the duration of that brief, electric experience. This deconstructive treatment of the text opened up narratives and experiences on different floors and behind every door, such as a silent interaction with the bartender of Hopper's painting *Nighthawks*. This play with duration heightened the sense of a kaleidoscopic turn within that world, elongating, contracting, coiling time into a helix.

The importance to Punchdrunk's work of sensory interaction, especially through touch, 'the most pure and potent sense', became paramount in *Faust* (Barrett in Machon, 2013, 162). Barrett and Doyle grappled with how to communicate some of the more complex academic ideas via movement language, and realized that it was the space that unlocked these conundrums. Ideas within the text were translated through the fusion of space, dance and scenography; the complexity of the source made palpable. The sensual signification processes took the audience directly into the physiological, psychological and philosophical world of Faust. Entering Faust's laboratory you could see equations worked out on walls, touch the experiments, discover him poring over these and follow him as he, literally, breaks free from the room and the confines of medical and academic life. The fleshliness of the Walpurgis atmosphere permeated the building, inviting tactile interaction with the scenographic design. All the senses were called into action including kinaesthetic awareness of one's own and others' bodily locomotion in space. You might be pulled into a sweaty duet with a reveller in the swirling jive of the Walpurgis dance, a physical possession by the piece that embodied the notion of leaving reality to enter a world of desire, mirroring the Faustian bond.

The fusion of space, sound and dance made narrative and theme multidimensional and experiential. Each environment held its own rules and regulations (sometimes explicit with the presence of masked attendants denying access to ensure safety, sometimes implicit in the intimacy of rooms devoid of live performers where you could enter, search the drawers, read the documents, be curious, find clues). Cramped motel rooms, vast cornfields and shadowy forests of fir trees provided settings for the looped narratives, exposing textual ideas and uncovering themes. For instance, Goethe's conceit of the devil existing in dangerous desire was made visceral in Gretchen's seduction. This scene was a physical, aural and visual reference to the audio-distorted bar scene of Lynch's film *Twin Peaks: Fire Walk with Me* (1992), palpably evoking its Faustian parallel: a moral vacuum of a place where corruption wins over purity, lust over love. Alternatively, the library, on the top floor of the building, touching the heavens, holding shelves of ancient, academic tomes on religion, knowledge, faith, contrasted with the physical descent to the cold, clammy, subterranean vault where Faust's naked, human frailty is exposed in every respect and where he meets his eventual doom. Unwittingly, voyeurs framed the sequences as they watched, choreographing themselves into carnivalesque sculptures around the space, anonymously, disquietingly complicit as they witnessed Gretchen's, and then Faust's, demise.

Faust has become a defining production in terms of the ways in which its artistic ambition began to shift company structures. It engaged key members of the ensemble, such as Fernanda Alba and Conor Doyle, performers who augmented 'the quality and standard of the work' (Doyle, 2013). It provided the first production where Barrett and Doyle were able to spend time casting and on research. Every element met the epic challenge of the building, from the complex readings that exist in the intertextualized form, to the massive scale of the performance across the building, to the power of the crescendo in the final sequence. Being still relatively unknown, the production was mainly 'marketed' by word of mouth, opening the work up to a National Theatre audience while mobilizing a non-theatre audience through underground networking:

> word spread naturally over the course of the six dark winter months
> … Much of the run was fittingly quite 'hellish' for the management
> team as we struggled to keep a project that had been set up to last
> six weeks, possibly twelve, on track over six months without any of
> the infrastructure and support it really needed. (Nightingale, 2013b)

It was crucial in pushing Punchdrunk into the mainstream in terms of public recognition. James Purnell, then Secretary of State for Culture, Media and Sport, announced that *Faust* was exemplary of work where accessibility and excellence were married, taking 'a canonical subject, "completely reinvent[ing] the genre", and attract[ing] an "audience of every single age and background"' (in Higgin, 2007). The hype surrounding *Faust* ensured that *The Masque of the Red Death* (October 2007–April 2008), co-produced with The National Theatre and BAC, was a sell-out before it opened.

Under the Eiderdown *(2009–)*

Under the Eiderdown was devised to address speaking, listening and creative writing in schools. A Punchdrunk Enrichment workshop, inspired by the book *Who Are You, Stripy Horse* (2008) by Jim Helmore, elicits from pupils what the bric-a-brac shop setting looks, smells, feels and sounds like. Designers observe the workshop, recording all of the pupils' suggestions and, unbeknownst to them, install the shop in the school over the weekend, complete with all the suggestions, with performers inserted as characters from the story. On the Monday, pupils receive a letter inviting them to come and visit the shop and to meet with the shopkeepers, the Weevils, who believe that every object in the world has a history and the potential to tell many stories, and that it is stories that keep the world and the shop alive. Pupils are entrusted with the job of looking after the shop for the next two weeks by writing stories about its objects. The shop remains in the school to facilitate imaginative learning and to inspire creative writing.

Punchdrunk's response to the site becomes a tool of empowerment in this regard; all members of the school community are encouraged to perceive spaces within the building as deregulated, reconditioned with new 'rules' of engagement and imagination. The immersive experience 'bleeds into the real world', initiated by the durational life of the event, but also lasting beyond it within the imagination and body of the pupils: 'the *feeling* you create within the school goes out of that shop and the pupils are in that world. They're *in* this story and this idea and this fiction. Once they've been in the shop they're in that state of mind' (Higgin, 2011, emphasis original). For Higgin, *Under the Eiderdown* became pivotal, establishing a prototype to which the Enrichment team return to rethink strategies, forms and content. It was vital in the way it offered structures for exploring a two-way immersive world, enabling Punchdrunk to plunge itself into the locations and experiences of the host community in order to create sensually inventive work with and for them in a meaningful and reciprocal manner.

Conclusion: Critical Reception, Future Evolutions

I remember Tom Morris saying years ago at a Board Meeting, 'well you will go and create a new form of theatre.' (Doyle, 2013)

Punchdrunk has been instrumental in opening up attitudes to what a theatre experience is, and stimulating the growing audience for non-traditional theatre experiences. It has provided existing audiences with a new perspective on the medium and offered an alternative format to those who are less keen on sitting in an auditorium to receive a work, resulting in both celebration and criticism. Responses to Punchdrunk's work are as diverse as the individuals who engage in the experience. Signature productions, while liberating for some, can be intimidating for others. Blogs and online comments record how the form can be frustrating when an audience member is unable to locate an expected storyline or when participants feel forced to wear an uncomfortable mask without experiencing its benefits. Some suggest the first thrilling experience of a Punchdrunk event can be dulled on subsequent visits to new pieces. Where the company has, arguably, overturned elitist forms and processes – those that only speak to an educated audience familiar with the conventions of traditional performance that occurs in regular theatres venues – it has instead established a form that might be viewed as 'cliquist', seized upon by exclusive groups who return again and again to unlock all aspects of the experience. Punchdrunk's practice polarizes its solid fan base, who will devour any offering with relish, and those who refuse to acknowledge it has complexity or value, regarding the work as style over content that is without political or philosophical integrity. Doyle argues that 'it's good and healthy to have work that divides people', although advises caution when responses come from a lack of appreciation of the processes involved in the work, or an in-built resistance to dance and interactivity. Pejoratives can also be levelled by those unwilling to let down a guard or play by the rules, thus preventing their full immersion in the work. For Doyle, the 'intellectual and physical graft' involved in Punchdrunk shows produces complexity, 'weight and gravitas', and requires equivalent risk and investment from its audience: 'that gravitas *allows* this vast audience, *allows* people to just fly around the edges of it or jump right into the middle ... There's so much to unveil, unravel and reveal in this work' (Doyle, 2013, emphasis original). *Sleep No More*, NY has expanded critical reception of Punchdrunk's work on an international scale, identifying both problems and pleasures in the work. Collette Gordon (2013) and Thomas Cartelli (2013) argue that the intimacy of the work and the licence to engage is questionable in terms of the voyeurism and misconstrued agency enacted (or not) by audience members. Alice Dailey (2013), Sivan Grunfeld (2013) and Pamela J. Rader (2013) suggest that Punchdrunk's deconstructed and sensory play with classic source material allows for an intertextual, intricate and sensual interpretation of the subject matter. However, concurring with British critic Michael Billington (see Billington, 2007, 2010, 2012), they argue that it comes at the expense of plot, character, dramatic cohesion and thus interpretative satisfaction on the audience member's part. Conversely, Sean Bartley (2013) emphasizes the audience empowerment that occurs, while Sophia Richardson and Lauren Shohet examine how Punchdrunk's transformations and transgressions in form, especially via the masked audience, thematize ideas around 'obscuring and revealing ... absence and presence that are inherent to performance and particularly to adaptive performances' (Richardson and Shohet, 2013). Throughout a range of Punchdrunk's work, Gareth White further illustrates how the mask facilitates interaction and exposes questions around 'community, public, audience and spectator' (White, 2009, 228).

W. B. Worthern argues that Punchdrunk's work is as complex as the human behaviour it examines; *Sleep No More*, NY deploys Shakespeare's *Macbeth* 'as an instrument for a critical, experiential reassessment of its own conditions of meaning' as well as 'an instrument for opening emerging practices of knowledge' (Worthern, 2012, 97). Through space, dance and audience interaction, Worthern argues, the characters are explored in a way that is both embedded in and detached from the dramatic logic of the play. The form encourages individual audience-participants to *feel* the interior and exterior worlds of the characters and, in so doing, to assemble their own logic during and following their journey through these worlds (Worthern, 2012). Similarly, White argues that the inherent 'invitations to explore and to try out different points of view in relation to the performance and its setting' enable an experiential appreciation of both form and subject matter (White, 2012, 225). This inevitably leads to an *affective* questioning of the implications and outcomes of form in a Punchdrunk event. What is apparent from the full range of criticism is the fact that Punchdrunk's practice activates debate around the problems, pleasures and politics of audience involvement in immersive work.

The impact of Punchdrunk's practice on a world stage is undeniable. Punchdrunk has revolutionized contemporary performance and, as Christopher McCullogh, Barrett's former Head of Drama at Exeter, puts it 'helped British theatre to break out of its corsets' (McCullogh, 2013). Punchdrunk events uphold a feel of the underground as a result of the secrecy that surrounds each new venture and the word-of-mouth way in which the work is still primarily received. Punchdrunk's relationship with the National Theatre, its global fan base established as a consequence of *Sleep No More*, NY, alongside its recognition across broadsheet and broadcast media, all point to the way in which Punchdrunk has moved from 'innovator outside the establishment to innovator within the establishment' (Yorke, 2013). This chapter is testament to the fact that Punchdrunk's unique approach, so vital in the current and future landscape of theatre, emerged from the fecund seeding beds of the British university system. It highlights the importance of academic institutions as training grounds for and motivators of innovation. In turn, a new generation of practitioners that have recently emerged from universities are citing Punchdrunk as a direct influence on their own practice, including Slung Low and Tin Box Theatre. In response to this, Milling instigated the Exeter University and Punchdrunk doctoral scholarship honouring Punchdrunk's practice via this mutually beneficial exchange, as 'a mechanism for giving proper attention to Felix' work' (Milling, 2013).

Punchdrunk's wider influence is not only discernible in current, innovative British practice, including that of Coney or Headlong, it has also had a direct impact on the aesthetic of popular culture: pop concerts and music festivals, fashion shows and advertising. Punchdrunk has reignited a passion for exploiting the visceral potential of live performance, whatever the event, and for taking theatre into unusual locations. It seems fitting that this should be written at a time when Punchdrunk is forging ahead with its pioneering practice by returning, in its current projects, to source material explored and techniques formed in the company's very earliest experimentations. *The Drowned Man* ambitiously reimagined *Woyzeck* on an epic scale in an enormous London site. *The Borough* developed *The Moonslave* model, blurring the real and the imagined by exploiting the potential of audio experiences and installation in 'real-world' environments. While inspiring new generations to experiment, Punchdrunk equally has no desire to be fixed in one formulaic way of producing work, but to evolve. Barrett's plans to test wearable technologies in performance, to further distort lines between art and the everyday by 'gamifying your life' (Barrett, 2012), accompany more outlandish explorations within festival environments and television, alongside an aim to establish Punchdrunk Travel, pushing forward the mission to offer *living* performances for participant-adventurers to be immersed for the duration of a weekend or longer in a Punchdrunk world. Ultimately, it is the passionate curiosity of Barrett's unceasing vision that continues to ignite and flame Punchdrunk's stove of ambition: 'I'm fascinated by that murky hinterland that is the space between the show and real life and how we can theatricalise that. There's a lot more in there for the future' (Barrett in Machon, 2013, 164).

Punchdrunk: Full Production History

The Cherry Orchard (2000), Poltimore House, Devon, UK

The Moonslave (2000), Exeter, UK

The Tempest (2001), commissioned by the National Trust. Yelverton, Dartmoor, UK

Johnny Formidable: Mystery at the Pink Flamingo (2001), Roborough Studio, Exeter, UK

The House of Oedipus (2002), Poltimore House, Pinhoe, Devon, UK

Chair (2002), an adaptation of *The Chairs* by Eugene Ionesco, commissioned by The Deptford X Festival of Contemporary Art. The Old Seager Distillery, Deptford, London, UK

The Tempest (2002), The Old Seagar Distillery, Deptford, London, UK

Midsummer Night's Dream: 'The Garden Party' (2002), created for garden designer Arne Maynard. Guanock House, Parsons Drove, Norfolk, UK

Sleep No More (2003), an adaptation of Shakespeare's *Macbeth*. The Beaufuoy Building, London, UK

Woyzeck (2004), The Big Chill Festival, Eastnor Castle, Herefordshire, UK

The Firebird Ball (2005), a fusion of Shakespeare's *Romeo and Juliet* and Igor Stravinsky's ballet *The Firebird*. The Offley Works, Oval, South London, UK

The Yellow Wallpaper (2005), a five-minute one-on-one. Battersea Arts Centre Attics, London, UK

Marat/Sade (2005), The Big Chill Festival, Eastnor Castle, Herefordshire, UK

Faust (October 2006–March 2007), co-produced with The National Theatre, 21 Wapping Lane, London, UK

The Masque of the Red Death (October 2007–April 2008), co-produced with The National Theatre and Battersea Arts Centre, London, UK

Under The Eiderdown (2009–ongoing), various schools across London, UK

Tunnel 228 (2009), a curational art and live performance installation, The Old Vic Tunnels, Waterloo, London, UK

Sleep No More (Boston, 2009–10), produced in association with the American Repertory Theatres, The Old Lincoln School, Brookline, Boston, USA

It Felt Like a Kiss (2009), commissioned by The Manchester International Festival, in collaboration with Adam Curtis and Damon Albarn. An experience for one audience member at a time in a deserted office block in Spinningfields, Manchester, UK

Holland Park Halloween (October 2009), Commissioned by The Royal Borough of Kensington Chelsea Arts Service, London, UK

The Duchess of Malfi (2010), an operatic adaptation of the play by John Webster, libretto by Torsten Rasch. Produced in collaboration with English National Opera, Great Eastern Quay, London, UK

Brixton Market Project (January–March 2010), The Granville Arcade, Brixton, London, UK

The Apricot Project (July 2010), the apricot orchard within the *The Duchess of Malfi* reimagined as a 'phonic orchard' for local pupils. Supported by Newham Council, Great Eastern Quay, London, UK

The Lambeth Walk (November 2010), created for primary schools in Streatham, London, UK

The Space Invaders Agency (May–June 2011), in collaboration with New Direction's London-wide Olympic Project: 'The Biggest Learning Opportunity on Earth'. The 'Space Invaders Agency', Waterloo Arches, Lower Marsh, London, UK

Sleep No More (New York, 2011–present), created and overseen by Punchdrunk, produced by Emursive, within a disused warehouse transformed into The McKittrick hotel, 530 W27th Street, New York City, USA

The Crash of the Elysium (2011), a one-hour show for children made in collaboration with the BBC and Manchester International Festival, Salford Quays, Manchester, UK

Black Diamond (2011), a 'travelling' piece, supported by Stella Artois, that combined a performance-soiree with a series of one-on-ones in cars and telephone booths across venues in East London, UK

And Darkness descended ... (2011), an underground performance in collaboration with Sony-Playstation. Waterloo Tunnels, Waterloo, London, UK

The Uncommercial Traveller (2011–ongoing), created in collaboration with Arcola 60+, Arcola Theatre, in Hackney, London. Reworked in a variety of international communities including Cape Town, Karachi, Melbourne, Penang and Singapore in collaboration with The British Council as part of the Dickens 2012 Programme

The Crash of the Elysium (2012), a reworking of the 2011 experience in collaboration with the BBC, the London 2012 Festival, the New Wolsey Theatre and Ipswich Borough Council, supported by Suffolk County

Council and Arts Council England as part of the Ipswich Arts and London 2012 Festivals, Ipswich, UK

Up Up and Away: The Last Story Balloonists (January–March 2012), London, UK

Grey's Printing Press (March 2012), Hackney Wick, London, UK

The House Where Winter Lives (November 2012–January 2013). For children aged three to six and their families. In collaboration with Discover, Stratford, London, UK

The Travelling Museum Society (February–March 2013), St Mary's School Hampstead, London, UK

The Borough (June 2013), a 50-minute adaptation of Benjamin Britten's *Peter Grimes* and George Crabbe's poem *The Borough*, commissioned by Aldeburgh Festival, 2013. A fusion of guided walk, living installation and audio/live performance for an individual audience member. Aldeburgh, UK

The Drowned Man: A Hollywood Fable (June 2013–July 2014), created by Punchdrunk. Presented by Punchdrunk and the National Theatre. Inspired by Georg Buchner's *Woyzeck*. Paddington, London, UK

NOTES

Chapter 3: Mind the Gap

1 Williams syndrome is a genetic condition that, along with early developmental delay and learning disabilities, often has characteristics of gregariousness, verbal articulacy and musicality.
2 The developing performance was trialled at the Cow and Calf, although poor weather forced the finished production to relocate for an indoor performance at the Silk Warehouse.

Chapter 4: Kneehigh

1 Rice appeared in Gardzienice's 1990 production *Carmina Burana*.
2 For example: 'We have always reinvented ourselves about every three years, which is one of the reasons we have gone on' (in Gardner 2004).
3 Even in 1947 Powell and Pressburger's life-affirming philosophical fantasy was an object of multiple interpretations. Due to the country's supposed after-war neutrality, the British Embassy in Moscow reacted with some alarm to an article in a Russian cultural magazine effectively dismissing *A Matter of Life and Death* as pro-American propaganda (Harper and Porter 1989). Ironically, when released in the States (as *Stairway to Heaven*) just weeks after its British premiere, the film was greeted by *Time* magazine with an equally scathing suspicion that the whole enterprise had been designed to tap into the US Box Office and fill the pockets of the British 'Cinemogul J. Arthur Rank' (no author, 1946).
4 Rice considers film 'one of the part of the [storytelling] armoury', however she acknowledges the irresistible appeal of this storytelling device: 'It can be addictive, because it is so stylish and because we all love film and you can make it – what I call "shiny" – "shiny theatre". And actually I am a great believer in theatre not being shiny and being a bit rough'. (Radosavljević, 2010, 95).

Chapter 6: Stan's Cafe

1 Sweeting is one of the founding members of Improbable Theatre and Told by an Idiot.
2 Barclays New Stages was an annual programme of funding of independent

theatre companies, culminating in a three-week season at the Royal Court Theatre that lasted for ten years.

3   In 2009, Stan's Cafe formed a three-year partnership with Domaine d'O, where they also presented *Of All the People: France* (2009), *The Cleansing* (2009) and *The Black Maze* (2010).

4   The company A. E. Harris and Co. produces metal pressings and laser cuttings and have often made set pieces for Stan's Cafe. In October 2013, they took back most of the performance spaces. Stan's Cafe kept the 50-seat space Australia, and announced their intention to focus on more intimate work.

5   China Plate is a partnership between producers Ed Collier and Paul Warwick, who offer opportunities to local artists in the West Midlands.

6   The company acknowledges the influence of Pete Brooks's Insomniac Productions *L'Ascensore* (1992) and *Clair de Luz* (1993), which used cinematic framings to play with the audience's gaze. Amanda Hadingue and Craig Stephens had previously collaborated with Insomniac.

7   So far, the piece has been presented in three different versions: small [city-specific], medium [continent-specific] and large [world-specific]. Each time, the number of people being represented determines the scale and therefore the quantities of rice being used. For their first world version, the company used 104 tons of rice.

8   This decision was inspired by Konstantin Lopushansky's film *Film Letters From a Dead Man* (Yarker, 2010b).

9   See, for instance, Stan's Cafe 2012; Stan's Cafe 2009a.

Chapter 7: Blast Theory

1   Other surveillance works that predate *Kidnap* are *ArTistheater* by Parkbench (1994), who claim to have created the first live web performance, and *Jennicam* (1996–2003), a durational self-surveillance project by Jennifer Ringley (Dixon, 2007, pp. 437–56).

2   The Red Army Faction (RAF), also known as the Baader-Meinhof gang in its early days, was a terrorist organization founded in West Germany in 1970 by Andreas Baader, Ulrike Meinhof and others. The group fought against a capitalist West German establishment killing more than 30 people over two years (BBC News website).

3   Created in 1919, the Irish Republican Army (IRA) was a paramilitary organization that sought the end of British rule in Northern Ireland and the reunification of Ireland (Encyclopaedia Britannica online).

Chapter 8: Punchdrunk

1 Founded in 2002 by Sally Scott, Joel Scott and Ian Summers, Goat and
   Monkey make immersive theatre, site-responsive productions and online
   stories, which aim to explore the potential of audience interaction within
   performance.

BIBLIOGRAPHY

Preface to Volume Three

Freeman, Sara (2006), 'Towards a Genealogy and Taxonomy of British Alternative Theatre', *New Theatre Quarterly* 22:4, pp. 364–78.

Kershaw, Baz (2004), 'Alternative Theatres, 1946–2000', in Baz Kersaw (ed.), *The Cambridge History of British Theatre Volume 3 Since 1895* (Cambridge: Cambridge University Press), pp. 349–76.

Chapter 1: Historical and Cultural Background

Allen, Chris (1997), 'Secretary-General's Report', *The Arts Council of England Annual Report 1996/97* (London: Arts Council of England).

—(2005), 'From Race to Religion: The New Face of Discrimination', in Tahir Abbas (ed.), *Muslim Britain: Communities under Pressure* (London and New York: Zed Books).

Arranz, José Igor Prieto (2006), 'BTA's Cool Britannia: British National Identity in the New Millennium', *Pasos* 4:2, pp. 183–200.

Arts Council England (1996), *The Policy for Drama of the English Arts Funding System* (London: Arts Council of England).

—(2000a), *Artstat: Digest of Arts Statistics and Trends in the UK 1986–87–1997–98* (London: Arts Council of England).

—(2000b), *Annual Review of the Arts Council of England 2000* (London: Arts Council England).

—(2008), *Arts Council England Annual Review 2008* (London: Arts Council England), www.artscouncil.org.uk/media/uploads/downloads/annualreview2008.pdf [accessed 23 June 2014].

—(2009), *Arts Council England Annual Review 2009* (London: Arts Council England), www.artscouncil.org.uk/media/uploads/downloads/annualreview2009.pdf [accessed 23 June 2014].

—(2013), *Annual Review 2012/13* (London: Arts Council England, www.artscouncil.org.uk/media/uploads/pdf/ACE_Annual_Report_2012-13_Interactive.pdf [accessed 23 June 2014].

Arts Council Wales (2002), *The Arts Council of Wales Annual Report 01/02* (Cardiff: The Arts Council of Wales), www.artswales.org.uk/c_annual-reports/annual-report-2001-2002 [accessed 23 June 2014].

—(2007), 'A National Theatre for Wales: Concept Paper', Cardiff: The Arts Council of Wales, 17 October 2007, www.theatre-wales.co.uk/news/newsdetail.asp?newsID=2360 [accessed 23 June 2014].

—(2013), *The Arts Council of Wales Annual Report 12/13* (Cardiff: The Arts
    Council of Wales), www.artswales.org.uk/c_annual-reports/annual-
    report-2012-2013 [accessed 23 June 2014].

Astle, Julian and Alasdair Murray (2006), 'Blair's Britain: An Audit', in Julian
    Astle, David Laws, Paul Marshall and Alasdair Murray (eds), *Britain after
    Blair: A Liberal Agenda* (London: Profile), pp. 13–73.

Batty, David (2011), 'Occupy the London Stock Exchange – Saturday 15
    October 2011', *Guardian,* 15 October, www.theguardian.com/global/2011/
    oct/15/occupy-movement-occupy-wall-street [accessed 23 June 2014].

BBC (2000), 'Arts Chief's Resignation Accepted', 25 September, news.bbc.
    co.uk/1/hi/wales/937282.stm [accessed 23 June 2014].

—(2005), 'Protests as BBC Screens Springer', 10 January, news.bbc.co.uk/1/hi/
    entertainment/4154071.stm [accessed 23 June 2014].

—(2006), 'Dramatic Changes to Arts Funding: Major Changes to the Way
    Companies are Funded by the Scottish Arts Council (SAC) have been
    Unveiled', 2 March, news.bbc.co.uk/1/hi/scotland/4764834.stm [accessed
    23 June 2014].

Boyden, Peter (2000), *A Review of the Roles and Functions of the English
    Regional Producing Theatres* (London: The Arts Council of England).

Calvi, Nuala (2005), 'Scottish Arts Makes Final Bid to Save Arm's-length
    Funding', *The Stage,* 21 June, www.thestage.co.uk/news/2005/06/scottish-
    arts-makes-final-bid-to-save-arms-length-funding/ [accessed 23 June
    2014].

Cantle, Ted (2008), *Community Cohesion: A New Framework for Race and
    Diversity* (Basingstoke: Palgrave Macmillan).

Close, Melanie (2011), 'Timeline History of the Disabled People's Movement',
    Disability Equality, www.disability-equality.org.uk/uploads/files/fb979acea
    0dfe4ec8163fc610ffcf305.pdf [accessed 23 June 2014].

Cockerell, Michael (2001), 'An Inside View on Blair's Number 10', in
    Anthony Seldon (ed.), *The Blair Effect* (London: Little, Brown and
    Company), pp. 571–79.

Creative Scotland (2013), *Annual Report and Financial Statements for the
    Year Ended 31ˢᵗ March 2013* (Edinburgh: Creative Scotland), www.
    creativescotland.com/resources/our-publications/annual-reports [accessed
    23 June 2014].

Curtice, John, Devine, Paula and Ormston, Rachel (2013), 'Identities and
    Constitutional Preferences Across the UK', in A. Park, C. Bryson, E. Clery,
    J. Curtice and M. Phillips (eds), *British Social Attitudes: The 30th Report*
    (London: NatCen Social Research), pp. 139–72, www.bsa-30.natcen.ac.uk
    [accessed 23 June 2014].

de Jongh, Nicholas (2008), 'Stop These Savage Cuts to London's Creative
    Gems', *Evening Standard,* 11 January, www.standard.co.uk/news/
    stop-these-savage-cuts-to-londons-creative-gems-6642412.html [accessed
    23 June 2014].

Eatwell, Roger (1989), 'The Nature of the Right, 1: Is There an "Essentialist" Philosophical Core?', in Roger Eatwell and Noël O'Sullivan (eds), *The Nature of the Right: American and European Politics and Political Thought Since 1789* (London: Pinter), pp. 47–61.

Edwardes, Jane (2008), 'Arts Council Funding Cuts', *Time Out*, 6 February, www.timeout.com/london/theatre/arts-council-funding-cuts [accessed 23 June 2014].

Elliott, Larry and Treanor, Jill (2013), 'Lehman Brothers Collapse: Five Years Later', *Guardian*, 13 September, www.theguardian.com/business/2013/sep/13/lehman-brothers-collapse-five-years-later-shiver-spine [accessed 23 June 2014].

Finney, Nissa and Simpson, Ludi (2009), '*Sleepwalking to Segregation'? Challenging Myths about Race and Immigration* (Bristol: The Policy Press).

FitzHerbert, Luke and Paterson, Mark (1998), *The National Lottery Yearbook 1998 Edition* (London: The Directory of Social Change).

Forgan, Liz (2010), 'Sustaining Artistic Excellence', *Arts Council England Annual Review 2010* (London: Arts Council England), www.artscouncil.org.uk/media/uploads/AC_annual_review_a4_online_final.pdf [accessed 23 June 2014].

—(2011), 'Seeds of Excellence', *Arts Council England Annual Review 2011* (London: Arts Council England), www.artscouncil.org.uk/media/uploads/pdf/ACEannual_review201011_Accessible_PDF.pdf [accessed 23 June 2014].

Frayling, Christopher (2005), 'Chair's Report', *Arts Council England Annual Review 2005* (London: Arts Council England), p. 2, www.artscouncil.org.uk/media/uploads/documents/publications/annualreviewpdf1_phpjBMziB.pdf [accessed 23 June 2014].

Gardner, Lyn (2007), 'The Arts Council Must Speak Up about Cuts', Theatre Blog, *Guardian*, 20 December, www.theguardian.com/stage/theatreblog/2007/dec/20/theartscouncilmustspeakup [accessed 23 June 2014].

Geddes, Andrew (2003), *The Politics of Migration and Immigration in Europe* (London: Sage).

Gidda, Mirren (2013), 'Edward Snowden and the NSA files – timeline', *Guardian,* 26 July, www.theguardian.com/world/2013/jun/23/edward-snowden-nsa-files-timeline [accessed 23 June 2014].

Government Equalities Office (2010), 'Equality Act 2010: What Do I Need to Know?', https://www.gov.uk/government/uploads/system/uploads/attachment_data/file/85028/vcs-service-providers.pdf [accessed 23 June 2014].

Gowrie, Lord (1996), 'An abridged version of a speech given in the House of Lords by Lord Gowrie, Chairman of the Arts Council of England, on 12 June 1996', *The Arts Council of England, Annual Report 1995/96* (London: Arts Council of England).

—(1998), 'Lord Gowrie's Review', *Annual Report of the Arts Council of England 1998* (London: Arts Council of England).

Guardian (2012), Technology Blog, 18 May, www.theguardian.com/technology/2012/may/18/facebook-ipo-stock-market-live [accessed 23 June 2014].

Hewison, Robert (1994), 'Public Policy: Corporate Culture: Public Culture', in Robert Freeman, Olin Robinson and Charles A. Riley (eds), *The Arts in the World Economy: Public Policy and Private Philanthropy for a Global Cultural Community* (Hanover: University Press of New England), pp. 26–32.

Hewitt, Steve (2008), *The British War on Terror: Terrorism and Counter-Terrorism on the Home Front since 9/11* (London and New York: Continuum).

Higgins, Charlotte (2012a), 'The arts funding row in Scotland – and why it matters to the rest of the UK', Culture Blog, *Guardian,* 9 June, www.theguardian.com/culture/charlottehigginsblog+uk/scotland [accessed 23 June 2014].

—(2012b), 'Rift deepens between Scottish artists and Creative Scotland, as despairing open letter is published', Culture Blog, *Guardian,* 9 October, www.theguardian.com/culture/charlottehigginsblog/2012/oct/09/open-letter-creative-scotland [accessed 23 June 2014].

Hiscock, John (2013), 'Julian Assange: My Life in the Embassy', *Telegraph,* 14 October, www.telegraph.co.uk/news/worldnews/wikileaks/10376799/Julian-Assange-my-life-in-the-embassy.html [accessed 23 June 2014].

Huntington, Samuel P. (1993), 'The Clash of Civilisations?', *Foreign Affairs* 72:3, pp. 22–49.

Husband, Charles and Alam, Yunis (2011), *Social Cohesion and Counter-Terrorism: A Policy Contradiction* (Bristol: The Policy Press).

Jeffers, Alison (2012), *Refugees, Theatre and Crisis: Performing Global Identities* (Basingstoke: Palgrave Macmillan).

Jones, George (2003), 'Blair Rejected Terror Warnings', *Telegraph,* 12 September.

Keat, Russell (2000), 'Market Boundaries and Human Goods', in J. Haldane (ed.), *Philosophy and Public Affairs* (Cambridge: Cambridge University Press), pp. 23–36.

Kilborn, Richard (2003), *Staging the Real: Factual TV Programming in the Age of Big Brother* (Manchester: Manchester University Press).

Leach, Robert (2007), 'The Short, Astonishing History of the National Theatre of Scotland', *New Theatre Quarterly* 23:2, pp. 171–83.

Leggett, Will (2005), *After New Labour: Social Theory and Centre-Left Politics* (Basingstoke: Palgrave Macmillan).

Leonard, Mark (1997), *Britain$^{TM:}$ Renewing Our Identity* (London: Demos).

Leys, Colin (2001), *Market-Driven Politics* (London and New York: Verso).

Liberty (2013), 'Overview of terrorism legislation', www.liberty-human-rights.

org.uk/human-rights/terrorism/overview-of-terrorism-legislation/index. php [accessed 23 June 2014].

Macpherson, William (1999), *The Stephen Lawrence Inquiry: Report of an Inquiry* (London: The Stationery Office, 1999), www.archive.official-documents.co.uk/document/cm42/4262/4262.htm [accessed 23 June 2014].

Marquand, David (1999), *The Progressive Dilemma: From Lloyd George to Blair*, 2nd edn, (London: Phoenix Giant).

Marr, Andrew (2007), *A History of Modern Britain* (London: Macmillan).

McKinnie, Michael (2004), 'A Sympathy for Art: The Sentimental Economies of New Labour Arts Policy', in Deborah Lynn Steinberg and Richard Johnson (eds), *Blairism and the War of Persuasion: Labour's Passive Revolution* (London: Lawrence & Wishart).

McMaster, Brian (2008), *Supporting Excellence in the Arts* (London: Department for Culture, Media and Sport).

McMillan, Joyce (2012), 'Creative Scotland's latest review endangers artists and betrays a total lack of imagination', *Scotsman*, 25 May, www.scotsman. com/lifestyle/arts/visual-arts/joyce-mcmillan-start-again-there-s-plenty-of-talent-around-1-2316426 [accessed 23 June 2014].

—(2014), 'Silence isn't Golden for the Arts', *Scotsman*, 10 April, www. scotsman.com/lifestyle/arts/news/joyce-mcmillan-silence-isn-t-golden-for-the-arts-1-3372802 [accessed 23 June 2014].

McVeigh, Karen (2011), 'Wall Street Protest Movement Spreads', *Guardian*, 4 October, www.theguardian.com/world/2011/oct/04/wall-street-protest-movement-spreads [accessed 23 June 2014].

Norris, Paul (1999), 'New Labour and the Rejection of Stakeholder Capitalism', in Gerald R. Taylor (ed.), *The Impact of New Labour* (London: Macmillan).

Osmond, John (2002), 'Welsh Civil Identity in the Twenty-first Century', in David C. Harvey, Rhys Jones, Neil McInroy and Christine Milligan (eds), *Celtic Geographies: Old Culture, New Times* (London and New York: Routledge), pp. 69–8.

Park, Alison, Bryson, C., Clery, E., Curtice, J. and Phillips, M. (eds) (2013), *British Social Attitudes: The 30th Report* (London: NatCen Social Research, 2013), www.bsa-30.natcen.ac.uk [accessed 23 June 2014].

Patten, Mags (2014), speaking at *In Battalions*, London, 4 July.

Pitcher, Ben (2009), *The Politics of Multiculturalism: Race and Racism in Contemporary Britain* (Basingstoke: Palgrave Macmillan).

Prasad, Raekha (2011), 'English Riots were "a Sort of Revenge" Against the Police', *Guardian,* 5 December, www.theguardian.com/uk/2011/dec/05/riots-revenge-against-police [accessed 23 June 2014].

Reid, Gavin (2007), 'Scottish Political Parties and Leisure Policy', in *Scottish Affairs* 59 (Spring), pp. 68–91.

Rhydderch, Francesca (2004), 'Devolution or Dissolution?', *New Welsh Review* 66, www.newwelshreview.com/article.php?id=61 [accessed 23 June 2014].

Robinson, Gerry (1998), 'Chairman's Introduction', *Annual Report of the Arts Council of England 1998* (London: Arts Council of England).

Ross, Andrew (2009), *Nice Work If You Can Get It: Life and Labor in Precarious Times* (New York: New York University Press).

Saunders, Graham (2008), 'Introduction', in Rebecca D'Monte and Graham Saunders (eds), *Cool Britannia: British Political Drama in the 1990s* (Basingstoke: Palgrave Macmillan), pp. 1–15.

Scottish Arts Council (2001) *Scottish Arts Council Annual Report 2000–01* (Edinburgh: The Scottish Arts Council)

—(2003), *Scottish Arts Council Annual Report 2002–03* (Edinburgh: The Scottish Arts Council).

—(2004a), *Corporate Plan 2004–2009: Key Themes – Championing the Arts for Scotland* (Edinburgh: Scottish Arts Council), www.scottisharts.org.uk/1/ information/publications/1001422.aspx [accessed 23 June 2014].

—(2004b) *Scottish Arts Council Annual Report 2003–04* (Edinburgh: The Scottish Arts Council).

—(2006), *Scottish Arts Council Cultural Successes List 2005/06* (Edinburgh, Scottish Arts Council).

—(2011), *Scottish Arts Council & Scottish Screen Joint Corporate Plan 2010/11* (Edinburgh: Scottish Arts Council and Scottish Screen), www.scottisharts. org.uk/resources/publications/Annual%20reports%20&%20plans/Pdf/ Corporate%20Plan%202010-11.pdf [accessed 23 June 2014).

Shaw, Eric (2007), *Losing Labour's Soul: New Labour and the Blair Government 1997–2007* (London and New York: Routledge).

Sierz, Aleks (2000), *In-Yer-Face Theatre: British Drama Today* (London: Faber).

Smith, Chris (1998), *Creative Britain* (London: Faber & Faber).

Spalek, B. and Lambert R. (2008), 'Muslim Communities, Counter-terrorism and Counter-radicalism: A Critical Reflective Approach to Engagement', *International Journal of Law, Crime and Justice* 36, pp. 257–70.

Spencer, Sarah (2011), *The Migration Debate* (Bristol: The Policy Press).

Stephens, Elen Closs (2006) *Wales Art Review: A Dual Key Approach to the Strategic Development of the Arts in Wales*, wales.gov.uk/depc/publications/ cultureandsport/arts/artsreview/reporte.pdf?lang=en [accessed 23 June 2014].

Theatre-Wales (1999), www.theatre-wales.co.uk/news/1999index.asp [accessed 23 June 2014].

Urban, Ken, (2008), 'Cruel Britannia', in Rebecca D'Monte and Graham Saunders (eds), *Cool Britannia: British Political Drama in the 1990s* (Basingstoke: Palgrave Macmillan) pp. 38–55.

Wade, M. (2002), 'Scottish Theatre Funding Left Trailing', *Scotsman*, 16 December.

Wright, A. (1986), *Socialisms* (Oxford: Oxford University Press).

Zerdy, Joanne (2013), 'Fashioning a Scottish Operative: *Black Watch* and

Banal Theatrical Nationalism on Tour in the US', *Theatre Research International* 38:3 pp. 181–95.

Chapter 2: British Theatre Companies: 1995–2014

Alexander, Jane (1988), 'My Pig Speaks Latin', *City Limits*, 14 January, www. faultyoptic.co.uk/mypigpage.htm [accessed 23 June 2014].

Arts Council England (2009), *Arts Council England Annual Review 2009* (London: Arts Council England), www.artscouncil.org.uk/media/uploads/ downloads/annualreview2009.pdf [accessed 23 June 2014].

Babbage, Frances (2004), *Augusto Boal* (London and New York: Routledge).

Bailes, Sara-Jane (2011), *Performance Theatre and the Poetics of Failure* (London and New York: Routledge,).

Baim, Clark, Brookes, Sally and Mountford, Alun (eds) (2002), *The Geese Theatre Handbook: Drama with Offenders and People at Risk* (Hampshire: Waterside Press).

Baraitser, Marion (1999), 'Introduction', *Contemporary Theatre Review*, 10:1, pp. 1–12.

Barker, Howard (2007), 'The Olympics Killed My Theatre', Theatreblog, *Guardian*, 5 June, www.theguardian.com/stage/theatreblog/2007/jun/05/ theolympicskilledmytheatre [accessed 23 June 2014].

BBC (2001), 'Census', news.bbc.co.uk/1/shared/spl/hi/uk/03/census_2001/ html/ethnicity.stm [accessed 23 June 2014].

Bennett, Stuart (ed.) (2005), *Theatre for Children and Young People: 50 years of Professional Theatre in the UK* (Eastbourne: Aurora Metro Press).

Billington, Michael (2003), 'Pericles', *Guardian*, 28 July, www.theguardian. com/stage/2003/jul/28/theatre.artsfeatures [accessed 23 June 2014].

Blind Summit (2013), *The Table* [extract], vimeo.com/44157302 [accessed 23 June 2014].

Boal, Augusto (1979), *Theatre of the Oppressed* (London: Pluto Press).

Boat Project website, www.theboatproject.com [accessed 23 June 2014].

Bolton, Jacqueline (2012), 'Capitalizing (on) New Writing: New Play Development in the 1990s', *Studies in Theatre & Performance* 32:2, pp. 209–25.

Bottoms, Stephen (2010), 'Silent Partners: Actor and Audience in Geese Theatre's *Journey Woman*', *Research in Drama Education: The Journal of Applied Theatre and Performance* 15:4, pp. 477–96.

Bourdieu, Pierre (1993), *The Field of Cultural Production*, trans. Randal Johnson (Cambridge: Polity Press).

British Council (2007), 'Edinburgh Showcase 1997–2007: Celebrating 10 Years of new UK Theatre on the World Stage' (London: British Council).

British Theatre Consortium and Rebellato, Dan (2009), *Writ Large: New Writing on the English Stage 2003–2009* (London: Arts Council England).

Brown, Ian, Robert Brannen and Douglas Brown (2000), 'The Arts Council Touring Franchise and English Political Theatre after 1986', *New Theatre Quarterly* 16:4, pp. 379–87.

Callery, Dymphna (2001), *Through the Body: A Practical Guide to Physical Theatre* (London: Nick Hern).

Cavendish, Dominic (2003), 'A Punishing, Purgatorial Meander with Pericles', *Telegraph*, 28 July, www.telegraph.co.uk/culture/theatre/drama/3599510/A-punishing-purgatorial-meander-with-Pericles.html#source=refresh [accessed 23 June 2014].

Clapp, Susannah (2001), 'Be Very Afraid', *Guardian,* 14 January, www.theguardian.com/theobserver/2001/jan/14/features.review87 [accessed 23 June 2014].

—(2006), 'So Long, Sooty', *Guardian,* 22 January, www.theguardian.com/stage/2006/jan/22/theatre [accessed 23 June 2014].

Curious Directive website, www.curiousdirective.com [accessed 23 June 2014].

Davis, Geoffrey and Fuchs, Anne (2006), '"We Have to Set our Stall out Artistically": An Interview with Felix Cross', in Geoffrey V. Davis and Anne Fuchs (eds), *Staging New Britain: Aspects of Black and South Asian British Theatre Practice* (Oxford: Peter Lang), pp. 219–38.

Dreamthinkspeak website, www.dreamthinkspeak.com, original article subscription only: www.thesundaytimes.co.uk/sto/culture/arts/theatre/article281485.ece [accessed 23 June 2014].

Duckie website, www.duckie.co.uk [accessed 23 June 2014].

Dunton, Emma, Nelson, Roger and Shand, Hetty (2009), *New Writing in Theatre 2003–2008: An Assessment of New Writing within Smaller Scale Theatre in England* (London: Arts Council England).

English, Carey (2005), 'Theatre for Special Audiences', in Stuart Bennett (ed.), *Theatre for Children and Young People: 50 Years of Professional Theatre in the UK* (Eastbourne: Aurora Metro Press), pp. 182–93.

Evaristo, Bernadine (1994), 'Going it … Alone: Solo Performers – The Art and the Ache', *Artrage* (November), pp. 14–15.

Freeman, Sara (2006), 'Towards a Genealogy and Taxonomy of British Alternative Theatre', *New Theatre Quarterly* 22:4, pp. 364–78.

Freshwater, Helen (2010), '*Delirium*: In Rehearsal with Theatre O', in Alex Mermikides and Jackie Smart (eds), *Devising in Process* (Basingstoke: Palgrave Macmillan), pp. 128–46.

Gardner, Lyn (2003) *The Quality of Children's Theatre: After the Birmingham Seminar* (London: Arts Council England).

—(2004), 'Slamdunk', *Guardian,* 1 March, www.theguardian.com/stage/2004/mar/01/theatre [accessed 23 June 2014].

—(2007), 'There is Something Stirring', in Daniel Brine and Lois Keidan (eds), *Programme Notes: Case Studies for Locating Experimental Theatre* (London: Live Art Development Agency), pp. 10–16.

—(2008), 'Contains Violence', *Guardian*, 5 April, www.theguardian.com/
stage/2008/apr/05/theatre2 [accessed 23 June 2014].

—(2009), 'Join in the Murder Game at Battersea Arts Centre', Guardian,
19 October, www.theguardian.com/stage/2009/oct/19/murder-game-
battersea-arts-centre [accessed 23 June 2014].

—(2010), 'Anthology', *Guardian*, 3 October, www.theguardian.com/
stage/2010/oct/03/anthology-liverpool-everyman-review [accessed 23 June
2014].

Goddard, Lynette (2007), *Staging Black Feminisms: Identity, Politics,
Performance* (Basingstoke: Palgrave Macmillan).

Grid Iron website, www.gridiron.org.uk [accessed 23 June 2014].

Gwent Theatre website, www.gwenttheatre.com [accessed 23 June 2014].

Harkins, Leigh, Pritchard, Cecilia, Haskayne, Donna, Watson, Andy and
Beech, Anthony R. (2011), 'Evaluation of Geese Theatre's Re-Connect
Program: Addressing Resettlement Issues in Prison', *International Journal
of Offender Therapy and Comparative Criminology*, 55:4, pp. 546–66.

Harman, Paul (2005), 'International Context', in Bennett, Stuart (ed.), *Theatre
for Children and Young People: 50 Years of Professional Theatre in the UK*
(Eastbourne: Aurora Metro Press), pp. 182–93.

Harpin, Anna (2010), 'Marginal Rxperiments: Peter Brook and Stepping Out
Theatre Company', *Research in Drama Education: The Journal of Applied
Theatre and Performance* 15:1, pp. 39–58.

Harvie, Jen (2005), *Staging the UK* (Manchester: Manchester University
Press).

Heddon, Deirdre and Milling, Jane (2006), *Devising Performance: A Critical
History* (Basingstoke: Palgrave Macmillan).

Higgins, Charlotte (2003), 'Open House', *Guardian*, 13 November, www.
theguardian.com/world/2003/nov/13/race.uk [accessed 23 June 2014].

Hingorani, Dominic (2010), *British Asian Theatre: Dramaturgy, Process and
Performance* (Basingstoke: Palgrave Macmillan).

Hodge, Stephen (2012), 'British Asian Live Art: motiroti', in Graham Ley
and Sarah Dadswell (eds), *Critical Essays on British South Asian Theatre*
(Exeter: The University of Exeter Press), pp. 196–206.

Ice and Fire website, iceandfire.co.uk [accessed 23 June 2014].

Keefe, John and Murray, Simon (eds) (2007), *Physical Theatres: A Critical
Reader* (London and New York: Routledge).

Kelly, Jem (2010), 'Three-way Inter-play: Devising Processes and Critical
Issues in Station House Opera's Telematic Performance, *The Other is
You*', in Alex Mermikides and Jacie Smart (eds), *Devising in Process*
(Basingstoke: Palgrave Macmillan), pp. 50–73.

Kershaw, Baz (1992), *The Politics of Performance: Radical Theatre as Cultural
Intervention* (London and New York: Routledge).

—(1999), *The Radical in Performance: Between Brecht and Baudrillard*
(London and New York: Routledge).

—(2004), 'Alternative Theatres, 1946–2000', in Baz Kersaw (ed.), *The Cambridge History of British Theatre Volume 3 Since 1895* (Cambridge: Cambridge University Press), pp. 349–76.

Khan, Keith (2007), 'Making Smaller', in *Programme Notes: Case Studies for Locating Experimental Theatre* (London: Live Art Development Agency), pp. 94–103.

Khan, Suhail (2006), 'Modern Dynamics of First and Second Generation Performance Artists', in Geoffrey V. Davis, and Anne Fuchs (eds), *Staging New Britain: Aspects of Black and South Asian British Theatre Practice* (Oxford: Peter Lang), pp. 161–76.

Klich, Rosemary and Scheer, Edward (eds) (2012), *Multimedia Performance* (Basingstoke: Palgrave Macmillan).

Lehmann, Hans-Thies (2006), *Postdramatic Theatre*, trans. Karen Jurs-Munby (London and New York: Routledge).

Ley, Graham and Dadswell, Sarah (eds) (2011), *British South Asian Theatres: A Documented History* (Exeter: The University of Exeter Press).

Lukowski, Andrzej (2009), 'A Small Town Anywhere', *Time Out*, 28 October, www.timeout.com/london/theatre/a-small-town-anywhere-3 [accessed 23 June 2014].

Mermikides, Alex and Smart, Jackie (2010), 'Introduction', in Alex Mermikides and Jackie Smart (eds), *Devising in Process* (Basingstoke: Palgrave Macmillan), pp. 1–29.

Mitchell, Bill (2014), *Wildworks: What we do*, vimeo.com/88911695.

Nathan, John (2008), 'Meet the Filthy Punk of Theatre', *Jewish Chronicle Online*, 28 March, www.thejc.com/arts/theatre/108/meet-%EF%AC%81lthy-punk-theatre%E2%80%99 [accessed 23 June 2014].

Neelands, Jonothan (2007), 'Taming the Political: The Struggle over Recognition in the Politics of Applied Theatre', *Research in Drama Education: The Journal of Applied Theatre and Performance* 12:3, pp. 305–17.

Nutkhut website, www.nutkhut.co.uk [accessed 23 June 2014].

Ockham's Razor website, www.ockhamsrazor.co.uk [accessed 23 June 2014].

Pearson, Mike and Michael, Shanks (2001), *Theatre/Archaeology* (London and New York: Routledge).

Pilot Theatre website, www.pilot-theatre.com [accessed 23 June 2014].

Preston, Sheila (2011), 'Back on Whose Track? Reframing Ideologies of Inclusion and Misrecognition in a Participatory Theatre Project with Young People in London', *Research in Drama Education: The Journal of Applied Theatre and Performance*, 16:2, pp. 251–64.

Radosavljević, Duška (2013), *Theatre-Making: Interplay Between Text and Performance in the 21ˢᵗ Century* (Basingstoke: Palgrave Macmillan).

Reason, Matthew (2010), *The Young Audience: Exploring and Enhancing Children's Experiences of Theatre* (Stoke-on-Trent: Trentham Books).

Red Room website, www.theredroom.org.uk [accessed 23 June 2014].

Reekie, Tony (2005), 'Revival of Theatre in Scotland: The Cinderella Story of Scottish Children's Theatre', in Stuart Bennett (ed.), *Theatre for Children and Young People: 50 Years of Professional Theatre in the UK* (Eastbourne: Aurora Metro Press), pp. 38–42.

Saunders, Graham (2015), *British Theatre Companies Volume 2* (London: Bloomsbury Methuen Drama).

Scullion, Adrienne (2008), 'The Citizenship Debate and Theatre for Young People in Contemporary Scotland', *New Theatre Quarterly* 24:4, pp. 379–93.

Swettenham, Neal (2005), 'Irish Rioters, Latin American Dictators, and Desperate Optimists' *Play-boy*', *New Theatre Quarterly* 21:3, pp. 241–54.

Tait, Peta (2005), *Circus Bodies: Cultural Identity in Aerial Performance* (London and New York: Routledge).

Theatr na n'Og website, www.theatr-nanog.co.uk [accessed 23 June 2014].

Theatre Wales website, www.theatrewales.co.uk/companies/company_details.asp?ID=2 [accessed 23 June 2014].

Tomlin, Liz (2013a), *Acts and Apparitions: Discourses on the Real in Performance Practice and Theory 1990–2010* (Manchester: Manchester University Press).

—(2013b), 'Foreword: Dramatic Developments', in Vicky Angelaki (ed.), *Contemporary British Theatre: Breaking New Ground* (Basingstoke: Palgrave Macmillan).

—(2015), 'The Academy and the Marketplace: Avant-garde Performance in Neo-liberal Times', in Kimberly Jannarone (ed.), *Vanguards of the Right* (Michigan: Michigan Press, 2015), pp.

Turner, Jeremy, 'Young People's Theatre in a Minority Language and Culture', in Stuart Bennett (ed.), *Theatre for Children and Young People: 50 Years of Professional Theatre in the UK* (Eastbourne: Aurora Metro Press), pp. 32–7.

Upswing website, upswing.org.uk [accessed 23 June 2014].

Visible Fictions website, visiblefictions.co.uk [accessed 23 June 2014].

Webb, Tim, 'Special Needs Audiences', in Stuart Bennett (ed.), *Theatre for Children and Young People: 50 Years of Professional Theatre in the UK* (Eastbourne: Aurora Metro Press), pp. 194–206.

White, Gareth (2010), 'Devising and Advocacy: The Red Room's *Unstated*', in Alex Mermikides and Jackie Smart (eds), *Devising in Process* (Basingstoke: Palgrave Macmillan), pp. 93–109.

Wilkie, Fiona (2002), 'Mapping the Terrain: A Survey of Site-Specific Performance in Britain', *New Theatre Quarterly* 18:2, pp. 140–60.

Williams, David and Carl Lavery (eds) (2011), *Good Luck Everybody: Lone Twin Journeys Performances Conversations* (Aberystwyth: Performance Research Books).

Wright, Beth-Sarah (2000), 'Dub Poet Lekka Mi: An Exploration of Performance Poetry, Power and Identity Politics in Black Britain', in Kwesi

Owusu (ed.), *Black British Culture and Society: A Text Reader* (London and New York: Routledge), pp. 271–88.

Chapter 3: Mind the Gap

Babbage, Frances (2004), *Augusto Boal* (Oxon: Routledge).
Berry, Kevin (2000), 'Of Mice and Men', *The Stage and Television Today*, 17 February, p. 15.
—(2005), 'On the Verge', online, 2005, www.thestage.co.uk/reviews/review.php/6538/on-the-verge [accessed 15 April 2014].
—(2009), 'Boo', online, www.thestage.co.uk/reviews/review.php/23699/boo [accessed 15 April 2014].
Boal, Augusto (2002), *Games for Actors and Non-Actors*, 2nd edn (London: Routledge).
Calvert, Dave (2009), 'Re-Claiming Authority: The Past and Future of Theatre and Learning Disability', *Research in Drama Education* 14:1, pp. 75–8.
Chesner, Anna (1994), 'An Integrated Model of Dramatherapy and its Application with Adults with Learning Disabilities', in Sue Jennings, Ann Cattanach, Steve Mitchell, Anna Chesner and Brenda Meldrum, *The Handbook of Dramatherapy* (London: Routledge), pp. 58–74.
Gee, Emma and Hargrave, Matt (2011), 'A Proper Actor? The Politics of Training for Learning Disabled Actors', *Theatre, Dance and Performance Training* 2:1, pp. 34–53.
Hargrave, Matt (2009), 'Pure Products go Crazy', *Research in Drama Education* 14:1, pp. 37–54.
—(2010), 'Side Effects: An analysis of Mind the Gap's *Boo* and the Reception of Theatre Involving Learning Disabled Actors', *Research in Drama Education* 15:4, pp. 497–511.
Jermyn, Helen (2001), *Arts and Social Exclusion: a Review Prepared for the Arts Council of England* (Arts Council).
Kempe, Andy (2013), *Drama, Disability and Education* (London: Routledge).
Kershaw, Baz (1992), *The Politics of Performance* (London: Routledge).
Megson, Chris (2012), *Modern British Playwriting: The 1970s* (London: Bloomsbury Methuen Drama).
Mind the Gap (2014a) *Jez Colborne – Acting Company*, online, www.mind-the-gap.org.uk/stories/jez-colborne-acting-company/ [accessed 11 March 2014].
—(2014b), *Gift (2014)*, online, www.mind-the-gap.org.uk/productions/gift-2014/ [accessed 11 March 2014].
Palmer, Jon and Hayhow, Richard (2008) *Learning Disability and Contemporary Theatre* (Huddersfield: Full Body and the Voice).

Ryan, Joanna and Thomas, Frank (1987), *The Politics of Mental Handicap* (London: Free Association Books).

Schechner, Richard (1985), *Between Theater and Anthropology* (Philadelphia: University of Pennsylvania Press).

Tomlinson, John (1996), *Inclusive Learning: Principles and Recommendations* (The Further Education Funding Council).

Tomlinson, Richard (1982), *Disability, Theatre and Education* (London: Souvenir Press).

Wheeler, Tim (2014), Personal interview with the author, 19 February.

Chapter 4: Kneehigh Theatre

Allfree, Claire (2007a), *Metro* in *Theatre Record*, 1–28 January, p. 52.

—(2007b), 'Rice Cooks up a Treat', *Metro*, 8 May, p. 29.

Annual Review (2004), Arts Council England, www.artscouncil.org.uk/media/uploads/past_annual_reviews/2004_annualreview.pdf [accessed 18 September 2013.

Anon. (1946), 'Stairway to Heaven', *Time*, 30 December, www.powell-pressburger.org/Reviews/46_AMOLAD/Time.html [accessed 26 June 2013].

Billington, Michael (1996), *Guardian*, in *Theatre Record*, 26 February–10 March, p. 285.

—(1999), 'The Riot', *Guardian*, 17 February.

—(2006) *Guardian*, in *Theatre Record*, 10–23 September, p. 1054.

Brown, Georgina (1999), 'The Riot', *Sunday Mail*, 21 February.

Butler, Robert (1996), *Independent on Sunday*, in *Theatre Record*, 26 February–10 March, p. 285.

Cavendish, Dominic (2006), *Daily Telegraph*, in *Theatre Record*, 10–23 September, p. 1055.

—(2010), 'Kneehigh: The Short Hop from Old Barn to Broadway', *Telegraph*, 2 August 2010, www.telegraph.co.uk/culture/theatre/theatre-features/7921964/Kneehigh-the-short-hop-from-old-barn-to-Broadway.html [accessed 14 June 2013].

Costa, Maddy (2008), 'Troupe Therapy', *Guardian*, 1 December, www.guardian.co.uk/stage/2008/dec/01/kneehigh-theatre-cornwall-maddy-costa [accessed 30 June 2013].

Craig, Sandy (ed.) (1980), *Dreams and Deconstructions: Alternative Theatre in Britain* (Ambergate: Amber Lane Press).

Curtis, Nick (1999), 'The Riot', *Evening Standard*, 12 February.

Dorney, Kate and Merkin, Ros (eds) (2010), *The Glory of the Garden: Regional Theatre and the Arts Council 1984–2009* (Newcastle: Cambridge Scholars Publishing).

Edge, Simon (2007), *Daily Express*, in *Theatre Record*, 7–20 May, p. 577.

Edmondson, Paul (2010), 'Not what we ought to say about the RSC?', *Blogging Shakespeare*, bloggingshakespeare.com/not-what-we-ought-to-say-about-the-r-s-c [accessed 26 June 2013].

Gardner, Lyn (2004), '"We like our plays to be foolish"', *Guardian*, Monday 19 July, www.guardian.co.uk/stage/2004/jul/19/theatre [accessed 12 June 2013].

Georgi, Claudia (2013), 'Kneehigh Theatre's Brief Encounter: "Live on Stage – Not the Film"' in Lawrence Raw and Defne Ersin Tutan (eds), *The Adaptation of History: Essays on Ways of Telling the Past* Jefferson (North Carolina: McFarland), pp. 66–78.

Halliburton, Rachel (2007), '*Time Out* London, 16.05.07' in *Theatre Record*, 7–20 May, p. 578.

Harper, Sue and Porter, Vincent (1989), 'A Matter of Life and Death – A View from Moscow', *Historical Journal of Film, Radio and Television* 9:2, p. 181, www.powell-pressburger.org/Reviews/46_AMOLAD/AMOLAD01.html [accessed 26 June 2013].

Hemming, Sarah (1996), *Financial Times*, in *Theatre Record*, 26 February–10 March, p. 286.

—(2007), *Financial Times*, in *Theatre Record*, 1–28 January, p. 52.

Hesse, Beatrix (2009), 'From Screen to Stage: The Case of *The 39 Steps*' in Monika Pietrzak-Franger and Eckart Voigts-Virchow (eds), *Adaptations: Performing Across Media and Genres* (Trier: Verlage), pp. 143–58.

Hytner, Nicholas (2007), 'What I really think about theatre critics', *Observer*, 3 June, www.guardian.co.uk/stage/theatreblog/2007/jun/03/whatireallythinkaboutthea [accessed 26 June 2013].

de Jongh (1996), Nicholas, *Evening Standard*, in *Theatre Record*, 26 February–10 March, p. 286.

—(2007), *Evening Standard*, in *Theatre Record*, 7–20 May, p. 575.

—(2008), *Evening Standard*, in *Theatre Record*, 11–24 February, p. 175.

Kershaw, Baz (1992), *The Politics of Performance: Radical Theatre as Cultural Intervention* (London: Routledge).

—(1999), *The Radical in Performance: Between Brecht and Baudrillard* (London and New York: Routledge).

Kirwan, Peter (2012), 'Cymbeline (review)', *Shakespeare Bulletin* 30:1, pp. 56–7.

Kneehigh Facts and Figures, infogr.am/Kneehigh-Facts-and-Figures/ [accessed 18 September 2013].

Lilley, Heather (2010), 'Vital Contact: Creating Interpretive Communities in a Moment of Theatrical Reception', in Gay McAuley and Laura Ginters (eds), *About Performance 10: Audiencing – The Work of the Spectator in Live Performance*, pp. 35–50.

Marmion, Patrick (2007), 'What's On in London,' in *Theatre Record*, 1–28 January, p. 52.

McKinnie, Michael (2004), 'A Sympathy for Art: The Sentimental Economies of New Labour Arts Policy', in Deborah Lynn Steinberg and Richard Johnson (eds), *Blairism and the War of Persuasion* (London: Lawrence & Wishart), pp. 186–204.

Morley, Sheridan (1996), 'Spectator, 16.03.96', in *Theatre Record*, 26 February–10 March, p. 285.

Nancy, Jean-Luc (1991), *The Inoperative Community* (Minneapolis and Oxford: University of Minnesota Press).

Radosavljević, Duška (2010), 'Emma Rice in Interview with Duška Radosavljević', *Journal of Adaptation in Film and Performance* 3:1, pp. 89–98.

—(2012), Interview with Mike Shepherd, 27 July.

—(2013a), *The Contemporary Ensemble: Interviews with Theatre-Makers* (London and New York: Routledge).

—(2013b), *Theatre-Making: Interplay Between Text and Performance in the 21st Century* (Basingstoke: Palgrave).

Rice, Emma and Grose, Carl (2007), *Cymbeline* (London: Oberon).

Shepherd, Mike (n.d.a), *Kneehigh Theatre: A History* (typed manuscript).

—(n.d.b), Notebook, University College Falmouth Library: Kneehigh Archive, Box 2.

—(n.d.c), Notebook, University College Falmouth Library: Kneehigh Archive, Box 73.

Smurthwaite, Nick (1999), 'Dark Age Drama', *The Stage*, 11 February.

Spencer, Charles (2007), *Daily Telegraph*, in *Theatre Record*, 7–20 May, p. 574.

—(2008), *Daily Telegraph*, 18.02.08, in *Theatre Record*, 11–24 February, p. 175.

Taylor, Paul (1996), *Independent*, 08.03.96, in *Theatre Record*, 26 February–10 March, p. 287.

—(2006), *Independent*, 27.09.06, in *Theatre Record*, 10–23 September, p. 1055.

—(2008), *Independent*, 19.02.08, in *Theatre Record*, 11–24 February, p. 176.

Turner, Adrian (2000), 'Brief Encounter', *The Criterion Collection*, 26 June, www.criterion.com/current/posts/88-brief-encounter [accessed 26 June 2013].

Waywell, Nicholas (1999), 'The Riot', *Times Literary Supplement*, 25 February.

Wayne, Valerie (2007), 'Kneehigh's Dream of Cymbeline', *Shakespeare Quarterly* 58: 2, pp. 228–37.

Chapter 5: Suspect Culture

Augé, Marc (1995), *Non-Places: Introduction to an Anthropology of Supermodernity*, trans. John Howe (London: Verso).

Bent, Simon (2006), *The Escapologist* (London: Oberon).

Billingham, Peter (2007), *At the Sharp End: Uncovering the Work of Five Contemporary Dramatists* (London: Methuen).

Brown, Mark (2004), 'High and Mighty', *Sunday Herald*, 1 February, www.

suspectculture.com/content/downloads/8000m/8000m_sundayherald.pdf [accessed 2 March 2013].

—(2007), 'A Study in Global Yawning', *Telegraph*, 13 April, www.telegraph. co.uk/culture/theatre/drama/3664458/A-study-in-global-yawning.html [accessed 10 October 2012].

—(2008), 'Static: Death by a Thousand Clichés', *Telegraph*, 28 February, www.telegraph.co.uk/culture/theatre/drama/3671476/Static-Death-by-a-thousand-cliches.html [accessed 7 March 2013].

Caldwell, Rebecca (2003), 'Sum of *Lament* Less than its Parts', *The Globe and Mail*, 30 January, www.theglobeandmail.com/arts/sum-of-lament-less-than-its-parts/article748551/ [accessed 10 October 2012].

Cooper, Neil (2000), 'Connecting with the Divine', *Scotsman*, 8 December, www.heraldscotland.com/sport/spl/aberdeen/connecting-with-the-divine-1.206670 [accessed 2 March 2013].

—(2006), 'Review of *The Escapologist*', *Herald Scotland*, 18 January, www.heraldscotland.com/sport/spl/aberdeen/theatre-the-escapologist-at-tramway-glasgow-4-5-1.31678 [accessed 2 March 2013].

—(2013), 'Still Timeless After All These Years', in Dan Rebellato and Graham Eatough (eds), *The Suspect Culture Book* (London: Oberon), pp. 49–52.

Coverley, Merlin (2006), *Psychogeography* (Harpenden: Pocket).

Cramer, Steve (2006), 'Review of *The Escapologist*', *The List*, 2–16 February, p. 2.

Crouch, Kristin A. (2007), 'Suspect Culture', in Gabrielle H. Cody and Evert Sprinchorn (eds), *The Columbia Encyclopedia of Modern Drama* (New York: Columbia University Press), pp. 1308–9.

Eatough, Graham (2013), personal communication, 25 April.

Fisher, Mark (2004), 'Review of *8000m*', *Guardian*, 27 January, www. theguardian.com/stage/2004/jan/27/theatre2 [accessed 10 October 2012].

—(2006), 'Review of *The Escapologist*', *Guardian*, 21 January, www. theguardian.com/stage/2006/jan/21/theatre2 [accessed 2 March 2013].

—(2007), 'Review of *Futurology*', *Guardian*, 13 April, www.theguardian.com/ stage/2007/apr/13/theatre [accessed 10 October 2012].

—(2011), 'Suspect Cultures and Home Truths: Interview with David Greig' in Anja Müller and Clare Wallace (eds), *Cosmotopias: Transnational Identities in David Greig's Theatre* (Prague: Litteraria Pragensia), pp. 14–31.

Good, Thelma (2002), 'Review of *Lament*', *Edinburgh Guide*, 4 April, www. edinburghguide.com/aande/theatre/reviews/l/lament.shtml [accessed 10 October 2012].

Graeae Theatre Company, www.graeae.org [accessed 7 March 2013].

Greig, David and Eatough, Graham (1998), *One Way Street*, in Philip Howard (ed.), *Scotland: Plays* (London: Nick Hern), pp. 227–60.

Haydon, Andrew (2008), 'Review of *Static*', *Financial Times*, 28 April, www.

ft.com/cms/s/0/089cbec6-12e4-11dd-8d91-0000779fd2ac.html [accessed 7 March 2013].

Jones, Sarah Unwin (2006), 'Deconstructing Harry Houdini', *Independent*, 24 January, p. 42.

Lehmann, Hans-Thies (2006), *Postdramatic Theatre*, trans. Karen Jürs-Munby (London and New York: Routledge).

Lumsden, Jaine (2007), '*Futurology* Scottish Arts Council Artistic Assessment' (Edinburgh: Scottish Arts Council), 21 May, www.scottisharts.org.uk/ resources/Organisations/Suspect%20Culture/2007_08/futurology%20 jl%2017%2004%2007.pdf [accessed 10 October 2012].

Mahoney, Elisabeth (2002), 'Review of *Lament*,' *Guardian*, 9 April, www. theguardian.com/stage/2002/apr/09/theatre.artsfeatures1 [accessed 10 October 2012].

McCarthy, Maxwell (2008), 'Lines of Enquiry: Extract from Recorded Conversation with Graham Eatough, Artistic Director of Suspect Culture, on *Static*', in Dan Rebellato, *Static* (London: Oberon), p. 11.

McMillan, Joyce (2002a), 'The Sad Case of Suspect Culture', *Scotsman*, 4 April www.scotsman.com/news/sad-case-of-suspect-culture-1-947258 [accessed 2 March 2013].

—(2002b), 'Haunted by Loss', *Scotsman*, 10 April, www.scotsman.com/news/ haunted-by-loss-1-502456 [accessed 2 March 2013].

—(2007), 'Party Like it's the End of the World', *Scotsman*, 13 April, www.scotsman.com/news/party-like-it-s-the-end-of-the-world-1-742734 [accessed 10 October 2012].

—(2008), 'Lacking Character', *Scotsman*, 22 February 8, www.scotsman.com/ news/lacking-character-1-1156161 [accessed 7 March 2013].

—(2013), 'One Way Street', in Dan Rebellato and Graham Eatough (eds), *The Suspect Culture Book* (London: Oberon), pp. 43–4.

Müller, Anja (2011), 'Cosmopolitan Stage Conversations: David Greig's Adapted Transnational Characters and the Ethics of Identity', in Anja Müller and Clare Wallace (eds), *Cosmotopia: Transnational Identities in David Greig's Theatre* (Prague: Litteraria Pragensia), pp. 82–102.

Paroni de Castro, Mauricio (2013), 'Theatre, Geography and Existence', in Dan Rebellato and Graham Eatough (eds), *The Suspect Culture Book* (London: Oberon), pp. 54–60.

Patience, Alexandria (2007), '*Futurology* Scottish Arts Council Artistic Assessment' (Edinburgh: Scottish Arts Council, 2 May), www.scottisharts. org.uk/resources/Organisations/Suspect%20Culture/2007_08/Suspect%20 Culture%20Futurology%20180407%20AP.pdf [accessed 10 October 2012].

Pope, Jon (2004), '*8000m*: Scottish Arts Council Artistic Assessment', Edinburgh: Scottish Arts Council, 6 February 2004, www.scottisharts.org. uk/resources/publications/Miscellaneous/Strategic%20Review%20papers/ CFOs/S/Suspect%20Culture/2004%20Suspect%20Culture%208000%20 metres%20(3).pdf [accessed 2 March 2013].

Quayle, Ged (2006), 'Review of *The Escapologist*', *The British Theatre Guide*, www.britishtheatreguide.info/reviews/escapologist-rev [accessed 2 March 2013].

Rebellato, Dan (2003), '"And I Will Reach Out my Hand with a Kind of Infinite Slowness and Say the Perfect Thing": The Utopian Theatre of Suspect Culture', *Contemporary Theatre Review* 13:1, pp. 61–80.

Rebellato, Dan and Eatough, Graham (eds) (2013), *The Suspect Culture Book* (London: Oberon).

Reid, Trish (2008), 'Scottish Arts Council Wields the Axe', *Contemporary Theatre Review* 18:3, pp. 398–401.

Schamberger, Magdalena (2004), '*8000m* Scottish Arts Council Artistic Assessment', Edinburgh: Scottish Arts Council, 18 February, www. scottisharts.org.uk/resources/publications/Miscellaneous/Strategic%20 Review%20papers/CFOs/S/Suspect%20Culture/2004%20Suspect%20 Culture%208000%20m%20(4).pdf [accessed 10 October 2012].

Scottish Arts Council (2008), 'Flexible Funding Assessment Reference number G201001009', Edinburgh: Scottish Arts Council, 24 April, www. scottisharts.org.uk/resources/publications/fxo%20assessments/Suspect%20 Culture%20FXO%20Assessment.pdf [accessed 10 October 2012].

—(2010), 'Past Grants Awarded', Edinburgh: Scottish Arts Council, July 2010, www.scottisharts.org.uk/1/funding/pastgrantsawarded.aspx [accessed 27 February 2013].

Suspect Culture, www.suspectculture.com, 2013 [accessed 7 March 2013].

Wallace, Clare (2013), *The Theatre of David Greig* (London: Bloomsbury Methuen Drama).

Wright, Isabel (2003), 'Working in Partnership: David Greig in Conversation', in Caridad Svich (ed.), *Trans-global Readings: Crossing Theatrical Boundaries* (Manchester: Manchester University Press), pp. 157–60.

Zaroulia, Marilena (2013a), 'Spinning Through Nothingness: Suspect Culture Travelling', in Dan Rebellato and Graham Eatough (eds), *The Suspect Culture Book* (London: Oberon), pp. 45–8.

—(2013b), '"Geographies of the Imagination" in David Greig's Theatre: Mobility, Globalisation and European Identities', in Clare Wallace (ed.), *The Theatre of David Greig* (London: Bloomsbury Methuen Drama), pp. 178–93.

Zenzinger, Peter (2005), 'David Greig's Scottish View of the 'New' Europe: A Study of Three Plays', in Christoph Houswitschka et al. (eds), *Literary Views on Post-Wall Europe: Essays in Honour of Uwe Böker* (Trier: Wissenschaftlicher Verlag Trier), pp. 261–82.

Chapter 6: Stan's Cafe

Arts Council England (2010), *Achieving Great Art for Everyone: A Strategic Framework for the Arts* (London: Gavin Martin, pp. 1–47, www. artscouncil.org.uk/media/uploads/achieving_great_art_for_everyone.pdf [accessed 13 March 2013].

—(n.d.), 'Stan's Cafe Theatre Company *Of All the People in the World*: To See the World in a Grain of Rice', pp. 10–15, www.artscouncil.org.uk/media/ uploads/documents/publications/phpf8M4q5.pdf [accessed 10 March 2013].

Auslander, Philip (1997), *From Acting to Performance: Essays in Modernism and Postmodernism* (London: Routledge).

Babbage, Frances (2000), 'The Past in the Present: a Response to Stan's Cafe's Revival of *The Carrier Frequency*', *New Theatre Quarterly* 16:1, pp. 97–9.

Bailes, Sara J. (2011), *Performance Theatre and the Poetics of Failure: Forced Entertainment, Goat Island, Elevator Repair Service* (London: Routledge).

Blackaby, Anna (2008), 'Stan's Cafe Wins Top Prize at Creative City Awards', *Birmingham Post*, 1 December, www.birminghampost.net/birmingham-business/birmingham-business-news/creative-industries-news/2008/12/01/ stan-s-cafe-wins-top-prize-at-creative-city-awards-65233-22374538/ [accessed 15 April 2013].

Cavendish, Dominic (2008), 'Review of *Of All the People in All the World*', *Telegraph*, 22 September, www.telegraph.co.uk/culture/theatre/ drama/3561114/Review-Three-Sisters-Of-All-The-People-in-All-the-World-and-Doug-Stanhope.html#mm_hash [accessed 25 April 2013].

—(2013), 'London International Mime Festival: *Popcorn Machine*; Purcell Room; *The Cardinals*, Roundhouse, Review', *Telegraph*, 16 January, www.telegraph.co.uk/culture/theatre/theatre-reviews/9806516/ London-International-Mime-Festival-Popcorn-Machine-Purcell-Room-The-Cardinals-Roundhouse-review.html [accessed 25 April 2014].

Gagen, Alison (2013), interview with the author. Arts Council England (West Midlands Office) 15 March.

Gardner, Lyn (2009), 'Theatre Preview: Spy Steps, Coventry', *Guardian*, 6 June, www.guardian.co.uk/stage/2009/jun/06/spy-steps/print [accessed 25 April 2013].

—(2011), '*The Cleansing of Constance Brown*: Review', *Guardian*, 14 March, www.theguardian.com/stage/2011/mar/14/cleansing-of-constance-brown-review [accessed 25 April 2014].

—(2013a), '*The Cardinals*: Review', *Guardian*, 15 January, www.theguardian. com/stage/2013/jan/15/cardinals-review [accessed 25 April 2014].

—(2013b), '*The Anatomy of Melancholy*: Review', *Guardian*, 27 November, www.theguardian.com/stage/2013/nov/27/anatomy-of-melancholy-review [accessed 27 April 2014].

Gorman, Sarah (2010), 'Theatre for a Media-Saturated Age', in Nadine

Holdsworth and Mary Luckhurst (eds), *A Concise Companion to British and Irish Drama* (London: Blackwell), pp. 263–82.

Harant, Marie-Christine (2009), 'Pouvoir and Purification à l'Anglaise', *Les Trois Coups*, 30 September, www.lestroiscoups.com/article-36741703.html [accessed 25 April 2013].

Harvey, David (1990), *The Condition of Postmodernity: An Enquiry into the Origins of Cultural Change* (Oxford: Blackwell).

Heddon, Deirdre and Milling, Jane (2006), *Devising Performance: A Critical History* (Basingstoke: Palgrave).

Jackson, Lorne (2010), 'Political Ideology Behind the Arts Cuts Says Stan's Cafe Artistic Director', *Birmingham Post*, 21 October, www. birminghampost.co.uk/whats-on/theatre/political-idealogy-behind-arts-cuts-3927185 [accessed 27 March 2014].

Jürs-Munby, Karen (2006), 'Introduction', in Hans-Thies Lehmann, *Postdramatic Theatre*, trans. and intro. Karen Jürs-Munby (London and New York: Routledge), pp. 1–15.

Kümmel, Peter (2005), 'Fresst uns nicht auf! Kämpfe im Wirbel der Globalisierung: Das Festival Theater der Welt hat in Stuttgart begonnen', *Der Zeit online*, 23 June, www.zeit.de/2005/26/Theater_der_Welt [accessed 3 May 2013].

Ledger, Adam (2013), 'Stan's Cafe: The Vision of the Ensemble', in John Britton (ed.), *Encountering Ensemble* (London: Bloomsbury Methuen Drama), pp. 152–66.

Lehmann, Hans-Thies (2006), *Postdramatic Theatre*, trans. and introd. Karen Jürs-Munby (London and New York: Routledge).

Paget, Derek (2009), '"The Broken Tradition" of Documentary Theatre', in Chris Megson and Alison Forsythe (eds), *Get Real: Documentary Theatre: Past and Present* (Basingstoke: Palgrave), pp. 224–38.

Parry, Simon (2010), 'Imagining Cosmopolitan Space: Spectacle, Rice and Global Citizenship', *RIDE: The Journal of Applied Theatre and Performance* 15:3, pp. 317–37.

Pavis, Patrice (1982), *Languages of the Stage* (New York: PAJ Publication).

Shaugnessy, Nicola (2012), *Applying Performance: Live Art, Socially Engaged Theatre and Affective Practice* (Basingstoke: Palgrave).

Stan's Cafe (2001), *Future Art Symposia* (Birmingham: Stan's Cafe).

—(2003), *Of All the People in All the World. Stan's Cafe*, www.stanscafe.co.uk/project-of-all-the-people.html#couldnt [accessed 10 April 2013].

—(2006a), *Home of the Wriggler, Stan's Cafe*, www.stanscafe.co.uk/project-home-of-the-wriggler.html [accessed 12 March 2013].

—(2006b), *Home of the Wriggler*, Birmingham: Stan's Cafe.

—(2007), *The Cleansing of Constance Brown, Stan's Cafe*, www.stanscafe.co.uk/project-constance-brown.html [accessed 10 September 2012].

—(2009a), *The Cardinals, Stan's Cafe*, www.stanscafe.co.uk/project-cardinals.html [accessed 7 April 2013].

—(2009b), '*Of All the People in All the World*: Bristol', 14–16 May, www.stanscafe. co.uk/project-of-all-the-people-bristol.html [accessed 12 April 2013].

—(2009c), *The Just Price of Flowers*, Stan's Cafe, www.stanscafe.co.uk/project-just-price-of-flowers.html [accessed 10 April 2013].

—(2009d), *The Smartie Mission*, Stan's Cafe, www.stanscafe.co.uk/project-smartie-mission.html [accessed 11 April 2013].

—(2012), '*Of All the People in All the World*: Stratford Upon-Avon', 14 –31 July 2012, www.stanscafe.co.uk/project-of-all-the-people-stratford.html [accessed 1 April 2013].

—(n.d.a.), '*It's Your Film*: Promoter Information, Programme Notes and Education Pack', *Stan's Cafe*, pp. 1–10, www.stanscafe.co.uk/images/ itsyourfilm.pdf [accessed 12 March 2013].

—(n.d.b.), 'We are Stan's Cafe: Introduction.' *Stan's Cafe*, www.stanscafe.co.uk/ about-us.html [accessed 10 September 2012].

—(n.d.c.), 'Helpful Things: FAQs', *Stan's Cafe*, www.stanscafe.co.uk/helpful-things.html#growbusiness [accessed 10 September 2012].

—(n.d.d.), 'About Us: Introduction', *Stan's Cafe*, www.stanscafe.co.uk/about-us. html [accessed 3 September 2012].

Tomlin, Liz (2004), 'English Theatre in the 1990s and Beyond', in Baz Kershaw (ed.), *The Cambridge History of British Theatre* Vol. 3 (Cambridge: Cambridge University Press), pp. 498–512.

Tushingham, David (n.d.), 'A Short Essay for the Vienna Festival', Stan's Cafe, www.stanscafe.co.uk/helpfulthings/essays-vienna-constance.html [accessed 13 February 2013].

Woolman, Natalie (2010), 'Stan's Cafe Awarded £60K to Remain at Birmingham Base', in *The Stage*, 1 November, www.thestage.co.uk/ news/2010/11/stans-cafe-awarded-60k-to-remain-at-birmingham-base/ [accessed 26 April 2013].

Yarker, James (1996), *Ocean of Storms*: post-show talk, The Royal Court, June. The British Library Sound Archive.

—(2001a), 'Audience as Collaborators', Stan's Cafe, www.stanscafe.co.uk/ helpfulthings/essays-audience-collaborators.html [accessed 30 March 2013].

—(2004), ' Technology and Perception', Stan's Cafe, www.stanscafe.co.uk/ helpfulthings/essays-technology-and-perception.html [accessed 1 February 2013].

—(2005), 'Making *Of All the People in All The World*', Stan's Cafe, www. stanscafe.co.uk/helpfulthings/makingofallthepeople.html [accessed 15 April 2013].

—(2006), 'Stan's Cafe and Education', Stan's Cafe, www.stanscafe.co.uk/ helpfulthings/essays-stan-education.html [accessed 12 April 2013.

—(2007a), 'Stan's Cafe and Site-Specific Performance', Stan's Cafe, www. stanscafe.co.uk/helpfulthings/sitespecificessay.html [accessed 1 September 2012].

—(2007b), 'MAC: An Arts Centre'. Stan's Cafe, www.stanscafe.co.uk/
helpfulthings/essays-mac.html [accessed 15 March 2013].

—(2007c), 'Set in Our Ways: Stan's Cafe's Sets and Set Design Strategies
Through the Years', Stan's Cafe, www.stanscafe.co.uk/helpfulthings/
essays-set.html [accessed 10 April 2013].

—(2008a), 'Artistic and Business Principles', Stan's Cafe, www.stanscafe.
co.uk/helpfulthings/essays-artistic-business.html [accessed 20 January
2013].

—(2008b), 'Stan's Cafe and Politics', Stan's Cafe, www.stanscafe.co.uk/
helpfulthings/essays-stan-politics.html [accessed 5 March 2013].

—(2008c), 'Stan's Cafe Leads the Call for a Return to Creativity', *Birmingham
Post*, 9 June, www.birminghampost.net/birmingham-business/
birmingham-business-news/creative-industries-news/2008/06/09/stan-s-
cafe-leads-the-call-for-a-return-to-creativity-65233-21043053/ [accessed 7
March 2013].

—(2010a), interview with *Time Out*, Beijing, Stan's Cafe, www.stanscafe.co.uk/
helpfulthings/essays-interview-beijing.html [accessed 5 April 2013].

—(2010b), 'Interview: *Home of the Wriggler* in China', Stan's Cafe, www.
stanscafe.co.uk/helpfulthings/essays-interview-wriggler.html [accessed 5
April 2013].

—(2013), interview with the author, Birmingham, 19 March.

Chapter 7: Blast Theory

Adams, Matt (2007), unpublished interview with author, 16 August.

Adams, Matt and Delahunta, Scott (2006) 'Day of the Figurines', *Performance
Research* 11: 4, pp. 148–51.

Adams, Matt with Rieser, Martin (2011), 'Blast Theory, Matt Adams:
Interview with Martin Rieser January 15 2005, Bath', in Martin
Rieser (ed.), *The Mobile Audience: Media Art and Mobile Technologies*
(Amsterdam: Rodopi), pp. 401–14.

Adams, Matt and O'Grady, Alice (2011), 'Interactivity and the Work of
Blast Theory: Matt Adams in Conversation with Alice O'Grady', in
Jonathan Pitches and Sita Popat (eds), *Performance Perspectives: A Critical
Introduction* (Basingstoke: Palgrave Macmillan), pp. 158–65.

Arts Council England website, www.artscouncil.org.uk/browse/?content=
NPO [accessed 20 December 2013].

Baudrillard, Jean (1991), *La Guerre du Golfe n'a pas eu Lieu* (Paris: Editions
Galilée).

BBC News (2007), 'Who were the Baader-Meinhof Gang?', BBC News,
12 February, news.bbc.co.uk/1/hi/6314559.stm [accessed 14 April 2014].

Beaver, Jacob, Gaver, William W. and Benford, Steve (2003), 'Ambiguity as a
Resource for Design', *CHI Letters* 5:1, pp. 233–40.

Benford, Steve and Giannachi, Gabriella (2011), *Performing Mixed Reality* (Cambridge, MA: MIT Press).

Blast Theory official website, www.blasttheory.co.uk/ [accessed 20 December 2013].

Blast Theory (1994), *Stampede*, video recording (Brighton: Blast Theory).

—(1996), *Something American*, video recording (Brighton: Blast Theory).

—(1998), *Kidnap*, video recording (Brighton: Blast Theory).

—(2000), *Selected Works 1994–2000*, video recording (Brighton: Blast Theory).

—(2004), *New Media, Art, and a Creative Culture*, Adelaide: Government of South Australia, www.thinkers.sa.gov.au/lib/pdf/blast_theory_final_report.pdf [accessed 20 December 2013].

—(2007), 'Report and Accounts: For the Year to 31 March 2007' (Brighton: Blast Theory).

Blast Theory and University of Nottingham (1999), *Desert Rain*, video recording (Brighton: Blast Theory).

Chatzichristodoulou, Maria (2009a) 'How to Kidnap your Audiences: An Interview with Matt Adams from Blast Theory', in Maria Chatzichristodoulou, Janis Jefferies and Rachel Zerihan (eds), *Interfaces of Performance* (Farnham: Ashgate), pp. 107–20.

—(2009b), 'When Presence and Absence Turn into Pattern and Randomness: *Can You See Me Now?*', *Leonardo Electronic Almanac* 16:4–5, n.p. www.leonardo.info/LEA/DispersiveAnatomies/DA_chatzichristodoulou.pdf [accessed 20 December 2013].

Clark, Liat (2014), 'City-wide Manhunt Turns Sheffield into Digital Stage', *Wired*, 20 February, www.wired.co.uk/news/archive/2014-02/20/sheffield-blast-theory/viewgallery/332643 [accessed 14 April 2014].

Crogan, Patrick (2011), *Gameplay Mode: War, Simulation, and Technoculture*, (Minneapolis: University of Minnesota Press).

CultureWatchEurope (2010), *CultureWatchEurope Conference Reader: Culture and the Policies of Change* (Brussels: Council of Europe).

Dekker, Annet with Somers-Miles, Rachel and Feuchtwang, Rachel (eds) (2011), *Virtueel Platform Research: Blast Theory* (Netherlands: Virtueel Platform) www.virtueelplatform.nl/blasttheory [accessed 20 December 2013].

d'Inverno, Mark and Prophet, Jane (2004), 'Creative Conflict in Interdisciplinary Collaboration: Interpretation, Scale and Emergence', in Ernest Edmonds and Ross Gibson (eds), *Interaction: Systems, Theory and Practice* (Sydney: Creativity and Cognition Studios), pp. 251–70.

Dixon, Steve (2007), *Digital Performance: A History of New Media in Theater, Dance, Performance Art and Installation* (Cambridge, MA: MIT Press).

Encyclopaedia Britannica (2014), 'Irish Republican Army (IRA)', *Encyclopaedia Britannica online*. www.britannica.com/EBchecked/topic/294148/Irish-Republican-Army-IRA [accessed 14 April 2014].

Flintham, Mark et al. (2007), 'Day of the Figurines: A Slow Narrative-
    Driven Game for Mobile Phones Using Text Messaging', *Proceedings of
    PerGames 2007*, Salzburg, Austria, April 2007, iperg.sics.se/Publications/
    Pergames2007-day-of-the-figurines.pdf [accessed 20 December 2013].

Foden, Giles (2012), 'ICT and Art Connect: Engaging Dialogues in Art and
    Information Technologies. A GD INFSO Workshop Report.' Brussels:
    Berlaymont/ Galerie Libre Cours/ iMAL Centre for Digital Cultures
    and Technology, 26–27 April, www.ucl.ac.uk/maths/steven-bishop/
    projects/dream_fellowship/ict-art_connect/ict-art_report [accessed 9 May
    2013].

Gaver, William W. (1991), 'Technology Affordances', *Proceedings of CHI
    91 Conference on Human Factors in Computing Systems*, New Orleans,
    Louisiana, April–June, dl.acm.org/citation.cfm?id=108856 [accessed 6 May
    2014].

Giannachi, Gabriella (2007), *The Politics of New Media Theatre: Life®™*
    (Abingdon and New York: Routledge).

Gordon, Eric and de Souza e Silva, Adriana (2011), *Net Locality: Why
    Location Matters in a Networked World* (Oxford: Wiley-Blackwell).

Gunatillake, Rohan (2013), 'Digital Innovation in the Arts Must be
    About the Art', *Guardian*, 23 September, www.theguardian.com/
    culture-professionals-network/culture-professionals-blog/2013/sep/23/
    digital-innovation-arts-creative-practice [accessed 20 December 2013].

Loxton, Howard (2007), 'Rider Spoke', *British Theatre Guide* October 2007,
    www.britishtheatreguide.info/reviews/riderspoke-rev [accessed 15 April
    2014].

McGrath, John (ed.) (2010), 'Surveillance, Performance and New Media Art',
    Special Issue, *Surveillance & Society* 7:2, www.surveillance-and-society.org/
    ojs/index.php/journal/issue/view/Performance/showToc [accessed 9 May
    2013].

Mixed Reality Laboratory official website, www.mrl.nott.ac.uk/ [accessed 9
    May 2013].

Palmer, Judith (1998), 'Lost in Cyberspace and a Hostage to Fortune', *The
    Independent Weekend Review*, 18 July.

Participate project official website, www.participateonline.info/ [accessed 9
    May 2013].

Rampton, James (1998), 'Kidnapped! And all in the Name of Art', *The
    Independent*, 3 June].

Shaw, Jeffrey, Heike, Staff, Farr, Ju Row, Adams, Matt, vom Lehm, Dirk,
    Heath, Christian, Rinman, Marie-Louise, Taylor, Ian and Benford, Steve
    (2000), 'Staged Mixed Reality Performance "Desert Rain" by Blast Theory',
    eRENA Deliverable 7b.3, www.nada.kth.se/erena/pdf/D7b3K.pdf [accessed
    9 May 2013].

Stuart, Keith (2011), 'Blast Theory Brings Interactive Art to Exeter',
    Guardian Games Blog, 4 October, www.theguardian.com/technology/

gamesblog/2011/oct/04/blast-theory-survey-exeter [accessed 15 April 2014].

Tait, Simon (2014), 'I've Seen the Future of Theatre ...', *The Stage*, 17 February, www.thestage.co.uk/columns/funding-matters/2014/02/ive-seen-future-theatre/ [accessed 15 April 2014].

The Times (2000), on Blast Theory website, 10 May, www.blasttheory.co.uk/projects/desert-rain/ [accessed 15 April 2014].

Walwin, Jeni (2003), 'Blast Theory', *Artists Talking: Exposing Contemporary Visual Artists' Practice*, London: a-n, www.a-n.co.uk/artists_talking/artists_stories/single/82463 [accessed 9 May 2013].

Wright, Alexa and Linney, Alf (2009), 'The Art and Science of a Long-Term Collaboration', Conference Paper, Belfast: ISEA, www.ucl.ac.uk/conversation-piece/Wright_Linney%20N_Cpaper.pdf [accessed 9 May 2013].

Chapter 8: Punchdrunk

Alston, Adam (2012), 'Funding, Product Placement and Drunkenness in Punchdrunk's *The Black Diamond*', *Studies in Theatre and Performance* 32:2, pp. 193–208.

—(2013) 'Audience Participation and Neoliberal Value: Risk, Agency and Responsibility in Immersive Theatre', *Performance Research: A Journal of the Performing Arts* 18:2, pp. 128–38.

Barrett, Felix (2012), unpublished interview with Josephine Machon, National Theatre Studios, London, 18 September.

—(2013a), unpublished interview with Josephine Machon, Young Vic, London, 5 February.

—(2013b), personal conversation with Josephine Machon, Farringdon, London, 2 May.

Barrett, Felix and Machon, Josephine (2007), 'Felix Barrett in Conversation with Josephine Machon', *Body, Space & Technology Journal* 7:1, people. brunel.ac.uk/bst/vol0701/home.html [accessed May 2013].

Bartley, Sean (2013), 'Punchdrunk: Performance, Permission, Paradox', *The Journal of Shakespeare and Appropriation* 7:2, www.borrowers.uga.edu [accessed July 2013].

Billington, Michael (2007), 'The Masque of the Red Death', *Guardian Online*, Thursday 4 October, www.theguardian.com/stage/2007/oct/04/theatre [accessed November 2013].

—(2010), 'The Duchess of Malfi', *Guardian Online*, Wednesday 14 July, www. theguardian.com/stage/2010/jul/14/duchess-of-malfi-review [accessed November 2013].

—(2012), 'E is for Experiment', *Guardian Online*, Tuesday 10 January, www. theguardian.com/stage/2012/jan/10/e-for-experiment-modern-drama [accessed November 2013].

Cartelli, Thomas (2013), 'Punchdrunk's Sleep No More: Masks, Unmaskings, One-on-Ones', *The Journal of Shakespeare and Appropriation* 7:2, www.borrowers.uga.edu [accessed June 2013].

Dailey, Alice (2013), 'Last Night I Dreamt I Went to Sleep No More Again: Intertextuality and Indeterminacy at Punchdrunk's McKittrick Hotel', *The Journal of Shakespeare and Appropriation* 7:2, www.borrowers.uga.edu [accessed June 2013].

Doyle, Maxine (2013), unpublished interview with Josephine Machon, 9 April 2013.

Doyle, Maxine and Machon, Josephine (2007), 'Maxine Doyle in Conversation with Josephine Machon', *Body, Space & Technology Journal* 7:1, people.brunel.ac.uk/bst/vol0701/home.html [accessed June 2011].

Gardner, Lyn (2003), 'Sleep No More', *Guardian Online*, 17 December, www.theguardian.com/stage/2003/dec/17/theatre2 [accessed November 2013].

Gillinson, Miriam (2012), 'Punchdrunk's Sleep No More: Is This a Sell-out Which I See Before Me?' *Guardian* Theatre Blog, Monday 6 February, www.guardian.co.uk/stage/theatreblog/2012/feb/06/punchdrunk-sleep-no-more-commercial [accessed May 2013].

Gordon, Collette (2013), 'Touching the Spectator: Intimacy, Immersion, and the Theater of the Velvet Rope', *The Journal of Shakespeare and Appropriation* 7:2, www.borrowers.uga.edu [accessed June 2013].

Grunfeld, Sivan (2013), 'Fractured Realities: A Receptive Review of Punchdrunk's *Sleep No More*', *The Journal of Shakespeare and Appropriation* 7:2, www.borrowers.uga.edu [accessed June 2013].

Harrison, Connie (2013), unpublished interview with Josephine Machon, London, 9 April.

Higgin, Pete (2011), unpublished interview with Josephine Machon, Elfrida Primary School, Lewisham, London. 10 March.

—(2012), personal email correspondence with Josephine Machon, 13 April.

—(2013a), unpublished interview with Josephine Machon, London, 11 April.

—(2013b), unpublished interview with Josephine Machon, London, 15 April.

Higgins, Charlotte (2007), 'Overthrow the Tyranny of Targets: Minister's Message for the Arts', *Guardian*, July 6, www.guardian.co.uk/politics/2007/jul/06/artsfunding.politicsandthearts [accessed February 2013].

Machon, Josephine (2011), *(Syn)aesthetics Redefining Visceral Performance* (Basingstoke: Palgrave).

—(2013), *Immersive Theatres: Intimacy and Immediacy in Contemporary Performance* (Basingstoke: Palgrave).

McCullogh, Christopher (2013), unpublished telephone interview with Josephine Machon, 30 April.

Milling, Jane (2013), unpublished telephone interview with Josephine Machon, 19 April.

Nightingale, Colin (2013a), unpublished interview with Josephine Machon, London, 8 April.

—(2013b), personal email correspondence with Josephine Machon, 16 April.

Nightingale, Colin and Balfour, Katy (2013), unpublished interview with Josephine Machon, Shoreditch, London, 26 March.

Punchdrunk website, www.punchdrunk.com.

Radar, Pamela. J (2013), 'The Murder of a Tale', *The Journal of Shakespeare and Appropriation* 7:2, www.borrowers.uga.edu [accessed June 2013].

Richardson, Sophia and Shohet, Lauren (2013), 'What's Missing in *Sleep No More*', *The Journal of Shakespeare and Appropriation* 7:2, www.borrowers.uga.edu [accessed July 2013].

Silvestre, Agnès (2012), 'Punchdrunk and the Politics of Spectatorship', *Culturebot*, November 14 [accessed November 2013].

White, Gareth (2009), 'Odd Anonymized Needs: Punchdrunk's Masked Spectator', in Alison Oddey and Christine White (eds), *Modes of Spectating* (Bristol: Intellect), pp. 219–29.

—(2012), 'On Immersive Theatre', *Theatre Research International* 37:3 (October), pp. 221–35.

Worthen, W.B. (2012) '"The Written Troubles of the Brain": *Sleep No More* and the Space of Character', *Theatre Journal* 64:1, pp.79–97.

Yorke, Griselda (2013), unpublished interview with Josephine Machon, London, 10 April.

NOTES ON CONTRIBUTORS

Dave Calvert is Senior Lecturer in Drama, Theatre and Performance at the University of Huddersfield, UK. Previously, he was Director of Theatre Education at Mind the Gap, where he led the design and delivery of two extensive training programmes for actors with learning disabilities, Making Waves and Making Theatre. His research is focused primarily on the work of learning-disabled performers, and he has also written on the tradition of the British seaside pierrot and other troupes in popular entertainment.

Maria Chatzichristodoulou [aka Maria X] is a cultural practitioner (curator, performer, writer) and Lecturer in Performance and New Media at the University of Hull, UK. She is co-editor of the volumes *Interfaces of Performance* (2009) and *Intimacy Across Visceral and Digital Performance* (2012). She was co-founder and co-director of the international media art festival Medi@terra and Fournos Centre for Digital Culture (Athens, Greece, 1996–2002); co-convener of the Thursday Club (Goldsmiths University of London, 2006–9); initiator and co-director of the festival and symposium Intimacy: Across Visceral and Digital Performance (London, 2007); and co-director/ co-convener of Becoming Nomad (York St John University, 2013). She is currently working on her monograph *Live Art in Network Cultures* and on the edited collection *Live Art and Performance Art in the UK: A Reader*; both expected to be published in 2016.

Marissia Fragkou is Senior Lecturer in Performing Arts at Canterbury Christ Church University, UK. Her research interests include feminist nomadic politics, ethics of responsibility, precarity and citizenship in contemporary British and European performance. She has published articles in *Contemporary Theatre Review* and *Performing Ethos* and contributed chapters in edited collections on contemporary theatre. She is a member of the early-career research network Inside/ Outside Europe and CDE (Contemporary Drama in English) and an associate member of the European Theatre Research Network (ETRN) based at the University of Kent.

Josephine Machon is the author of *Immersive Theatres: Intimacy and Immediacy in Contemporary Performance* (2013) and *(Syn)aesthetics:*

Redefining Visceral Performance (2009, 2011). She has written widely on immersive and experiential practices. Josephine is also Joint Editor for the Palgrave Macmillan Series in Performance & Technology, which includes her co-edited collections on this subject. She is the Senior Research Fellow in Contemporary Performance at Middlesex University, London, UK.

Duška Radosavljević is a Lecturer at the University of Kent, UK. She has worked as the Dramaturg at the Northern Stage Ensemble, an education practitioner at the Royal Shakespeare Company, and a theatre critic for The Stage Newspaper. Duška is the author of *Theatre-Making: Interplay Between Text and Performance in the 21st Century* (2013) and editor of *The Contemporary Ensemble: Interviews with Theatre-Makers* (2013). In addition, she has published numerous academic articles on contemporary British theatre, remains active as a theatre-maker, and is working on a Methuen Bloomsbury volume on theatre criticism.

Liz Tomlin is a senior lecturer at the University of Birmingham, UK. She is the author of *Acts and Apparitions: Discourses on the Real in Performance Practice and Theory 1990–2010* (2013). From 1999–2009 she was co-founder and co-director of Point Blank Theatre, and writer of the company's performance texts, available in the critical edition on the company's work, *Point Blank* (2007). She was associate editor of the journal *Performing Ethos* from 2011–13, and publishes widely on contemporary performance and political theory, as well as continuing to write for the theatre, most recently, *The Pool Game* produced by Geiger Counter in 2012.

Clare Wallace is an associate professor at the Department of Anglophone Literatures and Cultures at Charles University in Prague, Czech Republic. She is author of *The Theatre of David Greig* (Bloomsbury Methuen Drama, 2013) and *Suspect Cultures: Narrative, Identity and Citation in 1990s New Drama* (2006) and is editor of *Monologues: Theatre, Performance, Subjectivity* (2006) and *Stewart Parker Television Plays* (2008). Co-edited books include *Cosmotopia: Transnational Identities in David Greig's Theatre* (2011) with Anja Müller, *Stewart Parker Dramatis Personae and Other Writings* (2008) with Gerald Dawe and Maria Johnston, *Global Ireland: Irish Literatures for the New Millennium with Ondřej Pilný* (2006) and *Giacomo Joyce: Envoys of the Other* with Louis Armand (2002). She is a member of the editorial board of the *Journal of Contemporary Drama in English*.

INDEX

This index covers English, Scottish and Welsh theatre companies, genres, access and inclusive practice, in all chapters; these topics are categorized by further headings. Terms are indexed by commonly known abbreviation or in full.